ISRAELITE RELIGION

THE AUTHOR

Helmer Ringgren, former teacher at Garrett Theological Seminary, Evanston, Illinois, is presently professor of Old Testament at the University of Uppsala in Sweden. He is the author of FAITH OF THE PSALMISTS, FAITH OF QUMRAN: THEOLOGY OF THE DEAD SEA SCROLLS.

Israelite Religion

by

HELMER RINGGREN

translated by

DAVID E. GREEN

FORTRESS PRESS PHILADELPHIA

This book is a translation of *Israelitische Religion* published by
W. Kohlhammer Verlag, Stuttgart, 1963.

Biblical quotations from the Revised Standard Version of the
Bible, copyrighted 1946 and 1952 by the Division of Christian
Education of the National Council of the Churches of Christ
in the United States of America, are used by permission.

2893B66   Printed in U.S.A.   UB21

FOREWORD

Whoever enters upon the study of Israelite religion can easily lose his way in a jungle of diverse scholarly opinions and dogmatically conditioned judgments. In view of this situation, the primary purpose of the present book is simply to provide orientation. It does not set out to present any sensational new solutions, but above all to present facts and show what we really know and what we do not. Therefore passages from the text are cited verbatim as often as possible. Where our knowledge is inadequate or precarious, this fact is always indicated so that the reader may know where he is dealing with hypotheses.

It is not the purpose of this book to represent one-sidedly a particular school or scholarly tendency, although the author is consciously allied with the so-called Uppsala school. Divergent opinions could not always be discussed; this deficiency will, I hope, be made up by the notes, which refer to works representing the most diverse scholarly tendencies.

The reader will not find in this book a theology of the Old Testament, but a history of the Israelite religion, with primary emphasis on a descriptive presentation of the religion during the period of the monarchy. It is directed primarily not to theologians, who will find in it much that is obvious and superfluous, but to all who are interested in the history of the religion of the Old Testament. Theologians will also miss points of view based on *Heilsgeschichte*; these points of view have their place, but only within a theological presentation. On the other hand, I hope that theologians will find some value in the comparative approach, which is extremely important for determining, among other things, the uniqueness of the Old Testament religion.

I cannot see this history of Israelite religion published without expressing a word of thanks to the general editor of the Kohlhammer series, *Die Religionen der Menschheit*; Dr. Christel Matthias Schröder not only provided the stimulus for this book but also furthered my work in many ways.

Åbo, Finland   HELMER RINGGREN
May, 1963

PREFACE TO THE ENGLISH EDITION

The appearance of this English translation has afforded me the opportunity to correct some mistakes that were pointed out to me by reviewers of the German original. I have also made a few brief additions to the text and the notes without, however, aiming at complete coverage of the last three years. I should like to thank the translator, David Green, for his excellent work, and especially for his valuable notes.

Åbo, Finland
April, 1965

H. R.

TRANSLATOR'S NOTE

All quotations from the Bible, including the Apocrypha, are from the Revised Standard Version, except where its translation differs in substance from that of the author. In such cases the vocabulary and style of the RSV have been changed to conform to the translation given by the author, and a footnote added to explain the difference. In some cases, the rendering of the RSV margin has been used; these cases are not separately noted. In accord with the author's practice, one major alteration has been made in the RSV translation: the divine name, Hebrew *yahweh,* which is rendered "the LORD" by the RSV, is here rendered as "Yahweh."

All chapter and verse references are to the Hebrew text; where the English enumeration differs, the English reference has been added parenthetically. In the Apocrypha, the chapter and verse numbering of the RSV has been followed without further note; in some cases it differs from that of other standard editions.

Works in other languages cited by the author have been referred to here in their English translations, where such exist; in each case, the translation has been checked to assure the accuracy of the English rendering.

D. E. G.

CONTENTS

ABBREVIATIONS

AAF	*Annales Academiae Fennicae*
AcOr	*Acta Orientalia*
AELK	*Allgemeine evangelisch-lutherische Kirchenzeitung*
AfO	*Archiv für Orientforshung*
AJSL	*American Journal of Semitic Languages and Literatures*
ANEP	J. Pritchard (ed.), *The Ancient Near East in Pictures* (Princeton: Princeton University Press, 1955)
ANET	J. Pritchard (ed.), *Ancient Near Eastern Texts* (Princeton: Princeton University Press, 1955)
ARW	*Archiv für Religionswissenschaft*
AT	Altes Testament, Ancien Testament
BA	*Biblical Archaeologist*
Bar.	Baruch
BASOR	*Bulletin of the American Schools of Oriental Research*
BIFAO	*Bulletin de l'institut français d'archéologie orientale*
BJRL	*Bulletin of the John Rylands Library*
BR	*Biblical Research*
BWANT	*Beiträge zur Wissenschaft vom Alten und Neuen Testament*
CBQ	*Catholic Biblical Quarterly*
Chron.	Chronicles
CIS	*Corpus Inscriptionum Semiticarum*
Dan.	Daniel
Deut.	Deuteronomy
DT	*Deutsche Theologie*
Eccles.	Ecclesiastes
Ecclus.	Ecclesiasticus
Eng.	English
Esd.	Esdras
ET	*Expository Times*
ETh	*Evangelische Theologie*
Eth. Enoch	Ethiopic Enoch

Exod.	Exodus
Ezek.	Ezekiel
Gen.	Genesis
Hab.	Habakkuk
Hag.	Haggai
Heb.	Hebrew
Hos.	Hosea
HR	*History of Religions*
HTR	*Harvard Theological Review*
HUCA	*Hebrew Union College Annual*
ICC	*International Critical Commentary*
IDB	G. Buttrick (ed.), *The Interpreter's Dictionary of the Bible* (Nashville: Abingdon, 1962)
IEJ	*Israel Exploration Journal*
IIJ	*Indo-Iranian Journal*
Isa.	Isaiah
JBL	*Journal of Biblical Literature*
JCS	*Journal of Cuneiform Studies*
Jer.	Jeremiah
JJS	*Journal of Jewish Studies*
JMEOS	*Journal of the Manchester University Egyptian and Oriental Society*
Jn.	The Gospel of John
JNES	*Journal of Near Eastern Studies*
Jon.	Jonah
Josh.	Joshua
JPOS	*Journal of the Palestine Oriental Society*
JQR	*Jewish Quarterly Review*
JSS	*Journal of Semitic Studies*
Jth.	Judith
JTS	*Journal of Theological Studies*
Jub.	Jubilees
Judg.	Judges
Lam.	Lamentations
Lev.	Leviticus
Lk.	The Gospel of Luke
LQR	*Lutheran Quarterly Review*
LXX	The Septuagint
Macc.	Maccabees
Mal.	Malachi
Mart. Isa.	Martyrdom of Isaiah
MGKK	*Monatsschrift für Gottesdienst und kirchliche Kunst*
Mic.	Micah
Mk.	The Gospel of Mark
Mt.	The Gospel of Matthew

MT	Massoretic Text
MUST	*Melanges de l'université Saint-Joseph,* Beyrouth
MVÄG	*Mitteilungen der vorderasiatischen und ägyptischen Gesellschaft*
Neh.	Nehemiah
NKZ	*Neue kirchliche Zeitschrift*
NRT	*Nouvelle Revue Theologique*
Num.	Numbers
Obad.	Obadiah
OT	Old Testament
OTS	*Oudtestamentische Studien*
PEQ	*Palestine Exploration Quarterly*
Pr. Man.	Prayer of Manasses
Prov.	Proverbs
Ps.	Psalms
Ps. Sol.	Psalms of Solomon
RB	*Revue biblique*
RGG	K. Galling (ed.), *Religion in Geschichte und Gegenwart* (3rd ed.; Tübingen: Mohr, 1955—)
RHPR	*Revue d'histoire et de philosophie religieuses*
RHR	*Revue d'histoire des religions*
RQ	*Revue de Qumran*
RSR	*Recherches de science religieuse*
RSV	The Revised Standard Version of the Bible
RTP	*Revue de théologie et de philosophie*
Sam.	Samuel
SEÅ	*Svensk exegetisk årsbok*
Song	Song of Solomon
SOSOF	*Studia Orientalia,* Helsinki
SP	*Sacra Pagina*
SPAW	*Sitzungsberichte der preussischen Akademie der Wissenschaften*
STh	*Studia Theologica*
STU	*Schweizerische theologische Umschau*
SVT	*Supplements to Vetus Testamentum*
Test. Dan	Testament of Dan
Test. Jud.	Testament of Judah
Test. Levi	Testament of Levi
Test. Reub.	Testament of Reuben
Test. Sim.	Testament of Simeon
Test. Zeb.	Testament of Zebulun
ThR	*Theologische Rundschau*
TLZ	*Theologische Literaturzeitung*
Tob.	Tobit
TQ	*Theologische Quartalschrift*

TWNT	G. Kittel (ed.), *Theologisches Wörterbuch zum Neuen Testament* (Stuttgart: Kohlhammer, 1933—)
TZ	*Theologische Zeitschrift*
UM	C. Gordon, *Ugaritic Manual* (Rome: Pontifical Institute, 1955)
UUÅ	*Uppsala Universitets Årsskrift*
VT	*Vetus Testamentum*
Wisd. of Sol.	Wisdom of Solomon
WZKMU	*Wissenschaftliche Zeitschrift der Karl-Marx Universität, Leipzig*
WZUH	*Wissenschaftliche Zeitschrift der Universität Halle*
ZA	*Zeitschrift für Assyriologie*
ZAW	*Zeitschrift für die alttestamentliche Wissenschaft*
ZDMG	*Zeitschrift der deutschen morgenländischen Gesellschaft*
ZDPV	*Zeitschrift des deutschen Palästina-Vereins*
Zech.	Zechariah
Zeph.	Zephaniah
ZK	*Zeitschrift für Kirchengeschichte*
ZNW	*Zeitschrift für die neuttestamentliche Wissenschaft*
ZThK	*Zeitschrift für Theologie und Kirche*

INTRODUCTION

1. Problems and Methods

The study of the religion of ancient Israel has probably given rise to more discussions of basic questions than has the study of any other religion. The reason is that the written sources upon which such a study must be based constitute on the one hand the Holy Scriptures of Judaism, and on the other a part of the Christian canon, the so-called Old Testament. Theological interest is the usual reason a person concerns himself with the sacred documents of a religion, not the desire to subject them to historical criticism. For this reason, investigation of the faith of the Old Testament was carried on for a long period as Old Testament theology, by which is meant a study of the Old Testament having in view a systematic presentation of its basic theological ideas.[1]

Considered as a Christian discipline, Old Testament theology is probably conceivable only as one aspect of biblical theology: the Old Testament must be understood as a part of the Christian Bible, specifically as a preparation and prototype for the definitive revelation in Christ.[2] On the other hand, it would be possible to write a theology of the Old Testament in the same sense one speaks of the theology of Augustine or Luther, that is, a systematic presentation of the religious ideas of the Old Testament ignoring the question whether these ideas could be rendered serviceable for Christian theology. One would then ask what the Old Testament says about God, about the creation of the world, about man, etc., without taking into account how these

---

[1] For a thorough discussion, consult especially the Introductions to the various theologies of the Old Testament, e.g., L. Köhler, *Old Testament Theology,* trans. A. S. Todd (London: Lutterworth, 1957); E. Jacob, *Theology of the Old Testament,* trans. A. W. Heathcote and P. J. Allcock (New York: Harper, 1958); T. C. Vriezen, *An Outline of Old Testament Theology,* trans. S. Neuijen (Newton: Branford, 1958).

[2] Cf., for example, W. Vischer, *The Witness of the Old Testament to Christ,* trans. A. B. Crabtree (London: Lutterworth, 1949); G. A. F. Knight, *A Christian Theology of the Old Testament* (London: SCM, 1959).

1

ideas are related to the teaching of the New Testament. Thus under-stood, Old Testament theology is purely descriptive.

In his *Old Testament Theology*, G. von Rad supports a different point of view. He points out that the documents of the Old Testament were written, not as systematic expositions of the Israelite faith, but in order to emphasize particular aspects of Israel's religious experience. The historical books, for example, were written to provide a theological interpretation of history; they must therefore be read and evaluated in terms of this interpretation, not with reference to their idea of God or their understanding of man. The question, though, is whether this view does not place an unnecessary limitation on Old Testament theology. Behind the theology of history of the Old Testament writers there are certainly ideas about God, man, etc. The documents may not express these ideas directly but thorough analysis brings them to light.

Another difficulty in the theological approach, which is probably responsible at least in part for von Rad's new definition of Old Testament theology, consists in the observation that there is actually not one theology of the Old Testament, but a multiplicity of theologies. The Old Testament is a collection of writings dating from very different periods, and the faith of Israel by no means remained un-changed during all these periods. Any presentation of Old Testament theology that treats the religion of Israel as a constant must disregard the historical development of that religion. It may be true in a sense that the elements common to the various epochs of Israel's religious history are more important than the differences among them.[3] Never-theless, any presentation of the Israelite religion must be incomplete and distorted if it neglects the historical development on the one hand and the tensions between various parties within Israel on the other.

Desirable as an Old Testament theology written from the theological point of view may appear, the variety of religious phenomena in Israel must be the decisive factor in a religio-historical study. Despite the deficiency of the sources, particularly for the earlier periods, an attempt must be made to write a history of the Israelite religion utilizing a critical evaluation of the documents. To do so means also that we may not look upon the writings of the Old Testament as being basically different from other religious documents. They must be taken primarily as human, historical documents, which can and must be examined with the methods of historical criticism.[4] The question of divine inspiration or revelation does not fall within the

[3] This is the basic idea represented by J. Pedersen, *Israel, Its Life and Culture* (London: Oxford, 1959; corrected reprint of the original edition 1926-40).

[4] Cf. J. Pedersen, "Die Auffassung vom Alten Testament," *ZAW*, XLIX (1951), 161 ff.; I. Engnell, "Methodological Aspects of Old Testament Study," *SVT*, VII (Congress Volume, 1960), 13 ff.

scope of the history of religions. If the religio-historical method can neither presuppose nor prove the revelational nature of the Old Testament writings, neither does it exclude such an interpretation on the part of faith. The history of religions simply cannot deal with this question as long as it seeks to retain the character of a strict scientific discipline. It should be added that a purely descriptive theology of the Old Testament also comes very near this goal if it does not overlook the variations within Israelite religion.

A different methodological problem has to do with the use of extrabiblical comparative material to explain religious phenomena in Israel. It is self-evident and does not need to be stressed that a presentation of Israelite religion must be based primarily on Israelite material, i.e., the Old Testament. But this statement does not answer our question. Two observations on this point are of particular importance. First, in many details remarkable similarities can be observed between the Israelite religion and other ancient Near Eastern religions. It is obvious that the Israelite and Assyrian accounts of the deluge go back to a common ancient deluge tradition. The description of the mythical sea monster Leviathan in Isaiah 27:1 coincides almost word for word with a passage from the ancient Canaanite Ras Shamra texts. These and many other examples show that Israel by no means developed in a religious vacuum, but stood in close relationship to its neighbors in the religious as well as the cultural domain. Second, our sources do not provide a complete picture of the Israelite religion. Many details that are difficult to understand on the basis of Israelite material alone can often be explained when comparative material is brought to bear on the question. The Leviathan passage from Isaiah just mentioned above, for example, has become much clearer since the discovery of the Ras Shamra texts than it was before. Ideas only alluded to in the Old Testament appear in their proper context in the light of comparative material. Furthermore, our sources are often much more recent than the periods they depict; as a consequence, their conceptions are often influenced by the ideas of their own time. Occasionally, traces of deliberate censorship have been suggested.[5] In such cases, traces of older ideas and customs that have been preserved in the text can be discovered and interpreted with the aid of comparative material.

What we have said shows that the comparative method is both desirable and necessary. In addition, it plays an important role in determining the uniqueness of the Israelite religion. Things that sound similar do not always mean the same as they do in the context of an alien culture. A rite or religious practice can be variously interpreted, depending on its environment. Only precise analysis can determine in each case the nature and meaning of such correspondences.

---

[5] See, for example, I. Engnell, *Studies in Divine Kingship* (Uppsala: Almqvist & Wiksell, 1943), p. 174.

It follows from what has been said about the comparative method that the general similarity between the Israelite religion and its neighbors must not be made use of in such a way that religious elements found in the other religions of the ancient Near East are also postulated in the case of Israel. The so-called pattern theory, which presupposes the presence of a common structure of myth and ritual (a "pattern") throughout the entire ancient Near East,[6] has occasionally induced some of its adherents to assume that elements of this pattern not specifically attested were nevertheless present in Israel. In such cases, the extrabiblical material should be used only with extreme caution.[7] The comparative method can often determine the origin and original meaning of a religious phenomenon, but it must never determine the way the present function and meaning of the phenomenon are understood. The following presentation will furnish more than enough examples to illustrate this rule.

2. The Sources

As sources for the Israelite religion the writings of the Old Testament are by far the most important. As is well-known, however, the Old Testament is not one document, but a collection of writings from very different periods. Only their position as the Holy Scriptures of the Jewish religion holds them together. For just this reason their value for the history of religions differs widely: some writings, such as the Psalms, are direct evidence for the Israelite religion; others merely depict indirectly the circumstances of past ages. These latter can be used for a presentation of the history of the Israelite religion only when they have been subjected to correction by historical criticism and comparative material.

There are two versions of the Old Testament canon: the Palestinian, which was given its final form at the Synod of Jamnia about 100 A.D. and is composed in Hebrew; and the Alexandrian, which is represented by the Septuagint, the Greek translation of the Bible that came into being in Alexandria in the second century B.C. The latter, which also entered the Greek canon of early Christianity, contains several later writings lacking in the Hebrew canon.

The Jewish canon consists of three major divisions, called the law (tôrâ), the prophets (nᵉbî'îm), and the writings (kᵉtûbîm).[8]

---

[6] See S. H. Hooke (ed.), *Myth and Ritual* (London: Oxford, 1933); *The Labyrinth* (New York: Macmillan, 1935); *Myth, Ritual and Kingship* (Oxford: Clarendon, 1958); also the work of such Scandinavian scholars as I. Engnell, G. Widengren, A. Haldar, and G. W. Ahlström.

[7] For a criticism of this school, a criticism which unfortunately goes a bit too far, see K. H. Bernhardt, *Das Problem der Altorientalischen Königsideologie im Alten Testament* (*SVT*, VIII), 1961.

[8] For a discussion of literary questions, the reader is referred to the standard introductions to the Old Testament, e.g., O. Eissfeldt, *Einleitung*

The Hebrew term for the law is *tôrâ*, "instruction, oracle, law." In the Jewish canon, this term refers to the so-called Pentateuch ("five books") or the five Books of Moses, which contain a mixture of historical narratives and legal formularies.

Genesis ("Beginning") or the First Book of Moses contains the primal history (chapters 1—11: creation of the world, paradise, the fall, the deluge, etc.) and the history of the patriarchs (chapters 12—50: the ancestors of the Israelite people, Abraham, Isaac, Jacob, and Jacob's twelve sons).

Exodus ("Departure") or the Second Book of Moses depicts the deliverance of the Israelites out of Egypt under Moses and the covenant between Yahweh and Israel at Mount Sinai. Various legal formularies constitute the rest of the book.

Leviticus ("Book of the Levites") or the Third Book of Moses consists primarily of legal formularies, mostly ritual and cultic, but some ethical.

Numbers (the title refers to the census of the people) or the Fourth Book of Moses combines narratives from the period of Israel's desert wanderings with law of various kinds.

Deuteronomy ("Second Law") or the Fifth Book of Moses purports to be a speech delivered by Moses to the tribes of Israel shortly before their entry into Palestine. Here the aging leader discusses how God has guided the history of Israel, exhorts the people to obey the law, and repeats certain legal formularies in parenetic style. The book ends with the account of Moses' death.

Jewish and Christian tradition considered the Pentateuch the work of Moses. But it has long been recognized that the materials contained in the Pentateuch are of quite various origin and that the final collection of this material took place much later, during or after the Babylonian exile. Opinions differ as to the exact process. For a long time the Kuenen-Wellhausen documentary hypothesis was accepted almost universally. According to this theory, the Pentateuch came into existence during the postexilic period through a combination of four source-documents, which precise literary analysis of the present day text can recognize. Since the authors of the four source-documents were unknown, they were designated by letters or by quite general names:

---

in *das Alte Testament* (3rd ed.; Tübingen: Mohr, 1964); A. Weiser, *The Old Testament: Its Formation and Development,* trans. D. M. Barton (New York: Association, 1961); A. Bentzen, *Introduction to the Old Testament* (3rd ed.; Copenhagen: Gad, 1957). [At the time of writing, Eissfeldt's work is also scheduled to appear soon in English translation. Reference should also be made to J. Bewer, *The Literature of the Old Testament* (3rd ed., revised by E. G. Kraeling; New York and London: Columbia, 1962); and R. H. Pfeiffer, *Introduction to the Old Testament* (2nd ed.; New York: Harper, 1948).—Trans.]

J, or the Yahwist (after the spelling "Jahwe"), is looked upon as the oldest source (tenth or ninth century B.C.). It prefers the divine name Yahweh and represents an older, simpler theological position. E, or the Elohist, is somewhat later, and perhaps originates in northern Israel. It favors the divine name Elohim ("God") and takes a particular interest in dreams. P, or the Priestly Document, appears to be the latest source. It has a pronounced priestly character and is interested in cultic and legal questions. In addition, it bears a strongly systematic stamp, which appears in numerous genealogies, lists, inventories, etc. D, or Deuteronomy, is found almost exclusively in the book of the same name. In all probability, this document is not itself a unity, but rather derives from two or more sources. It or its central section is usually identified with the book of the law found in the Temple during the reign of King Josiah.

Several objections have recently been raised against this theory. It now presents a much more complicated picture than the simple outline given above.[9] Gunkel was one of the first to direct attention, not at the source-documents, but at their smallest components, the individual traditions.[10] The first questions he asked of each narrative were: Why was it told? By whom? In what context? In other words, he tried to discover the function of each individual story. He frequently concluded that the original function of a story differed from its later function in the context of the Pentateuchal narrative. It became clear, furthermore, that most of the stories had gone through a stage of oral transmission during which they had frequently been more or less thoroughly transformed before they became part of the written sources. Other scholars continued and refined the methods of this form-critical approach, which groups the material into myths, tales, fables, legends, etc.[11] For our purposes, it suffices to note that the statements of the

---

[9] See C. R. North, "Pentateuchal Criticism," *The Old Testament and Modern Study,* ed. H. H. Rowley (London: Oxford, 1951), pp. 48-83; H. J. Kraus, *Geschichte der historisch-kritischen Erforschung des Alten Testaments* (Neukirchen: Erziehungsverein, 1956), pp. 399 ff.

[10] H. Gunkel, *Genesis übersetzt und erklärt* (Göttingen: Vandenhoeck & Ruprecht, 1902). [The Introduction of this work was translated into English as *The Legends of Genesis,* trans. W. H. Carruth (Chicago: Open Court, 1907).—TRANS.]

[11] [The vocabulary of form-criticism is notoriously difficult to translate adequately. Its primary exponents were and are German scholars, and the problem is one of finding adequate equivalents for German words that have become technical terms in the field. There is still no consensus about proper English renderings, and many people writing in English use the German words as they stand. The reader is warned that the technical use of these terms, whether German or English, does not always correspond to general usage. It is probably best to think of them merely as more or less arbitrary labels attached to literary genres that are ultimately self-defining. The very term "form-criticism" is an inadequate rendering of the German *Formgeschichte,* which should mean "form-history"; but the latter word has not established itself.—TRANS.]

Pentateuch about the religion of the patriarchs and of the Mosaic age can by no means be accepted as historically accurate. Even though oral tradition may well have preserved many accurate reminiscences, the power of time to transform the narratives must be reckoned with. The views of later ages have had opportunity to influence them.

The laws, also, can be separated into smaller units that must once have had independent existence. These units cannot be immediately understood as integral parts of any of the source-documents. Examples of these legal codes are the Decalogue (The Ten Commandments, Exod. 20 and Deut. 5), the Book of the Covenant (Exod. 20:22—23:33), and the Holiness Code (Lev. 17—26).

Finally, Noth in particular has pointed out that Deuteronomy is not very closely connected with the four other Books of Moses, but rather constitutes an introduction to the so-called Deuteronomistic History (see below).[12] Many scholars have accepted this theory.[13]

The question of how the texts of the Pentateuch were transmitted has been reopened in recent years by the so-called Uppsala school (Engnell and others).[14] They assert that the three sources J, E, and P were not independent written documents, but rather represent the work of various "schools" within the stream of oral tradition. According to them, the Tetrateuch (Genesis—Numbers) represents a "priestly" redaction of material handed down by oral tradition.[15] Even though it is impossible at this time to say that the problem has been conclusively solved, one thing is certain: oral tradition played a much more important role in the transmission of the Pentateuch than the old documentary hypothesis assumed.

That major division of the canon referred to as the Prophets really comprises two collections: the Former Prophets and the Latter Prophets. The first collection is the so-called Deuteronomistic History, consisting of the books of Joshua, Judges, First and Second Samuel, and First and Second Kings. We have here a large-scale

---

[12] M. Noth, *Überlieferungsgeschichte des Pentateuch* (Stuttgart: Kohlhammer, 1948).

[13] See, e.g., I. Engnell, *Gamla Testamentet* (Stockholm: Svenska kyrkans diakonistyrelses bokförlag, 1945), I, 209 f.

[14] For discussion and bibliography, see E. Nielsen, *Oral Tradition,* (Chicago: Allenson, 1954); A. H. J. Gunneweg, *Mündliche und schriftliche Tradition der vorexilischen Prophetenbücher* (Göttingen: Vandenhoeck & Ruprecht, 1959); cf. also G. Widengren, *AcOr,* XXIII (1960), 201 ff.

[15] See the survey by C. R. North mentioned above (note 9). I. Engnell's most recent discussion of this question can be found in an article in *Religion och Bibel,* XVIII (1959), 3 ff. More recent traditio-historical studies of the Pentateuch include: R. Rendtorff, *Die Gesetze der Priesterschrift* (Göttingen: Vandenhoeck & Ruprecht, 1954); J. Hoftijzer, *Die Verheissungen an die drei Erzväter* (Leiden: Brill, 1956); K. Koch, *Die Priesterschrift von Ex. 25 bis Lev. 16* (Göttingen: Vandenhoeck & Ruprecht, 1959); W. Beyerlin, *Herkunft und Geschichte der älteren Sinaitradition* (Tübingen: Mohr, 1961).

historical work, depicting the history of Israel from the time it occupied the land of Canaan under Joshua until the fall of Jerusalem in 586 B.C. This work is constructed from sources of various kinds; it utilizes both local oral traditions and written records. It views and interprets history primarily on the basis of a theological viewpoint very close to that of Deuteronomy. Yahweh, the God of Israel, reveals himself in the history of Israel, guiding, repaying, rewarding. When the people forsake Yahweh and serve other gods, national catastrophe overtakes them; when the people repent and turn to Yahweh, he helps them and sends deliverance from their peril. The entire history of Israel thus becomes a continuing interplay between apostasy and punishment on the one hand and repentance and deliverance on the other.[16]

It is obvious that such a construction of history is not exactly advantageous when the material is to be used for a religio-historical study. It is absolutely essential to distinguish the contribution of the Deuteronomistic editor from the material of ancient traditions, of which there is quite an abundance, particularly in the books treating the earlier period. It is often very difficult, however, to distinguish these components. Extreme caution is necessary, particularly in those questions about which the Deuteronomist has strong feelings. The Deuteronomistic picture of the relationship between the worship of Yahweh and the Baal cult, for example, is greatly simplified: it is painted exclusively in black and white, whereas the reality of the situation must have been much richer in nuances. The Deuteronomist frequently passes critical and negative judgment on the kingship, in contrast to the Psalms, which ascribe to it a positive religious value.

The term "Latter Prophets" applies to the books that are prophetic in the strict sense, namely, those that contain the words of the persons known as prophets. These writings, therefore, are primary sources, direct documents of religious personalities, whose views on various questions of the period are herein set down. As sources for the prophetic movement in Israel, these books are of course extremely valuable. In using them to cast light on general religio-historical questions, however, one must bear in mind that the prophets often held very one-sided views and often exaggerated when they were attacking certain religious abuses.

The way in which the prophetic books have been transmitted creates another difficulty. The prophets were not primarily writers, but preachers. Much that they said was collected and written down only by their disciples.[17] Furthermore, in the course of transmission

---

[16] G. von Rad, *Old Testament Theology*, trans. D. M. G. Stalker (Edinburgh and London: Oliver and Boyd, 1962), pp. 334 ff.

[17] See, e.g., C. Kuhl, *The Prophets of Israel*, trans. R. J. Ehrlich and J. P. Smith (Edinburgh and London: Oliver and Boyd, 1960); J. Lindblom, *Prophecy in Ancient Israel* (Philadelphia: Fortress, 1962).

of the prophets' words additions were often made that apply the oracle in question to a new situation.[18] As a consequence, it is often difficult if not impossible to determine the precise original form of a prophetic oracle.[19] In many cases, however, an entire section stands out so distinctly from its context that it is easily recognizable as coming from another author and another time. Chapters 40—55 of Isaiah, for example, clearly presuppose the situation at the time of the Babylonian exile, and consequently must be dated about two centuries later than the prophet Isaiah. This does not necessarily mean that they are a forgery. It shows only that the prophetic word remained alive, that people meditated upon it and worked with it, perhaps even that the prophet had a circle of disciples in which his words lived on while new oracles were appended to them.

The Book of Isaiah, therefore, derives only in part from the prophet Isaiah, who was active in the period 748—700. In fact, "genuine" oracles of Isaiah are found only in chapters 1—39, and even here they are lumped together with later additions and historical material. Chapters 24—27, the so-called Isaiah Apocalypse, which describes the fall of a great city (probably Babylon), are considerably later and certainly postexilic. Both style and content show chapters 40—55 to be exilic. Because of their literary unity, they must be ascribed to an unknown author, whom we call Deutero-Isaiah (the "second" Isaiah). The last eleven chapters, 55—66, are postexilic. Although they resemble more an anthology than the work of one author, they are usually called Trito-Isaiah (the "third" Isaiah).

The Book of Jeremiah contains not only oracles of the prophet Jeremiah, who appeared in the last decades before the Exile, but also a great quantity of biographical material that may go back to his scribe Baruch. There is some secondary material, particularly in the latter portion of the book (chapters 46—52).

Ezekiel carried out his prophetic ministry in Babylon among the Jews who had been deported in 596 B.C.; he was there when Jerusalem fell in 586. His book is by and large a literary unity, and for the most part can be viewed as genuine. The presence of secondary material can be assumed with assurance only in the final chapters (40—48), which contain a program for rebuilding the Temple and the nation.

The Book of the Twelve is a collection of shorter prophetic books, combined into one scroll perhaps only for practical reasons. It contains the following:

Hosea, who comes from the Northern Kingdom, composed his

---

[18] G. von Rad, *Theologie des Alten Testaments* (Munich: Kaiser, 1960), II, 45 f.

[19] I. Engnell would prefer to give up all attempts to recover the *ipsissima verba* of the prophets; see, for example, his "Profetia och tradition," *SEÅ*, XII (1947), 134.

book roughly between 750 and 725 B.C. The book must for the most part be considered genuine, because no additions of any significance can be shown. It exists only in a Jerusalem recension, however.

Amos, the earliest of the writing prophets, was active around 750. His book contains very few secondary additions. Portions of the final chapter (9:11 ff.) in particular are of dubious authenticity.

Joel is a short book describing a plague of locusts as the harbinger of the ultimate catastrophe. According to some, the first section of the book is early, the second section late (postexilic); according to others, the book as a whole is contemporary with Jeremiah.[20]

Obadiah is a postexilic oracle against Edom, an enemy of Israel.

Jonah is a legend that tells about the prophet Jonah and his preaching in Nineveh. Historically the book is worthless; but it is of great interest as evidence of a universalistic movement in postexilic Israel. A psalm inserted in the text is early, at least based on an early model.

Micah was a contemporary of Isaiah. His book contains several disputed passages, but only a few can be declared secondary with assurance.

The Book of Nahum contains an oracle against Nineveh in three chapters, and is of interest because of the pronounced liturgical strain in its style.[21]

Habakkuk devotes two chapters to the coming destruction of the Chaldeans (Babylonians). Chapter three is in the style of a hymn.

Zephaniah, an earlier contemporary of Jeremiah, devotes three essentially genuine chapters for the most part to Yahweh's Day of Wrath. A few positive oracles are often thought secondary.

Haggai made his appearance in 520 B.C. among the Jews who had returned from Babylon. His purpose was to speed up the work on the Temple. His oracles, which are precisely dated, are contained in two chapters.

Zechariah was a contemporary of Haggai. He proclaimed the speedy coming of a new and better age. His message is contained primarily in the peculiar visions described in chapters 1—8. The latter portion of the book (chapters 9—14), the so-called Deutero-Zechariah, is as a whole a later composition, but may contain a few earlier prophetic oracles, originally anonymous.

Malachi is probably a pseudonym ("my messenger"; cf. 3:1). The book is postexilic.

The third section of the canon, the so-called Writings, is the most varied in content and in many respects the most interesting from the point of view of the history of religions. It comprises the following writings:

---

[20] A. Kapelrud, *Joel Studies* (Uppsala: Lundeqvist, 1948).

[21] This strain is especially emphasized by A. Haldar, *Studies in the Book of Nahum* (Uppsala: Lundeqvist, 1946).

The Book of Psalms is a collection of 150 religious poems, of which at least the majority were meant for cultic use. David, Solomon, Moses, Asaph, the sons of Korah, etc., are mentioned as composers of the Psalms; but these references are obviously not primary. It is even possible that they were not intended originally to indicate authorship, since, for example, linguistically speaking *"le dāwîd"* can mean not only "of David" but also "for" or "to David" or "belonging to the David collection."[22]

Present day study of the Psalms does not seek to determine who composed each individual psalm and in what historical situation. It is much more interested in their type or literary genre and also in the cultic function (or, as Gunkel put it, the *Sitz im Leben*) of each genre.[23] Each of the three most important genres, the hymn, the psalm of lament, and the psalm of thanksgiving, is connected with a particular cultic ceremony.

The age of the individual psalms is frequently indeterminable. In this area, scholars hold the most diverse opinions. When the theory of Davidic origin had been given up, most of the psalms were ascribed for quite a while to the postexilic period, especially the Maccabean period. Recent years have seen a strong reaction against this late dating of the psalms, and today many scholars consider the majority of the psalms pre-exilic.[24] In actual fact, the thanksgiving psalms from Qumran (the *hôdāyôt*) show that Maccabean psalms differ greatly from those of the Old Testament.

Comparative material outside the Bible also supports an earlier dating of most of the psalms. The biblical psalms evidence a remarkable similarity to Assyro-Babylonian and Canaanite psalms; it is therefore quite improbable that Israel learned the art of psalm composition only in the postexilic period.

The psalms are significant for the history of religions for two particular reasons: they can serve as a basis for reconstructing certain cultic ceremonies of the pre-exilic period,[25] and they provide valuable documentation for the piety of pre-exilic Israel as nourished by the

[22] S. Mowinckel, *Psalmenstudien* (corrected ed.; Amsterdam: Schippers, 1961), VI, 72 ff.; G. W. Ahlström, *Psalm 89* (Lund: Gleerup, 1959), p. 171.

[23] The pioneering work in this field is H. Gunkel and J. Begrich, *Einleitung in die Psalmen* (Göttingen: Vandenhoeck & Ruprecht, 1933).

[24] For an extreme position in this respect, see I. Engnell, *Studies in Divine Kingship* (Uppsala: Almqvist & Wiksell, 1943), p. 176, n. 2; cf. A. R. Johnson, "The Psalms," *The Old Testament and Modern Study,* ed. H. H. Rowley (London: Oxford, 1951), p. 185.

[25] For example, S. Mowinckel, *op. cit.,* II; H. J. Kraus, *Die Königsherrschaft Jahwes* (Tübingen: Mohr, 1951); A. R. Johnson, *Sacral Kingship in Ancient Israel* (Cardiff: University of Wales, 1955); G. W. Ahlström. *op. cit.*

official cult.[26] In what follows, we shall have to make copious use of this source.

The Book of Proverbs is a collection of wisdom aphorisms, reminiscent in many ways of Egyptian and Babylonian proverbs. Tradition names Solomon as their author or redactor, but the collection as a whole is considerably more recent than his period. The first nine chapters, which furnish more or less connected discourses on the value of wisdom, represent a point of view more advanced theologically than the rest of the book, and should probably be ascribed to the early postexilic period. The remaining sections can easily be pre-exilic. Nothing stands in the way of supposing that the nucleus of the collection comes from Solomon or from the Solomonic period. The section 22:17—23:14 is of particular interest, since in large part it corresponds verbatim with an Egyptian wisdom book, the "thirty chapters" of Amen-em-opet.

The Book of Job discusses in dialogue form the problem of theodicy, especially the suffering of the righteous. It has no real literary or form-critical parallels. It shares the dialogue form—with prologue, concluding speech of God, and epilogue—with Sumerian disputations,[27] but the content is completely different. The material treated in the book has points of contact with certain Sumerian and Babylonian poems,[28] but only with respect to the problems posed; the solution is peculiar to Job. Chronologically, the Book of Job probably belongs to the early postexilic period.[29] But it presupposes the existence of an earlier Job legend, which served as the author's point of departure for his discourses.

The Five Megilloth or festal scrolls are five short books, each of which is read in the synagogue on one of the great feasts. They are as follows:

The Song of Solomon is a collection of love poetry that has been interpreted in a variety of ways. The traditional interpretation sees in the Song of Solomon an allegory of God's love toward the people of Israel or the church. More recently many have considered it secular love poetry; others think the original *Sitz im Leben* of these love songs was a *hieros gamos* festival. Abundant parallels support this latter view, which seems constantly to be gaining ground.

The Book of Ruth is a short story about a Moabitess who became one of David's ancestors as a result of her marriage to an Israelite

[26] H. Ringgren, *The Faith of the Psalmists* (Philadelphia: Fortress, 1963).

[27] J. J. van Dijk, *Sagesse Suméro-accadienne* (Leiden: Brill, 1953).

[28] For additional bibliography, consult H. Gese, *Lehre und Wirklichkeit in der alten Weisheit* (Tübingen: Mohr, 1958), pp. 51 ff.

[29] W. F. Albright, "An Ostracon from Calah and the North-Israelite Diaspora," *BASOR,* CXLIX (1958), 33 ff., and D. N. Freedman, "The Massoretic Text and Qumran Scrolls," *Textus,* II (1962), 89 f., argue for the North-Israelite diaspora after the fall of Samaria in 722.

from Bethlehem. The purpose and point of the book are disputed, and opinions are divided as to its age.

The Book of Lamentations, wrongly attributed to Jeremiah, contains five laments on the destruction of Jerusalem in 586.

Ecclesiastes (Hebrew *qōhelet*) is a wisdom writing from the late postexilic period. Under the name of Solomon it develops a pessimistic doctrine of the meaninglessness of existence, or at least the incomprehensibility of whatever meaning there may be. God's existence is not denied, but his actions are incomprehensible; man does not understand the course of the world, but must adjust himself to it as well as possible.

The Book of Esther tells of a young Jewish woman who becomes the wife of the Persian king Ahasuerus (Xerxes) and prevents a persecution of the Jews. It was written to explain the late Jewish feast of Purim. Historically, however, it is of little value.

The Book of Daniel falls into two sections. The first recounts episodes from the life of Daniel, a wise and religious Jew in Babylon; its purpose is obviously to show that God protects and preserves whoever remains true to him even in the midst of trouble. The second section contains apocalyptic visions of the course of history from the Neo-Babylonian empire to Antiochus Epiphanes, one of the Seleucidae. It voices the hope that God will soon conquer all his enemies and set up his kingdom. The book obviously was written during the insurrection against Antiochus, in order to strengthen the faith and courage of the religious Jews. It is the only book in the Old Testament that is explicitly apocalyptic (see pp. 333 ff.).

The final books of the Writings are the Chronicler's history: First and Second Chronicles, Ezra, and Nehemiah. The two books of Chronicles are a retelling of the history of the Southern Kingdom from a priestly and cultic point of view. The Temple and the cult are the center of interest. The history of the Northern Kingdom is omitted, as having nothing to do with Jerusalem and the Temple. The books of Samuel and Kings are used as sources, but there is much additional material from other sources. These books provide a new religious interpretation of history, perhaps influenced by specifically Messianic expectations.[30] It is difficult to date Chronicles precisely; since it belongs together with Ezra and Nehemiah, a time of origin in the fourth or third century B.C. seems probable. It is possible, however, that Chronicles in its present form is the revision of a somewhat earlier prototype. These books can be used as historical or religio-historical sources only with extreme caution. They do, however, furnish abundant information about the religion of the period from which they date.

---

[30] D. N. Freedman, "The Chronicler's Purpose," *CBQ*, XXIII (1961), 436 ff.

The books of Ezra and Nehemiah provide an account, based on extracts from earlier documents, of those events following the return of the Jews from exile that the Chronicler considered important. The chronological data are confused, nor is there any attempt to provide a connected history. These books are nevertheless very significant, because they constitute our only source for an extremely important epoch in the history of Israel's religion.

The term "Apocrypha" applies to a few books and parts of books that do not occur in the Palestinian canon but were included in the Alexandrian canon. Most are extant only in Greek, and belong to the third and second centuries B.C.

In this category are the two books of the Maccabees, which provide an account of the Maccabean revolt against Antiochus Epiphanes and its consequences; Judith, a completely legendary story of a Jewish woman who killed the "Assyrian" general Holofernes; Tobit, a legend about miraculous cures; Sirach (more properly, Jesus the son of Sirach, or Ben Sira), a collection of wisdom aphorisms; Baruch, a didactic penitential poem from the first century B.C.; and, finally, a few additions to the books of Daniel and Esther, and the Prayer of Manasses.

From the late Judaean period come also a few writings that never achieved canonicity, but were read in certain circles and to an extent preserved in the Christian church. They are often called "pseudepigrapha," since they purport to have been written by early religious heroes. Most of them are apocalyptic. Among them we should mention here the two books of Enoch, the first of which is preserved primarily in Ethiopic, the second in Old Slavonic; IV Esdras; the Book of Jubilees; the Testaments of the Twelve Patriarchs; etc. These are of course significant for the religious history of late Judaism, although they were never recognized in "orthodox" circles, having circulated only within certain sects. They are comparable to the Essene writings found in the caves at Qumran, which will be discussed later.

I.
THE PRE-DAVIDIC
PERIOD

1.

THE RELIGION OF THE PATRIARCHS

Tradition is quite positive in placing at the beginning of Israel's history a series of patriarchal figures: Abraham, Isaac, Jacob, and Jacob's twelve sons, each standing as the representative of one of the twelve tribes of Israel. Before a real Israel existed, God chose from among the peoples of the world a particular individual, whom he called to be the father of a great people and to take possession of the land of Canaan. This man was Abraham. The story of his life and travels, and of his son Isaac and Isaac's son Jacob, is recounted in the various traditions of Genesis.

How much history lies behind these patriarchal narratives? It is obvious that they cannot be used as historical sources just as they stand. Whatever position one may take on the controverted question of the sources of the Pentateuch, one thing is certain: these narratives have come down to us through centuries of oral tradition and through the literary activity of one or more writers, and thus reflect the thoughts and ideas of much later periods as well. It is difficult if not impossible to determine what part of the traditional materials is really ancient and genuine. To be sure, the extreme views of the pan-Babylonian school, which interpreted the patriarchs as figures out of astral mythology, are rejected universally today. Yet in spite of the unprecedented progress of modern archaeology, there is still complete disagreement as to the historical reality underlying the patriarchal narratives.[1]

One fact seems to have been pretty well established: the twelve sons of Jacob are not merely individual tribal ancestors; they stand as actual representatives of the later tribes of Israel. They are figures that reflect the history of a people or a tribe, and as such are com-

---

[1] See M. Noth, *The History of Israel*, trans. S. Godman and P. R. Ackroyd (2nd ed.; New York: Harper, 1960), pp. 110 ff.; J. Bright, *A History of Israel* (Philadelphia: Westminster, 1959), pp. 60 ff.; also H. H. Rowley, "Recent Discovery and the Patriarchal Age," *BJRL*, XXXII (1949—50), 44 ff. (reprinted in *The Servant of the Lord* [London: Lutterworth, 1952], pp. 271 ff.); V. Maag, "Der Hirte Israels," *STU*, XXVIII (1958), 2 ff.

parable to the so-called Great Sheikhs of the modern Bedouins. Among the Bedouins, the history of the tribe is often recounted as if it were lived by the tribal ancestor or the Great Sheikh himself.[2] But is the same thing true of any of the patriarchs besides these twelve? Jacob of course represents the people of Israel as a whole, but there is no mention whatever of a tribe named Abraham or Isaac. On the other hand, names such as Peleg, Serug, Nahor, and Terah, from the genealogy of Abraham, have been encountered as place-names among the Amorites on the upper Euphrates.[3] It is therefore possible, at least in some cases, that hidden behind the stories even of Abraham and Isaac there lie historical reminiscences of the pre-history of Israel.

Now we actually know that the Amorites made an incursion into Palestine in the twentieth or nineteenth century B.C.; it is therefore tempting to try to establish a connection between this incursion and the patriarchal narratives. If such a connection exists, it does not matter so much whether the patriarchs actually led the migrating groups or were simply Great Sheikh figures representative of such groups; the important thing is that they are depicted as more or less representing these groups. In any event, there does seem to be at least a kernel of historical fact in the patriarchal narratives.

This of course raises a question: To what extent may we regard as historical the picture of the religion of these ancestors of Israel as portrayed in the patriarchal narratives? Do these narratives pre-suppose and reflect a religion that actually existed at the time, or do they simply mirror the views of later periods? On this point, too, present day scholars are in complete disagreement. Rost, for example, thinks that the three source-documents in Genesis present merely their own idealized pictures of the patriarchs' worship of God, and that they contain hardly anything of historical value.[4] A scholar like Albright, on the other hand, is inclined to view the religious data in the patriarchal narratives as generally trustworthy and historically valuable.[5] Maag finds the basic traits of the patriarchs' religion accurately depicted.[6]

It must be admitted, of course, that we do not have any of the patriarchal narratives in its original pristine form. Moreover, the picture of the patriarchs' religion given by these stories is not at all

---

[2] E. Bräunlich, *Islamica*, VI (1934), 68 f., 182 f.

[3] Bright, *op. cit.*, p. 70.

[4] L. Rost, "Die Gottesverehrung der Patriarchen im Lichte der Penta-teuchquellen," *SVT*, VII (Congress Volume, 1960), 346 ff.

[5] W. F. Albright, *From the Stone Age to Christianity* (2nd ed.; Garden City: Doubleday, 1957), pp. 243 ff.

[6] Maag, *loc. cit.*

unified—a fact that of itself would seem to point to a more or less deliberate alteration of the material. On the other hand, archaeology has shown in the last few decades that the patriarchal stories witness quite faithfully to customs and laws that were present in the second millennium B.C. Certain proper names used in these narratives, for instance, such as Abraham, Jacob, Laban, and Zebulun, have been shown by the Mari texts (eighteenth century) to be genuine Amorite (West Semitic) names. The cuneiform documents from Nuzu (fifteenth century) reflect the customary law of the patriarchs (on concubinage, adoption, inheritance, etc.).[7] Many portions of the Joseph stories have a local color that is distinctly Egyptian.[8] All of this seems to allow the conclusion that, in spite of everything, the patriarchal narratives have preserved genuine reminiscences. Is this true also with respect to the traditions that have been handed down concerning the religion of the patriarchs? Such a possibility cannot be dismissed out of hand, for the narratives in Genesis do in fact present much material that is not in agreement with later Yahwism. If it can be shown that, under similar circumstances elsewhere in the ancient Near East, the religious situation was much the same, then it must be regarded as very probable that we are dealing here with an authentic tradition. Maag even assumes that the traditions of the patriarchs lived on at the local sanctuaries as late as the time of David.[9]

The narrators of Genesis unquestionably consider that the god who speaks to and deals with the patriarchs is Yahweh. It is all the more remarkable, therefore, that he is so frequently given other divine names. For example, we frequently encounter the name *ēl*, "God," and the various names compounded with it: *ēl 'elyôn*, "God Most High" (Gen. 14:18 ff.); *ēl bêt'ēl*, "God (of) Bethel" (Gen. 31:13; 35:37); *ēl šadday*, "God Almighty" (Gen. 17:1; *passim*); *ēl 'ôlām*, "The Everlasting God" (Gen. 21:33); *ēl rŏ'î*, "God of seeing" (Gen. 16:13). We shall return to these names later. Another peculiarity is the frequent designation of this god as the "God of Abraham, the God of Isaac, and the God of Jacob" (Exod. 3:6; cf. Gen. 24:12; 26:24; 28:13; 31:53; etc.) or as "the God of my [or your, etc.] father" (Gen. 31:5, 29; 43:23; *passim*). Occasionally he is also called *paḥad yiṣḥāq*, "Fear of Isaac" (or more correctly, "Kinsman of Isaac"[10]), and *ăbîr ya'ăqōb*, "The Mighty One of Jacob."

Now there is precedent elsewhere in the ancient Near East for an

<hr />

[7] A bibliography on these matters can be found in E. L. Ehrlich, *A Concise History of Israel* (London: Darton, Longman & Todd, 1962), p. 6.

[8] This has been shown most recently by J. Vergote, *Joseph en Égypte* (Louvain: Publications Universitaires, Institut Orientaliste, 1959).

[9] Maag, *op. cit.*, p. 5.

[10] See below, p. 21.

individual to speak of a god as his own personal god. Thus the Sumerian king often calls the tutelary deity who watches over him and his family "my god." In the Old Assyrian texts from Cappodocia, an individual god is either referred to by name (e.g., Il-abrat) or called "your god" (*ilka*) or "the god of your father" (*il abīka*).[11] Alt has further shown that the Semitic and Greek inscriptions of the Nabataeans from the Hellenistic period frequently speak of the god of a particular individual.[12] For example, they mention the god of *QSJW*, the god of Aumos, and the god of Arkesilaos.[13] In a few cases, this god of a particular individual came to be acknowledged as the god of a whole region or was absorbed into one of the great gods, such as Zeus Helios.[14] Developments of this kind are attested also in the documents from Nuzu (fifteenth century) and in Aramaic inscription from the eighth century.[15]

Thus the god of an individual or the "god of the father" represents a type by no means uncommon in the ancient Near East. It is safe to assume that the god of the patriarchs was of the same type.

We also know that proper names from the Old Akkadian period (25th—23rd centuries) and the Old Assyrian period (20th—19th centuries) very frequently designate the divinities as "father," "brother," or "kinsman" of the individual so named. Proper names of this type were very popular among the Amorites in the period between 2100 and 1600.[16] This seems to indicate that a god was looked upon as a kinsman of the tribe that worshiped him. Now such proper names are also found among the Israelites in the earliest period: Eli-ab, "my god is father" (Num. 1:9 *et al.*); Ammi-el, "my kinsman is El" (Num. 13:12); Ahi-ezer, "my brother (god) is help" (Num. 1:12 *et al.*); etc. We may assume, therefore, that the pre-Mosaic Hebrews shared this same conception.

The names of some of the tribes of Israel present a particular problem, e.g., Asher, Gad, Zebulun, and Dan. A few scholars have interpreted them as divine names.[17] In fact, at least the name Gad appears elsewhere (for example, in Isa. 65:11) as the name of a god (the

---

[11] J. Lewy, *RHR*, CX (1934), 51, 53.

[12] A. Alt, *Der Gott der Väter* (Stuttgart: Kohlhammer, 1929); reprinted in A. Alt, *Kleine Schriften* (Munich: Beck, 1953), I, 1 ff.

[13] *Ibid.*, pp. 35 ff. (*Kl. Schr.*, I, 32 ff.).

[14] *Ibid.*, pp. 39 ff. (*Kl. Schr.*, I, 37 ff.).

[15] Albright, *op. cit.*, p. 249.

[16] *Ibid.*, pp. 244 f.; cf. E. Dhorme, *La religion des Hébreux nomades*, Vol. I: *L'évolution religieuse d'Israel* (Brussels: Nouvelle Société d'Editions, 1937), pp. 313 ff.

[17] E. Meyer; this theory has been supported most recently by G. Hölscher, *Geschichtsschreibung in Israel* (Lund: Gleerup, 1952), pp. 61 f.; cf. also I. Engnell, *Gamla Testamentet* (Stockholm: Svenska Kyrkans diakonistyrelses bokförlag, 1945), I, 123; T. J. Meek, *Hebrew Origins* (2nd ed.; New York: Harper, 1950), p. 111.

god of fortune).[18] Dan ("judge") could have been a Canaanite god. Asher might be taken as the male counterpart of Asherah, and Zebulun is reminiscent of the divine epithet *ba'al-zabul* from Ras Shamra. Now are these to be explained as tribal or family gods, regarded as being not simply kinsmen to but actually identical with the patriarch of the tribe (and hence really deified ancestors)? It is impossible to say with certainty at this time, but the possibility cannot be denied.

This is also the context in which to discuss the divine name *pahad yishāq* mentioned above. If that name is to be interpreted not in the usual fashion as "fear" of Isaac, but, following the analogy of the Arabic *fahid*, "hip, thigh," and the Palmyrene *pahda*, "family, tribe," as "Kinsman" of Isaac,[19] then it is in effect a precise designation of the god as kinsman of the tribe Isaac. The case of *ăbîr ya'ăqōb* is different. The Hebrew word *ăbîr* means "strong," but it also frequently has the meaning "bull" or "steer."[20] It is therefore not impossible to see here a reference to a symbolic bull; in the Canaanite religion, the bull as a symbol of strength and fertility is connected with El as well as Baal. We might mention by way of comparison the name "Shepherd of Israel" (Gen. 49:24).[21]

The divine names compounded with El are of a different sort entirely. In the first place, El is also familiar as the highest god of the Canaanites (as of most of the Semitic peoples). In the second place, these names are never associated with the patriarchs, either as individuals or as tribes; instead, with the exception of El Shaddai, they are always linked to specific cultic sites.

ēl 'elyôn is mentioned only once in the patriarchal narratives, in Genesis 14:18-22, where he appears as the god of Salem (i.e., Jerusalem) worshiped by Melchizedek. There is considerable evidence that the story of Melchizedek was composed at the time of David and actually reflects the conditions of that period.[22] Abraham represents David, and Melchizedek the contemporary city prince of Jerusalem. *ēl 'elyôn* would then have been the city god of Jerusalem as late as the time of David. The name *'elyôn* appears also in the Phoenician region; Philo Byblius, in his genealogy of the gods, calls him the father

---

[18] Cf. M. Noth, *ZDPV*, LXXV (1959), 26 f.; J. J. Stamm, "Der Name des Königs David," *SVT*, VII (Congress Volume, 1960), 179 f.

[19] Albright, *op. cit.*, p. 248; cf. Alt, *Kl. Schr.*, I, 26; O. Eissfeldt, "El and Yahweh," *JSS*, I (1956), 32.

[20] [Strictly speaking, the noun **ăbîr* occurs only in the construct form *ăbîr*, and then only in the phrase *ăbîr ya'ăqōb* or *ăbîr yiśrā'ēl*, both divine appellatives. Elsewhere the form is *abbîr*, which can mean both "strong" and "bull." For the most recent discussion connecting these two words on the basis of Ugaritic evidence, see B. Vawter, "The Canaanite Background of Genesis 49," *CBQ*, XVII (1955), 11.—TRANS.]

[21] Maag, *op. cit.*, p. 8.

[22] See below, pp. 60 f.

21

of all the divinities. In addition, the name 'elyôn is found once as a divine name in an Aramaic inscription.[23]

In Genesis he is called merely "maker [or "acquirer"] of heaven and earth"; this description is accorded him in such a way that it seems to be a more or less stock epithet.

ēl 'ôlām, "the Everlasting God," appears in Genesis 21:33 in connection with Beer-sheba. ēl rŏ'î, "God of seeing," appears in Genesis 16:13 at another sanctuary in southern Palestine. Beyond this, we have no information about these two divinities—or perhaps better, these two localized forms of a single great divinity.

ēl šadday is mentioned five times in Genesis (17:1; 28:3; 35:11; 43:14; 48:3; to these should probably be added 49:25). The original meaning of the name has not yet been explained. The most probable etymology derives the name from a word related to the Akkadian šadū, "mountain." If this is true, the name would mean something like "god of the mountain(s)."[24] It happens rather frequently that gods are called "mountain" or "rock." This is true both in the Old Testament and in Sumero-Babylonian religion, where Enlil is often called "the great mountain." A few Hyksos proper names also appear to contain the element har, "mountain," used as a divine name.[25] In the Old Testament we must probably understand this term primarily as a metaphor; it serves to express power and strength. Similarly in the case of Enlil, who is, after all, a god of the air, no identification with a mountain is presumably intended. If the name šadday actually has anything to do with "mountain," the most likely conclusion would seem to be that we are dealing with a god of the air like Enlil or Hadad; this supposition, of course, does not immediately exclude the possibility that such a god can reveal himself upon mountains. The passages in Genesis offer no clue as to the nature of this god; the other passages, particularly those in Job, are late, and give us no information about the original nature of the god. All in all, the Old Testament does not seem to connect any particular conception with this name.[26] The antiquity of the name is nevertheless demonstrated by the proper names Shedeur, Zurishaddai, and Ammishaddai contained in the lists of Numbers 1:5-15.[27] Furthermore, there is evidence for the existence of the name outside Israel during the Late

---

[23] J. Hempel, review of P. S. Ronzevalle's "Fragments d'inscriptions Araméennes des environs d'Alep," MUST, XV (1931), 237–60, in ZAW, L (1932), 182.

[24] Albright, op. cit., p. 244; see also his article "The Names Shaddai and Abram," JBL, LIV (1935), 173–204.

[25] Ibid., p. 246.

[26] L. Köhler, Old Testament Theology, trans. A. S. Todd (London: Lutterworth, 1957), pp. 46 f.

[27] E. Jacob, Theology of the Old Testament, trans. A. W. Heathcote and P. J. Allcock (New York: Harper, 1958), p. 46, n. 3; Albright, op. cit., p. 245.

Bronze Age.[28] In the fourteenth century, we find in Egypt the proper name *sadde ʿammi*.[29]

We come finally to the name *ēl bêtʾēl*, found in Genesis 31:13 and later in the Elephantine texts. It also occurs once at Tyre, in an Assyrian cuneiform document. This god is probably only a local form of Hadad, the great wind and storm god of the Amorites and Syrians —once more, a god of the air. No explanation has yet been given of the relationship between this name and the phrase *bêt ēl*, "house of God," which designates the stone set up as a symbol of the god (see below.)[30]

This discussion seems to indicate that the names compounded with El designate various local forms of the Canaanite storm god—or perhaps better, the great god of the air. The patriarchal narratives obviously reflect a merging or identification of the god of the fathers with the great Canaanite god.[31] Now it is difficult to decide to what extent the god of the fathers is similar in nature to this Canaanite god. Nabataean family gods were identified with the god of the heavens (Zeus or Baal-shamin); but this fact in itself does not prove anything, since these illustrations are so much later, and since, furthermore, there were other family gods that did not merge with the great god. The god of the patriarchs could equally well have been of this latter type. It must be admitted, nevertheless, that such an identification as that of the god of the fathers with the Canaanite El presupposes at least a certain similarity between the two divinities.

Although we can thus say certain things about the religious beliefs of the patriarchs with some assurance, there still remains the question of what we know about the cult and religious practices of that period. In this question we must rely once more on comparative data drawn from related religious forms. If we can demonstrate that a particular phenomenon at variance with the later practice of Israel existed among other peoples who were Israel's historical or cultural neighbors, there is a certain probability that it really was peculiar to the patriarchal period. If, on the other hand, we find the closest parallel later in Israel or even later among the Canaanites, we cannot say with assurance that the phenomenon in question was not read back anachronistically into the patriarchal period. There is one method that must be rejected at the outset. It is not possible simply to select those elements of the patriarchal stories, or of Israelite religion in a later period, that agree

---

[28] L. Rost, "Gottesverehrung der Patriarchen," *SVT*, VII (Congress Volume, 1960), 356, n. 1; no further details given.

[29] Ehrlich, *op. cit.*, p. 11; Albright, *op. cit.*, p. 243.

[30] O. Eissfeldt, "Der Gott Bethel," *ARW*, XXVIII (1930), 1 ff.; R. Dussaud, *Les origines cananéennes du sacrifice israélite* (2nd ed.; Paris: Leroux, 1921), pp. 231 ff.

[31] O. Eissfeldt, "El and Yahweh," *JSS*, I (1956), 35 f., makes a clear distinction between El and the god of the fathers.

with some theoretically reconstructed picture of a "primitive" religion, assemble them, and transfer them to the patriarchal period as the religion of the nomadic Hebrews. Each case must be examined individually to see where there is real evidence and where there is none. It is our intention in what follows, to discuss some particular points in greater detail.

Three times in the course of the patriarchal narrative we read that Jacob sets up a stone at a place where God revealed himself or that he wants to mark particularly. Once, the narrative is probably describing an ordinary funerary monument (Gen. 35:20, Rachel's tomb; cf. II Sam. 18:18). In another passage (Gen. 31:45 ff.), two traditions are woven together: the one speaks of a pillar, the other of a heap of stones; but both presume a ceremony in which a covenant is concluded, in other words, a sacral act. The third occasion is the well-known Bethel story (Gen. 28:10-22). In a dream, Jacob sees God and his angels; in the morning he takes the stone he had put under his head and sets it up as a pillar, pours oil on the top of it (v. 18), and calls the name of the place Bethel, because it is "God's house" or dwelling place. In verse twenty-two he adds that the stone is to be a "house of God." There is a similar account in another story at Genesis 35:14: "And Jacob set up a pillar . . . and he poured out a drink offering on it, and poured oil on it."[32]

Now we know that such pillars or massebahs (Hebrew *maṣṣēbâ*) were in use especially in the Canaanite religion, from which they were borrowed (see below); but we also know that these massebahs were strongly condemned by the prophets (Hos. 10:1 f.; Mic. 5:12 [Eng. 5:13]; Jer. 43:13; Deut. 7:5; 12:3; 16:22). The asherah represented the female divinity; the massebah beside it served as a symbol of the presence of the male god. These stones were smeared with blood or fat, moistened with drink offerings, or kissed by the worshiper. Excavations have unearthed several such massebahs. The Greeks saw them in Phoenicia and Syria and gave them the name *baitulos* or *baitulion*, a word that retains a reminiscence of the term *bêt'ēl*, "house of God."[33]

Now the question is, were such massebahs really already present in the patriarchal period, or were they later read back into that period? As far as the Bethel story is concerned, it is pretty clear that we have to do with a legend describing the origin of a cult and that the shrine of Bethel is very ancient. The stone was certainly already there when the story was framed, but of course we have no evidence for its existence in the patriarchal period. At this point, though, a parallel Arabic phenomenon comes to our aid. The pre-Islamic Bedouins had stones set up at their cultic sites; they called these stones *nuṣb*, and

[32] Dhorme, *op. cit.*, pp. 159 ff.
[33] *Ibid.*, p. 166.

worshiped them in a manner similar to that of the Canaanites.[34] *nuṣb*
and *maṣṣēbâ* both derive from the same root. There is also a similar
word in Phoenician.[35] Thus we probably have here another ramifica-
tion of the same phenomenon; and these—stones set up as pillars go
back to a time when the ancestors of the Canaanites, Hebrews, and
Arabs still shared the same culture. This might mean, of course, that
we are here dealing with what was originally a worship of holy stones
having nothing to do with any divinity. That is quite another question,
and each person must answer it according to the theory of the origin
of religion he happens to prefer.

On the other hand, it is doubtful whether the references to setting
up an altar are original. Altars are unknown among other Semitic
nomads, and plainly are characteristic of settled life.

The patriarchal narratives also contain several references to trees
that for some reason seemed to have particular significance.[36]
Shechem, for example, boasted a terebinth reputed to have played a
significant role as early as the time of Abraham and Jacob (Gen.
12:6; 35:4). A couple of times it is even called an oracle-terebinth
(*ēlôn môreh*, "teacher's terebinth," in Gen. 12:6; or *ēlôn meʻônenîm*,
"diviners' terebinth," in Judg. 9:37).[37] At Hebron, Abraham dwelt
by the terebinth of Mamre (Gen. 13:18; 14:13; 18:1; the Hebrew
text mentions "trees" in the plural, the LXX only one tree). Abraham
is said to have planted a tamarisk at Beer-sheba, and to have called
there on the name of *ēl ʻôlām*, "the Everlasting God" (Gen. 21:33).
Even if we explain these stories as aetiologies of later cultic practices,
there is actually nothing in itself improbable about the assumption that
holy trees existed as early as the time of the patriarchs. In ancient
Canaan, the green tree served as a symbol of fertility; fertility rites
were performed under green trees, as the prophets frequently attest
(e.g., Jer. 2:20; 3:6; Ezek. 6:13; Isa. 57:5). The pre-Islamic Bedouins
of Arabia also were familiar with sacred trees.[38] Right down to our
own day, such trees in Palestine are festooned with articles of clothing
or rags (clearly intended as sacrificial offerings).[39]

We must emphasize that this entire discussion by no means demonstrates the literal historicity of these references in the patriarchal

---

[34] J. Wellhausen, *Reste arabischen Heidentums* (2nd ed.; Berlin: Reimer,
1897), pp. 101 ff.

[35] Phoenician *nṣb* and *mṣbt* are found in funerary monuments published
in *CIS*, I, 123a, 139, and in *CIS*, I, 44, 46, 58, etc., respectively.

[36] Dhorme, *op. cit.*, pp. 149 ff.

[37] [The word *ēlôn* is translated "oak" by the RSV, with "terebinth" as
a footnote. On the confusion between the various words represented in
English by "oak" and "terebinth," see J. C. Trever's articles: "Oak," *IDB*,
III, 575; and "Terebinth," *IDB*, IV, 574.—TRANS.]

[38] Wellhausen, *op. cit.*, pp. 104 f.; W. Robertson Smith, *The Religion of
the Semites* (3rd ed.; New York: Macmillan, 1927), pp. 185 ff.

[39] R. Kriss and H. Kriss-Heinrich, *Volksglaube im Bereich des Islam*
(Wiesbaden: Harrassowitz, 1960-62), I, 20 f., 39 f.

narratives. Only one thing can be said with assurance: sacred stones and sacred trees played a part in the religion of that period. It is quite possible, however, that details of the stories in question reflect conditions of a much later period.

The so-called "teraphim" present a special problem.[40] They are mentioned in Genesis 31:19, 30 ff.: when Rachel and Jacob flee from Paddan-aram, Rachel steals her father's teraphim and hides them under the camel saddle. In verse thirty, Laban calls them "my gods." This description suggests that they are images of gods, but neither this text nor the other passages in the Old Testament mentioning teraphim provide more detailed information. They are mentioned several times in connection with seeking oracles (Ezek. 21:26 f. [Eng. 21:21 f.]; Zech. 10:2; cf. II Kings 23:24; Hos. 3:4; probably also Judg. 17:5). Even the etymology of the word is uncertain: Does it derive from rp', "heal," or from trp, "decay"? Some think the word designates the small female figurines from various periods that have been found in great abundance in Palestine. These figurines probably functioned as amulets.[41] More recently, in order to illuminate the pericope in question (Gen. 31), an adoption certificate from Nuzu is usually cited. According to this document, the adopted son must divide the inheritance with any other son who might be born later, but must let the latter have possession of the gods (presumably the images).[42] This would mean that by stealing the teraphim Rachel laid claim to the right of inheritance. If the teraphim were amulets, this parallel would be less informative. Since, however, the comparison with the Nuzu document is not completely assured,[43] it cannot be cited as an argument against the explanation given above. Nevertheless, how these amulets might have been used for divination remains a question. No positive answer can be given at this time. And if the Nuzu text turns out to be a false parallel, then there is no real evidence left for the existence of the teraphim in the patriarchal period.[44] Theoretically, they could quite as well have been introduced later. Nevertheless, the details of the narrative give such an impression of originality that the possibility does remain that we have here an ancient reminiscence.

This exhausts our material on the religion of the patriarchs. It is

[40] For a detailed discussion and bibliography, see A. R. Johnson, *The Cultic Prophet in Ancient Israel* (2nd ed.; Cardiff: University of Wales, 1962), p. 32, n. 4.

[41] This is the opinion of Albright, *op. cit.*, p. 311.

[42] This theory was first proposed by C. Gordon, *BA*, III (1940), 1 ff.

[43] The right of inheritance gives claim to the gods, not vice versa! Cf. M. Greenberg, "Another Look at Rachel's Theft of the Teraphim," *JBL*, LXXXI (1962), 239 ff.

[44] The attempt to demonstrate the occurrence of the word in the Ras Shamra texts has been unsuccessful. The form in 67 (= I* AB), I, 4 is verbal (*ttrp*).

not worth the effort to isolate those religious concepts and practices of later Israel that somehow agree with our picture of a "primitive" religion and read them back into the patriarchal period. There is no proof in any case that we could really discover the religion of the patriarchal period by this method. Such traits could have invaded Israel quite as easily from other sources. In the last analysis, all reconstructions of the primitive religion remain hypothetical. It should be noted further that what we have been able to discover with reference to the religion of the patriarchs by no means deserves the name "primitive"; neither was the environment of the patriarchs "primitive."

Of course, it may be possible that Maag is right in his reconstruction of the patriarchs' religion.[45] In his opinion, he can show certain correspondences between the patriarchs and pastoral tribes of the present day. Just as the patriarchs set out at the command of their god to seek a new land, so the Bakhtiari of Iran obey their leader, who is inspired by God, and set out in search of new pastures. And for them, as in the case of the patriarchal narratives, the important thing is trust and obedience; there is an assurance of being under the special protection of the deity. The weakness of this reconstruction, of course, lies in the distance, both temporal and spatial, separating the two quantities being compared.

---

[45] *Op. cit.*, pp. 2 ff.; see also his discussion in *SVT*, VII (Congress Volume, 1960), 138, n. 1.

2.

THE BEGINNINGS OF
ISRAEL'S RELIGION: MOSES

The biblical account of how the Israelite religion began is simple enough. Israel came into being as a people in Egypt, where their ancestor Jacob had emigrated with his sons because of a famine in Palestine. When the Israelites became more and more numerous and powerful, the Pharaoh subjected them to forced labor and finally gave orders that all the newborn sons of the Israelites should be killed. Nevertheless, one of these children, Moses, was miraculously saved and brought up at the court of the Pharaoh. The god of the patriarchs appeared to him in the desert of Midian, revealed his name Yahweh, and commissioned him to deliver the people of Israel from its bondage in Egypt. As the result of a miracle, the Israelites succeeded in crossing the Reed Sea,[1] while the Egyptians drowned in the sea. Then at Mount Sinai or Horeb, Yahweh appeared to the people and concluded a covenant with them, according to which Israel was to be his people and he Israel's god. After forty years of wandering in the desert and after the death of Moses, Israel, under the leadership of Joshua, conquered the land that had been promised beforehand to the fathers and settled there.

Moses was therefore the political and religious leader of the people of Israel, who left Egypt and migrated to Palestine. He was the mediator of the covenant between his people and Yahweh, his god; he laid down for his fellow Israelites the conditions of the covenant in the form of specific legal ordinances. In other words, he was the founder of the Israelite religion.

Now behind this apparently quite simple narrative there lies, however, a very complicated process of transmission, the course of which we can only guess. For this reason, the actual historical events on

---

[1] [Hebrew *yām sûp*, "sea of reeds." The LXX interpreted the Hebrew expression as referring to *thalassa eruthra,* the "Red Sea"; the Vulgate followed this interpretation, which passed thus into the English Bible.—TRANS.]

which this account is based are, for the most part, obscure.[2] On the one hand, that national entity that we call Israel first took shape on Palestinian soil; on the other hand, the Exodus tradition is so firmly rooted in the traditions of Israel that it can hardly be rejected as unhistorical. Furthermore, a nation is unlikely to invent a period of slavery in its past. It is possible, though, that only one of the groups that later united to form Israel actually underwent the experience of slavery in Egypt and subsequent liberation. Since the majority of the twelve tribes may have taken on tribal character only in Palestine, we cannot even identify those who were liberated with one or more of these tribes. There is a tradition, it is true, that Moses belonged to the tribe of Levi, and several Egyptian personal names occur in this tribe (Phinehas, Pashhur, Hophni, Merari, and Putiel, as well as Moses). These facts might support Meek's assumption that Levi represents this group.[3] But since the prehistory of the tribe of Levi is particularly enigmatic, it is impossible to say anything with assurance. There remains the possibility and even probability that other groups were also in Egypt.

Von Rad has made another important observation. The earliest credal summaries of Yahweh's mighty acts in history (Deut. 26:5-9; 6:20-24; cf. Josh. 24:2-13) do not mention Sinai; they place all their stress on the deliverance from Egypt and guidance into the promised land. As von Rad has correctly seen, this failure to mention Sinai is connected with the fact that the Sinai traditions were handed down within the framework of a covenant-renewal festival, while the Exodus traditions are rooted in other contexts,[4] the most important of which was probably the Passover cult-legend. This does not necessarily mean that the story of Sinai—although "traditio-historically secondary"—is unhistorical. It is even arguable that the Sinai story is just as "primary" as the Exodus traditions; it was only handed down in a different context.[5] It is a well-known fact in the history of religions that certain complexes of ideas are actualized only in certain situations and at certain times.[6]

In this discussion we must keep in mind a further fact. The historical Israel of the time of David and Solomon was made up of

---

[2] For a more detailed discussion of these problems, consult the various presentations of Israel's history, e.g., those of Noth and Bright.

[3] T. J. Meek, *Hebrew Origins* (2nd ed.; New York: Harper, 1950), p. 32.

[4] G. von Rad, *"Das formgeschichtliche Problem des Hexateuchs,"* BWANT, IV: 26 (1938), pp. 3-23. See also M. Noth, *Überlieferungsgeschichte des Pentateuchs* (Stuttgart: Kohlhammer, 1948), pp. 63 ff.; cf. M. Noth, *Exodus,* trans. J. S. Bowden (London: SCM, 1962), p. 11.

[5] Cf. H. Wildberger, *Jahwes Eigentumsvolk* (Stuttgart & Zürich: Zwingli, 1960); W. Beyerlin, *Herkunft und Geschichte der ältesten Sinaitraditionen* (Tübingen: Mohr, 1961).

[6] Cf. Å. Hultkrantz, "Configurations of Religious Beliefs," *Ethnos,* 1956, pp. 194 f.

two major components: a northern group of tribes, given the name Israel, with the two Joseph-tribes Ephraim and Manasseh as its nucleus; and a southern group, to which belonged primarily the tribe of Judah and also a few smaller groups such as the Kenites and the Calebites. Now the covenant-renewal festival is quite plainly peculiar to the northern tribes; Deuteronomy 27 and Joshua 24 unambiguously point to Shechem as the site of the festival. As we shall discuss later, the Israelite covenant form is similar to that of Hittite treaties; this fact might lead us to consider a northern origin for the entire covenant idea. Reminiscences of a stay at the oasis of Kadesh-Barnea play an important part in the traditions of the southern group, with its center at Hebron. Guthrie thinks that the Exodus traditions spread out from this group and only later were connected with the covenant tradition of Shechem. The combined traditions of these two groups gave the impression of a single chain of events including the deliverance from Egypt, the theophany at Sinai, and the conclusion of the covenant.[7] It is debatable, of course, whether such a clear distinction is possible. The southern group as well as the northern possesses the tradition of the theophany upon the holy mountain; in other words, this tradition forms a part of both the southern "Yahwistic" and the northern "Elohistic" and Deuteronomistic traditions. The southern tradition calls the mountain Sinai, the northern calls it Horeb. The encounter with God upon the mountain is therefore as secure a component of the tradition as is the Exodus, and cannot be ascribed to a particular group of tribes.[8]

Attempts have likewise been made to determine the role of Moses on the basis of similar traditio-historical considerations. Noth observes the presence of Moses in all the different traditions. Since, however, these traditions are by origin separate and distinct units, he thinks the figure of Moses must have been introduced into them at a later time. Moses is "not especially firmly rooted in the Sinai theme," and he "had no historical connection with the event which took place on Sinai." "It is therefore hardly justifiable to describe him as the organiser and law-giver of Israel," and "to describe him as the 'founder of a religion' . . . is quite misleading."[9] It is nevertheless doubtful whether this conclusion is really necessary or even admissible. If we admit, with Noth, that there is an historical event at the center of the Sinai tradition, the presence of an individual leader remains a very probable assumption. The fact that all the traditions speak of Moses could also be interpreted as meaning that he was so

---

[7] H. H. Guthrie, *God and History in the Old Testament* (Greenwich: Seabury, 1960), pp. 16 ff.

[8] Cf. also Beyerlin, *op. cit.*, pp. 165 ff.

[9] M. Noth, *The History of Israel*, trans. S. Godman and P. R. Ackroyd (2nd ed.; New York: Harper, 1960), p. 136, where he refers to his *Überlieferungsgeschichte*, pp. 172 ff.

universally known and recognized a figure that he quite naturally had a place both in the Exodus traditions and in the Sinai story. If in addition we refuse to draw a sharp line between the northern and southern streams of tradition, Noth's major argument breaks down. No doubt the unanimity of Israelite tradition with respect to the person of Moses has particular significance. If the historicity of the Mosaic traditions is denied, this means only that some other figure must be invented to explain the existence of the nation of Israel and its religion.[10]

But even if it is not really possible to doubt the existence of Moses, this fact is still far from proving that the whole Moses story contained in the book of Exodus should be considered historical. It is better viewed as a legend that has been considerably amplified in the course of time.

Now this legend (Exod. 2) relates that a woman from the tribe of Levi gave birth to Moses—whose name, by the way, is a good Egyptian name containing the element *msi*, "to bear," "to beget" (as in Ramses, Egypt. *r³-ms-sw*, "Ra is the one who begot him," or *i'ḥ-ms*, "the moon-god was born"). Since the Pharaoh was seeking to kill all Israelite boys, Moses was at first kept hidden and then set out on the Nile in a basket made of bulrushes. The daughter of the Pharaoh found him there, adopted him, and had him brought up at court. This story has many parallels in antiquity. The earliest is the legend of the birth of Sargon, the first Semitic king of Babylon. Similar stories are also told of Cyrus (by Herodotus, I, 108 ff.), Perseus, and the two founders of Rome, Romulus and Remus. We obviously have here a widespread legendary motif intended to show how divine providence protects a future ruler. The remarkable thing is that Moses is not a king or a ruler; but other traits of royal ideology seem also to have been connected with Moses.[11]

When he was a young man, Moses got into a quarrel with an Egyptian overseer and killed him. This led to his banishment. In this way he came to Midian—probably in northwest Arabia—where he married Zipporah, the daughter of a Midianite priest called either Reuel or Jethro by the tradition. Here the god of the patriarchs appears to him in a burning bush and commissions him to lead the Israelites out of Egypt. At the same time, God reveals to Moses his name Yahweh, or at least an explanation of this name. When Moses asks what God's name is, he receives the startling answer, "I am who I am" (Heb. *ěhyeh ăšer ěhyeh*, Exod. 3:14). Moses hesitates—

---

[10] N. Söderblom, *Das Werden des Gottesglaubens* (Leipzig: Hinrichs, 1916), p. 310, quoted with approval by I. Engnell, *Gamla Testamentet* (Stockholm: Svenska kyrkans diakonistyrelses bokförlag, 1945), I, 129.
[11] See, for example, I. Engnell, *Studies in Divine Kingship* (Uppsala: Almqvist & Wiksell, 1943), pp. 174 f.; G. Widengren, *The Ascension of the Apostle and the Heavenly Book* (Leipzig: Harrassowitz, 1950), p. 28.

as do the prophets Isaiah and Jeremiah later—but gives in and returns to Egypt after he has received the power to work wonders and the promise that he would have an assistant in his brother Aaron.

This story raises two immediate questions. First: How are we to understand the revelation of the name of God? And second: How much historical reality is there behind the tradition of Moses' stay in Midian?

The first question can be given a definite answer to this extent: the sentence "I am who I am" is intended beyond all doubt to be an explanation of the divine name Yahweh. But scholars are a long way from reaching agreement on the origin and original meaning of this name. The text alludes to a derivation from the root *hwy*, which is equated with *hyy*, "be." This derivation is frequently doubted. If it is accepted, the question remains whether the name is to be understood as a substantive formed with the prefix *ya-*, meaning "he who is" or "he who calls into being,"[12] or as a verbal form in the imperfect meaning "he is" or more probably, as the vocalization seems to suggest, "he who causes to be," i.e., "he who creates."[13] If this derivation is rejected, possible cognates include the Arabic *hawā*, which can mean "cause to fall" or "blow." The former is interpreted as a reference to Yahweh as a god of the thunderstorm,[14] the latter as a reference to him as a god of the windstorm.[15] It is probably impossible to reach a definite decision; but this does not matter particularly, since there is no other reference in the Old Testament to the meaning of the name, nor does the Old Testament conception of God depend in any way on the meaning of the name Yahweh.[16] Attempts to cite occurrences of the name outside Israel must probably be judged failures.[17] The closest parallel is the Ugaritic *yw*, which occurs once as a son of El;[18] but he is obviously identical with *ym*, the personified sea,[19] and therefore irrelevant on technical grounds.

---

[12] L. Köhler, *Die Welt des Orients*, I, 5, 1950, p. 405; cf. J. Obermann, "The Divine Name YHWH in the Light of Recent Discoveries," *JBL*, LXVIII (1949), 301 ff., with the suggested meaning "Sustainer," "Maintainer," "Establisher."

[13] W. F. Albright, "The Names 'Israel' and 'Judah,' etc.," *JBL*, XLVI (1924), 168 ff., following many earlier scholars. [See also F. M. Cross, Jr., "Yahweh and the God of the Patriarchs," *HTR*, LV (1962), 225 ff.—TRANS.]

[14] I. Engnell, *Gamla Testamentet*, I, 262, following Wellhausen *et al.*

[15] P. de Lagarde, *Übersicht*, p. 137; *Orientalia*, II, pp. 27 ff.

[16] Cf. L. Köhler, *Old Testament Theology*, trans. A. S. Todd (London: Lutterworth, 1957), p. 43.

[17] A. Murtonen, "The Appearance of the Name YHWH outside Israel," *SOSOF*, XIV (1951), 3. For a discussion of the entire question, see also A. Murtonen, *A Philological and Literary Treatise on the Old Testament Divine Names* (Helsinki: Societas Orientalis Fennica, 1952).

[18] *UM 'nt* (V AB), IV, 14.

[19] G. R. Driver, *Canaanite Myths and Legends* (Edinburgh: Clark, 1956), p. 12, n. 4.

Linguistic evidence, accordingly, does not solve the problem of the origin of Yahweh. Neither is it possible to decide definitely whether the full form *yahweh* is original, or whether the original form is the shorter *yah, yāhû,* or *yô-,* of which the latter two occur only in theophorous personal names.[20]

The fact that the answer "I am who I am" sounds somehow like an evasion also creates difficulties. We are left with the impression that this god does not want to surrender his name to men. The widespread conception that whoever knows a person's name has power over that person makes this evasion intelligible. The name of God, and therefore God himself, is simply not at man's disposal. Similarly, the god that wrestles with Jacob at the Jabbok refuses to reveal his name (Gen. 32:29). But this is only one side of the explanation. As a matter of fact, Yahweh reveals himself to Moses as the god who will help him and his people. It has been argued that the Hebrew verb *hāyâ* does not refer only or even primarily to mere being, but often has a dynamic, active character[21]; it would then be possible to translate: "I will be present on your behalf, I will be with you in the way that you will learn."[22] In view of recent semantic studies, however, it is uncertain whether this translation captures the real meaning of the name.[23]

With respect to the second question, too, we can only express conjectures. Midian was a Bedouin tribe with its home in northwest Arabia. There must have been some sort of connection between it and the emigrating Israelites, for the linking of God's revelation to the Midianite territory appears to be an original part of the tradition. Another tradition in Exodus 18 confirms this assumption: after the Exodus, Moses' father-in-law comes to meet the Israelites; and when he discovers what has happened, he acknowledges Yahweh to be the greatest of all gods and offers a burnt offering to him. Many scholars have concluded from this account that Jethro was a priest of Yahweh

---

[20] G. R. Driver, "The Original Form of the Name 'Yahweh': Evidence and Conclusions," *ZAW*, XLVI (1928), 7 ff.; K. G. Kuhn, *Orient. Stud. E. Littmann*, 1935, pp. 25 ff.

[21] T. Boman, *Hebrew Thought Compared with Greek*, trans. J. L. Moreau (London: SCM, 1960), pp. 38 ff.

[22] G. von Rad, *Old Testament Theology*, trans. D. M. G. Stalker (Edinburgh and London: Oliver and Boyd, 1962), pp. 180 f.; cf. M. Noth, *Exodus*, pp. 42 ff.; T. C. Vriezen, "EHJE 'AŠER 'EHJE," *Festschrift für Alfred Bertholet* (Tübingen: Mohr, 1950), pp. 498 ff. On the meaning of the construction "I am who I am," see E. Jacob, *Theology of the Old Testament*, trans. A. W. Heathcote and P. J. Allcock (New York: Harper, 1958), pp. 51 ff.; D. N. Freedman, "The Name of the God of Moses," *JBL*, LXXIX (1960), 151 ff. The case for the translation "I am the one who is" is argued by J. Lindblom in "Noch einmal die Deutung des Jahwe-Namens," *Annual of the Swedish Theological Institute* (Leiden: Brill, 1964), III, 4 ff.

[23] J. Barr, *The Semantics of Biblical Language* (London: Oxford, 1961), pp. 68 ff.

and that Moses had become acquainted with this god through him. Additional support for this theory has been found in the fact that the description of the subsequent events at Sinai suggests a volcanic mountain, and that volcanoes, though not found on the Sinai peninsula, are found in the Midianite region.[24] In addition, Judges 4:11 calls Moses' father-in-law a Kenite, and the Kenites are known to be nomads connected with the tribe of Judah. It is therefore not out of the question that relationships of a religious nature existed between the southern Israelite tribes and nomadic tribes like the Midianites and Kenites. We know at least that the Kenites worshiped Yahweh, and that their ancestor Cain received the mark of Yahweh upon his forehead (Gen. 4:15). This by no means proves, however, that Yahweh was originally the god of the Kenites or Midianites and that Moses took him over from those tribes. But the possibility should not be rejected out of hand. Of the many theories explaining the origin of the religion of Yahweh, the Kenite hypothesis is the only one to which a certain probability attaches.[25]

Now the story continues. Moses appears before Pharaoh and demands that he let the Israelites go, but Pharaoh refuses. A series of nine plagues (water changed to blood, frogs, gnats, flies, murrain, boils, hail, locusts, and darkness) with which Yahweh afflicts Egypt fails to move his heart. Then Yahweh announces the tenth visitation: in one night he will slay all the first-born in Egypt. The Israelites are to hold themselves in readiness to leave the land in great haste, for now Pharaoh will finally relent. So as not to be touched themselves by this plague, the Israelites are to slaughter a lamb and smear some of its blood on the doorposts of their houses, so that Yahweh will pass them by.

The plan succeeds, and the Israelites begin their march. But then Pharaoh changes his mind and decides to pursue them. He overtakes them just as they reach the shore of the "Reed Sea." Then Yahweh comes to their aid with a new wonder. He causes the water to recede, so that the Israelites can march across the bottom of the sea. When the Egyptians attempt to pursue them, the water rushes back and drowns the Egyptians. But the Israelites continue on into the desert, and finally arrive at the "mountain of God," Sinai.

This whole story obviously owes its form to its being a legend to

---

[24] Cf. M. Noth, *Exodus,* p. 156: "These [volcanoes] might have a bearing on the question if the description . . . in Exod. 19 does not merely represent the acceptance of traditional elements of a theophany description. . . ." It should be remarked that volcanoes are not found in Midian proper, but somewhat further south.

[25] For a detailed discussion with bibliography, see H. H. Rowley, *From Joseph to Joshua* (London: Oxford, 1950), pp. 149 ff.; cf. also M. Noth, *Exodus,* pp. 30 ff., 145 ff.

be read at the Passover festival.[26] On the one hand, the rites of Passover have been so framed as to imitate the events of the story; on the other hand, the ceremonies of the festival have probably influenced the narrative. In addition, the narrative combines several different traditions.[27] It is therefore difficult to uncover whatever historical nucleus there may be in the narrative. So-called natural explanations of the miracle at the Sea of Reeds overlook its nature: the account is not history but a festival legend, and concerns itself particularly with the religious meaning of the events.

More or less the same thing holds true for the Sinai pericope (Exod. 19, 20, and 24). When the Israelites have assembled at the foot of the mountain, Yahweh appears to them accompanied by smoke, fire, and thunder, and concludes a covenant with them: he will be their God and they will be his people. The basis of the covenant is laid out: first the Ten Commandments (the Decalogue), then the so-called Book of the Covenant (Exod. 20:22—23:33), probably a somewhat later composition. Here, too, the account clearly shows cultic influence: the preparations made by the Israelites to receive God's revelation are conceived as a process of self-sanctification (Exod. 19:10-14), that is, a kind of cultic purification; and the appearance of God is depicted in terms of a traditional cultic theophany. Probably the Sinai narrative is to be understood as the festival legend of a covenant renewal festival like that celebrated at Shechem, for example.[28]

Somewhat later, Moses climbs up the mountain into God's presence and receives two stone tablets on which God himself has written the law. These are the so-called tables of the testimony (Exod. 31:18; 32:15 ff.). Strangely enough, a different tradition tells us that after Moses, enraged at the apostasy of the Israelites, had broken the tables, he himself made new ones (Exod. 34:1-28). Perhaps this incident represents an earlier stage of the tradition, and the miraculous element in the giving of the law was later enhanced, so that God himself is now pictured as writing the law.

Mendenhall has pointed out that the form of the covenant is reminiscent of Hittite suzerainty treaties, in which a king enters into a covenant with a vassal.[29] Such a treaty document usually exhibits the following structure: (1) introduction—"Thus says N, the great

---

[26] J. Pedersen, *Israel, Its Life and Culture* (rev. ed.; London: Oxford, 1959), III-IV, Excursus I.

[27] See the standard commentaries (M. Noth, G. Beer, etc.).

[28] See below, pp. 192 ff.

[29] G. E. Mendenhall, *Law and Covenant* (Pittsburgh: Biblical Colloquium, 1955 [Reprinted from *BA*, XVII (1954)]). Now see also K. Baltzer, *Das Bundesformular* (Neukirchen: Erziehungsverein, 1959) [and D. J. McCarthy, *Treaty and Covenant* (Rome: Pontifical Biblical Institute, 1963).— TRANS.].

king . . ."; (2) an account of the relationship previously obtaining between the two parties; (3) the conditions of the treaty; (4) a provision that the document is to be deposited in a temple and regularly read in public; (5) a list of gods acting as witnesses; and (6) formulas of cursing and blessing. To a remarkable extent the Sinai covenant is described in the same categories. It is difficult to determine whether this phenomenon really shows Hittite influence in northern Israel or whether we are dealing with a treaty form common throughout the ancient Near East. But the analogies at least prove that the covenant concept is not necessarily a late idea, since it was known to the Hittites in precisely this form as early as the fourteenth century B.C.

We cannot say definitely, of course, to what extent the Israelite covenant idea goes back to Moses. Since this conception was so basic to the Israelite religion and tradition unanimously connects it with Moses, the possibility of Mosaic origin must be considered seriously.[30] The fact that the present form of the Sinai narrative in all probability goes back to a north Israelite source does not prove the contrary, since the form of a tradition is not the determining factor in deciding its origin. If Moses is really to be considered the founder of the Israelite religion, it is quite possible to connect the making of the covenant with him.

When the Hittites concluded a treaty, the conditions were always made public. We must therefore consider whether some part of the Book of the Covenant (Exod. 20:22—23:33) or at least the Decalogue (Exod. 20:1-17) derives from Moses.[31] Nothing can be proved on this point, of course. Today, the Book of the Covenant is usually ascribed to the period of the Judges; and, in fact, it probably does reflect circumstances that are somewhat later than the time of Moses. The Decalogue can be dated only with difficulty. A few details, such as the mention of ox and ass or the "sojourner who is within your gates," obviously presuppose the conditions of settled life in Canaan; but these can be explained as a secondary revision. It remains probable that the ancient covenant festival from the very beginning possessed a short summary of the covenant conditions. If Moses concluded the covenant, it probably follows that the obligations of the people must have been proclaimed to them in some form. And since tradition presents the Decalogue as such a summary, the original covenant must probably also have contained something at least very similar to our Decalogue. This prototype of the Decalogue, or perhaps better of the covenant conditions, obviously cannot now be reconstructed.

The events at Sinai are followed by the period of wandering in the

---

[30] Cf. Beyerlin, *op. cit.*, pp. 165 ff.
[31] *Ibid.*, pp. 169 f., and also pp. 59 ff.

desert. The Israelites spent forty years in the desert before they finally were allowed to take possession of the Promised Land. Numbers 14:26 ff. explains that this period of wandering was due to Israel's lack of faith, but this narrative looks more like a later explanation. In fact, the tradition of a fairly long stay at the oasis of Kadesh-Barnea does seem based on historical reality. This site, possibly identical with the modern 'Ain Qedeis,[32] apparently had particular significance for a part of the tribes that later migrated to Canaan.[33] This group probably lived there for some time; it was there they formed their religious traditions. A few scholars have even looked upon Kadesh as the place where the religion of Yahweh originated and look for Sinai very close by. Meek, for example, views the tribe of Levi—which later became a priestly group—as the possessors of the Kadesh tradition.[34] Much evidence, in his opinion, points in this direction: for example, the connection of Levi in Deuteronomy 33:8 with Massah and Meribah, where several desert traditions are localized (Exod. 17:7; Num. 20:13); and the appearance of the Levites in south Palestinian traditions such as Judges 17:7 and 19:1.[35] Meek assumes that the tribal god of Levi was a serpent divinity, which can still be glimpsed in the narrative of the bronze serpent Nehushtan (Num. 21:5-9)—this serpent having been made by Moses, who was of the tribe of Levi. Meek points out that several personal names in the tribe of Levi can be traced back to words for "snake": Nahshon (Exod. 6:23), Nahash (I Chron. 26:4, LXX), Shuppim (I Chron. 26:16). In the story of the golden calf (Exod. 32:25-29), the Levites appear as champions of the Yahweh cult, in contrast to the bull worship introduced by Aaron, which is obviously of Canaanite origin.[36] This argument shows that the story of the golden calf, like so many others of the desert period, is a retrojection of a later situation into the proto-history of Israel, but does not decide the question of its historical credibility.

According to another theory, the Levites were originally priests of a non-Israelite shrine at Kadesh who accepted the religion of

---

[32] [Or 'Ain el-Qudeirat; cf. E. G. Kraeling (ed.), *Historical Atlas of the Holy Land* (Chicago: Rand McNally, 1959), p. 55 (with map); B. Rothenberg and Y. Aharoni, *God's Wilderness* (London: Thames & Hudson, 1961), pp. 121 ff.; N. Glueck, *Rivers in the Desert* (New York: Farrar, Straus & Cudahy, 1959), p. 73 and *passim*. The identification with 'Ain Qedeis was first made by Trumbull in 1881, that with 'Ain el-Qudeirat by Woolley and Lawrence in 1913.—TRANS.]

[33] Beyerlin, *op. cit.*, pp. 165 f.

[34] *Op. cit.*, pp. 119 ff.

[35] On the other hand, Meek's assertion that the word *lawi'u* occurs in Minaean inscriptions from northern Arabia as the term for a priest has been proved wrong. See R. de Vaux, *Ancient Israel,* trans. John McHugh (New York: McGraw-Hill, 1961), pp. 358 f.

[36] Aaron as Moses' brother is traditio-historically secondary; see M. Noth, *Exodus*, pp. 46 f., 122.

Yahweh and later became his champions. Probably only one fact can be stated with assurance: the Levites were somehow connected with Kadesh and came to the fore as opponents of the bull cult. We must also assume that the traditions of a stay in Kadesh reflect historical facts. Perhaps the Israelites coming out of Egypt joined here with other tribes, bringing into being the first larger association of tribes with common religious obligations.

Then, according to Pentateuchal tradition, Moses died before the people migrated into Canaan from Transjordan. It was not granted him to enter the Promised Land; he was only allowed to look upon the land from Mount Nebo, east of the Jordan. Significantly, the site of his grave is not indicated; this fact shows that there was no local tradition about a burial place of Moses.[37]

Although Moses definitely played an extraordinarily important role as the principal figure in the beginnings of the Israelite religion, our sources fail us when we try to define this role more closely. It is probable that to him, as to so many other prophets, like Zoroaster or Mohammed, there was granted a soul-shattering experience of the God who acts; but the brief story of his call, even should it be historical, does not provide any clues for a thorough evaluation of this experience. He united a number of tribes into a league sharing a common religion, and concluded a covenant between them and the god Yahweh who appeared to him. But we cannot say what tribes made up this league, since the twelve-tribe system only came into being in Canaan. Probably the idea of the covenant itself has been transformed by later influences, so that we cannot determine the original nature of this covenant. But we must assume, as the tradition presupposes, that the covenant conditions contained certain ethical and cultic requirements. We do not have most of the laws in their original form, however; they have been revised and adapted to later conditions. All these considerations make any reconstruction of the Mosaic religion hazardous and probably of mere theoretical interest.

We must probably take the requirement that Israel should worship no other gods and the prohibition of images as original data. These two traits are very characteristic of the religion of Israel; it would be hard to derive them from other religions. It would surely be wrong to call the Mosaic religion monotheistic. The existence of other gods is not denied. A watered-down definition of monotheism (like that of Albright, for example: "belief in the existence of only one God, the creator of everything, the source of justice, who is equally powerful in Egypt, in the desert, and in Palestine, who has no sexuality and no

---

[37] The opposite view is espoused by Noth, *History of Israel,* p. 136, n. 2: "But perhaps the most concrete fact of all is the tradition of the tomb of Moses which was situated in a very definite spot." But it is just this spot that, according to tradition, is unknown.

mythology"[38]) serves only to make it possible to apply a word with positive overtones to the Mosaic religion.

One question comes to mind at once: Is there any connection between the Egyptian monotheism of Akh-en-Aton and the Mosaic religion? It is well known that Psalm 104 in the Old Testament shows remarkable similarities to the great hymn to the sun of Akh-en-Aton. The answer is rather simple. Apart from this isolated correspondence, we must conclude that the differences are greater than the similarities.[39] Above all, the "Mosaic" Yahweh is not a sun god.

The absence of images in the Israelite cultus is perhaps its most striking feature and must probably belong to its initial phase. The prohibition of images in Exodus 20:4 f. stands unique in the ancient world. Our sources are probably not sufficient for us to determine unambiguously whether this prohibition points to a spiritualized conception of God or whether, as von Rad thinks, it refers to the fact that God is not at man's disposal.[40] One thing, however, is certain: the gods of other religions, represented by images, can seem much more vividly present; they might therefore seem more easily susceptible to human influence. Yahweh was present only as the invisible God; he was the Lord, and Israel could not influence his decisions.

Later, in the Jerusalem Temple, the ark located in the holy of holies symbolized the presence of Yahweh. The existence of the ark even in the desert period is not in itself impossible, especially since there is evidence of portable shrines among the pre-Islamic Arabs.[41] There are nevertheless many indications that it made its first appearance in Canaan,[42] or, more likely, acquired new significence there.[43]

According to the priestly tradition, the ark was kept in the innermost room of a tent sanctuary as early as the desert period.[44] The earliest traditions call this tent either the tent of meeting (*ōhel mô'ēd*) or the tent of the testimony (*ōhel 'ēdût*), and do not connect it with the ark. P gives a detailed description of it as a portable sanctuary, similar in all essentials to the later temple in Jerusalem. This tent has therefore usually been assumed to represent nothing more than a retro-

---

[38] *From the Stone Age to Christianity* (2nd ed.; Garden City: Doubleday, 1957), p. 272.

[39] Albright remarks that the religion of Akh-en-Aton is called "teaching" (*sb³yt*), just as the documents of the Mosaic faith are called *tôrâ*, "instruction," "teaching." *Ibid.*, p. 270.

[40] *Op. cit.*, pp. 212 ff.

[41] See J. Morgenstern, "The Ark, the Ephod, and the 'Tent of Meeting,' " *HUCA*, XVII (1942/43), 153 ff.; XVIII (1943/44), 1 ff.

[42] This is the opinion of M. Dibelius, *Die Lade Jahves* (Göttingen: Vandenhoeck & Ruprecht, 1906); also G. von Rad, "Zelt und Lade," *NKZ*, XLII (1931), 476 ff. (reprinted in G. von Rad, *Gesammelte Studien zum Alten Testament* [Munich: Kaiser, 1958], pp. 120 ff.).

[43] W. Beyerlin, *op. cit.*, pp. 168, 176.

[44] G. von Rad, *Old Testament Theology*, I, 234 ff.; R. de Vaux, *op. cit.*, pp. 294 ff., with additional bibliography.

jection of later conditions into the early desert period. But even though this detailed description is found in the latest strata of the Pentateuch, it should be noted that the earlier traditions also mention a tent, though without providing an exact description. In addition, there is evidence for portable sanctuaries in the form of tents both among the pre-Islamic Arabs and also among the modern Bedouins. Among the former, the *qubbah* was a small tent of red leather in which the stone images of the tribal gods were carried with the tribe when traveling. During religious ceremonies and military marches it was transported on the back of a camel; in camp, it was set up beside the sheikh's tent and served as an oracle sanctuary.[45] The modern Bedouins have a similar tent sanctuary that they call *'utfah* or *markab*; when they travel, this tent is transported by camel.[46] Furthermore, Diodorus (XX. 65. 1) reports that the ancient Carthaginians had in their camp a small sacred tent beside the tent of their chief. A picture from Palmyra portrays a religious procession with a camel carrying a small tent; there is even evidence for the word *qubbah* in Palmyrene inscriptions.[47] We must conclude, therefore, that there is nothing improbable in the Israelite traditions of a tent sanctuary if we disregard the late description, which obviously represents only an idealized picture patterned after the Temple. That the tent of meeting was an oracle sanctuary is indicated by its very name. In addition, Exodus 33:7 states expressly that people went to the tent to seek Yahweh, i.e., to obtain an oracle. There Yahweh spoke to Moses "face to face" (Exod. 33:11); Moses therefore functions here as the mediator of divine decrees.

Besides this, we have little definite information about the cultus of the desert period. In spite of Jeremiah 7:22 f., it remains probable that sacrifices were offered, since sacrifices were customary among all Semitic peoples. Later Israelite sacrificial practice, however, is so much under Canaanite influence that we cannot draw any safe conclusions about the earliest period.

And so what we really know about Moses and his period is not much, and the little that we can say remains more or less hypothetical. Nevertheless, as has been said, we cannot dispense with Moses. The uniqueness of the Israelite religion remains inexplicable if we are forbidden to presuppose the existence of a creative personality. N. Söderblom has said, "If Moses did not exist, we should have to invent him."[48] Even if this is not a scientific argument, there is truth in it.

---

[45] H. Lammens, "Le culte des bétyles," *BIFAO*, XVII (1919), 39 ff. (also: *L'arabie occidentale avant l'hégire* [Beyrouth: Imprimerie catholique, 1928], pp. 101 ff.).

[46] De Vaux, *op. cit.*, p. 296.

[47] *Ibid.*, p. 297.

[48] *Das Werden des Gottesglaubens* (Leipzig: Hinrichs, 1916), p. 310.

3.

THE OCCUPATION OF CANAAN
AND THE PERIOD OF THE JUDGES

a. General

As is well-known, the Old Testament, particularly the Book of Joshua, shows all Israel migrating into Canaan under the leadership of one man, Joshua. In a series of military campaigns based on one coherent plan, they conquer the land and apportion it among the twelve tribes. However, the beginning of the book of Judges shows that the course of events was manifestly much more complicated. Even if archaeology can prove that a series of Canaanite cities were destroyed in the twelfth century B.C. and then occupied by a people with a much simpler material civilization—probably Israelites—there remain so many discrepancies between the findings of archaeology and the biblical narrative that no simple solution to the problem of how Canaan was occupied can prove satisfactory. More detailed discussion of this question must be left to presentations of Israel's history.[1] Here we can only emphasize that Canaanites and immigrating Israelites probably lived side by side in the land for a considerable time. During this time, the two peoples surely established relationships in many religious and cultural areas. Furthermore, we must emphasize once again that the complete twelve-tribe system took final shape only on the soil of Canaan. In all likelihood, the immigrating groups of Israelite tribes found that there were tribes related to them already in the land. These latter also joined the covenant of the god Yahweh. In this fashion, the people of Israel gradually came into being.

We do not know how the Israelites in the desert were organized. We must assume that the new religion was the bond uniting them and that the tribes joined together about the ark and the tabernacle. In Canaan

---

[1] M. Noth, *The History of Israel,* trans. S. Godman and P. R. Ackroyd (2nd ed.; New York: Harper, 1960), pp. 53 ff.; J. Bright, *A History of Israel* (Philadelphia: Westminster, 1959), pp. 117 ff.; cf. also Y. Aharoni, "Problems of the Israelite Conquest," *Antiquity and Survival,* II (1957), 131 ff.

we find the division into twelve tribes. It is remarkable how firmly fixed this number remains while the tribes themselves can change. For example, the division of the tribe of Joseph into the two tribes of Ephraim and Manasseh made up for the loss of the tribe of Levi (still present in Gen. 49:5). The number twelve obviously had special significance. This fact has attracted the attention of many scholars to the Greek amphictyonies, leagues of twelve cities united about a common sanctuary. Each city was responsible for maintaining the cultus at this shrine for one month of the year.[2] Such amphictyonies existed in Greece, one of them centered on Delphi, and among the Etruscans, one centered on Voltumna. Similar leagues have recently been brought to light among the Sumerians.[3]

Settling down in Canaan involved all kinds of social and religious problems. The Canaanites were settled farmers; their religion was a fertility cult appropriate to the needs of an agricultural civilization. The immigrating Israelites, in contrast, were probably nomads or semi-nomads; their civilization was primarily pastoral, and their religion was in no position to satisfy the demands made by agriculture. The inevitable result was syncretism: the Israelites took up religious practices and ideas found among the Canaanites that were appropriate to their new situation.

Thanks to the discovery of the Ras Shamra texts and other material, we are now rather well informed about the religion of the Canaanites. At the head of their pantheon stood the god El,[4] who is called King, Father, and Bull. He seems to a certain extent a *deus otiosus*. Under the name *ēl 'elyôn*, he seems to have been especially popular in Jerusalem; there is also evidence for this name among the Phoenicians. Beside El stands the young god Baal,[5] the god of fertility, who also appears as a dragon slayer. Baal is worshiped in many local guises, such as Baal-berith, the baal of the covenant (Judg. 9:4)[6] and Baal-zebub, the baal of flies (II Kings 1:2 ff.);[7] he is also worshiped as *ba'al šāmayim*, the baal of the sky.[8] This latter attribute brings him very close to El and has led some scholars to conceive of him as the hypostatization of one aspect of El.[9] At Ras Shamra he appears as

2 M. Noth, *Das System der zwölf Stämme Israels* (Stuttgart: Kohlhammer, 1930).
3 W. W. Hallo, "A Sumerian Amphictyony," *JCS*, XIV (1960), 88 ff.
4 O. Eissfeldt, *El im ugaritischen Pantheon*, 1951; M. Pope, *El in the Ugaritic Texts* (*SVT*, II [Leiden: Brill, 1955]); F. Løkkegaard, "A Plea for El," *Studia Orientalia Joanni Pedersen dicata* (Hauniae: Munksgaard, 1953), pp. 219 ff.
5 A. Kapelrud, *Baal in the Ras Shamra Texts* (Copenhagen: Gad, 1952).
6 Probably Baal-berith is identical with El-berith (Judg. 9:46).
7 Perhaps a distorted form of Baal-zebul; *zbl* occurs as a divine appellative at Ras Shamra.
8 O. Eissfeldt, "Ba'al šamēm und Jahwe," *ZAW*, LVII (1939), 1 ff.
9 I. Engnell, *Studies in Divine Kingship* (Uppsala: Almqvist & Wiksell, 1943), pp. 171 f.; cf. pp. 21 f.

Aliyan (puissant) Baal, the god of vegetation who dies and comes back to life. He is killed by the god Mot ("Death"), but is restored to life when his sister Anath has conquered Mot. This myth, which mirrors the changing cycle of the seasons, was probably actualized in a vivid ritual.[10]

Besides Anath, we know of two other goddesses among the Canaanites: Athirat (Asherah), the consort of El; and Athtart (Astarte). The distinctions between the three goddesses remain vague. They should all be looked upon as manifestations of the great mother-goddess of love and war.

We have considerable evidence of sun worship: place-names like Beth-shemesh (shemesh = sun), archaeological finds of sun symbols (at Hazor),[11] texts from Ras Shamra that mention a goddess Shapshu (Sun). Some scholars also think that $\bar{e}l$ '$elyôn$ of Jerusalem was a solar divinity,[12] but this identification remains doubtful.[13] A moon god is also known through place-names (Beth Jerach, Jericho) and is probably also attested in the Ugaritic texts.

The cultic drama of the dying and rising fertility god clearly played an essential role in the cultus. There was, in addition, sacral prostitution, considered very important because it was felt to promote fertility. A sacred marriage, which combined these two aspects, was a part of the cultic drama.

It is easy to see that this religious world was alien to primitive Yahwism. There were some points of contact, however. According to the early Sinai tradition, Yahweh appeared surrounded by fire, clouds, lightning, and thunder; these features recur regularly in archaic depictions of a theophany, such as Judges 5:4–5 and Psalm 68:8 ff. (Eng. 68:7 ff.). In the latter passage, furthermore, we find the epithet $rōkēb$ $bā'ărābôt$ (68:5 [Eng. 68:4]); this was formerly interpreted quite commonly as meaning "he who rides through the deserts" (RSV margin); but it is remarkably reminiscent of an epithet of Baal that occurs in the Ras Shamra texts: rkb 'rpt, "he who rides upon the clouds" (RSV text; cf. KJV).[14] Obviously both Yahweh and Baal were divinities associated with atmospheric phenomena like lightning and thunder. The question naturally could arise whether the Israelite conception of a theophany shows Canaanite influence; but the definite geographic location in the south found in the earliest texts as well as the lack of real parallels among the Canaanites indicate that we are

---

[10] See Kapelrud, *op. cit.*
[11] Y. Yadin, "The Fourth Season of Excavations at Hazor," *SEÅ*, XXIV (1959), 25.
[12] I. Engnell, *Gamla Testamentet* (Stockholm: Svenska kyrkans diakonistyrelses bokförlag, 1945), I, 119; G. W. Ahlström, *Psalm 89* (Lund: Gleerup, 1959), p. 95.
[13] Pope, *op. cit.*, pp. 82 f.
[14] See the commentaries of A. Weiser and H. J. Kraus.

probably dealing with an element that is genuinely Yahwistic. Since, however, it would have been difficult to apply an epithet to Yahweh if a certain similarity between him and Baal had not already been present, we must assume that the Canaanite baal of the sky and Yahweh both belonged to the same phenomenological type and that this very fact made an adjustment possible.

During the period of the Judges, proper names formed with the element "baal" occur even in families that were apparently strict Yahwists. This fact indicates that Yahweh and Baal were not always sharply distinguished in this period.[15] Gideon, for example, is also called Jerubbaal, i.e., "Baal contends" (Judg. 6:32); and the fourth son of Saul is called Ishbaal, i.e., "man of Baal" (cf. I Chron. 8:33; Samuel alters this name to Ishbosheth, "man of shame"). Therefore "Baal" (meaning "lord") is understood as an epithet of Yahweh, or else the people worshiped Baal beside Yahweh without sensing any contradiction. In the beginning, the Israelites took Baal as the natural representative of fertility and worshiped him as the god specializing in agriculture and similar matters. Only later did Baal become the archenemy of Yahweh.

The situation with El is totally different.[16] The Old Testament contains no polemic against El. He is simply represented as being identical with Yahweh. Only two passages show traces of a different conception. In the so-called Song of Moses, Deuteronomy 32, the original text of verses eight f. states that 'elyôn gave the lands to the peoples according to the number of the sons of El (RSV "God"; the MT reads "Israel"), and that Israel is Yahweh's portion. This passage seems to subordinate Yahweh to El.[17] In a similar vein, Psalm 82:1 states that El (RSV "God") takes his place in the divine council in order to hold judgment in the midst of the gods. It does not state expressly that Yahweh is among those gods,[18] but the idea of an assembly of the gods corresponds exactly to the situation depicted in the Ras Shamra texts (*UM* 51 [II AB], III, 14; 2, 17, 34; 107, 3). But in the Psalm we are probably to think of El as being identical with Yahweh.

We may presume that it is essentially this same El with whom Jacob strives at the Jabbok (Gen. 32:22-32). El is the lord of the land; through his struggle, Jacob wins the right to dwell in the land, and is now recognized as a citizen of the land.[19]

---

[15] Cf. S. Linder, "Jahwe und Baal im alten Israel," *Gedenkschrift A. von Bulmerincq*, 1938, pp. 98 ff.

[16] O. Eissfeldt, "El and Jahwe," *JSS*, I (1952), 25 ff.

[17] *Ibid.*, p. 29. Another interpretation is also possible: Yahweh-El distributes the lands and retains Israel for himself; see now G. W. Ahlström, *Aspects of Syncretism in Israelite Religion* (Lund: Gleerup, 1963), pp. 73 f.

[18] As Eissfeldt states; *ibid.*, pp. 29 f.

[19] For a discussion of this passage, see K. Elliger, "Der Jakobskampf

A further noteworthy fact should be mentioned here. Genesis 14:19 calls ēl 'elyôn "maker[20] of heaven and earth." The Hebrew verb used here, qānâ, is rare; but it occurs in Phoenician and Palmyrene inscriptions precisely in the phrase "El, maker of the earth."[21] In addition, El appears in the Ras Shamra texts as "creator of creatures" (bny bnwt). In this case the Israelite religion has obviously appropriated ancient Canaanite material and applied it to Yahweh.

It is impossible to fix definitely the time when the final identification of El with Yahweh took place. Perhaps it first took place in the Davidic period. The fact remains, however, as Eissfeldt has emphasized, that no hostility was ever felt between El and Yahweh, whereas Baal and Yahweh were very early considered irreconcilable foes.[22]

Having made these introductory remarks, we will examine several traditions from the period of the Judges in order to discover their religious significance, hoping in this way to learn something about the religion of this period.

b. The Concept of God

The Song of Deborah (Judges 5) is generally considered the earliest or at least one of the earliest documents of the Bible. It is probably contemporary with the events it depicts, or almost contemporary. It gives us some important evidence for the concept of God current in that period.

In the first place, Yahweh is here the God of Israel (vss. 3, 5), who acts on behalf of his people. The poem depicts his appearance in the form of the theophany on Sinai: he comes from the mountains of Edom, the earth trembles, the clouds drop water, the mountains quake before him (vss. 4, 5). Here, then, atmospheric traits are dominant; Yahweh is the God of thunder and rain. But he is also the God of Sinai—for this is surely the proper translation of the phrase zeh sînay in verse five.[23] The revelation on Sinai remains a living memory and,

---

am Jabbok," *ZThK*, XLVIII (1951), 1 ff.; H. J. Stoebe, "Der heilsgeschichtliche Bezug der Jabbok-Perikope," *ETh*, XIV (1954), 466 ff.; O. Eissfeldt, "Non dimittam te nisi benedixeris mihi," *Mélanges bibliques rédigés en l'honneur de André Robert* (Paris: Bloud & Gay, 1956), pp. 77 ff.

[20] Or "acquirer." For a discussion of the problem, see H. Ringgren, *Word and Wisdom* (Lund: Ohlsson, 1947), p. 101; Katz, *JJS*, V (1954), 126 ff. For a different view, see W. A. Irwin, "Where shall Wisdom be Found?" *JBL*, LXXX (1961), 133 ff.

[21] See below, pp. 104 f.

[22] O. Eissfeldt, "El and Jahwe," p. 26. Another way of accounting for this would be to assume that Yahweh was originally an epithet of the Canaanite El (cf. F. M. Cross, Jr., "Yahweh and the God of the Patriarchs," *HTR*, LV [1962], pp. 250 ff.). But it has to be admitted anyhow that Yahweh, with his active and dynamic character, is not simply and generally identical with El.

[23] H. Grimme, *ZDMG*, L, p. 573, n. 1; W. F. Albright, "The Names Shaddai and Abram," *JBL*, LIV (1935), 204.

with the passage of time, becomes stylized into a traditional theophany description, such as we find later in Psalm 18:8 ff. (Eng. 18:7 ff.), 68:8 ff. (Eng. 68:7 ff.), and Habakkuk 3:3 ff. We shall devote further attention to examining the cultic *Sitz im Leben* of the theophany.

This Yahweh intervenes as an ally in battle. The poet praises Yahweh's victorious deeds as expressions of his "righteousness" (*ṣᵉdāqâ*), or rather of his might: they are triumphant acts of deliverance (vs. 11: ". . . there they repeat the triumphs of the Lord"). In other words, he is the war god who leads the holy wars of his people. His enemies perish, but his friends are "like the sun as he rises in his might" (vs. 31). Here the picture is dominated by God's dynamic, even terrifying, traits. There is no contradiction between this picture and the expression "his friends," for in this context "his friends" are "those who fight on his side."

This does not simply mean that Yahweh was only or even primarily a warlike national god with atmospheric traits. It is the situation that leads to emphasis on these characteristics. In any case, however, we see here one essential side of Yahweh as he originally was.

Unfortunately, there are no authentic texts that might enlighten us about other characteristics of Yahweh. The Song of Hannah, I Samuel 2, which otherwise preserves a very archaic conception of God, comes from the period of the monarchy, as is shown by I Samuel 2:10. The statement of Samuel in I Samuel 15:22-23 stressing obedience at the expense of sacrifices cannot conclusively be proved ancient. If we want to learn something about the religion of the period of the Judges, therefore, we must have recourse to inferences drawn from later circumstances. We may consider it probable, for example, that the commandments of the Decalogue were not made up out of whole cloth in the period of the monarchy, but presuppose an earlier tradition. Therefore ethical demands presumably had an important place in the religion of the period of the Judges. It is even possible that the so-called Book of the Covenant (Exod. 20:22—23:33) came into being in the period of the Judges. If so, then we could add the following remarks to what has been said above about Yahweh: Yahweh is to be worshiped as the only god of Israel; idols are not to be tolerated (Exod. 20:23). Sacrifices are to be offered to Yahweh alone, not to any other gods (Exod. 22:20). Yahweh is concerned for the well-being of strangers, widows, and orphans; his wrath will be upon anyone who infringes upon the rights of these people (Exod. 22:21-24). Yahweh will bless and protect whomever serves him (Exod. 23:25). All these basic principles are also typical of the later religion of Israel.

Other sources again emphasize Yahweh's warlike traits. The historical traditions of the Book of Judges stress particularly his divine help in Israel's wars against its enemies: the Spirit (*rûaḥ*) of Yahweh gives Gideon power to overcome the Midianites and the Amalekites

46

(Judg. 6:34). The same is true of Jephthah (Judg. 11:29) and Samson (Judg. 14:6). The Israelites fight "for Yahweh and for Gideon" (Judg. 7:18, 20), etc. In Judges 6:22 and 13:22 we come across the idea that to "see" the holy God involves mortal danger; Exodus 33:20 witnesses to the same thought: ". . . man shall not see me and live."

We encounter a remarkable notion in Judges 9:23: Yahweh sends an "evil spirit" between Abimelech and the men of Shechem. Of course this expression means nothing more than a hostile attitude; but it is remarkable that Yahweh is looked upon as its source. This means that he is a God from whom come good and "evil" alike. We hear elsewhere that he hardens Pharaoh's heart (Exod. 7:3; 9:12, etc.), that he incites David to number the people even though such a numbering is looked upon as something forbidden (II Sam. 24:1). He "kills and brings to life, . . . makes poor and makes rich; he brings low, he also exalts." Thus says the Song of Hannah (I Sam. 2:6 f.; this psalm is admittedly somewhat later). This duality has often been pointed out as a characteristic of so-called high gods.[24]

As was stated above, in the earliest period Yahwism and the Canaanites religion stood independently side by side. Then a gradual amalgamation took place. In agricultural matters men probably at first called upon the Canaanite gods, particularly Baal. These gods were the proprietors of the land and were specialists, so to speak, in this area. At the same time, Yahweh was worshiped at the Canaanite sanctuaries, and probably took over other traits of the Canaanite gods along with the appropriate cultic practices. Unfortunately, we know very little about the course taken by this syncretism. Actually we only know the final result. It is impossible to say exactly to what extent the Israelites worshiped Canaanite gods. As we have seen, personal names indicate a certain identification of Yahweh with Baal. In addition, such a name as Samson (šimšôn) could point to sun worship. But apart from the name there is hardly anything in the Samson story to make us think of a sun cult. It is possible, however, that the account of Samson's tying burning torches to the tails of three hundred foxes (Judg. 15:1-6) is comparable to a similar custom that took place at the Roman Cerialia; this latter custom is usually explained as frightening away the rays of the sun.[25] Then "the little foxes that spoil the vineyards" (Song 2:15) might also be placed in this context.[26]

c. *The Cult*

There are only isolated references to the cult during the period of

[24] See, for example, G. Widengren, *Hochgottglaube im alten Iran,* 1938, pp. 100 ff., 194 ff., 277, and *passim.*
[25] K. Latte, *Römische Religionsgeschichte,* 1960, p. 68.
[26] H. Ringgren, *Das Hohe Lied* (Göttingen: Vandenhoeck & Ruprecht, 1958), p. 13.

the Judges. It is therefore impossible to make a complete reconstruction, and we must be content with a few remarks.

The central shrine of the Israelite amphictyony was the ark,[27] which is frequently mentioned in traditions referring to the period of the Judges. Now the ark traditions of the Old Testament, however, are not at all homogeneous; for the most part, they reflect conditions of later periods. I Samuel 4:6, though, is surely an ancient account. At the news that the ark has been brought into the camp of Israel, the Philistines say, "The gods have (or: God has) come into the camp." The ark therefore represents the presence of Yahweh, particularly in military undertakings. The two ancient formulas connected with the ark that are found in Numbers 10:35 f. show the same thing. There we read that whenever the ark set out, Moses said, "Arise, Yahweh, and let thy enemies be scattered; and let them that hate thee flee before thee"; when the ark rested, he said, "Return, Yahweh, to the ten thousand thousands of Israel." In I Samuel 4:4, the ark is called "the ark of the covenant of Yahweh of hosts, who is enthroned on the cherubim." According to Exodus 25:10 ff., two winged cherubim were located either above or beside the ark.[28] In Psalm 18:11 (Eng. 18:10), Yahweh's riding upon a cherub is linked with his appearance in wind and storm. It follows that the ark is a symbol of the presence of the god of air who stands in covenant-relationship with Israel. Psalm 24:7 ff. connects the entrance of the ark into the sanctuary with the idea of Yahweh's kingship. This idea is admittedly early,[29] but it probably arose under Canaanite influence.[30] Whether it was already present in our period cannot definitely be determined. In any case, the interpretation of the ark as the throne of Yahweh seems to have its roots in the settled situation of Canaan.

Obviously the ark did not remain in the same place throughout this period. After the crossing of the Jordan, the sources first mention the ark in connection with the camp at Gilgal, a site that later served as a cultic center and shrine (Josh. 4:19; 7:6; Josh. 5:13-15; I Sam. 11:15; 13:8; 15:21). Joshua 8:33 finds the ark located at Shechem;

---

[27] G. von Rad, "Zelt und Lade," *NKZ*, XLII (1931), 476 ff. (reprinted in G. von Rad, *Gesammelte Studien zum Alten Testament* [Munich: Kaiser, 1958], pp. 109 ff.; cf. particularly pp. 121 f.); R. de Vaux, *Ancient Israel* (New York: McGraw-Hill, 1961), pp. 297 ff.

[28] Cf. K. Koch, *Die Priesterschrift von Ex. 25 bis Lev. 16* (Göttingen: Vandenhoeck & Ruprecht, 1959), p. 12. For more detailed discussion of the cherubim, see below, pp. 100 f.

[29] A. Alt, "Gedanken über das Königtum Jahwes," *Kleine Schriften zur Geschichte des Volkes Israel* (Munich: Beck, 1953), I, 345 ff.; according to H. Wildberger, *Jahwes Eigentumsvolk* (Zürich: Zwingli, 1960), p. 29, this is a genuinely Yahwistic idea.

[30] J. Gray, "The Kingship of God in the Prophets and Psalms," *VT*, XI (1961), 1 ff.; V. Maag, "Malkut Jahwe," *SVT*, VII (Congress Volume, 1960), 147 ff.; W. Schmidt, *Königtum Gottes in Ugarit und Israel* (Berlin: Töpelmann, 1961).

but this passage is part of the Deuteronomic redaction, and in all probability does not report a genuine tradition.[31] In contrast, the statement of Judges 20:27 that the ark was in Bethel seems to be more reliable (cf. Judg. 2:1, 5, where Bochim, a place in the vicinity of Bethel, is mentioned). Finally, I Samuel 3:3 mentions its presence at Shiloh, where it is located in a proper temple.[32] During the Philistine wars, it is captured and carried off by the enemy. Since, however, it causes disease among the Philistines, it is first sent back to Beth-shemesh and then remains at Kiriath-jearim until brought by David to Jerusalem. At Shiloh we also find the tabernacle or "tent of meeting" (Josh. 18:1; 19:51; I Sam. 2:22), but it is not connected with the ark. Probably the later narrator thinks that the ark is inside the tent. It must be remembered, however, as von Rad has shown, that the ark and the tent represent two traditions originally independent of each other.[33]

Our sources also mention several other cultic sites, most of which were probably taken over from the Canaanites.[34] Besides Gilgal,[35] Bethel,[36] and Shiloh,[37] already mentioned, we know that Mizpah,[38] Gibeon,[39] Ophrah,[40] and Dan[41] were sacred spots. The sacredness of such cultic sites is based on legends of theophanies and the like. Jacob had his dream at Bethel (Gen. 28:10-22); Gilgal is the place, marked by a circle of stones, where Israel crossed the Jordan (Josh. 4:20) and perhaps also the place where "the commander of the army of Yahweh" showed himself to Joshua, calling the place holy (Josh. 5:13-15); at Ophrah the "angel of Yahweh" appeared to Gideon (Judg. 6:11-24). In other cases, the sacredness of the spot is simply taken for granted; the Canaanites sacrificed there, and the immigrating Israelites simply took over these cultic sites from the Canaanites.

---

[31] E. Nielsen, *Shechem* (Copenhagen: Gad, 1955), p. 77.

[32] Or is this an anachronism?

[33] Von Rad, *op. cit.*, pp. 122 f.

[34] De Vaux, *op. cit.*, pp. 302 ff.

[35] K. Galling, "Bethel und Gilgal," *ZDPV*, LXVI (1943), 140 ff., LXVII (1944-45), 21 ff., 34 ff.; H. J. Kraus, "Gilgal," *VT*, I (1951), 181 ff.

[36] K. Galling, *op. cit.*; C. A. Keller, "Über einige alttestamentliche Heiligtumslegenden: c. Die Legende von Bethel," *ZAW*, LXVII (1955), 162 ff.

[37] O. Eissfeldt, "Silo und Jerusalem," *SVT*, IV (Congress Volume, 1957), 138 ff.

[38] H. W. Hertzberg, "Mizpa," *ZAW*, XLVII (1929), 161 ff.; J. Muilenburg, "Mizpah of Benjamin," *STh*, VIII (1954), 25 ff.

[39] M. Noth, "Lehrkursus für 1956," *ZDPV*, LXXIII (1957), 7 ff.; K. Elliger, "Beeroth und Gibeon," *ibid.*, pp. 125 ff.

[40] Keller, *op. cit.*, pp. 154 ff.; E. Kutsch, "Gideons Berufung und Altarbau," *TLZ*, LXXXI (1956), cols. 75 ff.

[41] C. Hauret, "Aux origines du sacerdoce danite," *Mélanges bibliques rédigés en l'honneur de André Robert* (Paris: Bloud & Gay, 1956), pp. 105 ff.

At these sanctuaries sacrifices were offered. The sources contain several references to this fact. Gideon offers a sacrifice upon the altar of Baal that he has pulled down (Judg. 6); Samson's father, Manoah, offers a burnt offering to Yahweh upon a rock (Judg. 13); Samuel's father, Elkanah, offers a sacrifice every year at Shiloh (I Sam. 1:21; cf. also 1:3); at Shiloh Eli the priest and his sons perform sacrifice (I Sam. 2:21 ff.); Samuel frequently appears in charge of sacrificial worship (I Sam. 7:9 f.; 9:12 f.); etc. It is probable that the Israelites offered sacrifices at all periods. But, as Dussaud has shown,[42] the terminology and classification of Israelite sacrifice as found in the laws evidence such a remarkable similarity to Canaanite and Phoenician sacrificial practice that considerable Canaanite influence must be imputed to the Israelite practice.

The problem of human sacrifice is particularly difficult. Judges 11 relates how Jephthah, after his victory over the Ammonites, sacrifices his only daughter in consequence of an oath he had sworn. Amazingly, this story is told without the slightest reproach, as though we were here dealing with a completely natural and obvious situation. Since there is evidence for human sacrifice among the Canaanites, it has been assumed that the Israelites took over this custom from them. We shall return to this question later.[43] Here we shall only note that the actual purpose of the Jephthah story is to explain a cultic practice at Mizpah: the young women weep upon the mountains there for four days. This custom is probably connected in the first instance with the Canaanite fertility cult, and does not necessarily have anything to do with human sacrifice. The fact remains, nevertheless, that the narrative mentions such a sacrifice quite ingenuously. There are no other accounts of human sacrifice in the period of the Judges.

Besides performing sacrifices, the Israelites also celebrated pilgrimage festivals.[44] Judges 21:19-21 tells of such a festival (Heb. ḥag) at Shiloh, during which the young women danced in the vineyards. Here we probably have what was originally a Canaanite practice. The Book of the Covenant (Exod. 23:14-17), like the ancient festival calendar in Exodus 34:18-24, lists three yearly feasts: the feast of unleavened bread (ḥag hammaṣṣôt) in the spring, the feast of weeks (ḥag šābû'ôt) seven weeks later at the beginning of the wheat harvest, and the feast of ingathering (ḥag hā'āsîp) "at the end of the year, when you gather in from the field the fruit of your labor." They are all pilgrimage festivals, at which all the males in Israel are required to see "the face of Yahweh," i.e., visit the sanctuary. It is noteworthy that all three are agricultural festivals; either they first

---

[42] R. Dussaud, Les origines cananéennes du sacrifice israélite (2nd ed.; Paris: Leroux, 1921), pp. 160 f. For further discussion, see below, pp. 176 f.

[43] See below, pp. 174 f.

[44] For a bibliography on the festivals, see below, pp. 186 ff.

came into being in Canaan or they were borrowed there. Only Pass-over, which is not mentioned but belongs together with the feast of unleavened bread, has traits that point to a nomadic situation, above all the sacrifice of a lamb. Sheepshearing (I Sam. 25:4, 11) may also have been a religious festival.[45]

The festival mentioned in Judges 21 is probably the autumn festival (the feast of ingathering); it may well be identical with the annual sacrificial festival in I Samuel 1:3, 21.

Although this is not explicitly stated, a covenant renewal ceremony probably took place at the autumn festival.[46] Deuteronomy 31:9-13 admittedly speaks of such a custom only every seven years; the focal point was the public reading of the law and the recognition by the people of their obligation to obey it. But there is much in favor of the theory that earlier this ceremony took place every year. In all proba-bility, the narrative of the assembly at Shechem in Joshua 24 depicts the course of such a covenant renewal festival: the major components were the recounting of Yahweh's gracious acts in history, the renun-ciation of foreign gods,[47] and the obligation to serve Yahweh exclu-sively. In all probability, these covenant renewal festivals were more important than sacrifices in the cultic life of the amphictyony.[48] This would mean that, besides the fertility rites taken over from the Canaanites, the recounting of historical facts played an important role in the cultic life of Israel from the very beginning.

At the cultic sites, in addition, Yahweh's will was determined by the casting of lots. Saul was chosen king in this fashion at Mizpah (I Sam. 10:17-24). Before a military venture, Yahweh's will was ascertained through oracles at Bethel (Judg. 20:18-23); unfortu-nately, we are not told how Yahweh gave his answer.

Whether a priesthood already existed in the desert period cannot be determined. The references of the Pentateuch to Aaron and the Levites reflect the conditions of a much later period. The earliest sources show that individuals could offer sacrifice without the assistance of a priest (Judg. 6:25 ff.; 13:15 ff.; and probably also I Sam. 16:5 ff., since Samuel is not called a priest). But priests are also mentioned, for the first time in Judges 17—18.[49] Micah, a wealthy farmer (or prince?)

---

[45] Note that there is evidence for a feast of sheepshearing in Sumerian Lagash. (B. Landsberger, *Der kultische Kalender der Babylonier und Assyrer,* 1915, pp. 48 ff.).

[46] G. von Rad, *Das formgeschichtliche Problem des Hexateuch* (Stutt-gart: Kohlhammer, 1938), pp. 29 ff. (reprinted in G. von Rad, *Gesam-melte Studien,* pp. 41 ff.).

[47] E. Nielsen, *op. cit.,* pp. 103 f., 133 f., 238 f.; *idem,* "The Burial of the Foreign Gods," *STh,* VIII (1955), 103 ff.

[48] Bright, *op. cit.,* p. 149.

[49] Cf. J. Pedersen, *Israel, Its Life and Culture* (London: Oxford, 1959), III-IV, 150 f., 221 f.; E. Nielsen, *Shechem,* pp. 195 f.; A. Haldar, *Asso-ciations of Cult Prophets Among the Ancient Semites* (Uppsala: Almqvist & Wiksell, 1945), pp. 146 f.; Ahlström, *op. cit.,* pp. 25 ff.

in Ephraim, built a shrine with an image and installed his son as priest. When a Levite from Bethlehem came by, however, the man replaced his son with this Levite. Whether the Levites were simply members of the tribe of Levi or constituted a priestly group from the very beginning,[50] this story seems to indicate that as early as the period of the Judges they were considered specialists in cultic questions. In other words, we have evidence for the gradual development of a priesthood. It should be noted that the story obviously depicts a syncretistic cult.

After this account, we hear of priests once more in the story of Eli and his sons at Shiloh (I Sam. 1—2; 4). Here we learn that the sons —who bear Egyptian names—abused their priestly position by stealing the sacrificial meat; for this they were punished. Whether Eli really belonged to the tribe of Levi, as I Samuel 2:27 seems to indicate, is doubtful. This reference could also be an *ex post facto* justification of his priesthood, since later the Levitical descent of all priests was taken as a matter of course.

In all probability most priests were attached to specific sanctuaries as custodians. In addition to their sacrificial duties, they also furnished oracles. Passages like I Samuel 14:36-42; 23:12; 30:8 show that an oracle was a yes or no answer to a question directed to God. In most cases, lots were cast to determine the answer (as also in I Sam. 10:17-24). The Urim and Thummim mentioned in the laws (Exod. 28:30; Num. 27:21) were probably also a provision for such an oracle; they were two stones kept in the pocket of the breastpiece of the high priest, used for obtaining an oracle (cf. I Sam. 28:6).[51] We have already mentioned tree oracles in our discussion of the religion of the patriarchs.[52]

Besides the priests, there were also people who functioned specifically as seers (Heb. *ḥōzeh, rō'eh*).[53] Unfortunately, our sources contain only very meager references to their activity, and even these references are obscured by the influence of later conceptions. It remains extremely difficult to determine their exact function.

In I Samuel 9, Samuel appears as a prophet and seer—verse nine takes the two expressions as being equivalent—to whom people come "to inquire of God." The narrative best describes a clairvoyant who is able to recover lost asses. Somewhat later we find a "prophet" (*nābî'*), Gad, as "David's seer" (II Sam. 24:11); he looks into the future and proclaims the will of Yahweh.

As we have already seen, Samuel also functions as a sacrificial

[50] See pp. 378, 210.
[51] See below, pp. 205 f.
[52] See above, pp. 25 f.
[53] A. R. Johnson, *The Cultic Prophet in Ancient Israel* (2nd ed.; Cardiff: University of Wales, 1962), pp. 9 ff.; H. H. Rowley, *The Servant of the Lord* (London: Lutterworth, 1952), pp. 99 ff.

priest; in addition, he is called a prophet (*nābî'*). I Samuel 10 shows him as the leader of a band of prophets coming down from the high place in a state of ecstasy. Saul also lapses into ecstasy, giving rise to the proverb, "Is Saul also among the prophets?" (cf. also I Sam. 19:18-24).

Here we are obviously dealing with various strata of tradition, each of which conceives the role of Samuel somewhat differently. Great caution is therefore necessary in drawing conclusions about the nature of a seer.

We shall later discuss the prophets in a broader context.[54] Here we shall only note two things. First, ecstatic prophetism obviously has its roots in the Canaanite religion. Second, "prophets" and "seers" (*nābî'*, *ḥōzeh*, and *rō'eh*) are more or less synonymous terms for an office that very early came to play an important role in Israel, in addition to the priests who served at sanctuaries, offering sacrifice and supervising technical oracles.

There is incontestable evidence for one further religious institution in the period of the Judges: the holy war[55] and the *ḥerem*, the ritual destruction of everything taken in the name of Yahweh. Ancient Israel knows a kind of war that is a sacred obligation of the chosen people, bound up with special religious observances. Admittedly, later theories have to some extent influenced and stylized the accounts of such wars contained in the historical books; but the antiquity of the institution shines clearly through these accounts, and is further supported by the presence of a similar situation among the pre-Islamic Bedouins. We may summarize the most important elements of the tradition, following von Rad's analysis.[56]

The trumpet is sounded to summon men to the holy war (Judg. 3:27; 6:34 f.; I Sam. 13:3). The men are sanctified (*qiddēš*, "to make holy"; Josh. 3:5; I Sam. 21:6 [Eng. 21:5]) and must be subject to certain prescriptions guaranteeing ritual purity (e.g., sexual abstinence; I Sam. 21:6 [Eng. 21:5]; II Sam. 11:11 f.; cf. Deut. 23:9-14). God is consulted before battle (Judg. 20:23, 27; I Sam. 7:9; 14:37; 23:2-4, 9-12; etc.); if the answer is favorable, the leader proclaims, "Yahweh has given the enemy into your hand" (Josh. 6:2; 8:1, 18; Judg. 4:7, 14; 7:9, 15; etc.). The wars are the wars of Yahweh (I Sam. 18:17; 25:28) and Yahweh fights for Israel (Exod. 14:14; Josh. 10:14, 42; Judg. 20:35; etc.); therefore Israel must not fear, but be strong and of good courage (Josh. 8:1; 10:8, 25; Judg. 7:3; etc.). During the battle, Yahweh brings confusion and panic upon the enemy (Josh. 10:10; Judg. 4:15; 7:22; I Sam. 14:15, 20). The high point and conclusion of the war, finally, is the ban (Heb.

---

[54] See below, pp. 212 ff. and 248 ff.
[55] G. von Rad, *Der heilige Krieg im alten Israel* (Zürich: Zwingli, 1951).
[56] *Ibid.*, pp. 6 ff.

ḥerem), which in most cases involves the total destruction of all the booty. But this word is connected with a root that means "holy" elsewhere in west Semitic territory (Arabic *ḥaram*, "the holy place"; *iḥrām*, "the holy or sanctified state of pilgrims"; Nabataean *ḥrm*, "holy";[57] this root also occurs in the name Hermon, "the holy mountain"). What we have here is therefore a consecration or dedication of these things to Yahweh. One account actually states that silver and gold were consecrated to Yahweh, i.e., surrendered to him (Josh. 7:18 f.).[58]

This holy war is obviously a typically Israelite phenomenon. Up to now no evidence of anything comparable has been discovered in Canaan, though the word for "ban" occurs once on the Moabite stone, and perhaps also in a Nabataean inscription. The holy war is more likely connected with nomadic life than with the settled life of Canaan, although its aftereffects last well into the period of the monarchy and are especially apparent in the Deuteronomic writings.

As we have seen, the scattered references to the religion of Israel in the period of the Judges can scarcely be combined to provide a general picture. Quite probably there was no religious unity. The genuine traditions of Israel came into conflict with indigenous Canaanite traditions. Sometimes these traditions became confused, sometimes they remained independently side by side; the final outcome was inconclusive. Only the beginning of the monarchy, with the introduction of kingship, the conquest of Jerusalem, and the building of the Temple, created the conditions necessary for a synthesis.

---

[57] C.-F. Jean and J. Hoftijzer, *Dictionnaire des inscriptions sémitique de l'ouest* (Leiden: Brill, 1962—), *s.v. ḥrm*.

[58] H. Ringgren, *The Prophetical Conception of Holiness* (Leipzig: Harrassowitz, 1948), pp. 12 ff.

II.

THE RELIGION IN THE PERIOD OF THE MONARCHY

1.

INTRODUCTION

a. Basic Questions

The period of the monarchy is the classic epoch of the Israelite religion. Here our sources provide incomparably more abundant information than for the earlier periods. Despite this fact, we encounter many difficulties in describing the religion of this period.

In the first place, our sources are almost exclusively of Judean or Jerusalemite origin, or have come down to us only in a Judean recension. We can therefore learn from them very little that is reliable about the religious situation of the Northern Kingdom, although it is an unmistakable fact that on many points there was a considerable difference between the Northern and the Southern kingdoms. The material referring directly to the religion of the north is very fragmentary, nor is it by any means possible simply to supplement it with Jerusalemite material.

In the second place, the sources are partially of postexilic origin and to a certain degree reflect later conditions. This is particularly true for the Pentateuch. The final redaction of the laws took place in the exilic or postexilic period. Therefore the laws pertaining to sacrifices and feasts, for example, although they contain ancient material, have been assimilated to the customary practice of the later period. If we are to use these sources for describing the pre-exilic period, we must first examine them critically and compare them with material known to be pre-exilic.

We encounter a third problem in the difficulty of dating the sources, especially the psalms. Modern study is inclined to ascribe most of the psalms to the pre-exilic period, but in many cases it is difficult or even impossible to fix their dates precisely.[1] This uncertainty must naturally affect the picture we paint ourselves of the religion during the period of the monarchy.

Finally, the pre-exilic religion was by no means the homogeneous

---

[1] See above, p. 11.

57

entity that the present scriptures of the Old Testament make it out to be.[2] The conflict and compromise between Canaanite and Israelite traditions was still far from over. The struggle between the religion of Yahweh and the religion of Baal continued with unabated vigor. As a result, there existed in pre-exilic Israel several divergent tendencies that cannot be understood simply as manifestations of a single homogeneous faith. There existed side by side, for example, the so-to-speak official religion of the Temple and monarchy (in the Southern Kingdom), a popular syncretistic religion, the religion of the great literary prophets, and the religion of the Deuteronomistic circle. A uniform authoritative dogma did not yet exist; there were different theories of creation, the conception of God had not yet been codified in definitive propositions, opinions differed with regard to the so-called principle of retribution. If we nevertheless undertake to give a coherent description of the religion during the period of the monarchy, we must keep these facts constantly in mind and pay close attention to the variations within the religion of Israel. A certain basic unity, in spite of all this, dominates the diversity. Even if the ancient religion of Yahweh did not remain unchanged through the centuries, it still was powerful enough to prevail in most areas, transforming the borrowed Canaanite elements into something new, something that strikes us as being specifically Israelite. But the unity resides more in the final outcome than in the competing tendencies of the period of the monarchy.

b. The Kingship, the New Capital, and the Temple

The introduction of the kingship was one of the three events of the tenth century B.C. that put a new stamp upon the Israelite religion. The system of government during the period of the Judges was based upon the tribal organization; a common shrine (the ark) and a common faith constituted the only bond uniting all the tribes. To these are added now not only the kingship, but Jerusalem as the new capital, and the Temple.

I Samuel contains at least two different accounts of the introduction of kingship in Israel; they represent divergent estimations of this institution.[3] Chapter 11 may contain yet another tradition: after Saul succeeds in liberating Jabesh-gilead, which the Ammonites had been besieging, Saul's kingship is "renewed"—but many scholars view this chapter as a reference to the events that brought Saul to the throne.

---

[2] This fact is particularly emphasized by S. H. Hooke (ed.), *Myth, Ritual, and Kingship* (London: Oxford, 1958), pp. 13 ff.; and I. Engnell, "Methodological Aspects of Old Testament Study," *SVT*, VII (Congress Volume, 1960), 17.

[3] See the commentaries, e.g., H. W. Hertzberg, *Die Samuelbücher* (Göttingen: Vandenhoeck & Ruprecht, 1960), pp. 54 ff., 103 ff.

According to I Samuel 8 and I Samuel 10:17-27, the people demand that Samuel give them a king "like all the nations." Samuel condemns this demand as apostasy from Yahweh, the true king, but unwillingly grants their request. According to I Samuel 9 and I Samuel 10:1-16, Yahweh gives Samuel a direct commission to anoint Saul king and then pours out his spirit upon Saul. These accounts make two points clear: first, kingship was introduced after the pattern of the surrounding nations; and second, there were circles that for religious reasons looked upon kingship with suspicion and condemned it. It is obvious that the institutions connected with kingship and the conception of the meaning of kingship had to be borrowed from outside Israel. We shall later study the royal ideology in more detail, with attention to the extrabiblical parallels. At this point we shall only mention that the king, as Yahweh's anointed (*mᵉšîaḥ yahweh*), was considered sacrosanct, and that the anointing, as we have seen, was connected with the gift of the spirit, enabling the king to perform extraordinary acts.

Theoretically and ideologically, then, sacral kingship already existed in the person of Saul; in practice, however, it was his successor David who made the kingship an influential institution. First, at Hebron, David was elevated to kingship over the southern tribes; later the northern tribes also recognized him as their ruler. He thus united in his own person the royal authority over the two tribal groups that together constituted all Israel. Even during his own lifetime, though, he was to experience painfully the gulf that actually separated the two groups (II Sam. 19). It would even be more accurate to say that during the reigns of David and Solomon there existed a personal union between Judah and Israel than that they constituted a real political unity.

David presumably played an important role in the development of the royal ideology. He probably found his models for the most part among the Canaanites—thereby to an extent borrowing indirectly from Mesopotamian royal ideology—but there is also evidence of Egyptian traits. The significance of the kingship for the further religious development in Israel can hardly be overestimated. The king became the dominant and unifying figure both religiously and politically; the people looked upon him as the mediator of divine blessing, and the royal ideology later gave rise to the Messianic hope. These developments must of course be treated elsewhere.

The second decisive event that transformed the religion of Israel was David's conquest of Jerusalem and transfer of the ark there from Kiriath-jearim. In the eyes of both tribal groups constituting Israel, Jerusalem was neutral ground. On the other hand, though, it was also a Canaanite—or more precisely, Jebusite—cultic center, a shrine of *ēl ʿelyôn*. David had to accommodate himself to these facts. By bringing the ark up to Jerusalem, he made this city the religious center of his kingdom. In addition, a compromise must have been struck between Canaanite and Israelite religious traditions. Yahweh seems to have been identified with the high god of Jerusalem, *ēl ʿelyôn*; and certain Canaanite cultic practices seem to have been borrowed by the Israelite cult. The details of this process have not yet been explained definitively.[4] Three biblical narratives in particular bear on this question.

First, II Samuel 6 tells how the ark was brought to Jerusalem, where it remains for a while outside the city in the house of Obed-edom, finally to be brought into the so-called city of David amid jubilation and the sounding of trumpets (vss. 15 f.). There David pitched a tent for it—probably not the ancient tabernacle of the desert period, as some think—and offered sacrifices and performed a cultic dance. Although we have here the description of an historical event, the account of the celebration is probably based on later processions with the ark. II Samuel 6 may possibly even reflect a Canaanite New Year's ritual introduced into the Israelite cult by David, traces of which also remain in Psalm 132.[5] An oracle given to David through Nathan the prophet is also mentioned in connection with this event; this oracle promises him and his dynasty that they shall reign forever in Jerusalem and be Yahweh's sons (II Sam. 7; see below). In addition, Nathan's prophecy includes a prohibition: David must not build a house for the ark, since Yahweh prefers to dwell in a tent—as during the period of wandering in the desert—and has never demanded a temple. It is possible that this reason for the prohibition reflects a later Yahwistic and anti-Canaanite tradition, and that the actual reason was different, namely, that Nathan belonged to a Jebusite party hostile to any Yahweh temple.[6] In any case, David did not build a temple.

Second, II Samuel 24 tells how David brought a threshing floor to the north of the city from Araunah, a Jebusite—the king (v. 23)?[7]— in order to build an altar there. This was the place where Solomon was later to erect his temple. Now there are several passages in the Old Testament that mention a threshing floor as a cultic site or at least a sacred precinct (Gen. 50:10; I Kings 22:10; Hos. 9:1 ff.; *et al.*); this makes it probable that in this case David took over a local sanctuary. But to what extent did he also take over Jebusite cultic practice?

Our third passage gives us a little more information on this point. The enigmatic story of Abraham and Melchizedek in Genesis 14 has

---

[4] For a discussion of the entire question, see G. W. Ahlström, *Aspects of Syncretism in Israelite Religion* (Lund: Gleerup, 1963), pp. 34 ff.

[5] J. R. Porter, "The Interpretation of 2 Samuel vi and Psalm cxxxii," *JTS*, V (1954), 161 ff.; H. W. Hertzberg, *op. cit.*, p. 228.

[6] G. W. Ahlström, "Der Prophet Nathan und der Tempelbau," *VT*, XI (1961), 113 f.

[7] This is the view of Ahlström; *ibid.*, pp. 117 f.

Abraham give tithes to the priest-king of Salem, i.e., Jerusalem. Abraham thereby recognizes him and his worship of *ēl 'elyôn*; Melchizedek in return recognizes Abraham as a full citizen of Canaan. Now Psalm 110:4 emphasizes that the Israelite king of Jerusalem was considered the legitimate successor of Melchizedek. The possibility should be considered, therefore, that the account in Genesis 14 is intended as a justification of David's religious politics; in that case, its actual purpose would be to show that even Abraham recognized *ēl 'elyôn* of Jerusalem.[8] In addition, the name Melchizedek ("my king is Zedek") demonstrates the existence of a god Zedek (Heb. *ṣedeq*, "righteousness")[9] at Jerusalem, just as the name of the city contains the divine name Salem. Many scholars see a reference to this same divine name in the name of Zadok the priest, who later played an important role under David and Solomon. This would mean that a worshiper of Zedek became the high priest of Solomon. A few scholars even think that he formerly had been the priest-king of Jebusite Jerusalem, who, after the conquest of the city, had helped David and Solomon weld the elements of the Canaanite and Israelite religions into a unity.[10] Others, on the contrary, think that the rather unusual name Ahio in II Samuel 6:3 really refers to Zadok. The name, according to these scholars, should be read *āḥiw*, "his brother"; this would make Zadok the brother of Uzzah and the son of Abinadab, a Gibeonite.[11] In any case, Zadok, the ancestor or at least nominal ancestor of the later Israelite priesthood, did not come from the tribe of Levi, as tradition asserts. Further detail can only be conjectured.

Finally, Solomon's building of the Temple was of crucial importance. It is obvious that the Temple was built more or less according to Canaanite models.[12] It therefore represents yet another contact with the religion and cult of the earlier population of the country. In addition, the setting up of the ark in the Temple meant that the palladium of the Israelite tribes was now housed in the sanctuary of a royal palace —which is what the Solomonic Temple originally was. The king was responsible for the cult at this central sanctuary. This event marks the beginning of the course of development that was to culminate in the claim of the Jerusalem Temple to be the only legitimate cultic site in Israel.

It is difficult to determine in detail the effect the Temple had on the enrichment of the cult, but we must assume that it exercised some

---

[8] H. S. Nyberg, "Studien zum Religionskampf im alten Israel," *ARW*, XXXV (1938), 37 f.; G. von Rad, *Genesis*, trans. J. H. Marks (Philadelphia: Westminster, 1961), pp. 175 f.

[9] H. Ringgren, *Word and Wisdom* (Lund: Ohlsson, 1947), pp. 85 f.

[10] H. H. Rowley, "Melchisedek and Zadok," *Festschrift für Alfred Bertholet* (Tübingen: Mohr, 1950), pp. 461 ff.

[11] K. Budde, "Die Herkunft Sadok's," *ZAW*, LII (1934), 48 f.

[12] See the detailed discussion below at pp. 158 ff.

influence. We know, of course, only the final result, the cult during the period of the monarchy; we are even better acquainted with the cult of the postexilic Temple.

An exact definition of the relationship between Yahweh and ēl 'elyôn would be extremely interesting, but at this point our sources fail us. With the exceptions mentioned above,[13] all the biblical texts treat ēl 'elyôn as identical with Yahweh. In other words, the assimilation is complete. There may be truth in the observation that the Temple was oriented in such a way that at the equinoxes the sun rising over the Mount of Olives could shine into its inner chamber.[14] But does this prove that ēl 'elyôn was a sun god and that Yahweh took over his functions? In fact, the evidence that ēl 'elyôn was a sun god is not convincing.[15] Hollis says that sun worship was attacked several times by the reforming kings.[16] But three of the four passages he cites do not mention the sun at all, and the fourth (II Kings 23:4 ff.) speaks in quite general terms of "the sun, and the moon, and the constellations, and all the host of the heavens." It is true that the other evidence he brings forward supports the existence of sun worship in Canaan; but it does not connect this worship with ēl 'elyôn (or Yahweh).[17] Oesterly refers to Psalm 80:2 (Eng. 80:1), which reads, "Thou who art enthroned upon the cherubim, shine forth"; he states that the verb used here is applied only to Yahweh and the sun.[18] But this is not true. The verb hôpîaʻ is never used to refer to the sun (in Job 3:4 it refers to daylight); once (Job 37:15) it is even used of lightning. On the other hand, zāraḥ, "shine forth," which is used of the sun eleven times, is also applied to the appearance of Yahweh: Deuteronomy 33:2; Isaiah 60:1 f. It is correct to say that a theophany is often described in terms of light, for example in Habakkuk 3:3-4:[19]

> His glory covered the heavens,
>   and the earth was full of his praise.
> His brightness was like the light,
>   rays flashed from his hand. . . .

But the theophanies must all be studied together. When this is done, it will be seen that the traits that might possibly be derived from a sun god do not, so to speak, set the style; they only appear

---

[13] See p. 44.
[14] F. J. Hollis, "The Sun-Cult and the Temple at Jerusalem," in S. H. Hooke (ed.), *Myth and Ritual* (London: Oxford, 1933), pp. 87 ff.
[15] This is also the opinion of M. Pope, *El in the Ugaritic Texts* (*SVT*, II [Leiden: Brill, 1955]), pp. 82 f.; cf. above, p. 42.
[16] *Op. cit.,* pp. 88 f.
[17] *Ibid.,* p. 89, n. 1.
[18] W. O. E. Oesterly, "Early Hebrew Festival Rituals," in S. H. Hooke (ed.), *Myth and Ritual,* p. 115.
[19] *Ibid.,* p. 119.

more prominently in some cases than in others.[20] In any case, they do not prove that *ēl 'elyôn* was in any way connected with the sun. Even the prayer of dedication of the Temple in I Kings 8:12 f. says nothing about Yahweh's being a sun god;[21] it says rather that he has set the sun in the heavens. Psalm 19, which contains a few lines that seem to be borrowed from a hymn to the sun, never equates Yahweh with the sun; instead, Yahweh (or El) is the creator of the sun:

> In them he hath set a tent for the sun, which comes forth like a bridegroom leaving his chamber, and like a strong man runs its course with joy. (vss. 5 f. [Eng. 4 f.])

Thus traces of sun worship exist in the Old Testament, but they are not connected with *ēl 'elyôn*. El appears instead to be the old, venerable, and wise god, the creator of heaven and earth, the gentle and merciful father. He stands in contrast to the wild and dynamic Yahweh, whose realm is windstorm and thunderstorm. Probably the element of exalted peace and the striving for universality are the primary Canaanite contribution to the nature of the Israelite God.[22]

c. The Division of the Kingdom and Its Religious Consequences

From the very beginning a tension existed between the northern Israel tribes and the southern Judah tribes. As we have seen, David united both halves of the nation by means of a personal union. This union, however, very soon threatened to break up. Solomon tried by administrative reforms to abolish the tribal organization and replace it with a territorial organization. But after his death the northern tribes revolted against his son and successor Rehoboam and chose their own king, Jeroboam. This event is important for the history of the Israelite religion in at least three respects.

First, at Bethel and Dan Jeroboam created new, national shrines, where Yahweh was obviously worshiped in the image of a bull.[23] This was definitely a Canaanite feature; at Ras Shamra, El is called "the bull El," and Baal has intercourse with a heifer. Jeroboam's action violated the prohibition of images and produced an unbridge-

---

[20] See below, p. 194.

[21] F. J. Hollis, *op. cit.,* p. 90.

[22] Cf. O. Eissfeldt, "El and Yahweh," *JSS,* I (1956), 25 ff.; F. Løkkegaard, "A Plea for El," *Studia Orientalia Joanni Pedersen dicata* (Hauniae: Munksgaard, 1953), pp. 219 ff. (especially pp. 232 f.); A. Kapelrud, *Central Ideas in the Book of Amos* (Oslo: Oslo University Press, 1961), pp. 44 ff.

[23] At least according to the narrator. More recently, some scholars (H. T. Obbink, "Jahwebilder," *ZAW,* XLVII [1929], 264 ff.; W. F. Albright, *From the Stone Age to Christianity* [Garden City: Doubleday, 1957], pp. 299 f.) have suggested that the bulls served rather as a pedestal upon which the invisible God was thought to be enthroned. Cf. M. Weippert, "Gott und Stier," *ZDPV,* LXXVII (1961), 93 ff.

able gulf between the Northern Kingdom and Jerusalem. Since the ark remained in Jerusalem, the Northern Kingdom was denied access to the common central shrine of Israel, and the religious development of the north went its own way. The new shrines at Bethel and Dan were intended to replace Jerusalem (I Kings 12:28 ff.); the ancient local shrines also continued to exist. Deuteronomy demonstrates the importance of Shechem by reporting a covenant renewal festival celebrated there (Deut. 27—28). I Kings 12:32 informs us that a new feast was introduced, which was intended to replace "the feast that was in Judah."[24] We are not expressly told how viable these innovations were; but there is plenty of evidence that syncretistic elements were not lacking. In the time of Ahab, Elijah is embroiled in a furious struggle with the Baal cult. Amos condemns the cult at Bethel (Amos 4:4; 5:5). Hosea, the only literary prophet to exercise his ministry in the Northern Kingdom exclusively, inveighs against Baal with particular vehemence. In addition, the Elephantine papyri, from a Jewish military colony in Egypt, are acquainted with other divinities besides Yahweh; these have names like Ashim-bethel, Herem-bethel, and Anath-bethel (Anath-jahu),[25] which obviously point to some sort of connection with Bethel. Thus when the Assyrians settled people from various countries in the territory of the Northern Kingdom after the fall of Samaria, as II Kings 17 reports, people who brought their own cults with them, the ground had already been prepared for a mixture of religions.[26] We shall come back to these questions later.

Second, the kingship took a different course of development in the Northern Kingdom. While the Davidic dynasty reigned for the entire period in the Southern Kingdom in consequence of Yahweh's covenant with David, so that the royal dignity was hereditary, no dynasty was ever able to endure in the Northern Kingdom. Prophets participated in the choice of a remarkably large number of kings. In the Northern Kingdom, therefore, the kingship was to a certain extent charismatic; in the Southern Kingdom, on the contrary, it was an hereditary institution.[27] Unfortunately, the documents at our disposal for a study of the kingship in Israel are exclusively southern, from Judah and Jerusalem, so that in fact we are really acquainted with the royal ideology only of the Southern Kingdom.

Third, whatever religious traditions of northern Israel have been preserved in the writings of the Old Testament are extant only in a southern, Jerusalemite recension. We have North Israelite material in

---

24 H. J. Kraus, *Die Königsherrschaft Jahwes* (Tübingen: Mohr, 1951).

25 A. Vincent, *La religion des judéo-araméens à Eléphantine* (Paris: Guethner, 1937), pp. 593 ff.

26 Cf. below, p. 98.

27 See below, p. 221.

the "Elohistic" portions of the Pentateuch, in Deuteronomy, in certain passages in the Deuteronomistic history, and also in the book of Hosea. But seen as a whole, our Old Testament is a Jerusalemite product. If, then, we attempt to describe the religion during the period of the monarchy as the definitive religion of Israel, we must rely primarily on the Jerusalemite tradition, taking note of North Israelite material only occasionally.

2.

GOD

"Hear, O Israel: Yahweh our God is one Yahweh."[1] Thus Deuteronomy 6:4 expresses the basic tenet of the Israelite religion. The first commandment of the Decalogue puts it thus: "You shall have no other gods before [or 'besides'] me" (Exod. 20:3; Deut. 5:7). The statement is unambiguous: Israel must not worship any god but Yahweh. But this does not expressly deny the existence of other divinities. On the contrary: the continuation of the commandment forbids the worship of those other gods, whose existence is thus simply presupposed. It is possible, of course, that we have here merely an imprecise mode of expression. The prohibition could mean in reality, "You shall not worship any idols, for they are not real gods." But Judges 11:24 presupposes beyond any doubt that Chemosh is the god of the Moabites just as Yahweh is the god of Israel. Similarly, I Samuel 26:19 says that outside of Israel David would have to serve other gods; it does not question their existence. Psalm 82 even alludes to an assembly of the gods. On the other hand, a few psalms contain such statements as this:

> For all the gods of the peoples are idols;
> but Yahweh made the heavens. (Ps. 96:5)

In other words, Yahweh is the only real God. Deutero-Isaiah is the first biblical writer to deny completely the existence, or at least the authority, of the other gods. Either they do not exist, or they are powerless. An idol is only wood, stone, or metal; it is not a god at all (Isa. 41:7; 44:9-20).

> Behold, you are nothing,
> and your work is nought;
> an abomination is he who chooses you. (Isa. 41:24)

The religion of Israel, then, was originally not monotheistic in the sense of denying the existence of other gods. It would be more proper

---

[1] Or: Yahweh is our God, Yahweh is one. See the commentaries.

to call it monolatry or henotheism.[2] From a certain point of view, this is the characteristic position taken by a national religion: in practice, only the gods of one's own nation are significant; other gods may exist, but are of no consequence. But one of the distinguishing characteristics of the Israelite religion is the belief that there are not several gods of Israel, but only one, Yahweh, who claims exclusive devotion. The naïve conviction that Yahweh was the only God of Israel gave rise in the course of time to the belief that he was also the only God of the world. We encounter very early the idea that Yahweh is the creator of heaven and earth (Gen. 14:22; cf. also Gen. 2:4[J]), or that he is "the God of heaven and of the earth" (Gen. 24:3[J]). The psalms and Deutero-Isaiah develop this thought in the direction of a consistent monotheism that excludes the existence of any other gods.

The Hebrew word for God is *ĕlôah*; this word is also used occasionally to designate Yahweh, the only God. But in most cases the word used is *ĕlōhîm*. This latter word is morphologically a plural form, although it is always connected with a verb in the singular. Either the ending *-îm* is originally not a plural ending at all, but an expression of intensification, or else we are dealing here with the so-called plural of majesty. Be that as it may, this word in isolation is used to designate Yahweh, especially in certain circles.[3] No proper name is used; but there is no doubt who is intended.

The words *ĕlôah* and *ĕlōhîm,* and the corresponding Arabian *ilāh* (which occurs in "Allah," from *al-ilāh,* "the god") and Aramaic *ĕlāhā',* probably represent a secondary extension of the common Semitic "El" *(ilu, et al.).* There is no consensus on the derivation of this word. The root seems to be *'yl* or *'wl;* the basic meaning could be either "power, strength,"[4] or "the first, foremost."[5] Perhaps the word contains both these concepts. This by no means proves, however, that the Semitic concept of God can be derived from a belief in power or mana. A god called "the mighty one, the powerful one" is not necessarily the projection of an impersonal power.

The real, proper name of the Israelite God, however, is Yahweh. As we have seen,[6] the original meaning of this name is obscure. Neither do the extant sources seem to know what it means. The only interpretation given by the Old Testament is the one contained in Exodus 3:14, "I am who I am" (see above). But even this statement does not play any role elsewhere in the Old Testament. It is never again referred to, which probably proves that it is secondary. Yahweh

---

[2] See below, p. 99.
[3] The E-traditions in the Pentateuch and the so-called Elohistic Psalter.
[4] See, for example, L. Köhler, *Lexikon in Veteris Testamenti libros* (Leiden: Brill, 1950-53), *s.v. el.*
[5] T. Nöldeke, "Elohim, El," *SPAW,* 1882, pp. 1175 ff.
[6] See above, pp. 32 f.

is simply the proper name of the God of Israel; the Old Testament is not in the least concerned with what it may once have meant as a Hebrew word. The Septuagint simply translates it with *kurios*, "Lord," because at the time of translation motives of reverence prevented people from pronouncing the name of God; they replaced it instead with *ădônāy*, "the Lord (lit. 'my lord')."

The name Yahweh often appears in conjunction with "Sabaoth" (Heb. *ṣebā'ôt*).[7] This word means "hosts"; it occurs several times in the combination *yahweh ĕlōhê ṣebā'ôt*, "Yahweh, the God of hosts" (II Sam. 5:10; I Kings 19:10; Ps. 89:9 [Eng. 89:8]; Jer. 5:14; Hos. 12:6 [Eng. 12:5]; Amos 3:13; 6:14). The usual expression, though, is merely "Yahweh Sabaoth." At a pinch, this might mean "Yahweh of hosts"; it actually violates the rules of Hebrew grammar, however, since a proper name cannot be construed with a genitive. The real question, though, is *what* hosts are meant. Some think the phrase refers to the Israelite army. The appearance of the epithet several times in connection with the ark as a war shrine (II Sam. 6:2, 18; 7:2, 8, 26-27) seems to support this view. In addition, one passage (I Sam. 17:45) calls Yahweh "the God of the armies of Israel." But the ark, as we have seen, is also connected with the conception of Yahweh as an enthroned king; and the vast majority of occurrences of "Yahweh Sabaoth" as a divine name are found in the prophets, where emphasis upon the warlike aspects of Yahweh is not suggested by the context. Two other interpretations are therefore preferable: the one makes "Sabaoth" refer to the hosts of the stars (cf. Isa. 40:26); the other makes it refer either to angels or to other heavenly beings (cf. Ps. 103:21). Possibly these two interpretations can be combined; elsewhere in the ancient Near East the stars were considered to be gods, and therefore they might be taken as the servants of Yahweh. The idea of Yahweh's heavenly court could have contributed to this conception.[8]

Another interpretation has been suggested by F. M. Cross.[9] He thinks that *yahweh ṣebā'ôt* means "he who creates the (heavenly) armies," the *ṣebā'ôt* being the heavenly hosts or the "sons of God." Even if this be the original meaning, however, it is obvious that the actual use of the term in the Old Testament does not suggest such a meaning.

A fifth possibility would be to take the word "Sabaoth" as an abstract noun (in the plural); the epithet would then mean "the one

[7] B. N. Wambacq, *L'épithète divine Jahvé Sébaot*, 1947.
[8] W. Kessler, "Aus welchen Gründen wird die Bezeichnung 'Jahwe Zebaoth' in der späteren Zeit gemieden?" *Gottes ist der Orient* (Berlin: Evengelische Verlagsanstalt, 1959), pp. 79 ff., speaks of an integration or fusing of Canaanite numina.
[9] F. M. Cross, Jr., "Yahweh and the God of the Patriarchs," *HTR*, LV (1962), 256.

characterized by Sabaoth" or "the God of Sabaoth-ness," designating the God whose power is the epitome of all power.[10] It must be admitted, though, that such an adjectival use of a plural substantive would be unique.

In any case, "Sabaoth" is used particularly in those contexts that speak of Yahweh as the almighty Lord and king. The Septuagint accordingly often translates it as *pantokratōr*, "all-powerful."

Remarkably enough, the epithet is avoided in the later period. As early a writer as Hosea rejects it; Deuteronomy in particular avoids it, as do Ezekiel, Trito-Isaiah, and the other postexilic prophets. The question must remain open whether this avoidance really points to a polytheistic Canaanite origin for the expression.[11]

A third common designation for God is *ādôn*, "Lord," or—more commonly—*ădōnāy*, "my Lord(s)" (plural of majesty). As Köhler emphasizes, this word refers to the Lord in his capacity as ruler (while *ba'al* means the Lord as possessor and owner).[12] Hebrew also uses this word to refer to the master of a slave or a servant. It likewise occurs as a divine epithet in Phoenician and Punic inscriptions; it is applied, for example, to Baal, Baal Shamem, Resheph, Melkart, and Eshmun. The Greek designation for the west Semitic fertility god, Adonis, is derived from the same word. Yahweh, then, is Lord and ruler, e.g., "Lord of all the earth" (Josh. 3:11, 13). Man is his servant (*'ebed*), a feature found in most of the Semitic religions.

In addition, *ēl* ("God"), *ēl 'elyôn* ("God Most High"), and *ēl šadday* ("God Almighty") appear as epithets of Yahweh. As we have seen,[13] these were originally names of Canaanite gods; their application to Yahweh expresses the conviction that he is basically identical with those gods. "I appeared to Abraham, to Isaac, and to Jacob as 'God Almighty' [Heb. *ēl šadday*], but by my name Yahweh I did not make myself known to them," says Yahweh to Moses in Exodus 6:3. In the course of time, then, these divine names became mere epithets of Yahweh that could be applied to him without distinction.

Now if we ask how this God was conceived, the Old Testament does not give us an unequivocal answer. It is stated a few times that no man can look upon God (Exod. 33:20; Judg. 13:22); but this does not mean that God has no form, but rather that his divinity is so terrible that whoever sees him cannot remain alive (cf. Judg. 6:22; Deut. 5:26). Likewise the statement that God is spirit and

---

[10] O. Eissfeldt, "Jahwe Zebaoth," *Miscellanea Academica Berolinensia*, 1950, pp. 128 ff.; R. H. Pfeiffer supports a similar view in *Religion in the Old Testament* (New York: Harper, 1961), p. 92.

[11] Kessler, *op. cit.*

[12] L. Köhler, *Old Testament Theology*, trans. A. S. Todd (London: Lutterworth, 1957), p. 30.

[13] See above, pp. 21 f.

not flesh (cf. Isa. 31:3) can hardly mean that God is invisible; it rather indicates that he is totally different from man (cf. Num. 23:19). On the other hand, the fact that images of Yahweh in the form of a bull were set up in the Northern Kingdom should not lead us to conclude that Yahweh was pictured as a bull (I Kings 12:28). On the one hand, it is possible that the bull only served as a pedestal; on the other, we are dealing here with a Canaanite feature, and among the Canaanites the bull served only to symbolize in animal form gods that were otherwise thought of as being in human form. The prophets occasionally compare Yahweh to an animal (lion, bear, panther, e.g., Lam. 3:10; Hos. 5:14; 11:10; 13:7; an eagle in Deut. 32:11),[14] but these comparisons are of course only metaphorical. Many details suggest the assumption, however, that when anything at all is said about the appearance of Yahweh he is thought of as being like a man. For example, he created man in his own image (Gen. 1:27); the meaning of the words used, ṣelem and dᵉmût, hardly allows this statement to refer to anything but corporeal similarity. There is accordingly frequent mention of God's face, his eye, his mouth, his nose, and his hand. He walks about in the Garden of Eden and discovers the sinful couple (Gen. 3:8), he comes down to see the tower of Babel (Gen. 11:5), he shuts the door behind Noah (Gen. 7:16). Even if a few anthropomorphic expressions are to be understood metaphorically, the fact remains that God is often described in human terms and that the most distinct anthropomorphisms are found in the earliest strata of the Old Testament. Nevertheless, the universal prohibition of images (Exod. 20:4) places the strictest possible limitation upon anthropomorphism. Even if it was not always obeyed by everyone, this prohibition expresses plainly the transcendence of God to a degree not found in any of the other ancient religions. The God who forbids representation of himself cannot really be imagined as a human being. On the other hand, he could not be described without recourse to human features.[15]

Yahweh dwells in heaven. "Our God is in the heavens; he does whatever he pleases" (Ps. 115:3). Heaven is his throne and the earth his footstool (Isa. 66:1). He speaks to the Israelites out of heaven (Deut. 4:36); he fights for them from heaven (Judg. 5:20). Ezekiel sees him in the heavens: "The heavens were opened and I saw visions of God" (Ezek. 1:1). But Yahweh is not a God of the heavens in the sense that he is identical with the firmament. He dwells in heaven, but is not to be identified with heaven.

---

[14] J. Hempel, "Die Jahwegleichnisse der israelitischen Propheten," *ZAW*, XLII (1924), 74 ff.

[15] J. Hempel, "Die Grenzen des Anthropomorphismus Jahwes im Alten Testament," *ZAW*, LVII (1939), 7 ff.; W. Vischer, "Words and the Word," *Interpretation*, III (1949), 1 ff.; F. Michaeli, *Dieu à l'image de l'homme* (Neuchatel & Paris: Delachaux & Niestle, 1950).

At other times, Yahweh reveals himself in atmospheric phenomena. The traditional description of a theophany, such as we find, for example, in Judges 5:4-5; Deuteronomy 33:2; Psalm 18:8-10 (Eng. 18:7-9); Psalm 68:8-9 (Eng. 68:7-8), pictures Yahweh appearing accompanied by lightning, thunder, rain, and earthquake. Now this representation, it is true, has been developed in a cultic framework and cannot simply be explained as an echo of the revelation on Sinai (Exod. 19:16-19; 20:18) or as the description of a storm god; but the fact remains that Yahweh is connected with these natural phenomena. Possibly some of this description was borrowed from the Canaanite religion. We have seen, for instance, that the epithet *rōkēb bā'ărābôt*, "he who rides through the deserts [?]," in Psalm 68:5 (Eng. 68:4) should probably be understood as a reinterpretation of the Canaanite epithet *rākib 'arpāti*, "he who rides upon the clouds."[16] Elsewhere, too, in the Old Testament we read that Yahweh rides in the heavens or upon clouds (Ps. 18:11 f. [Eng. 18:10 f.]; 68:34 [Eng. 68:33]; Deut. 33:26; Isa. 19:1). Psalm 29, which describes the thunder as Yahweh's voice and the storm as a manifestation of his power, contains a wealth of stylistic features that are also typical of Canaanite poetry.[17] Even if this psalm is not a revision of a Canaanite original, it nevertheless demonstrates that Canaanite elements have contributed to the development of the conception of God. These traits, however, could not simply have been ascribed to Yahweh if points of contact were not already present in his original nature. Yahweh's association from the very beginning with atmospheric phenomena is established beyond question.

His close connection with fertility can be derived from this function but is probably a secondary feature. Hosea 2:10 (Eng. 2:8) emphasizes that Yahweh provides grain and wine and oil; but this view is obviously a polemic against Canaanite ideas, which looked on Baal as the god of fertility. In Psalm 65:10 ff. (Eng. 65:9 ff.), however, Yahweh appears quite naturally as the giver of rain, who causes the grain to grow:

> Thou visitest the earth and waterest it,
> thou greatly enrichest it;
> . . . .
> Thou waterest its furrows abundantly,
> settling its ridges,
> softening it with showers,
> and blessing its growth.

---

[16] See above, p. 43.

[17] F. M. Cross, "A Note on a Canaanite Psalm in the Old Testament." *BASOR*, CXVII (1949), 19 ff.; T. Gaster, "Psalm 29," *JQR*, XXXVII (1946), 54 ff.

This idea followed naturally from serious belief in Yahweh as creator; but the religion of Baal probably led to a considerable accentuation of this feature.

The idea of Yahweh as the God of the land of Canaan is also linked with this development. The theophanies pictured Yahweh as coming from Sinai; Psalm 68 and Habakkuk 3 show how this conception lived on. Now we also find passages that refer to Yahweh as lord and ruler of Israel's territory. When identified with the god that struggles with Jacob at the Jabbok (Gen. 32), he appears having the land of Canaan at his disposal; he is able to guarantee possession of the land to Jacob-Israel. According to Deuteronomy 32:8 f., Yahweh kept Israel as his inheritance when he distributed the peoples and nations. Now Yahweh dwells in Jerusalem; Zion is his holy mountain, from which he shines forth to destroy his enemies (Ps. 50:2-4; 48:3-8 [Eng. 48:2-7]). The theophany can therefore now be localized in Jerusalem and the Temple. This localization assigns to Yahweh the place previously occupied by the national gods of Canaan. Yahweh's link with the land of Canaan develops to such a degree that people occasionally think he cannot be worshiped outside Canaan. In order to be able to worship Yahweh in his own homeland, Naaman the Syrian must take earth from Canaan and erect an altar to Yahweh upon it (II Kings 5:17).

If we study the characteristics of this Israelite God, we immediately encounter a certain duality in his nature. The Song of Hannah, a thanksgiving psalm, states, for example:

> Yahweh kills and brings to life;
> he brings down to Sheol and raises up.
> Yahweh makes poor and makes rich;
> he brings low, he also exalts. (I Sam. 2:6 f.)

The context shows clearly that in this case the emphasis is upon bringing to life and exalting; but this passage nevertheless states unambiguously that everything, good and bad, good fortune and ill fortune, comes from Yahweh (cf. also Deut. 32:39: "I wound and I heal"). Deutero-Isaiah develops this thought into a statement of theoretical monism:

> I am Yahweh, and there is no other.
> I form light and create darkness,
> I make weal and create woe,
> I am Yahweh, who do all these things. (Isa. 45:6-7)

It is true that this passage might have been formulated in deliberate contrast to Iranian dualistic ideas. But it is in complete harmony with the general Israelite conception of God to say that everything, both good and "evil," comes from Yahweh. Now and then even a

72

"demonic" element has been found in Yahweh's nature.[18] This does not mean, of course, that Yahweh is somehow connected with demons; it means rather that there is something unfathomable and sinister about him and that, as we have seen, he can also bring disaster. Quite unexpectedly he wrestles with Jacob at the Jabbok, and afterwards blesses him (Gen. 32:24-30); without any apparent reason he attacks Moses and attempts to kill him (Exod. 4:24); he hardens the heart of Pharaoh (Exod. 9:12; 10:1; etc.) and smites the Egyptians; he induces David to number the people and then punishes him for doing so (II Sam. 24); he sends a spirit of enmity between Abimelech and the men of Shechem (Judg. 9:23); he sends an evil spirit into Saul and makes him mad (I Sam. 16:14; 19:9-10); he sends a spirit of false prophecy to entice Ahab to destruction (I Kings 22:19-23); the evil that befalls a city comes from him (Amos 3:6).

This duality in Yahweh's nature should not be effaced or softened; it is an original component of the Israelite faith in God. It is characteristic of a particular type of god, namely the so-called high gods, who are primarily gods of destiny exalted above the dualism of good and evil, sending both good fortune and ill fortune.[19] Having said this, however, we must not overlook the fact that Yahweh is not, like most such gods, an otiose god, but appears in furious activity.

This general description also holds true for one of the basic aspects of Yahweh's nature: his holiness.[20] The adjective "holy" is so frequently applied to Yahweh that—especially in later Judaism[21]—he is often called simply "the Holy One" or, especially in the book of Isaiah, "the Holy One of Israel." This latter usage obviously combines the concept of holiness with the idea that Yahweh is the national god of Israel.

The Hebrew word for "holy" is qādôš. The basic meaning of the root is usually said to be "set apart" (i.e., from everything profane and "ordinary"). This explanation, however, is based on the dubious assumption that in the Semitic languages a triconsonantal stem can be formed through arbitrary expansion of a biconsonantal root. In Hebrew, other words beginning with q-d refer to a separation; therefore, the argument runs, the same thing holds true also for q-d-š. But in Akkadian—the only language in which the root occurs independently of its biblical use—the word quddušu has the primary meaning "shining" or "gleaming," and is used in parallel with such

[18] P. Volz, *Das Dämonische in Jahwe* (Tübingen: Mohr, 1924).

[19] G. Widengren, *Hochgottglaube im alten Iran*, 1938, pp. 77, 390.

[20] W. W. von Baudissin, *Der Begriff der Heiligkeit im Alten Testament*, 1878; A. Fridrichsen, *Hagios—Qādōš*, 1916; N. H. Snaith, *The Distinctive Ideas of the Old Testament* (London: Epworth, 1944), pp. 21 ff.; H. Ringgren, *The Prophetical Conception of Holiness* (Leipzig: Harrassowitz, 1948).

[21] S. Esh, *Der Heilige (Er sei gepriesen)* (Leiden: Brill, 1957).

words as *ebbu,* "pure," and *ellu,* "pure, clear, shining."[22] Certainly Yahweh is frequently connected with light and brilliance. His "glory" (Heb. *kābôd*) is clearly associated with light phenomena (see, for example, Ezek. 1—2), and at least Isaiah 6:3 sees a close association between holiness and *kābôd*:

> Holy, holy, holy is Yahweh of hosts;
> the whole earth is full of his glory.

It is nevertheless not possible simply to restrict our definition of Yahweh's holiness to light or brilliance; neither, of course, can it be explained in all passages as separateness. In fact, the basic meaning we have assumed to exist has become so obscured that in biblical language "holy" is best understood as meaning "divine" or "wholly other." The holy God is the Terrible One, exalted and unapproachable, who stands far above everything human. God's name is holy and terrible (terrifying) (Ps. 111:9). In Hosea 11:9, Yahweh says, "For I am God and not man, the Holy One in your midst." And in I Samuel 6:20, we read, "Who is able to stand before Yahweh, this holy God?" In the presence of the holy God man's reaction is awe and dread (Isa. 8:13; 29:23).

When the Book of Isaiah uses the epithet "the Holy One of Israel," the phrase refers primarily to the greatness and majesty of God, particularly, as Fridrichsen has noted, to the divine majesty when offended.[23] But the Holy One of Israel is also the Maker to whom men look for help (Isa. 17:7), the God on whom the preserved remnant shall lean (Isa. 10:20) and in whom the poor shall rejoice (Isa. 29:19, perhaps a later passage?).

The holiness of God thus has a dual meaning. On the one hand, it signifies the unapproachability, the awesomeness, even the dangerousness of the God who is wholly other. On the other, it signifies beneficence: the Holy One is the kindly God who has chosen Israel and has mercy upon Israel.

God's holiness, however, is not directly associated with morality or ethics.[24] Isaiah's reaction, "I am a man of unclean lips, and . . . my eyes have seen the King, Yahweh of hosts!" (Isa. 6:5), refers primarily to the contrast between the majesty of God and human insufficiency. We perhaps come closest to an ethical significance in the so-called Holiness Code, where the admonition, "You shall be holy; for I Yahweh your God am holy" (Lev. 19:2), stands in conjunction with moral and ethical commandments.

---

[22] Ringgren, *op. cit.,* p. 6. On the use of *ebbu* and *ellu,* see A. Haldar, *Associations of Cult Prophets among the Ancient Semites* (Uppsala: Almqvist & Wiksell, 1945), pp. 202 ff.

[23] *Op. cit.,* p. 25.

[24] Ringgren, *op. cit.,* pp. 23 f.

To call persons or things holy means primarily that they are related to what is divine: that which is holy belongs to the divinity as his own personal property.[25]

On the purely descriptive side, then, the concept of holiness in the Old Testament is quite unambiguous. It nevertheless raises a religio-historical problem. The Israelite mind sees certain similarities between what is holy and what is unclean, since it also considers that what is unclean is dangerous and must not be touched. How are these two concepts related to the religio-historical concept of taboo? The evolutionistic theory of religion sought to explain taboo as attaching to objects fraught with mana, and supposed that "holy" and "unclean" developed through differentiation of the concept of taboo. As belief in mana gradually gave way to belief in gods, the mana associated with divine objects became holiness, while in Israel all other mana lived on as uncleanness. Later on (pp. 141 f.) we shall illuminate the concept of uncleanness more fully and shall see that in many respects it corresponds indisputably to holiness. Uncleanness and taboo nevertheless lack that positive aspect which we have found to such a high degree in holiness. Even if taboo and holiness originally belonged together—which is itself questionable—this is no longer true in any case for Israel and the Old Testament. On the contrary, holiness and uncleanness are irreconcilable opposites.[26]

Another characteristic is closely related to the holiness of Yahweh: his zeal or jealousy (Heb. *qin'â*).[27] Yahweh is a jealous God (Heb. *ēl qannā'*). This means in the first instance that he will not tolerate any other god beside him (Exod. 20:5), that he will give his glory to no other (Isa. 42:8; 48:11), so that neither god nor man may share his glory. "For you shall worship no other god, for Yahweh, whose name is Jealous, is a jealous God" (Exod. 34:14). "For Yahweh your God is a devouring fire, a jealous God" (Deut. 4:24). Therefore the jealousy of Yahweh is apt to be connected with his judgment and punishment of his enemies, as in Zephaniah 1:18:

> Neither their silver nor their gold
> > shall be able to deliver them
> > on the day of the wrath of Yahweh.
> In the fire of his jealous wrath,
> > all the earth shall be consumed;
> for a full, yea, sudden end
> > he will make of all the inhabitants of the earth.

[25] Baudissin, *op. cit.*, p. 45: "not a condition, but a relationship."

[26] R. Dussaud, *Les origines cananéennes du sacrifice israélite* (2nd ed.; Paris: Leroux, 1921), pp. 30 ff.; Ringgren. *op. cit.*, pp. 15 f.

[27] F. Küchler, "Der Gedanke des Eifers Jahwe im Alten Testament," *ZAW*, XXVIII (1908), 42 ff. [More recently, see H. A. Brongers, "Der Eifer des Herrn Zebaoth," *VT*, XIII (1963), 269 ff.—TRANS.]

On the other hand, Yahweh's jealousy also has a positive side, namely his passionate zeal for the well-being of his chosen people. Thus Isaiah's prophecy of the wonderful king (Isa. 9:1-6 [Eng. 9:2-7]) concludes with the words, "The zeal of Yahweh of hosts will do this" (cf. also Isa. 37:32; Ezek. 39:25; Zech. 1:14). Yahweh's jealousy, then, shows the same duality of the divine nature as does his holiness: positive towards friends, negative towards enemies.

The wrath of God goes hand in hand with the negative aspect of his jealousy.[28] These two concepts appear occasionally as being equivalent, for example in Zephania 3:8 (cf. Num. 25:11):

> . . . to pour out upon them my indignation,
>   all the heat of my anger;
>   for in the fire of my jealous wrath
>   all the earth shall be consumed.

Yahweh is a jealous God, avenging and wrathful, says Nahum (1:2).

The Hebrew language possesses a whole series of words for wrath, most of which allude to the accompanying physiological phenomena: *ap,* "anger," is connected with *ānap,* "snort"; *hēmâ* and *hārôn* actually mean "heat"; *qeṣep* probably is "eruption"; *'ebrâ* actually means "overflow." Most of these expressions are used to refer to both human and divine wrath. Thus here, too, human emotions are once more ascribed to God, as though to a human being. There are two words, however, that are applied only to God: *za'am,* "indignation," and *hārôn ap,* "burning anger." It is not altogether clear whether this restriction means that a distinction is made between human and divine wrath. In view of the fact that the heart is generally considered always to be the seat of the emotions, it is remarkable that the expressions referring to wrath are never connected with the heart. Emphasis seems to lie on the outward expressions of wrath.

The Bible accordingly follows the general practice of the Hebrew language, describing the wrath of Yahweh more as activity than as an emotion. Yahweh's wrath takes effect through actions. God pours it out (Ezek. 20:33; Lam. 4:11), he causes it to rise against the sinful people (II Chron. 36:16), he sends it forth (Job 20:23; Ps. 78:49), he "does" or executes it (I Sam. 28:18; Hos. 11:9).[29] In a few cases, wrath appears as an almost objective entity, absolutized or half personified. The characteristic Hebrew mode of expression pro-

[28] J. Boehmer, "Zorn," *ZAW,* XLIV (1926), 320 ff.; J. Gray, "The Wrath of God in Canaanite and Hebrew Literature," *JMEOS,* XXV (1954), 38 ff.; H. M. Haney, *The Wrath of God in the Former Prophets* (New York: Vantage, 1960); H. Ringgren, "Einige Schilderungen des göttlichen Zorns," *Tradition und Situation. A Weiser zum 70. Geburtstag* (Göttingen: Vandenhoeck & Ruprecht, 1963), pp. 107 ff.

[29] E. Jacob, *Theology of the Old Testament,* trans. A. W. Heathcote and P. J. Allcock (New York: Harper, 1958), p. 114.

vides a natural explanation for this objectification; it is not necessary to assume, with Boehmer, the existence of an original demon, "Great Wrath" (*qeṣep gādôl*; Deut. 29:27 [Eng. 29:28]; Jer. 21:5; 32:37; this expression is always connected with Yahweh, except in II Kings 3:27, where it occurs independently).[30]

On occasion the wrath of Yahweh is incomprehensible; it arises without apparent reason, e.g., II Sam. 24:1, "Again the anger of Yahweh was kindled against Israel, and he incited David against them. . . . " In other cases, the ostensible reason may seem insignificant to us, e.g., when Moses hesitates at his commission to free the Israelites (Exod. 4:14), or when the people in the desert weep and lament (Num. 11:10). These incidents probably all describe an offense to the divine majesty, e.g., through lack of trust. Usually divine wrath is quite clearly the appropriate reaction of the offended God to rebellion and enmity. He brings terrible disaster upon God's enemies (Ps. 2:5; 56:8 [Eng. 56:7]), frequently involving fire and heat, as in the theophany in Psalm 18:8 ff. (Eng. 18:7 ff.):

> Then the earth reeled and rocked;
>> the foundations also of the mountains trembled
>> and quaked, because he was angry.
> Smoke went up from his nostrils,
>> and devouring fire from his mouth;
>> glowing coals flamed forth from him.

But divine wrath is also directed against the nation of Israel when it has transgressed God's will through sin and disobedience (Lev. 26:28; Num. 32:14; Ps. 78:21; Josh. 7:1). The great prophets make this point especially clear (e.g., Isa. 10:17; Jer. 4:4; 7:20). In Isaiah 30:27 f., we read:

> Behold, the name of Yahweh comes from far,
>> burning with his anger, and in thick rising smoke;
> his lips are full of indignation,
>> and his tongue is like a devouring fire;
> his breath is like an overflowing stream. . . .

And in Isaiah 5:25:

> Therefore the anger of Yahweh was kindled against his people,
>> and he stretched out his hand against them and smote
>> them,
>> and the mountains quaked;
> and their corpses were as refuse
>> in the midst of the streets.
> For all this his anger is not turned away
>> and his hand is stretched out still.

---

[30] Boehmer, *op. cit.*, pp. 321 f.

(The last two lines also appear as a refrain in Isa. 9:11, 16, 20 [Eng. 9:12, 17, 21] and 10:4). These descriptions are obviously dependent upon cultic traditions (e.g., Ps. 18).[31]

For the prophets, the wrath of Yahweh is often more or less equivalent to terrible punishment. The great Day of Yahweh, on which he executes his judgment, is a day of wrath, e.g., Zephaniah 1:15 f.:

> A day of wrath is that day,
>   a day of distress and anguish,
> a day of ruin and devastation,
>   a day of darkness and gloom,
> a day of clouds and thick darkness,
>   a day of trumpet blast and battle cry. . . .

Here, too, dependence on cultic traditions is unmistakable.

In the Psalms and in prophetic texts we occasionally encounter another image that probably originates in the cult, namely the image of the cup of wrath.[32] In Psalm 75:9 (Eng. 75:8), we read:

> For in the hand of Yahweh there is a cup,
>   with foaming wine, well mixed;
> and he will pour a draught from it,
>   and all the wicked of the earth
>   shall drain it down to the dregs.

And in Jeremiah 25:15-27:

> Thus Yahweh, the God of Israel, said to me: "Take from my hand this cup of the wine of wrath, and make all the nations to whom I send you drink it. They shall drink and stagger and be crazed because of the sword which I am sending among them." So I took the cup from Yahweh's hand, and made all the nations to whom Yahweh sent me drink it . . . [here follows a list of the various nations] . . . "Then you shall say to them, ' . . . drink, be drunk and vomit, fall and rise no more, because of the sword which I am sending among you.' "[33]

In all probability, the point of this image is the helplessness of the drunken man: whoever stands under the judgment of God's wrath is irretrievably lost. Obviously some concrete reality must lie behind such a metaphorical expression; but unfortunately we are ignorant of any practice, secular or cultic, that could explain this mode of expression, either in Israel or in the neighboring religions. The use of this image in Psalm 75, as well as such passages as Obadiah 16,

---

[31] H. Ringgren, "Einige Schilderungen," *loc. cit.*
[32] H. Ringgren, "Vredens kalk," *SEÅ*, XVII (1953), 19 ff.
[33] Other examples are found at Hab. 2:15 f.; Jer. 51:7; Ezek. 23:31 ff.; Isa. 51:17 ff.; Lam. 4:21.

nevertheless suggest a cultic context; and the fact that we encounter the image of the cup in connection with God's court of judgment and theophany (as in Ps. 75 and Jer. 25:15-38) suggests the great autumn festival, at which, perhaps, a cup of wine somehow symbolized Yahweh's wrathful judgment.

But we have not yet exhausted the theme of Yahweh's wrath. There is in his nature an opposite tendency; in general, it outweighs his wrath. Yahweh is also patient and merciful. The Hebrew word for the former concept is *erek appayim*, i.e., "long with respect to anger, slow to anger" (e.g., Ps. 103:8). We also read that he will not keep his anger for ever (Ps. 103:9; Jer. 3:5, 12; Mic. 7:18). There is a great tension between these two character traits. We can see it with particular clarity in Hosea 11:8 f., where the prophet describes Yahweh as debating with himself whether or not he should punish his people in his wrath:

> How can I give you up, O Ephraim!
> How can I hand you over, O Israel!
> . . . .
> My heart recoils within me,
> my compassion grows warm and tender.
> I will not execute my fierce anger,
> I will not again destroy Ephraim;
> for I am God and not man,
> the Holy One in your midst,
> and I will not come with fire of wrath.[34]

It is remarkable that this passage sets holiness in contrast to wrath; for what is holy can also be terrifying and dangerous on occasion. Thus Yahweh is "a great and terrible God" (Deut. 7:21). He is a "dread warrior" (Jer. 20:11) or a God who is "feared . . . great and terrible" (Ps. 89:8 [Eng. 89:7]). But this feature, too, is ambiguous. When Yahweh does great and terrible things for his people Israel (II Sam. 7:23; cf. Exod. 34:10; Ps. 66:3, 5; 106:22), his deeds arouse fear and terror among his and Israel's enemies; but to the people of Israel they are deeds that bring salvation. Because Yahweh has chosen Israel to be his own possession, everything great, terrible, and wonderful that he does means salvation for Israel.

We must now examine a particular complex of ideas that is connected with the conception of Yahweh as king.[35] This concept and its related motifs occur above all in a particular group of psalms, the so-called enthronement psalms. Later, we shall discuss the cultic function

---

[34] On this translation of the last line see H. S. Nyberg, "Studien zum Hoseabuche," *UUÅ*, VI (1935), 52; and cf. L. Köhler, *Lexikon in Veteris Testamenti Libros* (Leiden: Brill, 1950-53), *s.v.* *'rⁿ*.

[35] See above, p. 48, where a bibliography is given.

of the psalms;[36] here only their objective content concerns us. In addition, these ideas are abundantly present outside of this particular group of psalms.

Three primary components constitute the idea of Yahweh's kingship: he is lord and king of the world, because he created it; he is the judge, who judges the nations with righteousness; and he is the mighty God, who smites all his enemies.

> Yahweh reigns; let the peoples tremble!
>> He sits enthroned upon the cherubim; let the earth quake!
> Yahweh is great in Zion;
>> he is exalted over all the peoples. (Ps. 99:1-2)

> For Yahweh is a great God,
>> and a great King above all gods.
> In his hand are the depths of the earth;
>> the heights of the mountains are his also.
> The sea is his, for he made it;
>> for his hands formed the dry land. (Ps. 95:3-5)

Thus Yahweh's superiority to all other gods is also connected with his kingship.

Isaiah also beholds the Lord as king: he was "sitting upon a throne, high and lifted up; and his train filled the temple . . . [and the seraphim sang:] 'Holy, holy, holy is Yahweh of hosts; the whole earth is full of his glory.' . . . And I said: 'Woe is me! For I am lost; for I am a man of unclean lips, and . . . have seen the King, Yahweh of hosts!' " (Isa. 6:1-5).

Gods were also saluted as kings outside of Israel. In Egypt, Horus of Edfu is celebrated as the king of all gods; and in Ras Shamra, El is called "the king, father of years,"[37] while Aliyan Baal is called "our king and judge."[38] Anu, the Sumerian god of the heavens, is the king of gods and men. Marduk, the national god of Babylon, is addressed as king in the creation epic. The same is true of Ashur in the Assyrian New Year's festival. We even possess a hymn to King Marduk from the Babylonian New Year's festival; it shows certain similarities to the Israelite enthronement psalms.[39] But the idea of kingship seems nowhere else to have played such an important and central role as it did in Israel.

At this point, the question arises whether the idea of Yahweh's kingship is ancient, or came into being after the introduction of the monarchy in Israel. According to Alt, this conception is by no means as late as might be supposed; it is already present as a part of the ark

---

[36] See below, pp. 191 ff.

[37] *UM* 49 (I AB), I, 8; 2 Aqht VI, 49.

[38] *UM* 'nt (V AB), V, 40.

[39] *ANET*, p. 332, ll. 222 ff.; the text is also found in F. Thureau-Dangin, *Rituels accadiens* (Paris: Leroux, 1921), pp. 127 ff.

tradition of the amphictyony. It derives from the universal Near Eastern conception that the world of the gods is organized as a monarchy, and probably goes back to Canaanite patterns.[40] Gray comes to a similar conclusion after examining the motifs connected with the idea of Yahweh's kingship.[41] It turns out that most of the psalms that speak of Yahweh as king contain allusions to a primordial battle between Yahweh and such chaos monsters as Rahab, Leviathan, *tannîn* ("dragon"), or simply the sea. The purpose of this battle is the establishment of the existing world order:

> Yet God my King is from of old,
> > working salvation in the midst of the earth.
> Thou didst divide the sea by thy might;
> > thou didst break the heads of the dragons on the waters.
> Thou didst crush the heads of Leviathan,
> > thou didst give him as food for the creatures of the
> > > wilderness.
>
> . . . .
>
> Thine is the day, thine also the night;
> > thou hast established the luminaries and the sun.
> Thou hast fixed all the bounds of the earth;
> > thou hast made summer and winter. (Ps. 74:12-17)

We shall later return to the various forms taken by this creation myth describing a battle with a dragon.[42] The important thing here is only that this battle myth occurs in the Ugaritic texts with the same names for the enemies (at least Lotan, Tannin, and the sea), even though the myth seems to have another function at Ugarit. This parallel demonstrates that the Israelites borrowed the myth from the Canaanites.

The battle motif is also used to describe the great events of Israelite history. Egypt appears as Rahab (Isa. 30:7); the Reed Sea, through which the Israelites were safely brought, is Yahweh's enemy the sea; etc. In Psalm 74, quoted above, creation and the deliverance from Egypt are so interwoven that it is impossible to separate the two elements. This is even clearer in Isaiah 51:9-11, where we have an imperceptible transition from creation to the deliverance from Egypt and the imminent deliverance from Babylon. In all three cases it is the mighty God, the king of the universe, that smites his enemies. The psalms in question for the most part juxtapose features from the original Canaanite creation myth and the specifically Israelite application of these features to history (e.g., Pss. 68; 77; 89; 93; 95; 97; 146);

---

[40] A. Alt, "Gedanken über das Königtum Jahwes," *Kleine Schriften* (Munich: Beck, 1953-   ), I, 345 ff.

[41] J. Gray, "The Kingship of God in the Prophets and Psalms," *VT,* XI (1961), 1 ff.

[42] See below, pp. 107 f.

only three psalms refer exclusively to the historical traditions of Israel (Pss. 47; 95; 114), to which should be added the victory hymn in Exodus 15. In other words, we definitely have here an application of elements and motifs from Canaanite mythology to the factual events of Israel's history. The kingship motif is therefore most probably also of Canaanite origin. The way in which Israel elaborated this theme nevertheless differs fundamentally from what we know of the corresponding phenomenon in the Canaanite religion.

King Yahweh appears above all as judge:

> At the set time which I appoint
> I will judge with equity.
> When the earth totters, and all its inhabitants,
> it is I who keep steady its pillars.
>
> . . . .
>
> For nor from the east or from the west
> and not from the wilderness comes lifting up;
> but it is God who executes judgment,
> putting down one and lifting up another.
> (Ps. 75:3 ff. [Eng. 75:2 ff.])

Or:

> Say among the nations, "Yahweh reigns!
> Yea, the world is established, it shall never be moved;
> he will judge the peoples with equity."
>
> . . . .
>
> . . . for he comes,
> for he comes to judge the earth.
> He will judge the world with righteousness,
> and the peoples with his truth. (Ps. 96:10, 13)

Similarly, the prophets often cast their sermons in the form of a trial, at which Yahweh functions as both plaintiff and judge (Isa. 1; Mic. 6; Jer. 2).[43]

Now the Hebrew word for "judge," *šāpaṭ*, has a double meaning; it can mean both "see that justice is done" and "inflict punishment."[44] Accordingly, Yahweh's enemies encounter his judgment as destroying punishment, while Yahweh's people Israel encounter it as salvation. Psalm 7:9-10 (Eng. 7:8-9) provides a clear illustration of this principle as applied to an individual:

---

[43] Cf. E. Würthwein, "Der Ursprung der prophetischen Gerichtsrede," *ZThK*, XLIX (1952), 1 ff.; G. E. Wright, "The Lawsuit of God," *Israel's Prophetic Heritage*, ed. B. W. Anderson and W. Harrelson (New York: Harper, 1962), pp. 26 ff.

[44] H. W. Hertzberg, "Die Entwicklung des Begriffs *mšpṭ* im Alten Testament," *ZAW*, XL (1922), 256 ff., and XLI (1923), 16 ff.; J. van der Ploeg, "sāpaṭ et mišpāt," *OS*, II (1943), 144 ff.

Yahweh judges the peoples;
>   judge me, Yahweh, according to my righteousness
>   and according to the integrity that is in me.
> O let the evil of the wicked come to an end,
>   but establish thou the righteous.

In the Babylonian religion, Shamash, the sun god, is the judge. But there the emphasis lies more on the mere fact of his being judge than on his active intervention.

As judge, Yahweh is righteous; he judges with righteousness (Ps. 98:9). But here we must be careful. The Hebrew word *ṣedeq* or *sᵉdāqâ* does not mean what we usually understand by the word "righteousness."[45] It is neither exclusively nor even primarily a juristic or moral concept. On the basis of Arabic, the original meaning of the root is something like "be right, stable, substantial." Jacob thinks these nuances can be derived from the definition "conformity to a norm."[46] In this case, though, we must remember that the norm is actually found within God's own nature. As Pedersen says, *ṣedeq* is "the assertion of one's own nature," consistency in what one does.[47] Yahweh is righteous when he punishes sin, he is righteous when he rewards the good, he is righteous when he is patient and merciful to the sinner. But he is also righteous when he destroys his enemies and delivers his people. Therefore *ṣedeq* and *sᵉdāqâ* must frequently be translated as "victory" or "deliverance." On the other hand, there is frequently a sociological aspect to *ṣedeq*: a man is righteous when he conducts his life in accordance with the norms of society.[48] But even these norms are based on the righteousness of God.

There is also a cosmic side to the concept of *ṣedeq*.[49] Psalm 72 links the righteousness of the king so closely with the fertility of the land that we are forced to ask whether "righteousness" cannot occasionally also refer to the proper ordering of nature. In fact, Joel 2:23 says that Yahweh sends the early rain *liṣdāqâ*, i.e., "at the proper time."[50] Psalm 85:12 f. (Eng. 85:11 f.) mentions in one breath good

---

[45] E. Kautzsch, *Die Derivate des Stammes ṣdq im alttestamentlichen Sprachgebrauch*, 1881; K. H. Fahlgren, *Ṣedākā nahestehende und entgegengesetzte Begriffe im Alten Testament* (Uppsala, 1932); cf. also J. Pedersen, *Israel* (corrected edition; London: Oxford, 1959), I-II, 336 ff.; N. H. Snaith, *op. cit.*, pp. 51 ff.; Jacob, *op. cit.*, pp. 94 ff.

[46] Jacob, *op. cit.*, p. 94.

[47] *Op. cit.*, p. 338.

[48] This is Fahlgren's basic thesis; *op. cit.*, pp. 78 ff.

[49] G. Widengren, *Religion och Bibel*, II (1943), 75; H. Ringgren, *Word and Wisdom* (Lund: Ohlsson, 1947), p. 87; G. Pidoux, "Un aspect négligé de la justice dans l'ancien Testament: son aspect cosmique," *RTP*, 1954, pp. 283 ff.

[50] [RSV: "for your vindication"; KJV: "moderately." The commentaries differ as to whether or not *sᵉdāqâ* here preserves "theological" overtones.—TRANS.]

crops and the righteousness that comes from heaven, another allusion to the order of nature that assists fertility.

Yahweh's righteousness is therefore the origin and source of all proper order in the world, both in nature and in human society. In this respect it is very similar to Babylonian *mēšaru* and Egyptian *m³'t*.[51] As an attribute of God, righteousness is primarily a positive quality: Yahweh is righteous and a savior (Isa. 45:21), his *ṣᵉdāqôt*, the expressions of his righteousness, are his victories over Israel's enemies (Judg. 5:11). Naturally there is also a negative side to this righteousness: the destruction of the enemies. Nevertheless, the use of "*ṣedeq*" to refer to distributive, punitive righteousness is late and uncommon. It refers predominantly to Yahweh's benevolent nature.

It is of particular interest that the concept of *ṣedeq* obviously stands in a special relationship to Jerusalem. Jerusalem is "the city of righteousness" (Isa. 1:26). Several persons whose names contain the root *ṣdq* are citizens of Jerusalem, e.g., Melchizedek, Adoni-zedek, and Zadok.[52] Perhaps Zedek is even the name of a Canaanite god worshiped in Jerusalem; there is further evidence pointing in this direction.[53] But probably there is no direct connection between the righteousness of Yahweh and the Canaanite god Zedek (in spite of Ps. 17:1, where Yahweh is apparently addressed as Zedek: "Hear, *yahweh ṣedeq*"[54]—probably through a textual error).[55]

The conception of Yahweh as king also lies behind those passages that depict Yahweh as a mighty warrior.[56] He is a warrior and a man of war (Exod. 15:3; Ps. 24:8; Zech. 9:13); he rises up to battle (Ps. 35:23; 59:6 [Eng. 59:5]; 68:2 [Eng. 68:1]); he bares his strong arm (Ps. 77:16 [Eng. 77:15]; 89:11 [Eng. 89:10]; Isa. 52:10; etc.). All these images may be understood as poetic metaphors, but they ultimately go back to the so-called myth of the battle with the nations: Yahweh, as king, conquers and destroys the hostile nations. Perhaps we have here a hidden connection with the conceptions linked to the holy war, which we have already discussed.

In a few passages, Yahweh is called "shepherd" (Ps. 23:1; 80:2 [Eng. 80:1]; cf. Ps. 100:3). Since "shepherd" is a common royal title in the ancient Near East (being found both in Egypt and in Babylon), we should expect that this term, also, is connected with the kingship of Yahweh. This does not seem to be the case, however; at least no connection is mentioned explicitly. Even Psalm 100, which has much

---

51 Ringgren, *Word and Wisdom*, pp. 49, 58.

52 *Ibid.*, p. 86.

53 *Ibid.*, pp. 83 ff.

54 G. Widengren, *The Accadian and Hebrew Psalms of Lamentation* (Stockholm: Thule, 1937), p. 71.

55 [Thus the RSV, which translates, "Hear a just cause, O Lord." Cf. LXX and possibly Ps. 4:2.—TRANS.]

56 H. Fredriksson, *Jahwe als Krieger* (Lund: Gleerup, 1945).

in common with the enthronement psalms, does not explicitly call
God king ("It is he that made us, and we are his; we are his people,
and the sheep of his pasture."). The salient points here—as is true,
of course, when "shepherd" is used as a royal title—are the care and
protection that the shepherd provides. A few statements of the
prophets make this same point even more emphatically. (Ezek. 34:12;
Mic. 7:14; Isa. 40:11).

The image of the rock is frequently used to characterize the God
who provides protection and safety:

> Yahweh is my rock, and my fortress, and my deliverer,
>   my God, my rock, in whom I take refuge,
>   my shield, and the horn of my salvation, my stronghold.

So says the writer of Psalm 18:3 (Eng. 18:2). It has been pointed
out that the Sumero-Babylonian god Enlil is often called the "Great
Mountain";[57] but in his case the meaning is different, since "mountain" probably has here a cosmic mythological significance. As the
example quoted plainly shows, the emphasis in the case of Yahweh
is upon the strength, the security, and the protection provided by the
God. The mythological background, which must not be overlooked in
the case of Enlil, is lacking in Israel.

We have gradually arrived at those attributes of Yahweh that are
unambiguously "good." In this category there are a few additional
concepts that are particularly significant and deserve a more extensive treatment. Above all there is Yahweh's "grace and truth." The
two Hebrew words usually so translated (*ḥesed* and *ĕmet*) are not
quite synonymous; neither do they possess exactly the meaning that
we usually read into these words. The former, *ḥesed*, is perhaps best
translated as "faithfulness to the covenant" or "loyalty" (cf. the RSV:
"steadfast love").[58] It refers to God's staunch fidelity to the promises
he made to Israel when he established his covenant with them, his
reliability vis-à-vis the other partner to the covenant. Only later did
the word take on the secondary meaning of benevolence, goodness,
and "grace." The other word, *ĕmet,* actually refers to that which is
secure and dependable, and accordingly comes to mean "fidelity" and
"truth." The latter, however, should not be understood as the theoretical concept of truth; it refers rather to that which has the inherent power to assert itself.[59]

---

[57] G. W. Ahlström, *Psalm 89* (Lund: Gleerup, 1959), p. 115 ("not
merely as a metaphor for strength and security").

[58] N. Glueck, *Das Wort Hesed im alttestamentlichen Sprachgebrauch*
(2nd ed.; Berlin: Töpelmann, 1961); H. J. Stoebe, "Die Bedeutung des
Wortes häsäd im Alten Testament," *VT,* II (1952), 244 ff.; A. R. Johnson,
"Ḥesed and ḥāsīd," *Interpretationes S. Mowinckel missae* (Oslo: Forlaget
land og kirke, 1955), pp. 100 ff.

[59] Pedersen, *op. cit.,* I-II, 338 f.; Fahlgren, *op. cit.,* pp. 142 ff.

A few verses from Psalm 89 show the connection between the covenant and Yahweh's fidelity and loyalty. In verses 29, 34 f. (Eng. 28, 33 f.), we read (referring to the king):

> My steadfast love [ḥesed] I will keep for him for ever,
> and my covenant will stand firm for him.
>
> . . . .
>
> But I will not remove from him my steadfast love,
> or be false to my faithfulness.
> I will not violate my covenant,
> or alter the word that went forth from my lips.

Thus Yahweh is the dependable God who stands by his word and loyally upholds the covenant by which he has engaged himself. He is a God merciful (raḥûm) and gracious (ḥannûn), "slow to anger, and abounding in steadfast love and faithfulness (ḥesed and ĕmet), keeping steadfast love for thousands, forgiving iniquity and transgression and sin" (Exod. 34:6 f.). Yahweh's fidelity is therefore not a static attribute, but the expression of a close relationship between him and the people of the covenant, a relationship that shows itself in acts of loyalty, in deliverance from danger, and in forgiveness of sins.

> Yahweh is merciful and gracious,
> slow to anger and abounding in steadfast love.
> He will not always chide,
> nor will he keep his anger forever.
> He does not deal with us according to our sins,
> nor requite us according to our iniquities.
>
> . . . .
>
> As a father pities his children,
> so Yahweh pities those who fear him. (Ps. 103:8-10, 13)

The covenant with Israel, within which Yahweh demonstrates his goodness and fidelity, is ultimately based upon his love. Yahweh chose Israel, not because it was greater or better than any other people, but because he loved Israel (Deut. 7:7 f.; 10:15). "I have loved you with an everlasting love; therefore I have continued my faithfulness to you" (Jer. 31:3). The passage from Psalm 103 just quoted uses the image of the father who loves his children to describe the relationship of Yahweh to those "who fear him." The same image is occasionally used elsewhere, e.g., Hosea 11:1; Deuteronomy 14:1; Isaiah 1:2. The expression is usually avoided, however, as Vriezen correctly states.[60] When it does occur, it is either used in similes ("*like* a father") or else applied to Israel as the son or sons of

---

[60] T. C. Vriezen, *An Outline of Old Testament Theology*, trans. S. Neuijen (Newton: Bradford, 1958), p. 145.

Yahweh. We obviously do not have here some sort of mythological conception of the divine origin of the people—which might, indeed, have been possible in earlier stages of the religion (see above); the purpose is rather to impress upon Israel the love and care of Yahweh. Isaiah 49:15 even compares the love of Yahweh to that of a mother.

Finally, something must be said here about Yahweh as the living God.[61] This expression (Heb. *ēl ḥay* or *ĕlōhîm ḥayyîm*) occurs eleven times in the Old Testament (thirteen times if two parallel passages are included). In the majority of cases it refers to the God whom one cannot offend with impunity and who intervenes actively in battle (Josh. 3:10; I Sam. 17:26, 36; II Kings 19:4, 16; Isa. 37:4, 17; cf. Jer. 23:36) or the God with whom one can enter into intimate relationship (Ps. 42:3 [Eng. 42:2]; 84:3 [Eng. 84:2]). Characteristically, we read in Jeremiah 10:10. "But Yahweh is the true God; he is the living God and the everlasting King. At his wrath the earth quakes." Here we have the active and operative God, the God who enters into communion with man. The living God is a person, an active person. Probably the expression also has overtones of the God who gives life. Furthermore, in Israel, as elsewhere,[62] mortality is man's lot, while life belongs to God (a conception, for instance, in Ps. 82:6-7).

In addition, the oath-formula *ḥay yahweh*, "[as surely as] Yahweh lives," occurs very frequently. This formula alternates with *ḥay ănî*, "as surely as I live," in the mouth of Yahweh, and with longer formulas like "as surely as Yahweh and the king live," etc. Now the question is, is there some connection between this formula and the outwardly identical expression *ḥy ălèyn b'l*, "Aliyan Baal lives," which in the Ras Shamra texts refers to the peripeteia in the myth and ritual of the dying and rising god: now the god who was dead is alive.[63] Once in the Old Testament *ḥay yahweh* occurs in a similar context, and is therefore not an oath-formula. The passage in question is Psalm 18:47 (Eng. 18:46): "Yahweh lives; and blessed be my rock. . . . " We are dealing here with Yahweh's mighty intervention to save the psalmist from deadly danger, in other words, with the peripeteia of the psalm. The prophet Hosea gives us a hint that the oath-formula is not completely inoffensive (4:15); perhaps he knows that the Canaanites have a similar formula. Amos censures a comparable formula in which the god in Dan and the *dôd*[64] of Beer-sheba are mentioned (8:14). But none of these data probably allow the

---

[61] Köhler, *op. cit.*, pp. 53 f.; A. R. Johnson, *The Vitality of the Individual* (Cardiff: University of Wales, 1949), pp. 105 ff.

[62] E.g., in the Gilgamesh Epic and the Myth of Adapa.

[63] G. Widengren, *Sakrales Königtum* (Stuttgart: Kohlhammer, 1955), pp. 69 ff.

[64] A very probable reading, supported by the LXX; MT texts reads *derek*, "way."

conclusion that certain circles looked upon Yahweh as a dying and rising God like Baal. Rather whoever takes this oath appeals to a particularly characteristic attribute of Yahweh: he is living, active, the well-spring of all life. Whether the conception of Yahweh as the living God represents a conscious protest against the dying gods[65] or rather alludes to life as a prerogative of divine beings as opposed to human beings can scarcely be determined on the basis of our material.

Somewhat more probability attaches to the claim that a few passages allude to the conception of a dying god. These are the passages in which we read that Yahweh awakes from his sleep or rises up like one who was drunk in order to do battle with his enemies (Ps. 7:7 [Eng. 7:6]; 35:23; 44:24 f. [Eng. 44:23 f.]; 78:65 f.). Sleep and drunkenness could be understood as metaphors for the condition of the dead god.[66] As long as these passages furnish our only basis for such an assumption, however, the fact that the entire Old Testament contradicts such a theory must lead us to doubt that Yahweh was ever looked upon as a dying and rising god. The expressions quoted can be explained quite satisfactorily as poetic metaphors, though it is of course entirely possible that these metaphors may ultimately derive from Canaanite tradition.

---

[65] W. W. von Baudissin, *Adonis und Eschmun* (Leipzig: Hinrichs, 1911), pp. 450 ff.

[66] Widengren, *Sakrales Königtum*, pp. 66 f.

3.

MANIFESTATIONS OF GOD

We have seen that Yahweh occasionally appears among men in human form: he walks through the Garden of Eden, he climbs down to be with the men who are building the Tower of Babel, etc. But this ancient anthropomorphic idea was obviously very early felt to be too naïve; and other, less objectionable, manifestations of Yahweh gradually came to the fore.

Among the earliest and most "primitive" of these is the idea of the angel or messenger of Yahweh (*mal'ak yahweh*).[1] Such an angel appears to Hagar and helps her when she is fleeing from Sarai (Gen. 16:7-13); he reveals himself to Moses in the burning bush (Exod. 3:2 ff.); he summons Gideon to save Israel (Judg. 6:11 f.); he appears to the wife of Manoah and announces the birth of Samson (Judg. 13:3 ff.); he strengthens the prophet Elijah (I Kings 19:7); he smites the army of the Assyrians (II Kings 19:35). He obviously takes human form. It is remarkable that in several of these passages the narrator alternates between "Yahweh" and "the angel of Yahweh," so that it remains uncertain whether the two are identical or different. Von Rad is probably right in explaining this state of affairs as the result of a revision of older traditions. Local traditions "told quite directly of extremely spectacular divine appearances at definite places. Those who came later, then, understood it in such a way that not Yahweh but Yahweh's angel appeared."[2] Perhaps even non-Israelite gods were subsumed into this angel of Yahweh. Naturally this conception is still far removed from the angels of later Judaism.

In other cases, Yahweh's presence is represented by his "counte-

---

[1] A. Lods, "L'ange de Yahweh et l'âme extérieure," *Studien zur semitischen Philologie . . . Julius Wellhausen* (Giessen: Töpelmann, 1914), pp. 265 ff.; F. Stier, *Gott und sein Engel im Alten Testament* (Münster: Aschendorff, 1934).

[2] G. von Rad, *Genesis,* trans. J. H. Marks (Philadelphia: Westminster, 1961), pp. 188 f.

nance."[3] This "countenance" should be understood as one of the forms in which Yahweh reveals himself, although any mention of its concrete appearance is lacking. It seems rather that "countenance" (pānîm) has in this case a different meaning than usual. There is a Punic expression that may be comparable: the goddess Tanit is called the "countenance" of Baal (tnt pn b'l), i.e., his manifestation. The basic meaning "front," i.e., the visible side, probably lies behind this expression.

A few examples will clarify what we have said. In Exodus 33:14, Yahweh promises that his countenance will go with the Israelites through the desert. This must somehow refer to a real presence.[4] Later on the expression "to behold the countenance of Yahweh" is frequently used to mean participation in the Temple cult.[5] "The countenance of Yahweh" in our passages might therefore refer to his cultic presence: after the overwhelming revelations on Sinai, Yahweh is present "only" in the cult.[6] But it is also possible that we are dealing here with his presence in the pillar of cloud or fire. In Deuteronomy 4:37 we read, "He . . . brought you out of Egypt with his own pānîm, by his great power"; here we must obviously understand "countenance" as the manifestation of God, or, more precisely, his power. An obscure passage, Isaiah 63:9, says, "Neither a messenger nor an angel, but his countenance (i.e., probably 'he himself') helped them."[7] This is more likely a metaphor than a concrete conception of a particular form of revelation. The same is true of the passages that speak of Moses seeing God face to face (Exod. 33:11; Num. 12:8; 14:14); their point is to describe personal association.

A particular group of traditions and statements, deriving from priestly circles (especially P and Ezekiel), describes the presence of Yahweh in terms of his glory or kābôd.[8] The basic meaning of kābôd is "heaviness," "weight"; it then comes to mean "honor." But strangely the kābôd of Yahweh is often associated with light phenomena. On Sinai, the glory of Yahweh manifests itself as a devouring fire (Exod.

---

[3] E. Gulin, "Das Antlitz Gottes im Alten Testament," AAF, 1923, pp. 21 ff.; A. R. Johnson, "The Use of pānîm in the Old Testament," Festschrift Otto Eissfeldt (Halle: Niemeyer, 1947), pp. 155 ff.

[4] [The RSV therefore translates pānîm in this and similar passages (such as those cited below) as "presence."—TRANS.]

[5] F. Nötscher, Das Angesicht Gottes schauen nach biblischer und babylonischer Auffassung, 1925.

[6] Cf. M. Noth, Exodus, trans. J. S. Bowden (Philadelphia: Westminster, 1962), p. 257.

[7] This translation, like that of most recent commentators, involves a slight repunctuation of the MT. Cf. the traditional rendering, followed by the RSV: "The angel of his presence (pānîm) saved them."

[8] H. Kittel, Die Herrlichkeit Gottes (Giessen: Töpelmann, 1934); L. H. Brockington, "The Presence of God: A Study of the Term 'Glory of Yahweh,'" ET, LVII (Oct., 1945), 21 f.; H. Riesenfeld, Jésus transfiguré (Uppsala, 1947), pp. 97 ff.

24:17). During the period of wandering in the desert, it occasionally appears as a pillar of cloud that accompanies the Israelites (Exod. 16:10; Num. 17:7 [Eng. 16:42]; etc.). In Exodus 33:18 ff., we read how Moses prays that he be allowed to see Yahweh's glory. His request is granted, but only with certain reservations. When the "beauty" of Yahweh passes by Moses, Moses may not see Yahweh's face—the brightness would have been too much for his eyes—but is allowed to see his "back." He has actually been granted a meeting with Yahweh.

In these instances we are dealing with particular appearances at specific times. But the glory of Yahweh is also thought of as being present constantly in the tent of meeting (Exod. 40:34 f.) and in the Temple at Jerusalem (I Kings 8:11).[9] In both passages a cloud also appears as a sign of God's presence. The relationship between the cloud and Yahweh's glory is not made quite clear, however. According to the former passage, the cloud covers the tent which is filled with the glory, so that Moses cannot enter it; according to the latter, the cloud fills the Temple so that the priests cannot enter, "for the glory of Yahweh filled the house of Yahweh."

We are obviously dealing here with specific cultic realities: perhaps a lamp or a flame and incense, intended to provide a vivid image of the divine presence.[10] It is impossible, however, to be more specific, although there is no lack of theories. I Samuel 3:3 and 4:21 have been taken as evidence for the presence of a lamp; Leviticus 9:23 f. suggests the fire upon the altar.[11]

Later on, when Ezekiel sees the glory of Yahweh, it appears as a light surrounding Yahweh's throne. As in the case of the angel of Yahweh, we can see here a certain vacillation between Yahweh himself and his glory (Ezek. 9:3 f.): where Yahweh's glory is, there is Yahweh himself. On account of the sins of Israel the glory departs from the Temple (Ezek. 11:22 ff.); in the distant future, when Israel is restored, the glory will return (Ezek. 43:2 ff.): Yahweh will once more dwell in the midst of his people. The *kābôd* is therefore a manifestation of God's presence, especially as represented in the Temple through certain symbols. But the glory of Yahweh also fills the whole earth, as many hymns affirm (Ps. 57:6, 12 [Eng. 57:5, 11]; Isa. 6:3; cf. Num. 14:21; Isa. 40:5; 58:8). This idea is closely linked with the kingship of Yahweh.

The Deuteronomistic books, on the other hand, represent a different theology of the divine presence: here we meet the name of God as

---

[9] G. von Rad, *Studies in Deuteronomy*, trans. D. Stalker (London: SCM, 1953), pp. 37 ff.

[10] Riesenfeld, *op. cit.*, especially pp. 99, 113.

[11] E. Jacob, *Theology of the Old Testament*, trans. A. W. Heathcote and P. J. Allcock (New York: Harper, 1958), p. 80, n. 2.

the symbol of his presence.[12] In ancient Israel—as is frequently the case with peoples in the early stages of cultural development—the name is the manifestation of the soul, a part of the personality, or even the person himself.[13] Whoever knows the name knows the person and has power over him. Where the name is, there is the person along with his influence and his authority. According to Deuteronomy, Yahweh chooses a place in order to cause his name to dwell there. In Deuteronomy 12:5, for example, we read that Yahweh "puts" his name in the Temple so that the Temple can be his habitation. In I Kings 9:3, Yahweh says his name will dwell in the Temple for ever. This expression is obviously intended to express something different from the priestly kābôd-theology. The presence of Yahweh in the Temple is not to be taken literally; he is present only through his name.[14]

The conception of the spirit of Yahweh is a different matter entirely.[15] Obviously we are not here dealing with anything comparable to the later Christian doctrine of the Holy Spirit. We have here rather in the first instance one of the ways in which God acts. To understand this concept, we must start with the basic meaning of the word rûaḥ, "spirit."

Sometimes rûaḥ means "wind," sometimes the divine life principle in man, which obviously was once connected with the breath. A man's spirit is given him by God, and God can take it back at any moment (Ps. 104:29 f.; Job 34:14 f.). "The vital spirit of living creatures is not thought of as a material, but as a manifestation of God's power."[16] Figuratively, then, rûaḥ comes to mean "disposition," "state of mind." Used in this sense, it refers primarily to expressions of the human will. The Bible speaks, for example, of a spirit of wisdom (Exod. 28:3, RSV "an able mind"; Deut. 34:9), a spirit of willingness (Ps. 51:14 [Eng. 51:12], RSV "a willing spirit"), a spirit of judgment (Isa. 4:4), or a spirit of confusion (Isa. 19:14); a new spirit is a new disposition (Ezek. 36:26).

Now we understand why "spirit" can mean both the life and activity of God and also, more commonly, the endowment of certain men with divine power. Just as there is something mysterious about the

---

[12] O. Grether, *Name und Wort Gottes* (Giessen: Töpelmann, 1934); G. von Rad, *Studies in Deuteronomy*, pp. 37 ff.

[13] J. Pedersen, *Israel* (rev. ed.; London: Oxford, 1959), I-II, 245 ff.

[14] G. von Rad, *Studies in Deuteronomy*, pp. 38 f.

[15] P. Volz, *Der Geist Gottes im Alten Testament und im Judentum* (Tübingen: Mohr, 1910); S. Linder, *Studier till Gamla Testamentets föreställningar om Anden* (Uppsala: Almqvist & Wiksell, 1926); J. Hehn, "Zum Problem des Geistes im Alten Orient und im AT," *ZAW*, XLIII (1925), 210 ff.; H. Ringgren, *Word and Wisdom* (Lund: Ohlsson, 1947), pp. 165 ff.; K. Koch, *Geist und Messias*, 1950.

[16] G. Gerleman, *RGG³*, II, col. 1270.

wind, so also there is something mysterious about the spirit of God.[17] Just as the spirit determines the life and capabilities of a human being, so the spirit of God is the concrete representation of his power and activity. The spirit of God is God's numinous action in specific situations.[18] Occasionally, the spirit even seems to be identical with God: "Whither shall I go from thy Spirit?" asks the psalmist (Ps. 139:7); he means God himself. Characteristically, he continues, "Or whither shall I flee from thy presence (*pānîm*)?" mentioning another manifestation of the divine presence. Now from time to time this activity of God is hypostatized. Whether "the Spirit of God . . . moving over the face of the waters" in the creation account (Gen. 1:2) should really be considered a creative principle remains doubtful;[19] but we can clearly recognize the working of the spirit among the judges, kings, and prophets. The verbs used to describe the activity of the spirit are illuminating. The spirit "clothes" Gideon (Judg. 6:34; Heb. *lābešâ*, RSV "took possession of"); it "comes mightily upon" (Heb. *ṣlḥ*) Samson (Judg. 14:6), Saul (I Sam. 10:6, 10; 11:6), and David (I Sam. 16:13); it falls upon Ezekiel (Ezek. 11:5). In all these cases the spirit enables the person in question to perform extraordinary deeds: to conquer enemies, to fall into prophetic ecstasy, etc.[20] In the case of the king, the gift of the spirit is connected with the anointing. The famous Messianic oracle Isaiah 11 connects the working of the spirit with the king's righteousness and judicial wisdom.

With the exception of the passage from Ezekiel, the examples cited belong to the early traditions of Israel. Obviously the conception of a violent divine force that takes possession of specific persons in specific situations also belongs to the early period. The idea that the king is endowed with the gift of the spirit already points to a more advanced degree of systematic thinking. And a few late passages that speak of the outpouring of the spirit (Isa. 44:3; Joel 3:1 [Eng. 2:28]; Ezek. 39:29) give us the impression that we are no longer dealing with a participation in a divine power but with a sort of fluid imbued with power. In this context belongs also the personification or hypostatization of the spirit that we encounter in late texts.[21] We read, for example, in Isaiah 63:14 that the spirit of Yahweh gave the Israelites rest in the wilderness. Haggai promises that the spirit of Yahweh will abide among the people (Hag. 2:5). In Psalm 143:10, the psalmist prays, "Let thy good spirit lead me on a level path"; here the spirit almost appears in the guise of a guardian angel.

---

[17] Jacob, *op. cit.*, p. 122.
[18] A. Neher, *L'essence du prophétisme* (Paris: Presses Universitaires, 1955), pp. 94 f.
[19] See below, p. 106; also K. Galling, *NKZ*, XLVII (1950), 145 ff.
[20] Cf. S. Mowinckel, "The Spirit and the Word," *JBL*, LIII (1934), 199 ff.
[21] Volz, *op. cit.*, pp. 145 ff.; Ringgren, *op. cit.*, pp. 165 ff.

The evil spirit mentioned in a few relatively early passages provides a special problem.[22] Yahweh sends "an evil spirit" between Abimelech and the men of Shechem (Judg. 9:23)—this could possibly refer to a contentious disposition. But in I Samuel 16:14, we read that "the Spirit of Yahweh departed from Saul, and an evil spirit from Yahweh tormented him." In other words, here an evil spirit, to be distinguished from the spirit of Yahweh, takes possession of Saul and makes him mentally ill. Two other passages (I Sam. 18:10; 19:9) describe the same occurrence as "an evil spirit from Yahweh" coming upon Saul. Two different conceptions have obviously been fused here: first, the conviction that everything, even what is "evil," comes from Yahweh; and second, the view that demonic possession is the cause of mental illnesses.

I Kings 22:19 ff., finally, paints a unique picture. The prophet Micaiah ben Imlah sees Yahweh sitting upon his throne, surrounded by all the host of heaven. Yahweh asks, "Who will entice Ahab, that he may go up and fall at Ramoth-gilead?" But no one is prepared to do so. Then "the spirit" (Heb. hārûaḥ, RSV: "a spirit") comes forward and offers "to become a lying spirit" and place false words in the mouth of the prophets, in order that Ahab may suffer a disastrous defeat. Do we have here merely a dramatization of the proceedings—since the spirit was the normal source of prophetic inspiration—or does there lie behind this account the conception of an evil spirit or demon, which here appears subordinate to Yahweh in the interests of monism? The latter possibility cannot be dismissed out of hand.

[22] Ringgren, op. cit., pp. 168 f.

4.

YAHWEH AND THE GODS: ANGELS AND SPIRITS

Yahweh is the only God of Israel. In the early period, as we have seen, this statement does not however exclude the existence of other divinities. In the course of time, though, the Israelite religion asserts its monotheistic character more and more strongly; and the relationship between Yahweh and the other gods becomes a problem. The identification of ēl 'elyôn or even Baal with Yahweh points out one path leading to the absolute sovereignty of Yahweh. Another is embodied in the degradation of alien gods to the status of divine beings of lesser rank.

The Babylonian and Canaanite religions are well acquainted with the concept of the assembly of the gods (puḫur ilāni, mpḫrt ilm). Nor is this conception unknown in Israel.[1] Psalm 82 begins:

> God [ĕlōhîm] has taken his place in the divine council ['adat ēl];
> in the midst of the gods [ĕlōhîm] he holds judgment.

Later, in verse six, the psalm calls these same gods "sons of the Most High," i.e., 'elyôn. In Israel, no one besides Yahweh can be "God." In all probability, the idea of the assembly of the gods should be considered a continuation of the corresponding Babylonian and Canaanite conception; but what was meant by this conception in Israel is not at once apparent. Occasionally the "sons of God"[2] make their appearance as Yahweh's heavenly court (Ps. 29:1; 89:7 [Eng. 89:6]; Deut. 32:8 LXX).[3] Yahweh is king, and it is therefore only natural for him to have a court. He sits upon his throne while the host of heaven waits upon him (I Kings 22:19). Job 15:8, a

---

[1] Cf. K. Schubert, "Der gegenwärtige Stand der Erforschung der in Palästina neu gefundenen hebräischen Handschriften," *TLZ*, LXXVIII (1953), cols. 502 f.

[2] [Or "sons of gods" (RSV margin); RSV text translates freely as "heavenly beings."—TRANS.]

[3] Cf. also Gen. 6:2 f. and Job 1:6.

passage permeated with ancient mythological material, mentions the council of God. But none of the divine beings is comparable to Yahweh. "Who in the skies can be compared to Yahweh?" asks Psalm 89:7 [Eng. 89:6]. In the strictest sense of the word, therefore, they are not gods. The term "sons of God," *bᵉnê ᵉlōhîm*, probably means something more like "divine, heavenly beings." In any case, they are only counsellors and servants of the one king. They are not worshiped as gods. But obviously we have here an imperfectly assimilated remnant of polytheistic ideas.

In addition, from the time the Israelites migrated into Canaan there was a syncretistic tendency characterized by the borrowing of Canaanite divinities.[4] Thus while Yahweh was coalescing with the Canaanite high god *ēl ʿelyôn* in Jerusalem, elsewhere in the land worship was being offered at the local cultic centers to Baal and the mother-goddess in one or more of her forms, such as Astarte, Asherah, or Anat.

Hosea clearly indicates the tension that existed between the local Canaanite cults and the cult of Yahweh. Israel did not know, the prophet has Yahweh say, "that it was I who gave her the grain, the wine, and the oil, and who lavished upon her silver and gold which they used for Baal" (Hos. 2:10 [Eng. 2:8]). Those Israelites took Baal to be the giver of fertility, and therefore they worshiped him; but in reality, says the prophet, Yahweh, the only God, is also the author of all increase.

The Old Testament contains quite a bit of evidence for this syncretism, but we are not able in every case to reconstruct a picture of the nature of this faith. The reason is that our sources represent the viewpoint of the religion of Yahweh that ultimately won out, and as a consequence are strongly tinged with polemic. The prophets attack the worship of Baal; the Deuteronomic history uses stereotyped formulas to describe the worship of other gods,[5] especially Baal or Baals (in the plural), the cult practiced upon the high places and under every green tree (i.e., the fertility cult),[6] or the sacrifice of children to Moloch.[7] Only rarely do our sources provide concrete details, and then always with polemic intent.

We are perhaps best informed about the cult of the mother-goddess. We know that the Jewish colonists at Elephantine, in Egypt, in the postexilic period worshiped several Canaanite gods besides Yahweh,

---

[4] G. W. Ahlström, *Aspects of Syncretism in Israelite Religion* (Lund: Gleerup, 1963), pp. 46 ff.

[5] C. Lindhagen, *The Servant Motif in the Old Testament* (Uppsala: Lundeqvist, 1950), pp. 120 ff.

[6] See below, pp. 157 f.

[7] See below, pp. 174 f.

especially the virgin Anat, the mother-goddess.[8] Since it is scarcely possible that they borrowed these divinities in Egypt, they must have brought them along when they emigrated from Palestine in the late pre-exilic or early postexilic period. The book of Jeremiah contains evidence of worship of a "queen of heaven" both in Jerusalem and also among the Jews who emigrated to Egypt (Jer. 7:18; 44:17, 19, 25). This "queen of heaven" could have been either Anat[9] or Astarte; in any case, she must have been a form of the Canaanite mother-goddess. In addition, the frequent mention of asherim (wooden pillars that served as symbols of the goddess) and the numerous finds of so-called Astarte figurines[10] provide conclusive evidence for the cult of the mother-goddess.

Other divinities are occasionally mentioned. Ashimah of Samaria and Dod of Beer-sheba are found in Amos 8:14 (emended); Ashimah also occurs in II Kings 17:30. She appears later at Elephantine as Ashembethel;[11] her precise nature has not been determined. Dôd may well have been a god of love and fertility, whose name is found in cuneiform texts as *dādi*.[12] The Hebrew word *dôd* means both "uncle" and "love, beloved." The word occurs on the Moabite stone as a divine appellative, but not as a proper name. The "*dôdî*" ("my beloved") of Song of Solomon 5:10 might be an allusion to this god. The assumption that "*dôd*" is somehow connected with the royal name (or title?) "David" (*dāwīd*) must be labeled doubtful. Even less probable is the theory that Dod was considered the son of Yahweh and was familiar as a dying and rising god, embodied in the ritual by the king.

Ezekiel mentions the worship of the Sumero-Babylonian Tammuz in the Jerusalem Temple (Ezek. 8:14), but this passage may refer to a Canaanite fertility god. The images of "creeping things and loathsome beasts" mentioned in the same chapter could represent Egyptian gods in animal form, but unfortunately we lack definite information on this point.[13]

The existence of sun worship is demonstrated by Job 31:26 f. (one salutes the sun by kissing one's hand), II Kings 23:11 (horses dedicated to the sun), and Ezekiel 8:16. In Psalm 19 we find several

---

[8] A. Vincent, *La religion des judéo-araméens à Elephantine* (Paris: Geuthner, 1937); W. F. Albright, *Archeology and the Religion of Israel* (3rd ed.; New York, 1935), pp. 168 ff.

[9] The identification proposed by G. Widengren in *The Accadian and Hebrew Psalms of Lamentation* (Stockholm: Thule, 1937), p. 72.

[10] Albright, *op. cit.*, pp. 114 f.; *idem, The Archaeology of Palestine* (Harmondsworth: Penguin, 1960), pp. 104 ff.

[11] Cf. Albright, *Archeology and the Religion of Israel*, pp. 169, 171.

[12] G. Ahlström, *Psalm 89* (Lund: Gleerup, 1959), pp. 163 ff.; cf. the remarks of Å. Sjöberg's review in *SEÅ*, XXV (1960), 104 ff. Sjöberg thinks the "name" is probably only an epithet.

[13] Albright, *Archeology and the Religion of Israel*, pp. 167 f.

verses that sound like a quotation from a hymn to the sun; here, though, they have been adapted to the religion of Yahweh, and the sun appears as Yahweh's creation. Deuteronomy 4:19 and 17:2-5 prohibit sun worship.

Nyberg has suggested that a few passages misunderstood by the Masoretes conceal the divine name '*al* (= *'elyôn*).[14] This suggestion is possible but remains unproven. If Nyberg's readings of the various texts are correct, " '*al*" would be an abbreviated form of " *'elyôn.*" This would mean that the Canaanite god lived on as an opponent of Yahweh. But in most cases, as we have seen, *'elyôn* and Yahweh fused together. Of the passages cited by Nyberg, at least I Samuel 2:10 equates '*al* with Yahweh. Widengren finds the divine name '*al* *ĕlōhîm* in Psalm 7:11 (Eng. 7:10);[15] the context shows that this name is to be understood as an epithet of Yahweh. It is hardly possible therefore to find any polytheistic conception here; what we have is an instance of what Bertholet called "*Göttervereinigung*" (a fusion of gods).[16] In the Northern Kingdom, where the coalescence did not take place as it did in Jerusalem, '*al-'elyôn* may possibly have been considered an opponent of Yahweh. At least Nyberg found his best examples in the book of Hosea, which originates in the Northern Kingdom (Hos. 7:16; 10:5; 11:7; in addition, I Sam. 2:10; Isa. 59:18; 63:7).

The Deuteronomistic historians expressly mention three particularly important instances of syncretism:

1. Jezebel the queen, Ahab's wife, who was of Phoenician descent, promoted the cult of Baal and even persecuted the prophets of Yahweh. In this instance, "Baal" is probably Melkart, the city-god of Tyre, whose cult Jezebel sought to introduce from her homeland.

2. After they had conquered Samaria in 722 B.C., the Assyrians repopulated the territory that had belonged to the Northern Kingdom with a pagan population; these newcomers brought their own gods with them, whom they worshiped alongside Yahweh. The historian writes:

> The men of Babylon made Succoth-benoth, the men of Cuth made Nergal, the men of Hamath made Ashima, and the Avvites made Nibhaz and Tartak; and the Sepharvites burned their children in the fire to Adrammelech and Anammelech, the gods of Sepharvaim. They also feared Yahweh, and appointed from among themselves all sorts of people as priests of the high places . . . (II Kings 17:30 ff.)

---

[14] H. S. Nyberg, *Studien zum Hoseabuche*, 1935, pp. 58 ff., 60, 74, 78, 90, 170; cf. also *idem*, "Studien zum Religionskampf in alten Israel," *ARW*, XXXV (1930), 329 ff.

[15] Widengren, *op. cit.*, p. 72.

[16] A. Bertholet, *Götterspaltung und Göttervereinigung* (Tübingen: Mohr, 1933).

The last sentence is significant. This is the way the Yahwistic author describes the fact of religious syncretism. Then he continues in verse thirty-three, "So they feared Yahweh but also served their own gods, after the manner of the nations from among whom they had been carried away." This marks the beginning of the Samaritan religious community.[17]

3. Finally, we read that Manasseh, king of Judah, rebuilt the high places (*bāmôt*), erected altars for Baal, and worshiped all the host of heaven (thus we have here an astral cult); we read further that he practiced all sorts of magical arts and even set up idol altars and an asherah in the Jerusalem Temple (II Kings 21:3-7). Manasseh seems therefore to have striven quite deliberately to bring about a union between the cult of Yahweh and the Canaanite religion. This attempt in turn furnishes the background for the reformation carried out by his grandson Josiah.

We do not know precisely how successful such efforts were in setting up an Israelite pantheon. We have already mentioned the pantheon of the Jewish military colony at Elephantine. Something similar must probably have been in Manasseh's mind. In general, of course, we must probably assume that religious syncretism came about without premeditation and was never theoretically systematized.

It is true that the Yahwistic sources are not strictly monotheistic, but any real polytheism is alien to them. The repeated affirmations of the psalms that Yahweh is the greatest and mightiest of the gods (Ps. 86:8; 89:7-9 [Eng. 89:6-8]; 95:3; 96:4; 97:9; 135:5) are evidence for the supreme significance of Yahweh; they leave no room for regular worship of other gods. We should not overlook the fact that the majority of our citations are from the enthronement psalms, which frequently stress the fact that Yahweh is the only God. In one of the psalms cited (96), the statement of Yahweh's superiority to the gods is even followed by a verse that states that the gods of the peoples are powerless idols, while it is Yahweh who made the heavens. Admittedly, this statement is not logical according to our way of thinking; for we cannot call these beings gods and at the same time say they are powerless without sensing a contradiction. But we are obviously confronted with a situation in which the worship of other gods by foreign nations is accepted as an empirical fact, while Yahweh alone is of significance for the Israelites. Using Widengren's expression, we can describe this as an "affective monotheism."[18]

Neither is polytheism present where abstract concepts such as "justice," "righteousness," etc. are personified or hypostatized. We

---

[17] See below, p. 300.
[18] Widengren, *op. cit.*, p. 72; seconded by Ahlström, *Psalm 89* (Lund: Gleerup, 1959), p. 62.

read, for example, "Righteousness will go before him" (Ps. 86:14 [Eng. 86:13]), or, "Steadfast love and faithfulness will meet; righteousness and peace will kiss each other" (Ps. 85:11 [Eng. 85:12]), or, "Oh send out thy light and thy truth, let them lead me" (Ps. 43:3). Even if we are not simply dealing here with poetic personifications, these entities are certainly not accorded an independent existence, nor are they worshiped or venerated. The fact that a god Zedek ("righteousness") really did exist in ancient Canaan does not affect our conclusions.[19] And even if such hypostases occasionally developed into independent divinities, this was unable to take place within the domain of the genuine religion of Yahweh.

In God's heavenly court we find several creatures that are not, in the strictest sense, divine. Most important are the angels (mal'ākîm, "messengers") (Ps. 103:20; 148:2); they are also called mighty warriors and servants. They are sent to protect and guard men (Ps. 34:8 [Eng. 34:7]; 91:11 f.). There is no information given about their form; but there is every reason to think that they—like the "angel of Yahweh"—were thought of as having human form. There are also angels that bring about destruction (II Sam. 24:16), a fact that comports very well with the already mentioned duality in Yahweh's nature.[20]

Other heavenly beings are also mentioned. Isaiah sees Yahweh surrounded by seraphim (Isa. 6:2), which are depicted as composite creatures, half bird, half man, with six wings.[21] Ezekiel sees half-human creatures with four faces and four wings about the throne of God (Ezek. 1:5 ff.). The cherubim appear as guardians of the Garden of Eden after man has been exiled from it (Gen. 3:4; they perform a similar function upon God's holy mountain in Ezek. 28:14, 16), but they are not described. Once we read that Yahweh rides on a cherub (Ps. 18:11 [Eng. 18:10]); the context suggests storm clouds. Elsewhere the word "cherub" refers to the two creatures that protect the ark of the covenant with their wings (Exod. 25:18-22). We therefore frequently read that Yahweh is enthroned upon the cherubim (I Sam. 4:4; Isa. 37:16; Ps. 80:2 [Eng. 80:1]; 99:1) or speaks from between the two cherubim (Exod. 25:22; Num. 7:89). Although none of this gives us a really clear picture of what is meant, it must be

---

[19] See above, pp. 61, 84.

[20] W. G. Heidt, *Angelology of the Old Testament* (Washington: Catholic University of America Press, 1949); cf. A. R. Johnson, *The One and the Many in the Israelite Conception of God* (Cardiff: University of Wales, 1942).

[21] Strangely enough, the serpents that beset the Israelites in the desert are also called *śerāpîm*. But this does not mean that we should picture to ourselves such hybrid creatures as serpent-men or serpent-birds (G. Fohrer, *Das Buch Jesaja* [Zürich: Zwingli, 1960-62], I, 23). The root *śrp* means "burn."

considered certain that we see here the embodiment of the same ideas
that appear in Babylonian figures of tutelary spirits in the shape
of animals with human faces. Etymologically, too, there is a connection: the Babylonian name for such a tutelary spirit is *"kuribu."*[22]

In addition, the Old Testament often speaks of demons, although
it never defines their function. In general, they should be thought of
as carriers of disease or bringers of calamity.[23] A characteristic
passage is Isaiah 13:21 f., which predicts the destruction of Babylon:

> But wild beasts will lie down there,
>> and its houses will be full of howling creatures;
> there ostriches will dwell,
>> and there satyrs will dance.
> Hyenas will cry in its towers,
>> and jackals in the pleasant palaces.

The juxtaposition of demons and desert animals is both remarkable
and significant; it provides a vivid impression of the sinister look of
the desolate land. The beings called in the RSV "wild beasts" (Heb.
ṣiyyîm) and "hyenas" (*iyyîm*) are possibly demons; they are mentioned elsewhere (Isa. 23:13; 34:14; Jer. 50:39) in similar fashion,
i.e., as inhabitants of the desert; but their appearance is never described.
The "satyrs" are called in Hebrew *śe'îrîm*, i.e., "hairy"—the idea that
they looked like goats is only derived from their name. If this conclusion is correct, we might have here the Hebrew counterpart to the
Greek satyrs. Worship of the *śe'îrîm* is even mentioned occasionally
(Lev. 17:7; II Chron. 11:15).

It is in general quite comprehensible that such ideas should be
linked with the desert, the sinister land in which everything evil
makes its home and which, in contrast to the settled regions, is considered the region of death. The Bedouins of Arabia also speak of a
desert demon, the so-called *ghūl*, who appears in various guises and
brings calamity.

In this context we should raise the question whether the occasional
description of enemies as wild animals somehow alludes to ideas of
demons. Psalm 22 offers a good example:

> Many bulls encompass me,
>> strong bulls of Bashan surround me;
> they open wide their mouths at me,
>> like a ravening and roaring lion.

. . . .

---

[22] R. Dhorme and A. Vincent, "Les cherubins," *RB*, 1926, pp. 320 ff.,
481 ff. [Cf. also W. F. Albright, "What Were the Cherubim," *BA*, I (1938),
1 ff.—TRANS.]

[23] H. Duhn, *Die bösen Geister im Alten Testament* (Tübingen: Mohr,
1904); A. Jirku, *Die Dämonen und ihre Abwehr im Alten Testament*,
1912.

> Yea, dogs are round about me;
> a company of evildoers encircle me. (vss. 13, 14, 17a
> [Eng. 12, 13, 16a])

Here the animals obviously represent quite generally what is evil and hostile to God. Even if they are not demons, there is something demonic about them: they represent a destructive element, the power of death and of chaos.[24] In another passage the gods of the pagan world have provided the colors used to depict the enemy; in Psalm 73, the evildoers are characterized as follows:

> They set their mouths against the heavens,
> and their tongue struts through the earth.

The Ras Shamra texts contain a passage that is identical almost to the word; it refers to evil gods that embody the powers of death.[25]

In certain cases, a borrowing of the demonic figures from other religions can be clearly demonstrated. Isaiah 34:14, for example, mentions a female demon of the wilderness by the name of Lilith (RSV "the night hag"). Beyond any doubt she is identical with the Babylonian storm demon Lilitu (from Sumerian *lil*, "wind"). Later Hebrew connects her with *layil*, "night," and thinks of her as a night demon. In later Judaism, she appears as Adam's first wife, who fell and was transformed into a demon.

Babylonian originals probably also lie behind the *šēdîm*, which are mentioned occasionally as recipients of (non-Yahwistic) sacrifices (Deut. 32:17; Ps. 106:37). The Septuagint obviously reads the same word in Psalm 91:6, and interprets it as a noon demon. In any case, it is linguistically identical with the Babylonian *šēdu* ("tutelary spirit"). The context also suggests that the *šēdîm* were considered beneficent.

Other traces of ideas of demons appear in certain psalms. Psalm 91:6, for example, speaks of pestilence and destruction in such a way that they can easily be considered demons, the more so because the same verse speaks of magical influences exercised by the sun and moon.[26]

Finally, Azazel, mentioned in the ritual of the Day of Atonement (Lev. 16), to whom the scapegoat is sent, is usually taken to be a desert demon. Later Judaism made him into a kind of devil. The text,

---

[24] H. Ringgren, *The Faith of the Psalmists* (Philadelphia: Fortress, 1963), p. 45.

[25] H. Ringgren, "Bemerkungen zum LXXIII. Psalm," *VT*, III (1953), 267 f.; *idem, The Faith of the Psalmists*, p. 44; cf. T. Worden, "The Influence of the Ugaritic Fertility Myth," *VT*, III (1953), 284; R. T. O'Callaghan, "Echoes of Canaanite Literature in the Psalms," *VT*, IV (1954), 169.

[26] Cf. also N. Nicolsky, *Spuren magischer Formeln in den Psalmen*, 1925, pp. 16 ff.; Widengren, *op. cit.*, pp. 201 f.

however, merely mentions the name, which some recent scholars interpret simply as a term for the trackless desert region.[27] Jewish tradition, nevertheless, quite definitely understood the word as a proper name.

But even if the existence of demons is never denied in principle, they are still basically alien to genuine Yahwism. Sacrifices to the *šēdîm* are as vigorously rejected as divination through spirits (perhaps spirits of the dead; Deut. 18:10 f.). A popular belief in demons along-side a belief in gods is quite conceivable; the one does not exclude the other. But the conviction that everything, both good and bad, comes from Yahweh actually made belief in demons superfluous. The exorcism of demons and the utilization of their knowledge for the purpose of divination were therefore considered irreconcilable with pure Yahwism. Even if Psalm 91 is formally reminiscent of an exorcism, we are not dealing here with a magical exorcism, but with a prayer directed to Yahweh for protection against the demonic powers in life.

---

[27] G. R. Driver, "Three Technical Terms in the Pentateuch," *JSS*, I (1956), 97 f.

5.

GOD AND THE WORLD:
CREATION AND HISTORY

a. Creation

Everyone knows the first words of the Bible: "In the beginning God created the heavens and the earth" (Gen. 1:1). No one doubts that, in the view of the Old Testament, Yahweh is the creator of the world. But on the one hand this idea is not uniform throughout the Old Testament, and on the other the age of the idea of creation is disputed.

Let us take up the second question first. The statement is often made that the idea of creation first acquired significance with Jeremiah, that it did not play any role in the early history of Israel or that it was even unknown then.[1] This view is based, however, on several dubious presuppositions. It is true that the account of creation in Genesis 1, in its present form, is of comparatively late date. But there are two other points to remember. First, recent studies show that the numerous psalms mentioning Yahweh as the creator of the world do not all come from a relatively recent period. Second, it is by no means a proven fact that the so-called doxologies of the book of Amos (4:13; 5:8; 9:5 f.), which extol Yahweh as creator, are later additions. In them we probably have quotations from an ancient hymn.[2]

The earliest evidence for the Old Testament creation ideology is the expression "God Most High, maker [or acquirer] of heaven and earth" (*ēl 'elyôn qōnēh šāmayim wā'āreṣ*) in Genesis 14:19. Even if this chapter cannot definitely be proved ancient, a shorter version of the same formula is attested several times outside of Israel. as the name of a pre-Canaanite or Aramaic god. The instances come from

---

[1] This view is supported, for example, by W. Foerster, in his article "ktizo," *TWNT*, III, 1004 ff.

[2] See below, pp. 265 f.

a period extending from the Hittite empire down to the Roman era.[3] Of course this only means that the Canaanite El (*'elyôn*) was viewed as a creator-god. But since Yahweh was identified with El at a very early period, he, too, must probably have been considered a creator-god.

The systematic account of the creation of the world is found in the first two chapters of Genesis. Traditio-historically, of course, this account is not homogeneous, but rather consists of two distinct narratives, the first of which, Genesis 1:1—2:4a, is ascribed to P, while 2:4b-25 belongs to J.[4]

The Yahwistic account of creation begins by describing a dry desert without plants, into which life is brought through water. Then Yahweh forms a man (Heb. *ādām*) from the dust of the earth and breathes the breath of life into his nostrils, bringing him to life. Then God plants a garden with all sorts of good trees for the man in Eden, and places the man in the garden "to till it and keep it." Only then does Yahweh create the animals and the birds, likewise from the dust of the earth. He brings them to the man, who gives them names and puts them to work for him. Finally, Yahweh takes a rib from the body of the sleeping man and makes it into a woman, who receives the name Eve (Heb. *ḥawwâ,* which is probably somehow connected with the word for life[5]).

It should be noted that this narrative does not present a complete account of creation. In the first place, we hear nothing of the origin of the heavens and the earth; in the second place, the focal point of the story is the creation of man. But it is noteworthy that this narrative presupposes at the outset the existence of a dry desert land, out of which living creatures gradually come into being in this order: man, plants (or are the plants already present before the man, so that only the garden comes after him?), animals, woman. This indicates that the story came into being in a region where drought appears as the enemy of life, i.e., probably in Palestine or somewhere on the edge of the desert. It should be emphasized also that this account is only slightly systematized, and leaves the impression of recounting ancient popular conceptions.

The so-called Priestly account in Genesis 1, which is relatively late, is completely different. Here everything is well ordered and

---

[3] We find the transcription *ilkunirša* in a Hittite mythological fragment, *'l qn 'rṣ* in the Karatepe inscription and in a Punic inscription, and *'lqwn 'rṣ* in Palmyra. For a presentation of the material, see H. Schmid, "Jahwe und die Kulttraditionen von Jerusalem," *ZAW,* LXVII (1955), 180.

[4] See the commentaries, e.g., H. Gunkel, *Genesis* (Göttingen: Vandenhoeck & Ruprecht, 1902), or G. von Rad, *Genesis,* trans. J. H. Marks (Philadelphia: Westminster, 1961). For a good general treatment of Israelite cosmogony, see S. G. F. Brandon, *Creation Legends of the Ancient Near East* (London: Hodder and Stoughton, 1963), pp. 118 ff.

[5] The word is probably not connected with the Aramaic *ḥiwyâ,* "serpent."

reduced to a logical system.[6] At the outset we have a primordial sea lying in darkness, while the wind ("spirit" is scarcely possible) of God blows over it.[7] All is chaos (*tōhû wābōhû*). But God is there. Unlike its neighbors, Israel is unacquainted with any theogony that starts with an account of the origin of the gods. Then God says (the name Yahweh is avoided), "Let there be light"; and it happens according to his word. Thus day and night are distinguished for the first time, and the rest of creation takes place within the next five days. Then, on the seventh day, God "rests." On the second day, the firmament of heaven is created—likewise through God's creative word —to separate the heavenly from the earthly waters (here the ancient Near Eastern conception of the world is clearly visible: the rain comes from the heavenly ocean). The third day brings the separation between land and sea, and the creation of plants. On the fourth day follows the creation of the heavenly bodies, the sun, the moon, and the stars; on the fifth, the creation of the birds and all that lives in the sea; and on the sixth, the creation of land animals and of man, who is here at once created as male and female "in the image of God," to rule over all creation.

Three striking facts are immediately apparent. First, eight acts of creation are distributed among six days. This is obviously because the story in its present form focuses on the seventh day as a day of rest, i.e., its purpose is partially to give a reason for observation of the Sabbath.[8] The original account probably contained only the eight stages of creation without the seven day schema. Second, the order of the stages is here completely different from that of the Yahwistic account; in particular, man, both male and female, appears as the culmination and goal of creation. At the outset there is a chaos consisting of water—the primordial sea—not a desert, as in the Yahwist's account.

Third, the creative word of God plays a crucial role. It is true that the idea of the creative power of the divine word is also familiar outside of Israel—it is found as early as the so-called Memphitic theology of the Egyptian Old Kingdom[9] and as a subsidiary motif in

---

[6] See especially von Rad, *op. cit.*, p. 45.
[7] K. Galling, "Der Charakter der Chaosschilderung in Gen. 1.2," *NKZ*, XLVII (1950), 145 ff. The word *merahepet* should not suggest any conception of the brooding world bird and the cosmic egg; cf. H. Ringgren, *SEÅ*, XIII (1948), 15.
[8] In agreement with Budde, A. Bertholet ("Zum Schöpfungsbericht in Genesis 1," *JBL*, LIII [1934], 237 f.), von Rad, *et al.* For the opposite view, see P. Humbert, "La relation de Gen. 1 et du Ps. 104 avec la liturgie du Nouvel-An israelite," *RHPR*, XV (1935), 1 ff.; Humbert interprets the seven days as a reflection of the seven feast days of the Feast of Tabernacles. Peters' comparison of the seven days with the seven tablets of the Babylonian creation epic ("The Wind of God," *JBL*, XXX [1911], 44 ff.) is irrelevant, since the tablets do not correspond to separate days.
[9] E.g., H. Junker, *Die Götterlehre von Memphis*, 1939.

the Babylonian creation epic[10]; but here it is given a fundamental significance that is without parallel. "For he spoke, and it came to be; he commanded, and it stood forth" (Ps. 33:9).

There is a fourth point, not immediately evident. A closer inspection shows that the author of Genesis 1 has utilized and transformed ancient mythological material.[11] The Hebrew word for the primordial sea is *tehôm*; it is etymologically identical with the Babylonian *tiāmat*. Now Tiamat is familiar as the primordial ocean of the Babylonian creation epic, which describes creation as the outcome of Marduk's victory over Tiamat. As a matter of fact, in Israel, too, the primordial sea is "conquered"; it is driven back, it is given a place of its own, a boundary is set for it that it may never pass (Ps. 104:9; cf. 148:6). In the biblical story, however, God's mighty word alone fights the battle.

Now several Old Testament passages contain clear allusions to mythological ideas that are connected with creation, ideas that stand much closer to the Babylonian account. In them we hear of a terrible battle fought by Yahweh against a dragon, which is called Rahab or Leviathan or else simply "the dragon" (*tannîn*).

> Thou didst divide the sea by thy might;
> > thou didst break the heads of the dragons on the waters.
> Thou didst crush the heads of Leviathan,
> > thou didst give him as food for the creatures of the
> > wilderness. (Ps. 74:13 f.)

> By his power he stilled the sea;
> > by his understanding he smote Rahab.
> By his wind the heavens were made fair;
> > his hand pierced the fleeing serpent. (Job. 26:12 f.)

The context shows that in each case the battle with the dragon goes together with the creation of the world. In Isaiah 27:1, Leviathan is called "the fleeing serpent, the twisting serpent, the dragon that is in the sea." The Ras Shamra texts apply exactly these same epithets to a creature named *ltn* (probably to be read *Lôtan*) conquered by Baal.[12] Obviously the two names are etymologically identical, and we are dealing with one and the same myth. At Ras Shamra, however, Baal's victory over the dragon is not connected with creation. Furthermore, only one passage in the Old Testament (Isa. 51:9 f.) mentions *tehôm*

---

[10] Tablet 4, 11. 19 ff. Cf. L. Dürr, "Die Wertung des göttlichen Wortes im Alten Testament und im alten Orient," *MVAG*, XLII (1938), 36.

[11] The basic work on this subject is H. Gunkel, *Schöpfung und Chaos in Urzeit und Endzeit* (Göttingen: Vandenhoeck & Ruprecht, 1895). Cf. also H. Ringgren, *Teol. Tidskrift—Teol. aikakauskirja*, LIII (1948), 128 ff.

[12] *UM* 67 (I* AB) I, 1 f.; cf. *'nt* (V AB) III, 32 ff., where Anat appears to slay the dragon.

together with Rahab. Perhaps we have here two variants of the same mythical motif, the one Canaanite and the other originally Babylonian, which were brought together in Israel and linked with the idea of creation. We should add that in another Canaanite variant the sea (*ym*) appears as a hostile figure, conquered by God.[13]

A remarkable variant of the creation narrative is found in the relatively late passage Proverbs 8:22-31. The point here is the glorification of (personified) wisdom, which is extolled as the first work of God at creation. In words reminiscent of Egyptian and Babylonian cosmogonies, the writer emphasizes that wisdom was present before everything else in the world was created, and that it was somehow beside God during his work of creation.[14] As far as the actual process is concerned, this account seems on the whole to agree with the others.

Psalm 104 occupies a position half way between mythological and theological cosmogony. It is a familiar psalm, primarily because it evidences remarkable similarities to the sun hymn of Pharaoh Akh-en-Aton. The battle motif appears somewhat more clearly here than in the account of Genesis 1, to which the content of the psalm otherwise corresponds closely:

> At thy rebuke they [the waters of the primordial sea] fled;
> at the sound of thy thunder they took to flight. (vs. 7)

But there is another, more important, observation: the religious significance of the Israelite belief in creation comes to light clearly in the following verses. The primary purpose is not to provide a theoretical explanation of how the world came to be, but to illustrate the enduring result of creation: God's handiwork, which is continually renewed. The poem moves almost imperceptibly from creation at the beginning of time to the creative activity of God in the present. God set a bound for the waters, says the psalmist, and then continues:

> Thou makest springs gush forth in the valleys . . . they give drink to every beast of the field . . . by them the birds of the air have their habitation . . . thou waterest the mountains . . . thou dost cause the grass to grow for the cattle, and plants for man to cultivate, that he may bring forth food from the earth. . . . (vss. 10 ff.)

Then he speaks of the sun and moon, which determine the alternation of day and night; it is noteworthy in this connection that the night, too, has its positive significance as the time for the beasts of prey,

---

[13] *UM* 68 (III AB A), 1 ff.; 137 (III AB B) 1 ff.; cf. the '*nt* passage mentioned in the preceding note; G. R. Driver, *Canaanite Myths and Legends* (Edinburgh: Clark, 1956), pp. 12 f., 20 f.; A. Kapelrud, *Baal in the Ras Shamra Texts* (Copenhagen: Gad, 1952), pp. 101 f.

[14] H. Ringgren, *Word and Wisdom* (Lund: Ohlsson, 1947), pp. 99 ff.; *idem, Sprüche* (Göttingen: Vandenhoeck & Ruprecht, 1962), p. 40.

while in the Egyptian sun hymn it is considered the evil, unfruitful time.[15] Summing up, the psalmist concludes:

These all look to thee,
to give them their food in due season.
. . . .
When thou hidest thy face, they are dismayed;
when thou takest away their breath, they die
and return to their dust.
When thou sendest forth thy Spirit, they are created;
and thou renewest the face of the ground. (vss. 27 ff.)

Here, then, we see revealed the central affirmation of the Old Testament belief in creation: the absolute dependence of all that lives upon Yahweh. Creation is a continuous activity, which man gratefully accepts. This idea refers not only to God's care for each individual, but also to the world order in general. The earth stands firmly upon its pillars, the mountains do not totter, the waters do not return to cover the land—all this is Yahweh's eternal work of creation, of which the psalmists never tire of singing (Ps. 24:2; 104:5, 9; 136:6).[16] The regular alternation of day and night, of winter and summer, is the work of the creator (Gen. 8:22; Ps. 74:16 f.). All this gives man a feeling of security. God protects the world against a renewed invasion of chaos; therefore man can live in safety. Knowledge of this state of affairs is a constant cause for thankfulness.[17]

b. Paradise

According to the Yahwist's account, the first man, Adam, lived with his wife, Eve, in the garden of Eden ("Eden" is probably not connected with the Sumerian *edin*, "steppe"; the Hebrews seem to have equated it with *'ēden*, "luxury").[18] The geographical location of "paradise" (a later Persian loan word) remains vague. The statement that four rivers flowed out of Eden has strong mythological over-

[15] H. Ringgren, *The Faith of the Psalmists* (Philadelphia: Fortress, 1963), pp. 119 f.
[16] This description is of course based on the ancient Near Eastern conception of the universe, according to which the earth is a flat disk floating on the world-ocean, supported by props or pillars.
[17] Cf. H. Ringgren, "Gammaltestamentlig skapelsetro," *Teol. Tidskr.—Teol. Aikakauskirja*, LIII (1948), 232 ff.
[18] T. C. Vriezen, *Onderzoek naar de Paradiesvorstelling bij de oude semitische Volken*, 1937; A. Weiser, "Die biblische Geschichte von Paradies und Sündenfall," *DT*, 1937, pp. 9 ff.; P. Humbert, *Études sur le récit du paradis et de la chute dans la Génèse* (Neuchâtel: Secreteriat de l'Université, 1940); for comparative material, see G. Widengren, *The King and the Tree of Life in Ancient Near Eastern Religion* (Uppsala: Lundeqvist, 1951). For the etymology of Eden, see Å. Sjöberg's review of the original German edition of this book in *SEÅ*, XXIII-XXIX (1964), pp. 145 ff.

tones, although two of them are the well-known Tigris and Euphrates. Babylonian reliefs contain pictures of life-giving water that divides into four branches, probably in order to bring life to all four corners of the world.[19] Obviously the author wants to indicate a location in the middle of the world. But the geographical details somehow point to Mesopotamia as the homeland of the story. In this garden all kinds of fruit were at the disposal of the man and his wife; they were only forbidden to eat of "the tree of the knowledge of good and evil." The narrative also mentions the tree of life. The role played by the tree of life in the story remains vague, however, and the relationship between it and the tree of knowledge of good and evil is not defined. Obviously two traditions have been brought together here in such a way that their relationship has been obscured.[20]

The happy life in Eden was soon interrupted. Enticed by the serpent, the man and his wife ate of the forbidden tree and were driven from the garden because of their disobedience. As punishment, they were forced to live their lives far from the tree of life and labor for their sustenance. In addition, the birth of their children was to be painful.

Obviously several motifs have been linked together here. The basic motif is man's forfeiture of life in paradise through his own disobedience. Many other peoples tell similar myths to explain the wretched lot of man. The serpent is clearly thought of as a real animal, for its punishment is to live in a way that is typical of serpents (creeping on its belly, etc.). In addition, the story in its present form may contain a polemic against the snake worship of the Baal religion.[21] The idea that the serpent is the devil is a later interpretation.

It would be most important to know what the tree of knowledge symbolizes. Many have suggested sexual knowledge: the man and his wife forfeit the life guaranteed by the tree of life, but receive instead the ability to reproduce.[22] But it is doubtful whether the expression "good and evil" really refers to sexual life. It is equally possible that "good and evil" stands for "everything," and that we are dealing with the desire to achieve divine omniscience.[23] Then man's sin would

---

[19] G. Cornfeld (ed.), *Adam to Daniel* (New York: Macmillan, 1961), p. 19, with a picture from Mari. For Iranian parallels, see G. Widengren, *Iranische Geisteswelt*, 1961, p. 32; cf. von Rad, *op. cit.,* pp. 77 f.

[20] See the commentaries, e.g., H. Gunkel, *Genesis,* pp. 21 f.; von Rad, *op. cit.,* pp. 76 f.; Brandon, *op. cit.,* pp. 133 ff.

[21] F. F. Hvidberg, "The Canaanite Background of Genesis I—III," *VT,* X (1960), 285 ff.

[22] This suggestion has been made most recently by I. Engnell, " 'Knowledge' and 'Life' in the Creation Story," *SVT,* III (1955), 103 ff.

[23] This suggestion has been made most recently by von Rad, *op. cit.,* pp. 86 f. H. J. Stoebe, "Gut und Böse in der Jahwistischen Quelle des Pentateuch," *ZAW,* LXV (1953), 188 ff., suggests "beneficial and detrimental to life" as a paraphrase of "good and evil." Cf. also J. Coppens, *La connaissance du bien et du mal et le péché du Paradis,* Louvain, 1958.

actually be hybris, the longing to be like God and control one's own destiny.[24]

In fact, the Old Testament contains other variants of the same story that suggest this interpretation. Ezekiel, for example, speaks of a primordial king who dwelt in glory in Eden, the holy mountain of God (!), but was cast down from the mountain because of his sin (Ezek. 28:11-19). If verses one to ten are connected with this passage, we can define this sin more precisely as hybris, because the king considers himself God. Another prophet compares the King of Babylon to a mythical figure that longed to sit on the mount of the assembly of the gods and be like God (Isa. 14:12-14). Above all, the book of Job alludes to the first man, who sought to acquire divine wisdom (Job 15:7-8). All this shows that the narrative contained in Genesis 3 was not the only myth of the first man known to Israel. It probably also demonstrates that the motif of hybris originally played a crucial role.[25]

One extrabiblical parallel is the Babylonian myth of the primal king Adapa, to whom Anu, the supreme god, offers the food of life. Through a misunderstanding, however, Adapa rejects this food and with it eternal life. The so-called Sumerian paradise myth[26] speaks of a happy land without death and pain, transformed into a garden by means of water; it also mentions the eating of eight forbidden plants that cause suffering. But it differs in all its details from the Hebrew narrative, and, at least in the form preserved to us, has a completely different *Sitz im Leben*: it serves as part of a charm against certain diseases.

c. The Deluge

The biblical writers next continue their account of how sin comes to prevail upon the earth. After the first act of disobedience, offenses follow each other in rapid succession. Cain, the elder son of Adam

---

[24] A Babylonian parallel suggests a possibility of combining these aspects. In the Gilgamesh epic the "wild man" Enkidu attains civilization through sexual intercourse with a temple prostitute, and she then addresses him: "You are wise, you have become like a god." If this combination is correct, it might be possible to find in the Israelite narrative a tacit polemic against the role of woman in the Canaanite fertility cult. See Brandon, *op. cit.*, pp. 131 f., and Ephraim Speiser, *Genesis* (Garden City: Doubleday, 1964), pp. 26 f.

[25] For a compilation of the variants of the motif, see Gunkel, *Genesis*, pp. 29 ff. On Ezek. 28, see G. Widengren, *Sakrales Königtum* (Stuttgart: Kohlhammer, 1955), pp. 26 f.; on Job 15, see Ringgren, *Word and Wisdom*, pp. 89 ff.; on the myth of the primal man, see I. Engnell, "Die Urmenschvorstellung und das Alte Testament," *SEÅ*, XXII/XXIII (1958), 265 ff.

[26] S. N. Kramer, *From the Tablets of Sumer* (Indian Hills: Falcon's Wing, 1956), pp. 170 ff.; see also the analysis by M. Lambert and R. Tournay, *Revue d'Assyriologie*, XLIII (1949), 105 ff.

and Eve, slays his younger brother Abel (Gen. 4; here the writer seems to have utilized an ancient poem recounting the enmity between farmer and herdsman[27]). The daughters of men have intercourse with heavenly beings (the "sons of God," Gen. 6:1 ff.) and give birth to giants, etc. When sin continues to increase upon earth, God finally decides to exterminate the whole human race. He punishes the earth with a devastating flood, so that all men perish. Only one single man, a righteous man named Noah, is saved, together with his family: at God's command he builds a ship, in which he also preserves two of every kind of animal.[28] After the flood, the ship comes to rest on a mountain in Ararat, i.e., Armenia. Noah offers sacrifice to his God and receives the pledge that God will never again permit such a flood to overwhelm the earth.

This narrative has naturally made use of ancient material that is best known to us from Sumerian and Assyro-Babylonian sources. The Sumerian account is independent;[29] the Assyrian account forms a part of the Gilgamesh epic (another account is included in the Atrahasis myth). Both tell how man is wiped out by a mighty flood. Interestingly, the Assyrian account also locates the story in Armenia. In Mesopotamia, however, the story of the flood remains an isolated episode; the deluge is the momentary inspiration of a god. The biblical account, on the contrary, is integrated into a larger whole; the flood is the punishment brought upon man for his sin (traces of this idea may be found also in the Atrahasis version). It is depicted as a temporary victory for chaos, and is followed by the restoration of the world order through the command of Yahweh. Such differences are much more significant than the purely superficial observation that the Sumero-Babylonian versions have a polytheistic background, while the biblical account of the deluge is thoroughly monotheistic.

A survey of the primal history (Gen. 1—11) makes one important point stand out: mythological material has here been placed in an historical framework. The creation is the beginning of history; the deluge is an event in the history of mankind.

d. God in History

The Israelites see history as controlled by Yahweh. He created the world and mankind, he sent the deluge to punish the sins of mankind. But despite everything sin continues to increase in the world. Then God chooses one man, Abraham, from Ur in Chaldea, to make him the father of a new nation through which all the families of the earth

---

[27] Cf. I. Engnell, *SVT*, III (1955), 118. Engnell sees in this story a reflection of an ancient ritual in which the king is slain and the priest who performs the action flees; cf. the Greek Bouphonia.

[28] According to P, seven pairs of clean animals only.

[29] Kramer, *op. cit.*, pp. 176 ff.

will be blessed (Gen. 12:1-4). At Yahweh's command, Abraham migrates to the land of Canaan (Palestine) and becomes the ancestor of the Israelites (and a few related peoples). His grandson Jacob has twelve sons—actually we have here a retrojection of the later twelve tribes of Israel—who emigrate to Egypt because of a famine. After several generations, the Israelites are finally led out of Egypt by Moses, and take possession of the land of Canaan once and for all. Thus Israel recounts its own history. Now the important question is not to what extent this account is real history or legendary elaboration; for the Israelites, the crucial fact is that all this was the work of Yahweh, their God.

Three creed-like passages in the Old Testament express this conviction clearly and unmistakably. One of them runs:[30]

> A wandering Aramean was my father; and he went down into Egypt and sojourned there, few in number; and there he became a nation, great, mighty, and populous. And the Egyptians treated us harshly, and afflicted us, and laid upon us hard bondage. Then we cried to Yahweh the God of our fathers, and Yahweh heard our voice, and saw our affliction, our toil, and our oppression; and Yahweh brought us out of Egypt with a mighty hand and an outstretched arm, with great terror, with signs and wonders; and he brought us into this place and gave us this land, a land flowing with milk and honey. (Deut. 26:5-9)

Thus everything Israel experienced in history is an act of Yahweh.[31] Israel's historians, both in the Pentateuch and in the so-called Deuteronomistic history, interpret events from this point of view. And if Yahweh is a righteous God, rewarding the upright and punishing the wicked, then the conduct of the people must have historical consequences. When the people sin and forsake Yahweh, enemies overrun the land and Israel is defeated; when the Israelites turn again to Yahweh, their lot becomes more favorable. This, in brief, is how the Deuteronomistic historians look upon history.[32] Even if this inter-

---

[30] The two others are Deut. 6:20-24 and Josh. 24:2-13. See G. von Rad, *Das formgeschichtliche Problem des Hexateuch* (Stuttgart: Kohlhammer, 1938), pp. 3 ff. (reprinted in *idem, Gesammelte Studien zum Alten Testament* [Munich: Kaiser, 1958], pp. 11 ff.)

[31] For a discussion of Israelite historiography, see E. Jacob, *La tradition historique en Israel* (Montpellier: Faculté de théologie protestante, 1946); C. R. North, *The Old Testament Interpretation of History* (London: Epworth, 1953); R. C. Dentan (ed.), *The Idea of History in the Ancient Near East* (New Haven: Yale, 1955); A. Malamat, "Doctrines of Causality in Hittite and Biblical Historiography: A Parallel," *VT*, V (1955), 1 ff.; H. Gese, "Geschichtliches Denken im alten Orient und im Alten Testament," *ZThK*, LV (1958), 127 ff.

[32] Cf. G. von Rad, *Old Testament Theology*, trans. D. M. Stalker (Edinburgh & London: Oliver and Boyd, 1962), I, 334 ff.

pretation of history is not quite unique,[33] it still represents the earliest consistent philosophy of history in antiquity. Later writers, such as the Chronicler, modified this basic point of view only slightly.

But the axiom that Yahweh is at work in history also has meaning in a larger context. In several passages from the prophetic literature we encounter the idea that Yahweh also controls the course of history for the entire world. Amos, for instance, emphasizes that Yahweh not only brought the Israelites up from the land of Egypt, but also brought the Philistines from Caphtor and the Syrians from Kir (Amos 9:7, if genuine). In the King of Assyria, Isaiah sees the instrument chosen by Yahweh to carry out his punishment against Israel; Yahweh then censures the king for having overstepped his commission, boasting that he is the master of his own deeds while in reality he is only performing Yahweh's purposes (Isa. 10:5-7, 15). In similar fashion, Deutero-Isaiah looks upon Cyrus, the Persian king, as the man commissioned by Yahweh to liberate Israel from captivity in Babylon (Isa. 44:28; 45:1-4). We find a characteristic statement in II Kings 10:32: "In those days Yahweh began to cut off parts of Israel. Hazael defeated them throughout the territory of Israel." In other words, Hazael is actually carrying out Yahweh's enterprise.

Does it follow, then, to the Israelite way of thinking, that even the Gentiles are responsible to Yahweh, whom they neither know nor worship? This is definitely not the view represented unanimously by all the Old Testament writers. But some of the prophets, at least, presuppose it. It is quite clearly the case in the passage from Isaiah just mentioned. And when Amos censures Damascus, the Philistine cities, Tyre, Edom, Ammon, and Moab for their sins (chapters 1 and 2), he obviously implies their responsibility to Yahweh. "Yahweh has power to act everywhere, and it is his right and duty to punish sin wherever it is found."[34] It has been suggested that Amos is here applying "a naive ethical criterion," according to which both the Israelites and the Gentiles are subject to the same basic demands.[35] More likely the prophet is here drawing the logical conclusion from his belief in Yahweh as creator and king of the world: if Yahweh created the world and rules it, his demands apply to everyone, and everyone is responsible to him.

---

[33] H. Güterbock, *ZA*, XLII (1934), 1 ff.; XLIV (1938), 45 ff.; see also Dentan, *op. cit.,* Gese, *op. cit.,* and J. J. Finkelstein, "Mesopotamian Historiography," *Proceedings of the American Philosophical Society,* CVII (1963), 461 ff.

[34] A. Kapelrud, *Central Ideas in Amos* (Oslo: Oslo University Press, 1961), p. 27.

[35] A. Weiser, *Die Profetie des Amos* (Giessen: Töpelmann, 1929), p. 112; cf. W. A. Irwin, "The Hebrews," in H. Frankfort (ed.), *The Intellectual Adventure of Ancient Man* (Chicago: University of Chicago Press, 1946), pp. 225 f., 228.

Finally, special significance attaches to the fact that history is occasionally depicted with the assistance of mythical categories.[36] This is true particularly for the deliverance from Egypt. The passage through the sea is described as a victory of Yahweh over the waters of chaos or over the dragon of the creation account. The clearest example is perhaps Isaiah 51:9 f., where the question, "Was it not thou that didst cut Rahab in pieces?" could be thought at first to refer to the battle at creation. But the prophet continues:

> Was it not thou that didst dry up the sea,
> the waters of the great deep;
> that didst make the depths of the sea a way
> for the redeemed to pass over?

This must refer to the exodus from Egypt, which is also thought of as a victory over the powers of chaos. The most appropriate form for representing the victory of God was precisely the ancient myth of the battle with the dragon. This process has sometimes been called an "historicization of the myth"; but we are probably not dealing primarily with a myth that has been reinterpreted in historical terms, but rather with an historical event, or at least an event thought to be historical, that has been interpreted in mythical categories. "Mythologization of history" would therefore be a more correct term.

e. The Election and the Covenant

For the Old Testament writers, Yahweh's action in history is concentrated in what he has done for Israel. Two concepts are of preeminent importance in this regard: election and covenant.

Yahweh elected Israel.[37] "You only have I known of all the families of the earth," Amos has Yahweh say (Amos 3:2). "Know" here does not mean the ordinary process of becoming acquainted with something. The prophet states with this expression that Yahweh chose Israel and entered into a particular kind of relationship with Israel. The verb *bāḥar* ("elect, choose") is especially frequent in Deuteronomy; its use in this connection does not seem to antedate Deuteronomy. There we read, for example, "For you are a people holy to Yahweh your God; Yahweh your God has chosen you to be a people for his own possession, out of all the peoples that are on the face of the earth"

[36] H. Ringgren, *Faith of the Psalmists*, pp. 93 ff.; G. Widengren, "Myth and History in Israelite-Jewish Thought," in S. Diamond (ed.), *Culture and History: Essays in Honor of Paul Radin* (New York: Columbia, 1960), pp. 467 ff.
[37] K. Galling, *Die Erwählungstraditionen Israels* (Giessen: Töpelmann, 1928); H. H. Rowley, *The Biblical Doctrine of Election* (London: Lutterworth, 1950); T. H. Vriezen, *Die Erwählung Israels nach dem Alten Testament* (Zürich: Zwingli, 1953); K. Koch, "Zur Geschichte der Erwählungsvorstellung in Israel," *ZAW*, LXVII (1955), 205 ff.; H. Wildberger, *Jahwes Eigentumsvolk* (Zürich: Zwingli, 1960).

(Deut. 7:6). It is emphasized that the election did not take place because of Israel's greatness or other merits of the people, but only "because Yahweh loves you" (Deut. 7:8).

Other Old Testament writers use other expressions. In the so-called Song of Moses, we read that Israel is Yahweh's portion or heritage: "He found him in a desert land . . . he encircled him, he cared for him . . . " (Deut. 32:9-11).

In the book of Hosea, Yahweh says:

> When Israel was a child, I loved him,
> and out of Egypt I called my son. (Hos. 11:1)

Ezekiel employs the allegory of a foundling, whom Yahweh discovered, brought up, and took as his wife (Ezek. 16).

Originally, the deliverance from Egypt and subsequent covenant upon Sinai were probably considered God's act of election. But the theology of election very soon was applied to the patriarchal traditions. The call of Abraham, demanding that he leave his own land in order to migrate to Canaan, was taken as the beginning, or at least a preliminary stage, of Israel's election. Traditio-historically, the patriarchal narratives are secondary. They were handed down separately, and then at a late date prefixed to the exodus and Sinai traditions.[38] But this very fact shows the power and significance of the idea of election. Every means was tried to get back to the first act of election, for there one could find the meaning of the entire history of Israel.

Although the word *bāḥar* first appears in Deuteronomy, the idea itself is probably considerably older. The conviction that a divine act made Israel the people with whom Yahweh entered into a special relationship probably goes back to the time of the Judges, when Israel was in the process of becoming a nation. This idea then gradually came to be described as "election."

But this brings us to a second point. Election implies a purpose.[39] And thus in the course of time Israel came to understand its election as being purposeful. Israel was chosen in order that a particular plan of God might be realized. The promises to the patriarchs define the purpose of the election as follows: "By you [or 'by your seed'] all the families of the earth will be blessed" (Gen. 12:3; cf. 18:18; 22:18; 26:4; 28:14). It is possible that, traditio-historically, these promises are of rather late date.[40] In fact, they are most closely related to the ideas of Deutero-Isaiah, when the latter says that Israel is to be "a light to the nations" (Isa. 42:6). But the well-known prophecy that all nations shall flow to Jerusalem, contained both in Micah 4 and

[38] G. von Rad, *Genesis,* pp. 20 f.

[39] Rowley lays particular stress on this fact in the work cited above.

[40] As is suggested by J. Hoftijzer, *Die Verheissungen an die drei Erzväter* (Leiden: Brill, 1956).

Isaiah 2, also provides a universal task for Israel: the transmission of the will and word of Yahweh to all nations. This prophecy is usually considered late; but it is clearly based on the conceptions of the so-called Zion hymns, which are certainly quite ancient.[41] In this instance, the national sanctuary has replaced the nation as the object of God's election. In both cases, however, the election is based on a definite divine purpose, which can be called universal. Strangely enough, though, the Israelites never really drew the logical conclusions that follow from this idea. Israel never attempted to contribute to the realization of this purpose through active missionary activity.

It would be difficult to separate the idea of election from the concept of the covenant.[42] At Sinai, Yahweh concluded a covenant with Israel. "Now, therefore, if you will obey my voice and keep my covenant, you shall be my own possession among all peoples; for all the earth is mine, and you shall be to me a kingdom of priests and a holy nation" (Exod. 19:5 f.). Jeremiah puts it this way: "Obey my voice, and I will be your God, and you shall be my people; and walk in all the way that I command you, that it may be well with you" (Jer. 7:23). The first half of the latter passage seems to reproduce a fixed covenantal formula, referred to specifically by Deuteronomy 26:17 f. in the ritual of the covenant renewal.

The covenant-concept clearly was extremely important for Israel's religious consciousness, and therefore demands our special attention.

The Hebrew word for "covenant" is *berît*. Despite many attempts, no one has succeeded in providing a convincing etymology for this word.[43] It can be applied both to agreements between human partners and to the covenant between Yahweh and Israel. A covenant implies definite obligations incumbent upon both parties.

When men conclude a covenant, the partners can occasionally be equals or almost equals (e.g., Laban and Jacob in Gen. 31:44); but in most cases the stronger offers to enter into a covenant with the weaker. The Israelites enter into a covenant with the Gibeonites that puts the latter under Israelite protection (Judg. 9); Nahash, the king of Ammon, concludes a covenant with the men of Jabesh-gilead

---

[41] H. Wildberger, "Die Völkerwallfahrt zum Zion," *VT,* VII (1957), 62 ff.

[42] J. Begrich, "Berit," *ZAW,* LX (1944), 1 ff.; J. van Imschoot, "L'alliance dans l'Ancien Testament," *NRT,* 1952, pp. 785 ff.; A. Jepsen, "Berith," in A. Kuschke (ed.), *Verbannung und Heimkehr* (Tübingen: Mohr, 1961), pp. 161 ff.

[43] For discussion of the etymology, see E. Nielsen, *Shechem* (Copenhagen: Gad, 1955), pp. 110 ff. Nielsen relates the word to Akkadian *birtu,* "middle, midst," and *ina birit,* "between." W. F. Albright, "The Hebrew Expression for 'Making a Covenant' in Pre-Israelite Documents," *BASOR,* CXXI (1951), 21 f., compares the Hebrew *kārat berît* to an Akkadian expression "to cut a *berîtu,*" deriving *"berîtu"* from *"birîtu,"* which means "chain" or "bond."

(I Sam. 11:1 ff.); Abimelech the king makes a covenant with Isaac (Gen. 26:28); etc.

A covenant between a human being and a divinity is not entirely unknown in the ancient Near East. We know of one, for example, that the Sumerian king Urukagina concluded with the god Ningirsu.[44] But two differences should be pointed out. First, the king seems to play a more active role here; second, the covenant idea is not accorded nearly the significance it is in Israel.

As we have seen, however, the Hittite suzerainty treaties do furnish an outward formal parallel to the covenant between Yahweh and Israel.[45] The accounts of the making of the covenant at Sinai (Exod. 19 f.) and of Joshua's renewal of the covenant at Shechem (Josh. 24) both follow this pattern. These two accounts lack the blessings and curses typical of the Hittite model, but Deuteronomy 27—28 contains such blessings and curses within the context of a covenant renewal ceremony. This ceremony also includes the public reading of the law, which contains the covenant stipulations (Deut. 31:10 ff.). From the point of view of theology and the history of religions, it is particularly significant that the initiative for making the covenant proceeds from Yahweh and that the covenant appears as a solemn pledge made by God.[46] Yahweh chose Israel from all the nations of the earth and entered into intimate relationship with it: "You shall be my own possession among all peoples." Thus Israel becomes a people belonging (which is what "holy" means in this context) to Yahweh, under his special protection, who may approach him as "priests" and who are to prosper. Their obligation is to keep the commandments of Yahweh: "... if you will obey my voice and keep my covenant" (Exod. 19:5 f.).

The parties to a covenant are expected to be loyal and true to their obligation. The Hebrew word for this loyalty is *ḥesed*.[47] This quality is ascribed above all to Yahweh. Since the covenant came into being through his initiative, the concept of loyalty to the covenant easily takes on the nuance of grace. The Septuagint therefore used *eleos* (mercy) or *charis* (grace) to translate the Hebrew word.

Now in the opinion of the prophets and the Deuteronomistic historians the Israelites broke the covenant. They did not live according to the commandments of God; in particular, they did not accept him as their only God. When a people fails to fulfill the obligations of the covenant, the covenant actually ceases to be in force. "They have gone after other gods to serve them; the house of Israel and the house of Judah have broken my covenant which I made with their

---

[44] H. Schmökel, *Geschichte des alten Vorderasiens* (Leiden: Brill, 1957), p. 27.

[45] See above, pp. 35 f.

[46] Jepsen, *op. cit.*

[47] Cf. above, pp. 85 f.

fathers. Therefore, thus says Yahweh, Behold, I am bringing evil upon them which they cannot escape" (Jer. 11:10 f.). The punishment is inescapable. Nevertheless a prophet like Jeremiah sees one hope: Yahweh will conclude a *new covenant* with Israel. For "behold, the days are coming, says Yahweh, when I will make a new covenant with the house of Israel and the house of Judah. . . . I will put my law within them and I will write it upon their hearts; and I will be their God, and they shall be my people. . . . They shall all know me, from the least of them to the greatest" (Jer. 31:31-34). In other words, the obligations of the new covenant will not be imposed from without: they will spring from the new character of the changed heart, intimate with God. Even so, the covenant is still connected with obligations in the form of a "law" (*tôrâ*).

The covenant idea, then, was so basic to Israel that even the restoration of the broken relationship with God was conceived as a covenant. The covenant became the normal form for Israel's association with God.

There are also certain individual aspects of the relationship between Yahweh and Israel that are themselves referred to as covenants. The covenant with Abraham and the other patriarchs (Gen. 15, 18, etc.) is of course probably to be understood merely as a retrojection of the Sinai covenant into the patriarchal period. By contrast, special significance attaches to the covenant with David.[48]

> I have made a covenant with my chosen one,
>   I have sworn to David my servant:
> I will establish your descendants for ever,
>   and build thy throne for all generations.
>
> (Ps. 89:4 f.; [Eng. 89:3 f.])

Here, as in the so-called last words of David (II Sam. 23:1), we have a reference to Yahweh's promise to David through the prophet Nathan that one of David's descendants should always sit upon the throne of Israel (II Sam. 7). In this case, too, according to the text before us the initiative proceeds from Yahweh and the covenant is a pledge.

On one point the references to the Davidic covenant are not in complete agreement. At times the continuance of the covenant is made to depend on the obedience of the kings, e.g., in Psalm 132:12:

> If your sons keep my covenant
>   and my testimonies which I shall teach them,
> their sons also for ever
>   shall sit upon your throne.

---

[48] Cf. L. Rost, "Sinaibund und Davidbund," *TLZ*, LXXII (1947), cols. 129 ff.; von Rad, *Old Testament Theology*, I, 308 ff.

At other times, however, the kingship as such is independent of the actions of the individual kings, e.g., in Psalm 89:31-35 (Eng. 89:30-34):

> If his children forsake my law
> and do not walk according to my ordinances,
> if they violate my statutes
> and do not keep my commandments,
> then I will punish their transgressions with the rod
> and their iniquity with scourges;
> but I will not remove from him my steadfast love,
> or be false to my faithfulness.
> I will not violate my covenant,
> or alter the word that went forth from my lips.

The point of II Samuel 7:14 f. is similar. Here, then, we have a tension between two conceptions: according to one, the kingship is in itself a permanent institution; according to the other, the kings are responsible for its continuance.

The tradition of the Davidic covenant is of course later than that of the Sinai covenant. In the period of the monarchy, however, both conceptions obviously stood side by side without any apparent contradiction. Historically speaking, the Sinai covenant is connected with the ancient tribal association or amphictyony, while the conception of the Davidic covenant is bound up with the development of Israel as a state, but somehow understood as a special agreement reached within the framework of the Sinai covenant. The king, who actually rules by virtue of the Davidic covenant, seems even to have been responsible for seeing to it that the people keep the Sinai covenant. He must have taken part in the cultic renewal of the covenant. Perhaps, as many think, he himself publicly recited the law, i.e., the covenant obligations.[49]

---

[49] Cf. also G. Widengren, "King and Covenant," *JSS*, II (1957), 1 ff.

6.

MAN[1]

The Hebrew word for "man" is ādām—the name given by Genesis 2:7 to the first man. The verse in question connects this name with ădāmâ, "soil," "earth," because man was made "of dust from the ground." Now this explanation of the word, like most of the etymologies provided by the Old Testament writers, is probably not scientifically correct. It is a play on the similarity of the two words and an attempt to derive a theological conclusion from this similarity. There is a possibility that both words can be derived from the root 'dm, with the meaning "red" or "brownish-red"; but this association was certainly not evident to the Hebrews.

On the other hand, the origin of man from earth or clay is mentioned several times in the Old Testament. After the fall, when Yahweh punishes Adam he says, "You are dust, and to dust you shall return or: . . . and you shall become dust once more" (Gen. 3:19). In the book of Job, the poet says that man is made from clay (Job. 10:9; 33:6). Similar ideas are found among the Babylonians.[2] The idea of a return to dust gives perfect expression to man's transitoriness and mortality.

Man is more than dust, however. "Then Yahweh formed man of dust from the ground, and breathed into his nostrils the breath of life (nešāmâ); and man became a living being (nepeš)," we read in Genesis 2:7. Elsewhere in the Old Testament this latter word is usually translated as "soul." In other words, the common idea that man consists of a body and a soul (nepeš) is a misconception: as a totality, as a living being, he is a "soul."

---

[1] General studies: W. Eichrodt, *Man in the Old Testament*, trans. K. and R. Gregor Smith (Chicago: Allenson, 1951); A. R. Johnson, *The Vitality of the Individual in the Thought of Ancient Israel* (Cardiff: University of Wales, 1949); L. Köhler, *Hebrew Man*, trans. P. R. Ackroyd (London: SCM, 1956); G. Pidoux, *L'homme dans l'Ancien Testament* (Paris: Delachaux & Niestle, 1953); J. Pedersen, *Israel* (London: Oxford, 1959), I-II, 99 ff.

[2] *La naissance du monde* (Paris: Editions du Seuil, 1959), p. 130.

The word *nepeš* has several meanings. Originally, it probably meant something like "throat"[3] (as it still does, for instance, in Ps. 69:2 [Eng. 69:1]). From this point, the meaning gradually changed to "breath" (that which goes through the throat; cf. perhaps Gen. 35:18; I Kings 17:22) and finally "life." But one can go on to say that the *nepeš*, i.e., the life, is in the blood (Gen. 9:4; Lev. 17:11, 14). On the other hand, from the basic meaning "throat" can be derived such meanings as "desire," "appetite." The word *nepeš* can also have the attenuated meaning of "person" or "self." The primary fact to keep in mind is that the "soul" is not looked upon as something that is added to the body; the word means man as a totality. A man does not *have* a soul, he *is* a soul.[4]

Genesis 2:7 calls the divine vital principle that makes man a "soul" *nešāmâ*, "breath." Elsewhere it is usually called *rûaḥ*, "spirit." We read, for example, in Ecclesiastes 12:7: "The dust returns to the earth as it was, and the spirit returns to God who gave it"; and in Psalm 104:29-30: "When thou takest away their breath, they die. . . . When thou sendest forth thy Spirit, they are created." The spirit, says Pedersen, "is the motive power of the soul. It does not mean the center of the soul, but the strength emanating from it and, in its turn, reacting upon it."[5] As a result, the "spirit" is very often connected with feelings and emotions. "But it is the spirit in a man, the breath of the Almighty, that makes him understand" (Job 32:8). In other words, without spirit there can be no life; without spirit the emotions cannot function.

The heart also appears as the locus of the emotions. To the Israelites, the heart is the organ of thought and feeling, "the set of a man's heart determines his actions." *Nepeš*, says Pedersen, "is the soul in its full totality; the heart is the soul in its inner content."[6] The heart receives impressions, the heart frames plans, the heart is the seat of religious knowledge.[7]

Besides the heart, the Old Testament also mentions the bowels, the kidneys (Jer. 11:20; 17:10; Ps. 7:10 [Eng. 7:9]; 26:2—all translated in the RSV as "mind"), and the liver (Lam. 2:11; perhaps also Gen. 49:6; Ps. 7:6 [Eng. 7:5]; 16:9; etc., where MT reads[8] *kābôd*, "glory," instead of *kābēd*, "liver"—RSV usually translates as "heart") as the

---

[3] P. Dhorme, *L'emploi métaphorique des noms de parties du corps* (Paris: Geuthner, 1923), p. 191 (= *RB*, XXIX [1920], 182 f.); L. Dürr, "Hebr. *nepeš* = akk. *napištu* = Gurgel, Kehle," *ZAW*, XLIII (1925), 262 ff.

[4] Pedersen, *op. cit.*, p. 99.

[5] *Ibid.*, p. 104 (the author's rendering of the Danish original).

[6] *Loc. cit.*

[7] Cf. also F. H. von Meyenfeldt, *Het hart (leb, lebab) in het Oude Testament* (Leiden: Brill, 1950).

[8] Against Pedersen, *op. cit.*, p. 519.

seat of the emotions. All these conceptions are held in common with the rest of the ancient Near East.

From another point of view, man is flesh (*bāśār*). God is spirit, man is flesh (cf. Isa. 31:3)—thus the difference between the divine and the human can be briefly put. But this contrast between spirit and flesh is not, as in the Hellenistic world, a contrast between the spiritual and the material, with the implication that there is something evil or sinful about the flesh per se. What our passage describes is the weakness of man in contrast to the power and might of God, or the transitoriness of man in contrast to the Eternal. Thus Jeremiah says:

> Cursed is the man who trusts in man
> and makes flesh his arm,
> whose heart turns away from Yahweh. (Jer. 17:5)

Help cannot come from men, nor should confidence be put in them; only Yahweh is reliable, because he always remains the same. Thus the Chronicler has king Hezekiah say of the Assyrian king, "With him is an arm of flesh; but with us is Yahweh our God, to help us and to fight our battles" (II Chron. 32:8).

The Old Testament makes frequent mention of the transitoriness of all flesh. In the remarkable narrative about the "sons of God," who in the primeval period had intercourse with the daughters of men (Gen. 6:1-4), Yahweh says, "My spirit shall not abide in man for ever, for he is flesh, but his days shall be a hundred and twenty years." Even though much of this verse is obscure,[9] this much is clear: the brief duration of man's life is connected with the fact that God's spirit will not remain within man forever, because he is flesh. In similar fashion, a prophet says, "All flesh is grass, and all its beauty is like the flower of the field" (Isa. 40:6). The psalms of lament and the book of Job stress this transitoriness of man over and over again:

> Thou turnest man back to the dust,
> and sayest, "Turn back, O children of men!"
> ·
>
> Thou dost sweep men away; they are like a dream,
> like grass which is renewed in the morning:
> in the morning it flourishes and is renewed;
> in the evening it fades and withers. (Ps. 90:3-6)

But God is the eternal and constant one. Man, who is nothing, flees to him; for he created man.

> Remember, O Lord, what the measure of life is,
> for what vanity thou hast created all the sons of men!
> (Ps. 89:48 [Eng. 89:47])

---

[9] [Cf. E. A. Speiser, *Genesis* (Garden City: Doubleday, 1964), pp. 44 ff.—TRANS.]

This, ultimately, is the basic difference between God and man: God is the creator, man his creature. Therefore man is dust, flesh, transitory, weak; but also for this reason God has pity on his creatures:

> As a father pities his children,
>> so Yahweh pities those who fear him.
> For he knows our frame;
>> he remembers that we are dust. (Ps. 103:13 f.)

The "priestly" account of creation in Genesis 1 puts special emphasis on a quite different aspect of man. In a poetic section he recounts the creation of man: "Then God said, 'Let us make man in our image, after our likeness. . . .' So God created man in his own image, in the image of God he created him; male and female he created them" (Gen. 1:26 f.).

Many exegetes have discussed this passage, without reaching a consensus. The old theological view that the image of God consists in man's spiritual ability to know God and to do his will has been given up as not doing justice to the context; but no one has been able to suggest a new interpretation that is immediately convincing.[10] This much is certain: elsewhere in the Old Testament, "image" (*selem*) refers to an actual copy. Accordingly, the word *demût*, "likeness," added interpretively to *selem* in verse twenty-six, should not be taken restrictively,[11] but as a more specific definition of what is meant by "image." Man is a likeness of God, similar to God. It is difficult to escape the conclusion that outward similarity in form is meant.[12] But another fact must also be kept in mind. The rulers of the ancient Near East set up images and statues of themselves in places where they exercised or claimed to exercise authority. The images represented the ruler himself as symbols of his presence and his authority.[13] Man accordingly should rule as God's representative upon earth. The priestly writer quite properly adds immediately: "Let them have dominion over the fish of the sea, and over the birds of the air, and over the cattle, and over all the earth, and over every creeping thing that creeps upon the earth." Thus man's similarity to God consists in

---

[10] J. Hehn, "Zum Terminus Bild Gottes," *Sachau Festscrift*, 1915, pp. 46 ff.; Bachmann, "Das Ebenbild Gottes," in *Das Erbe Martin Luthers* (Ihmels Festschrift), 1928; W. Caspari, "Imago Divina," in *Seeberg Festschrift*, I, 1929, pp. 190 ff.; L. Köhler, "Die Grundstelle der Imago-Dei-Lehre Gen. 1, 26," *TZ*, IV (1940), 16 ff.; G. von Rad, *Old Testament Theology*, trans. D. M. G. Stalker (Edinburgh and London: Oliver and Boyd, 1962), I, 144 ff. [Cf. also F. Horst, "Face to Face," *Interpretation*, IV (1950), 259 ff.—TRANS.]

[11] As is done by Köhler, "Die Grundstelle . . . ," pp. 20 f.

[12] Von Rad, *op. cit.*, p. 144: ". . . refer to the whole of man . . . to the splendor of his bodily form."

[13] E. Jacob, *Theology of the Old Testament*, trans. A. W. Heathcote and P. J. Allcock (New York: Harper, 1958), p. 167.

his dominion over the animal world, exercised by him as God's representative.[14]

In a similar vein, the poet of Psalm 8 speaks of man (*ĕnôš*) or the "son of man" (*ben ādām*):

> Yet thou hast made him little less than God,
>   and dost crown him with glory and honor.
> Thou hast given him dominion over the works of thy hands:
>   thou hast put all things under his feet,
> all sheep and oxen,
>   and also the beasts of the field,
> the birds of the air, and the fish of the sea,
>   whatever passes along the paths of the sea.
>   (Ps. 8:6-9 [Eng. 8:5-8])

Here, however, we encounter a special problem. Words like "crown," "glory," and "honor" immediately suggest a king; and the expression "little less than God" or "almost divine" could be most easily understood within the framework of the ancient Near Eastern royal ideology.[15] On the other hand, dominion over the animals is precisely what the creation story promises to man in general. Either this psalm must therefore have been used at an occasion when the king assumed the role of the first man, or else the first man is here described with the aid of royal terminology. Both possibilities are equally likely, and a decision must be reserved until our discussion of the kingship.

If we now bring together the ideas of man contained in the two creation accounts (Gen. 1 and 2), a certain duality emerges. On the one hand, man is dust—or, according to other passages, flesh—and as a consequence weak and transitory; he possesses life only through God's spirit. On the other hand, he is God's likeness, exercising dominion over nature; he possesses accordingly a certain majesty that definitely gives him a place above all other creatures. In other words, man is the supreme work of creation; but he still remains far inferior to the creator and dependent upon the creator in every respect.

---

[14] Von Rad, *op. cit.*, pp. 146 f.

[15] A. Bentzen, *Messias — Moses redivivus — Menschensohn* (Zürich: Zwingli, 1948), pp. 12 f.; H. Ringgren, *SEÅ,* XIII (1948), 18.

7.

MAN BEFORE GOD

Yahweh, as we have seen, is *ādôn*, a powerful lord. This is the basic tenet of the Israelite religion, but one shared with most other Semitic religions. Man is accordingly a *'ebed*, "slave," "servant." Man's proper conduct towards God is described by the word *'ābad*, "serve."[1] The proper attitude toward God is *yir'â*, "fear," "reverence," a word frequently used to designate the religious attitude in general. "You shall fear Yahweh your God; you shall serve him," we read in Deuteronomy 6:13. "Serve Yahweh with fear," says Psalm 2:11. "And now, Israel, what does Yahweh your God require of you, but to fear Yahweh your God, to walk in all his ways, to love him, to serve Yahweh your God with all your heart and with all your soul" (Deut. 10:12). In this last quotation, we find two new elements of man's relationship to God: obedience, which is of course a servant's duty, and love of God.

In this combination of fear and love we see clearly the characteristic ambivalence of religious experience. God is both *tremendum* and *fascinosum;* man, accordingly, must fear him and love him. With reference to Psalm 62:12 f. (Eng. 62:11 f.), "Power belongs to God; and to thee, Yahweh, belongs steadfast love," Weiser quite properly says, "It is in the union of power and grace that the essential nature of the Old Testament belief in God is truly expressed."[2] Fear and love, then, are the two poles between which man's appropriate reaction moves.[3]

Fear of God is occasionally a real fear and trembling:

> Let all the earth fear Yahweh,
> let all the inhabitants of the world stand in awe of
> [lit. tremble before] him! (Ps. 33:8)

---

[1] C. Lindhagen, *The Servant Motif in the Old Testament* (Uppsala: Lundeqvist, 1950), esp. pp. 152 ff.

[2] A. Weiser, *The Psalms,* trans. Herbert Hartwell (Philadelphia: Westminster, 1962), p. 452.

[3] H. Ringgren, *The Faith of the Psalmists* (Philadelphia: Fortress, 1963), pp. 48 f.

When Yahweh appeared on Mount Sinai, we read in the account of Exodus 20:18 f., the people trembled and stood far off and said to Moses, "You speak to us and we will hear; but let not God speak to us, lest we die." Again and again the appearance of the holy God inspires fear:

> But thou, terrible art thou!
> Who can stand before thee
> when once thy anger is roused?
> From the heavens thou didst utter judgment;
> the earth feared and was still. (Ps. 76:8 f. [Eng. 76:7 f.])

Accordingly, when God speaks in a theophany he usually begins, "Fear not" (e.g., Judg. 6:23; cf. Exod. 20:20; Isa. 41:14).

But usually the fear of God means reverence before God, the religious attitude in general: "But there is forgiveness with thee, that thou mayest be feared" (Ps. 130:4); "The fear of the Lord is the beginning of wisdom" (Prov. 9:10; cf. 1:7). The concept also includes a strong admixture of obedience. Abraham is said to fear God when he is prepared to sacrifice his son Isaac at God's command (Gen. 22:12). Job was "one who feared God and turned away from evil" (Job 1:1, 8). This term, in other words, refers not only to the experience of awe but also "to its consequence, i.e., to obedience." Von Rad has even tried "to interpret the phrase 'fear of God' simply as a term for obedience to the divine commands."[4]

Love of God is inculcated particularly in the parenetic passages of Deuteronomy.[5] "And you shall love Yahweh your God with all your heart, and with all your soul, and with all your might" (Deut. 6:5; cf. 10:12). The Psalms contain remarkably few applications of the word "love" to man's attitude toward God;[6] in fact, only Psalm 18:2 (Eng. 18:1) comes into consideration: "I love thee, O Yahweh, my strength" (Ps. 97:10 and 116:1 are textually doubtful). But the psalms contain much other evidence for a positive attitude: joy, confidence, satisfaction, etc. The same psalmist who asks at one point, "Who considers the power of thy anger, and thy wrath according to the fear of thee?" can also say, "Satisfy us in the morning with thy steadfast love, that we may rejoice. . . . Make us glad. . . . Let the favor of Yahweh our God be upon us" (Ps. 90:11 and 90:14, 15, 17). Here we see once again the combination of *tremendum* and *fascinosum*, of fear and love.

Another important point is the repeated emphasis on man's absolute dependence upon God. At creation, God breathed into man the

---

[4] G. von Rad, *Genesis,* trans. J. H. Marks (Philadelphia: Westminster, 1961), pp. 236 f.
[5] [Cf. W. Moran, "The Ancient Near Eastern Background of the Love of God in Deuteronomy," *CBQ,* XXV (1963), 77 ff.—TRANS.]
[6] Ringgren, *op. cit.,* p. 51.

breath of life and made him "a living being" (Gen. 2:7). This feeling of dependence is magnificently expressed in Psalm 104, as it was quoted above:

> These all look to thee,
>> to give them their food in due season.
> ....
> When thou hidest thy face, they are dismayed;
>> when thou takest away their breath, they die
>> and return to their dust.
> When thou sendest forth thy Spirit, they are created;
>> and thou renewest the face of the ground.
>
> (Ps. 104:27, 29 f.)

God is great, exalted, and eternal; man is insignificant, worthless, and transitory. "What is man that thou art mindful of him?" asks a psalmist (Ps. 8:5 [Eng. 8:4]). "Before the mountains were brought forth, or ever . . . the earth and the world" were formed, Yahweh was (Ps. 90:2). A thousand years in his sight are as a day. What is man? "Thou dost sweep men away; they are like a dream, like grass which is renewed in the morning; in the morning it flourishes and is renewed; in the evening it fades and withers" (Ps. 90:4-6).

It is fitting for man to recognize and acknowledge his dependence on God. Whoever does not is one of the wicked, rāšāʿ. The wicked are those who would be masters of their own fate, so to speak, without regard for God—an attitude called by the Babylonians "living ina ramānišu,"[7] and considered hybris by the Greeks. Psalm 10 describes the wicked as follows:

> In the pride of his countenance the wicked does not seek him;
>> all his thoughts are, "There is no God."
> He thinks in his heart, "I shall not be moved;
>> throughout all generations I shall not meet adversity."
> He thinks in his heart, "God has forgotten,
>> he has hidden his face, he will never see it."
>
> (Ps. 10:4, 6, 11)

The same idea appears in Psalm 30. The petitioner had been successful and was consequently full of self-confidence:

> As for me, I said in my prosperity,
>> "I shall never be moved."
> By thy favor, O Yahweh,
>> thou hadst established me as a strong mountain;
> thou didst hide thy face,
>> I was dismayed. (Ps. 30:7-8 [Eng. 30:6-7])

---

[7] G. Widengren, The Accadian and Hebrew Psalms of Lamentation (Stockholm: Thule, 1937), pp. 141 f.; cf. Ringgren, op. cit., pp. 35, 39.

As long as the psalmist prospered, he felt confident, trusting in himself and his own strength; he did not realize that actually all this had been granted him through God's grace and favor. Only when stricken by misfortune did he recognize that he had been wrong. Thus the author of Deuteronomy also warns his readers not to forget God in the days of prosperity, saying, "My power and the might of my hand have gotten me this wealth." It is Yahweh who gives the power to get wealth (Deut. 8:11-18).

The sin of the first man consisted in his desire to be like God. In Ezekiel 28, the king of Tyre, depicted as primal man and primal king, supposes that he has acquired his wealth through his own wisdom, and says in his pride, "I am a God," although he is only a man (Ezek. 28:4-9). For this reason he is cast down from God's holy mountain. The song of the Day Star in Isaiah 14, referring to the king of Babylon, expresses the same idea:

> You said in your heart,
>   'I will ascend to heaven;
> above the stars of God
>   I will set my throne on high;
> I will sit on the mount of assembly
>   in the far north;
> I will ascend above the heights of the clouds,
>   I will make myself like the Most High.'
> But you are brought down to Sheol,
>   to the depths of the Pit. (Isa. 14:13-15)

To trust in one's own strength means to make oneself equal to God; such pride is a sign of rebellion against God (cf. also Gen. 11:1 ff.; Ps. 52:7, 9 [Eng. 52:5, 7]).

The proper attitude toward God consists in man's recognition of his total dependence upon God and in confidence in God.

> Trust in him at all times, O people;
>   pour out your heart before him;
>   God is a refuge for us.
> Men of low estate are but a breath,
>   men of high estate are a delusion.
>
>   (Ps. 62:9-10 [Eng. 62:8-9])

It is better to take refuge in Yahweh than to put confidence in man or even in princes, says another psalmist (Ps. 118:8 f.).

> Cursed is the man who trusts in man
>   and makes flesh his arm,
>   whose heart turns away from Yahweh. (Jer. 17:5)

To rely upon one's own strength or upon human strength in general automatically means to abandon Yahweh.

Isaiah seeks to awaken in his hearers this attitude of trust in God; they are seeking help from men, but only Yahweh can really help them:

> In returning and rest you shall be saved;
> in quietness and in trust shall be your strength.
> And you would not, but you said,
> "No! We will speed upon horses." (Isa. 30:15 f.)

Salvation lies not in horses or other forms of military might, but in trust in Yahweh. Men cannot provide help, but only God. In another context, the same prophet says, "If you will not believe, surely you shall not be established" (Isa. 7:9). Faith and trust describe man's proper attitude. Abraham believes Yahweh, and it is reckoned to him as righteousness (Gen. 15:6).

The psalms bear frequent witness to this trust in God, e.g., "In God I trust without a fear. What can man do to me?" (Ps. 56:12 [Eng. 56:11]), or:

> For God alone my soul waits in silence;
> from him comes my salvation.
> He only is my rock and my salvation,
> my fortress; I shall not be greatly moved.
> (Ps. 62:2 f. [Eng. 62:1 f.])

On the other hand, there is in the Old Testament no *unio mystica* with the godhead. A few expressions recently quoted as evidence for a mystical relationship with God merely point to an intimate association with him, not to a real merging of the self with the godhead (e.g., Ps. 63:9 [Eng. 63:8]; 91:14; 25:14; 31:6 [Eng. 31:5]).[8] It is ultimately the Old Testament concept of God that stood in the way of any Israelite mysticism. It is impossible to become absorbed, in the mystical sense, in the personal, ruling lord of the Israelite religion.

What *is* possible and desirable, on the other hand, is knowledge of God. This does not mean simply intellectual knowledge about God,[9] but intimate association and familiarity with him, in the sense of the Hebrew verb *yāda‘*, "know," "be acquainted with."[10] Hosea declares lack of knowledge of God to be the most serious defect in the religious situation of the people. "My people are destroyed for lack of knowledge" (Hos. 4:6). But this lack also involves a lack of faithfulness

---

[8] H. J. Franken, *The Mystical Communion with Jhwh in the Book of Psalms* (Leiden: Brill, 1954); Ringgren, *op. cit.*, pp. 56 ff.

[9] This aspect is stressed by H. W. Wolff, *ETh*, XII (1952/53), 533 ff.

[10] J. Hänel, *Das Erkennen Gottes bei den Schriftpropheten* (Berlin & Stuttgart: Kohlhammer, 1923); S. Mowinckel, *Die Erkenntnis Gottes der alttestamentlichen Propheten* (Oslo: Grøndal, 1941); G. J. Botterweck, *Gott erkennen im Sprachgebrauch des Alten Testaments* (Bonn: Hanstein, 1951).

and kindness (*ĕmet, ḥesed,* Hos. 4:1). The restoration of the proper relationship is described thus: "I will betroth you to me in faithfulness; and you shall know Yahweh" (Hos. 2:22 [Eng. 2:20]). This passage clearly is speaking of an intimate association.

Knowledge of God also makes man acknowledge that God is indeed God. We read fifty-four times in Ezekiel, "You [they] shall know that I am Yahweh." By this the prophet obviously means that Yahweh's action in history is intended to make men recognize not only his existence, but also the fact that he is God, and therefore worship him.[11]

Thus both fear of God and knowledge of God ultimately produce obedience: to believe in God, to know God, and to fear God means to obey him, to do his will.

Later Judaism considers the law (*tôrâ*) to be the perfect expression of God's will. This word, however, has a long history. It is etymologically identical with the Babylonian *tērtu*, "oracle"; its original meaning was probably "direction," "instruction."[12] It still retains this more general meaning in several Old Testament passages. "For out of Zion shall go forth the law, and the word of Yahweh from Jerusalem," we read in Isaiah 2:3c; here "law" (*tôrâ*) is obviously more or less equivalent to "the word of Yahweh." In the wisdom literature, *tôrâ* frequently refers to the instruction given by the teacher of wisdom (Prov. 3:1; 4:2; 28:9; etc.).[13] Since divine instruction was often imparted through priests or cultic prophets, the word also took on the meaning of priestly instruction, e.g., concerning what is clean and unclean (Hag. 2:11 f.).[14] Individual divine precepts or commands are also called by this name (Exod. 16:28; 18:26; Isa. 8:12). Finally, "*tôrâ*" became the comprehensive designation for all divine precepts: the law. In Deuteronomy, "*tôrâ*" means the law code in question ("this law"—Deut. 1:5; 4:8; 17:18; etc.). In the postexilic period, it refers to the Pentateuch as a whole.

This word reveals to us an important principle of Israelite ethics: the law is the word of God; it expresses his will and claims divine authority. To live according to the law means to do God's will. Ethical conduct is determined by divine commandments. The law explains God's will, it enlightens man, makes him wise, admonishes him, it shows him the right way (Ps. 19:8-12 [Eng. 19:7-11]). It is God's gift for man's benefit.

---

[11] W. Zimmerli, *Erkenntnis Gottes nach dem Buche Ezechiel* (Zürich: Zwingli, 1954), reprinted in *idem, Gottes Offenbarung* (Munich: Kaiser, 1963), pp. 41 ff.

[12] Östborn, *Tōrā in the Old Testament* (Lund: Ohlsson, 1945), chaps. i and ii; I. Engnell, *Israel and the Law* (Uppsala: Wretmans, 1946), pp. 1 ff.

[13] Östborn, *op. cit.,* pp. 112 ff.

[14] *Ibid.,* pp. 89 ff.

Proper ethical conduct is often called justice (*mišpāṭ*) and righteousness (*ṣedeq, ṣᵉdāqâ*). *Mišpāṭ* is primarily a legal decision, a regulation, a commandment; its goal is the preservation of God's order. As Köhler stresses, it expresses the demanding, imperative nature of the law, God's demands.[15] Ezekiel says that God has given man his statutes; man must fulfill them in order to live (Ezek. 20:11). But in addition, especially for the prophets, *mišpāṭ* stands side by side with *ṣᵉdāqâ* as that which God demands of man (e.g., Amos 5:24). Amos 5:15 sounds almost like a definition: "Hate evil, and love good, and establish justice (*mišpāṭ*) in the gate."[16] This makes *mišpāṭ* the human will to love what is good and hate what is evil.[17] In this context, *mišpāṭ* also means social justice and the proper administration of justice. In brief, *mišpāṭ* is "the conduct one must observe as a member of a specific people related to a specific God" (cf. II Kings 17:24 f.).[18] It is "the principle according to which the conduct of man towards his fellow man and also his attitude toward God is judged" (Isa. 28:17 f.).[19] "The expression of God's will results in a claim made by God upon those who worship him; *mišpāṭ* becomes the binding law that contains the demands of Yahweh."[20]

Now what is meant by righteousness (*ṣedeq, ṣᵉdāqâ*)? We have already touched on this question in our discussion of the attributes of God. There we mentioned various attempts to define this concept as "conduct faithful to society" (Fahlgren), agreement with a norm (Jacob, Kautzsch), or faithfulness to one's own nature (Pedersen).[21] There is some truth in all of these explanations. From our point of view, the word *ṣᵉdāqâ* has so many meanings that no modern word can reproduce its content. In our present context we can disregard the *ṣᵉdāqâ* of God, in the sense of his self-assertion, and restrict ourselves to the ethical content of this concept.

The word *ṣaddîq*, "righteous," can refer to a man who wins a legal action, while the word *rāšāʿ*, "wicked," can refer to the guilty party, against whom judgment is given (e.g., Deut. 25:1; Prov. 17:15). In general, however, and perhaps originally, that man is *ṣaddîq* who lives according to the prevailing norms of society. Similarly *ṣᵉdāqâ*

---

[15] L. Köhler, *Old Testament Theology*, trans. A. S. Todd (London: Lutterworth, 1957), pp. 204 f.; see also K. H. Fahlgren, *sedākā* (Uppsala, 1932), pp. 120 ff.; W. Hertzberg, "Die Entwicklung des Begriffes *mišpāṭ* im Alten Testament," *ZAW*, XL (1922), 256 ff. For a general discussion, see J. Hempel, *Das Ethos des Alten Testaments* (Berlin: Töpelmann, 1938); E. Jacob, "Les bases théologiques de l'étique de l'A.T.," *SVT*, VII (1960), 39 ff.

[16] Cf. Hertzberg, *op. cit.*, pp. 274 f.

[17] *Ibid.*, p. 272.

[18] Fahlgren, *op. cit.*, p. 134; cf. Hertzberg, *op. cit.*, p. 283.

[19] Fahlgren, *op. cit.*, p. 137.

[20] Hertzberg, *op. cit.*, p. 283.

[21] See above, pp. 83 f.

is conduct faithful to society. It both presupposes and creates harmony in the life of the community; in fact, it is such harmony. It refers to the situation in which society as a whole lives according to the norm, "both faithfulness to society and the fruits of this faithfulness."[22] Pedersen points out that Job's concluding speech in chapter 29 depicts this ideal situation: the righteous man is the strong and responsible man who lives in a sound and happy society, for whom righteousness and success mean the same thing. "I put on righteousness, and it clothed me; my justice was like a robe and a turban" (Job 29:14).[23]

Soon, however, there set in a process of development the result of which is reflected in most of the Old Testament writings: man's ṣᵉdāqâ becomes restricted exclusively to his conduct according to the norm, while the results of this conduct are described as peace, blessedness, success, or salvation.[24] Now ṣᵉdāqâ has become obedience toward Yahweh; it comprises on the one hand certain duties toward God, and on the other certain duties towards one's neighbor. The important thing is precise observance of the commandments.[25] "And it will be righteousness for us, if we are careful to do all this commandment before Yahweh our God, as he has commanded us" (Deut. 6:25).

In the wisdom literature, especially in Proverbs, we see another side to the concept of righteousness. When the psalms contrast the righteous with the wicked, the wicked are primarily those who live or seek to live without God, those who are proud and defiant, those infected with hybris. In Proverbs, however, the wicked man is the fool who pays no heed to anything, the hotheaded man who continually loses his temper. The righteous man, in contrast, is the wise and thoughtful man, who always acts with foresight and prudence and consequently achieves success. It has become clear that the wisdom literature of Israel—like that of Egypt—seeks above all to discover the order that is inherent in the world and human life, making it possible for man to accommodate himself reasonably to this order.[26] This inherent order, however, is righteousness. That is to say, the Hebrew ṣᵉdāqâ corresponds in function to the Egyptian concept of $m^{3\prime}t$, "truth," or better "rightness," "orderly management."[27]

---

[22] Fahlgren, op. cit., p. 90.

[23] J. Pedersen, Israel (London: Oxford, 1959), I-II, 363 ff.

[24] Fahlgren, op. cit., p. 91; Pedersen, op. cit., pp. 374 f., 435 f.

[25] Fahlgren, op. cit., pp. 93 f.

[26] H. Gese, Lehre und Wirklichkeit in der alten Weisheit (Tübingen: Mohr, 1958), esp. pp. 33 ff.; cf. also H. Skladny, Die ältesten Spruchsammlungen in Israel (Göttingen: Vandenhoeck & Ruprecht, 1962), pp. 7 ff., 21 ff., 29 ff., 58 f.

[27] See H. Ringgren, Word and Wisdom (Lund: Ohlsson, 1947), p. 49; Gese, op. cit., pp. 11 ff.

According to Proverbs, in other words, the righteous man is he who conforms to the order of the world. This order is ultimately divine, instituted by God—even if the reasoning of Proverbs, which seems to be purely empirical, sometimes conceals this fact.[28] (These considerations have even led to the suggestion that the Old Testament, and particularly the book of Proverbs, contains no doctrine of divine retribution, but only an automatic law according to which sin creates a sphere of trouble that affects human life.[29]

As we have seen, however,[30] *ṣedeq* and *ṣedāqâ* refer to the divine order that regulates the world and the universe, expressed in the regular cycle of the seasons, in the alternation of day and night, heat and cold, and in the fertility of the earth. In other words, it is the order of creation. This means that the order of the world, instituted by God, and the ethical order demanded by him through his commandments are two sides of the same coin: divine "righteousness."

What is the will of Yahweh? The laws and the prophets answer this question with varying emphasis, but all agree in the general outline of the answer. There is no lack of attempts to reduce the will of God to the lowest common denominator. In Micah 6:8, for example, we read:

> He has showed you, O man, what is good;
> and what does Yahweh require of you
> but to do justice, and to love kindness,
> and to walk humbly with your God?

Thus God's revealed will lies behind the ethical demands. The so-called Holiness Code contains another summary, perhaps somewhat later: "You shall be holy; for I Yahweh your God am holy" (Lev. 19:2b). This passage is remarkable. In the first place, it is almost the only passage in the Old Testament in which "holiness" is expressly linked with ethical demands. In the second place, it demonstrates with absolute clarity that God is the ultimate ground for all ethical conduct. In the same chapter, furthermore, we find another rule, later made a general principle by the New Testament: "You shall love your neighbor as yourself" (Lev. 19:18). It should be pointed out, however, that the word *rēa'*, "neighbor," refers primarily or even exclusively to one's fellow Israelites. What we have here, then, is not love of one's neighbor in the Christian sense, but more a kind of national solidarity.

The so-called introit-liturgies also contain summaries of ethical demands. The question "Who may enter the sanctuary?" is answered

---

[28] Skladny, *op. cit.*, pp. 71 ff., 89 f.

[29] K. Koch, "Gibt es ein Vergeltungsdogma im Alten Testament?" *ZThK*, LII (1955), 1 ff.

[30] See above, pp. 85 f.

with a list of specific commandments. Psalm 15 is perhaps the best example:

> O Yahweh, who shall sojourn in thy tent?
> Who shall dwell on thy holy hill?
> He who walks blamelessly, and does what is right,
> and speaks truth from his heart;
> who does not slander with his tongue,
> and does no evil to his friend,
> nor takes up a reproach against his neighbor; etc.

(Ps. 15:1-3)

Psalm 24:3-6 provides another example, where the context clearly shows that the questions and answers are connected with the entrance of a religious procession into the Temple. Imitations of such liturgies are found in the prophets, e.g., Micah 6:6-8, quoted above, and Isaiah 33:14-16. The thing to note here is that quite obviously no basic distinction is felt between cult and ethics. Participation in the cult presupposes the satisfaction of certain ethical conditions. Cult without ethics is worthless; and when ethical demands have been neglected, cultic ceremonies are performed in vain. The prophetic emphasis on ethical demands has led many recent scholars to interpret the prophetic message as meaning that the cult is completely worthless, and that the fulfillment of the ethical commandments alone constitutes right religion. In actual fact, however, in the Israelite religion cult and ethics constitute an indissoluble unity.

We find pregnant formulations of God's demands especially in the so-called apodictic laws. Among the laws of the Pentateuch we find two basic kinds of legal material.[31] The first is apodictic. Here we read simply, "You shall . . . " or "You shall not . . . ," obviously because these commandments are conceived as being direct speech from the mouth of God; they confront man immediately with divine authority. Probably these commandments were originally called *tôrâ*, (divine) instruction. The other basic form is casuistic or conditional law. Here we read, "If a man (commits a certain crime), then he shall (be subject to such-and-such a punishment)," or, "Whoever does such-and-such a thing, shall. . . ." This latter form is shared by Israel with the other law codes of the ancient Near East (Sumerian, Akkadian, and Hittite), while apodictic law does not appear at all outside of Israel, or at least appears very rarely.[32]

The apodictic laws are by nature sacral laws, i.e., laws proclaimed at sanctuaries by divine authority; they therefore did not actually

---

[31] A. Alt, *Die Ursprünge des israelitischen Rechts* (Leipzig: Hirzel, 1934), reprinted in *idem, Kleine Schriften* (Munich: Beck, 1953—), I, 278 ff.; cf. G. Mendenhall, *Law and Covenant* (Pittsburgh: Biblical Colloquium, 1955), pp. 6 f.

[32] Mendenhall, *op. cit.*, p. 7.

need any motivation. They were the commandments of God, and God's commandments are not open to discussion.

The Old Testament contains several series of apodictic laws that give us a good idea of the ethical side of the Israelite religion. The so-called cultic decalogue, Exodus 34:14-26, contains primarily cultic prescriptions: prohibition of the worship of other gods, prohibition of idol worship, rules for feasts and sacrifices. In the so-called sexual dodecalogue, Deuteronomy 27:15-26, we have a collection of twelve curses referring to ethical sins, primarily dealing with sex. Cursed be the man who makes an image, who dishonors his parents, who removes a landmark, who misleads a blind man, who perverts the justice due to the fatherless and the widow, who commits certain sexual offenses, etc. Here, too, we have an ancient form of sacral law, expressed in (magically effective) curses. The mixture of religious, ethical, and ritual prescriptions is noteworthy.

The so-called Mosaic decalogue deserves particular mention in this context.[33] It exists in two somewhat different recensions, Exodus 20 and Deuteronomy 5, which clearly go back to a common original. The decalogue is obviously an ancient formula; most scholars today, however, deny its Mosaic origin, since several details presuppose the conditions of a settled population. Of course one must reckon with the possibility that an early prototype has been subjected to later revision; the nucleus of the Decalogue is certainly very old.

The Decalogue obviously came into being within the cult, and probably served as a basis for the annual cultic renewal of the covenant. Even the present context of both versions connects it with the conclusion of the covenant. It is significant that the Decalogue thus documents the ethical basis of the covenant relationship between Israel and Yahweh.

The original form of the Decalogue cannot be recovered in all its details, but in all probability it ran roughly as follows:[34] I am Yahweh your God, who brought you out of the land of Egypt.

1. You shall have no other gods besides me.
2. You shall not make yourself a graven image.
3. You shall not misuse the name of Yahweh your God.
4. Remember the sabbath day, to keep it holy.

---

[33] S. Mowinckel, *Le Décalogue* (Paris: Alcan, 1927); H. H. Rowley, "Moses and the Decalogue," *BJRL*, XXXIV (1951), 81 ff., reprinted in *idem, Men of God* (London: Nelson, 1963), pp. 1 ff.; J. J. Stamm, *Der Dekalog im Lichte der neueren Forschung* (2nd ed.; Bern: Haupt, 1962); E. Nielsen, *De ti bud* (Copenhagen: University, 1965).

[34] The enumeration presented here is probably the most natural; it is followed by the Orthodox and Reformed. The Lutherans and Roman Catholics take 1 and 2 as one commandment, dividing the commandment against coveting (10) into two. The Jews take the introduction as the first commandment, 1 and 2 as the second, etc.

5. Honor your father and your mother.
6. You shall not kill.
7. You shall not commit adultery.
8. You shall not steal.
9. You shall not bear false witness against your neighbor.
10. You shall not covet your neighbor's house.

The first commandment affirms the monotheistic, or perhaps better monolatrous, basis of the Israelite covenant religion. The existence of other gods is not denied, but Israel must worship only Yahweh. The prohibition of images means than man cannot have Yahweh at his disposal, so to speak, in the form of an image.[35] The third commandment protects the holiness and inviolability of the divine name: it must not be used for magic, or for any evil or unworthy purpose. The next commandment similarly protects the Sabbath, which is holy to the Lord, against profane use. The other commandments, which regulate relationships between men, are immediately clear. The only noteworthy point is that even coveting is forbidden. Probably the verb used also "includes the attempt to attach something to oneself illegally."[36] "House" must be taken in its widest sense as family and possessions. An addition develops this concept in more detail: wife, domestic animals, servants, etc.

After the second commandment both recensions insert a section that goes into what happens if the commandments are obeyed or disobeyed. Yahweh is a jealous God, punishing sin to the fourth generation, but "showing steadfast love" to those who love him and keep his commandments. Here, then, love of God is said to be the basic disposition that leads to obedience towards the commandments. We also see illustrated the general principle of collective responsibility: punishment for the sins of the fathers is visited upon their children and their children's children.[37] The family or clan constitutes a single unit within which each individual is responsible for the actions of the other members. Not only does this mean that children must answer for the sins of their fathers, but also that all the members of a clan, or even all the inhabitants of a city or of the whole land, share this responsibility. If a murder is committed in a city and the murderer remains unidentified, guilt rests upon the entire region and expiation

---

[35] G. von Rad, *Old Testament Theology*, trans. D. M. G. Stalker (Edinburgh & London: Oliver and Boyd, 1962), I, 212 ff.

[36] M. Noth, *Exodus*, trans. J. S. Bowden (Philadelphia: Westminster, 1962), p. 166, following J. Herrmann, "Das zehnte Gebot," *Sellin-Festschrift* (Leipzig, 1927), pp. 71 ff.

[37] Cf. J. Hempel, *op. cit.*, pp. 32 ff.; W. Eichrodt, *Theologie des Alten Testaments* (Göttingen: Vandenhoeck & Ruprecht, 1957), III, 1 ff.; J. Scharbert, *Solidarität in Segen und Fluch* (Bonn: Hanstein, 1958), I, 1 ff., 113 ff.

must be made (Deut. 21:1-9). The king's sin brings misfortune upon the entire land (II Sam. 24). On the other hand, however, the presence of a small number of righteous men can save an entire city, as the story of Abraham's intercession on behalf of Sodom presupposes (Gen. 18:23-33).

This idea of collective responsibility is an outgrowth of Israelite tribal solidarity. It must not be oversimplified as meaning that individual responsibility was unknown or that the individual was robbed of his individuality.[38]

The commandments, then, are an expression of God's will; they appear with divine authority. They demand obedience. As we have seen, this obedience can come from love of God. In Deuteronomy, we also find gratitude towards God as a motive for obedience, most clearly, perhaps, in chapter 7: Yahweh delivered Israel from Egypt and gave Israel the land, with all its fertility; now Israel must not forget him and serve other gods, but must observe his commandments and ordinances.

Every offense against the commandments is a sin. Hebrew has several words for this concept, each of which reflects one side of the Israelite conception of sin.[39] The commonest word for sin, *ḥaṭṭā't* or *ḥēṭ'*, is derived from a root that actually means "miss." The verb still occurs in the Old Testament with this original meaning (Job 5:24; Prov. 8:35 f.). This would mean that sin is a kind of lapse or failure. Pedersen is therefore partially right in declaring sin to be something empty and without content, the product of a divided and chaotic soul.[40] *Peša'* refers to sin as rebellion and disobedience toward God (e.g., Hos. 8:1, ". . . they have broken my covenant, and transgressed my law [*tôrâ*]"). Etymologically, *'āwôn* means "what is bent and twisted"; it can also be used to refer to the guilt that results from sin. There is, however, reason to doubt whether the Israelites were conscious of the original distinction among these three words. Very often the Old Testament uses two or even all three expressions in such a way that they must have been more or less synonymous.

There is a consensus that Genesis 3 depicts the origin of sin.[41] Tempted by the serpent, Adam and Eve rebel against God and, believing that they will thereby become like God, eat of the forbidden fruit of the tree of knowledge. The transgression of God's prohibition and the desire to become like God constitute sin. The corresponding punishment follows: man is banished from paradise and falls prey to

---

[38] *Pace* J. de Fraine, "Individu et société dans la religion de l'Ancien Testament," *Biblica*, XXXIII (1952), 324 ff., 455 ff.

[39] Köhler, *op. cit.*, pp. 169 ff.; von Rad, *op. cit.*, pp. 262 ff.

[40] *Op. cit.*, pp. 413 f.

[41] See above, pp. 109 f.

death. Now the serpent in this narrative is not the devil, as representative of evil; such an interpretation belongs to later Judaism and Christianity. In this narrative, though, the author or redactor of the Pentateuch does seem somehow to have seen the story of how sin began. The basic nature of sin would then be defined as the desire to be like God or as rebellion against his will.

The Genesis account goes on to tell how sin continues to spread upon the earth: Cain kills his brother Abel (Gen. 4:8 ff.), Lamech takes blood vengeance (Gen. 4:23 f.), the sons of God have intercourse with the daughters of men (Gen. 6:1-4), and finally, on account of man's wickedness, God must overwhelm the earth with the deluge (Gen. 6:5 ff.). Sin appears as something that comes from without, as an objective entity, an incarnation of all the powers in life that are hostile to God.[42] The story of Cain even depicts sin in the form of a demon: ". . . sin is couching at the door; its desire is for you, but you must master it" (Gen. 4:7). This passage raises many questions: Why is the word of sin, which is feminine, treated as a masculine noun? Why is this statement so similar to what is said of man and wife in Genesis 3:16? It is certain, however, that Isaiah 13:21 applies the verb *rābaṣ* to demons, and that the Babylonian *rabīṣu* is the name of a demon.[43]

On the other hand, sin is also a part of human nature, so to speak. Man is flesh, and therefore weak (Gen. 6:3). "The imagination [Heb. *yēṣer*, "form, purpose"] of man's heart is evil from his youth" (Gen. 8:21; cf. 6:5). "The heart is deceitful above all things, and desperately corrupt; who can understand it?" (Jer. 17:9). A psalmist laments that he was brought forth in iniquity and conceived by his mother in sin (Ps. 51:7 [Eng. 51:5]). The intention of this passage is neither to brand the entire sexual realm as sinful nor to proclaim a doctrine of original sin, but simply to describe the speaker as being totally sinful.

No man is without sin—this the Old Testament asserts repeatedly. In Solomon's prayer at the dedication of the Temple (Deuteronomistic), we read, "For there is no man who does not sin" (I Kings 8:46). In Proverbs, we find this statement:

> Who can say, "I have made my heart clean;
> I am pure from my sin?" (Prov. 20:9)

Psalm 130:3 expresses the same thought with more religious depth:

> If thou, O Yahweh, shouldst mark iniquities,
> Lord, who could stand?

---

[42] E. Jacob, *Theology of the Old Testament,* trans. A. W. Heathcote and P. J. Allcock (New York: Harper, 1958), p. 282.

[43] *Ibid.,* n. 1. [For a fuller discussion of this passage, see E. A. Speiser, *Genesis* (Garden City: Doubleday, 1964), pp. 32 f.—TRANS.]

Man, who is made of dust, cannot be pure before his Maker, says Eliphaz in the book of Job (4:17-21), and Job himself asks:

> Who can bring a clean thing out of an unclean?
> There is not one.　(Job 14:4)

But precisely because man is dust he can dare to beg for mercy. God has pity on man, "for he knows our frame; he remembers that we are dust" (Ps. 103:14). He restrains his anger because he remembers that man is but flesh (Ps. 78:39). No living man is righteous before him; for this very reason, man ventures to ask for mercy (Ps. 143:2).

In spite of this, the Old Testament is generally dominated by a mood of joyful optimism as to the possibility of a man's fulfilling the law. "See, I have set before you this day life and good, death and evil," Deuteronomy 30:15 has Moses say. Life is given to those who do what is good, death to those who work evil. There is not the slightest suggestion that man is incapable of doing what is good. The verses immediately preceding make this fact even clearer: "For this commandment which I command you this day is not too hard for you, neither is it far off. . . . But the word is very near to you; it is in your mouth and in your heart, so that you can do it" (Deut. 30:11, 14). Similarly, the discourse of the prophet Ezekiel in the eighteenth chapter also presupposes that man is capable of acting in righteousness. The introduction to the book of Proverbs, probably somewhat later, implies that whoever has understanding and knowledge will also do what is right.[44] In this latter case the explanation should probably be sought in the special significance of wisdom: wisdom is more than intellectual ability; it also includes practical knowledge. The wise man knows what is good and can act accordingly. Similarly, wisdom in the sense of skill is not mere intellectual knowledge, but also practical ability.

A complication arises in the case of unconscious sins.[45] "But who can discern his errors? Clear thou me from hidden faults," says a psalmist (Ps. 19:13 [Eng. 19:12]). The context shows that the hidden faults are precisely those sins which are not discerned. We find such statements rather often in Babylonian texts, which even provide means for discovering such unknown sins (see, e.g., the *Shurpu* series). Whenever a divine command has been transgressed, punishment follows immediately, whether the sinner is aware of his sin or not. This sin must therefore be determined in order that atonement can be made. In Israel, statements of this kind are infrequent. In addition to the passage just quoted from Psalm 19, a few other passages from the psalms are relevant in this connection, e.g., Psalm 90:8. This

---

[44] H. Ringgren, *Sprüche* (Göttingen: Vandenhoeck & Ruprecht, 1962), p. 13.

[45] Ringgren, *Faith of the Psalmists*, pp. 70 f.

latter passage, however, could just as well refer to sins that a man attempts to conceal from other men and from God. A few sacrificial laws in Leviticus presuppose that there exist sins that are unconscious, or perhaps better, unintentional (Lev. 4:2, 13, 22; 5:2; etc.).

In most cases when a man prays for forgiveness of his sins, however, he is well aware that he has sinned: "For I know my transgressions, and my sin is ever before me" (Ps. 51:5 [Eng. 51:3]). A few psalms contain protestations that the speaker is not guilty, for example, Psalm 17:3-5:

> If thou triest my heart, if thou visitest me by night,
>> if thou testest me, thou wilt find no wickedness in me;
>> my mouth does not transgress.
> With regard to the works of men, by the word of thy lips
>> I have avoided the ways of the violent.
> My steps have held fast to thy paths,
>> my feet have not slipped.

Here there can surely be no question of unwitting sins. Protestations of innocence would be senseless if unconscious sin were possible. H. Schmidt has attempted to interpret these psalms (e.g., 7, 17, 26, 59) as prayers of the accused,[46] seeking to show that they have to do with specific transgressions of which the speaker knows he is innocent. Many have disputed this theory, however, and it cannot be considered definitely established.

The idea of uncleanness causes a further complication. The term "unclean" (*ṭāmē'*) applies to specific animals that must not be eaten or touched (Lev. 11; Deut. 14); to everything having to do with the sexual life (Lev. 15), with the reproduction process (II Sam. 11:14), and with the birth of children (Lev. 12); to the disease known as leprosy (Lev. 13 f.);[47] and to everything connected with death, such as corpses, graves, etc. (Num. 19:11-16).

Uncleanness is contagious. Whoever comes into contact with anything unclean becomes unclean himself (Lev. 5:2; 15:21-24; Num. 19:22; Hag. 2:13). One gains the impression that this uncleanness is something physical, a kind of external maculation that can be removed by ablutions.

Uncleanness is primarily a cultic and ritual concept. A man who is unclean cannot participate in the cult (Lev. 22:3, 6 f.; Num. 9:6; I Sam. 20:26); he cannot even take part in the normal life of the community without damaging its "integrity." In general, everything is unclean that is foreign to the Israelite community and its God. Everything alien, everything foreign, is unclean (Amos 7:17; Hos.

---

[46] H. Schmidt, *Das Gebet der Angeklagten im Alten Testament* (Giessen: Töpelmann, 1928).

[47] It is doubtful whether the actual disease of leprosy is meant; cf. L. Köhler, "Aussatz," *ZAW*, LXVII (1955), 290.

9:3); so is all idolatry and everything connected with it (Ezek. 22:3; Ps. 106:39; Jer. 2:7; 13:27).

A reading of the lists of unclean animals shows that they consist in part of those animals that other religions favor for sacrificial purposes, e.g., the camel and the pig (there is evidence for the sacrificial use of camels among the Arabs and of pigs among the Canaanites;[48] camels are nevertheless mentioned without comment in the patriarchal narratives, which may mean that their designation as unclean is the result of a later development). In other cases, e.g., in the realm of sex and death, the concept of uncleanness should probably be seen as a kind of taboo. It is very doubtful, however, whether holiness and uncleanness can be understood as deriving from a differentiation of an original taboo concept. In any case, within the Old Testament holiness and uncleanness are absolute opposites (see, for example, Isa. 6:3 f.; 35:8; 52:1, 11).[49] The only evidence for a connection between uncleanness and holiness is a late passage from the Mishnah (Yadayim 3:2 f.) that states that the Holy Scriptures "make the hands unclean." This must either represent a late contamination on the analogy that what is unclean must not be touched or else the simple idea that these writings are so holy that they automatically make the reader's hands seem unclean.[50]

Since uncleanness is injurious to the healthy integrity of society, it can on occasion be called sin or guilt, even when a man has become unclean through "contagion" and not deliberately (Lev. 5:2, 4; Num. 19:19). This constitutes the basis for the religious and ethical evaluation of uncleanness. In Isaiah 6:5, the prophet says that his lips are unclean, whereupon Yahweh forgives him his sins. The psalmist can say, "Wash me thoroughly from my iniquity" (Ps. 51:4 [Eng. 51:2]), as though sin were uncleanness.

In fact, both sin and uncleanness can be viewed as expressions of the hostile reality that permeates life, attempting again and again to penetrate the sphere of what is divine and good. There is, so to speak, a sphere of evil and death that continually threatens man's life: it is called uncleanness, sin, chaos.[51]

We are obviously dealing with two different concepts of sin, between which there exists a certain tension. The mechanistic conception supposes that every deliberate or accidental violation of God's commandments represents as it were a transgression of the limits set by

---

[48] R. de Vaux, "Les sacrifices de porcs en Palestine et dans l'Ancien Orient," in J. Hempel (ed.), *Von Ugarit nach Qumran* (Berlin: Töpelmann, 1958), pp. 250 ff.

[49] R. Dussaud, *Les origines cananéennes du sacrifice Israélite* (2nd ed.; Paris: Leroux, 1921), pp. 30 ff.; H. Ringgren, *The Prophetical Conception of Holiness* (Leipzig: Harrassowitz, 1948), pp. 14 ff.

[50] A. J. Fridrichsen, *Hagios-Qādōš*, 1916, p. 30.

[51] Pedersen, *op. cit.*, pp. 453 ff.; von Rad, *op. cit.*, pp. 277 f.

God and creates a "sphere of evil" that results in punishment and suffering.[52] The personal conception, on the other hand, implies that a man knows when he breaks the law, and therefore feels responsible. A complete harmonization of these two conceptions is probably impossible. The mechanistic view is found not only in "primitive" contexts, like ordinances relating to taboo and ritual purity, but also in cases where a heightened awareness of the holiness of God leads to recognition of man's total sinfulness.

This tension, moreover, does not eliminate man's complete responsibility for his actions. He has a choice between good and evil. The prophetical calls to repentance and to righteousness would make no sense if man were not a responsible being, possessed of free will.

The consequences of ethical actions have already been suggested in part. Even such a short resumé of ethical demands as the Decalogue contains promises: "Honor your father and your mother, that your days may be long in the land . . . " (Exod. 20:12). In other words, long life is the reward of obedience. The Old Testament views long life as one of God's greatest gifts (cf. Ps. 34:13 [Eng. 34:12]; 91:16) and looks upon a premature death as a great misfortune (Ps. 55:24 [Eng. 55:23]; 89:46 [Eng. 89:45]; Isa. 38:10). In Psalm 19:12b (Eng. 19:11b) we read, "In keeping them [the commandments] there is great reward." When Deuteronomy places before Israel the alternatives of obedience and disobedience, this means at the same time the choice between life and death, between blessing and curse (Deut. 28; 30:15 ff.).

As we have seen, the word ṣᵉdāqâ, "righteousness," originally included in its meaning the happy consequences of righteousness. We also have a whole series of other expressions that describe the blessings following upon righteousness. Two words in particular should be mentioned as terms for a prosperous and happy life: šālôm and bᵉrākâ.

The usual translation of šālôm is "peace," but this translation comes nowhere near exhausting the content of the term. This concept includes everything pertaining to a peaceful life. The basic meaning is something like integrity, intactness, harmony; but šālôm also means prosperity and happiness, victory and peace. It refers to the condition of perfect communion with God and man.[53]

The meaning of bᵉrākâ, "blessing," is even wider in scope, if such a thing is possible. It includes such concepts as numerous descendants, fertility, wealth, victory over foes, and success in general. Blessing is

---

[52] K. Koch, "Gibt es ein Vergeltungsdogma im Alten Testament?" *ZThK*, LII (1955), 1 ff.; but cf. F. Horst, "Recht und Religion im Bereich des Alten Testaments," *ETh*, XVI (1956), 71 ff., reprinted in *idem, Gottes Recht* (Munich: Kaiser, 1961), pp. 260 ff.

[53] Pedersen, *op. cit.,* pp. 243 ff.

therefore not a "spiritual" thing; it refers rather to the total wealth of a successful and happy life. In ancient Israel, the concept of blessing is very close to the "mana" of comparative religion, if the personal side of the concept of mana is emphasized. *Berākâ*, then, is man's excellence, his ability to achieve success.[54] It should not be forgotten, of course, that "blessing" does not stand as an independent entity; it is always viewed as the gift of God. No man possesses blessing in his own right. It is God's blessing that crowns man's work with success (e.g., Ps. 127:1).[55]

Evil is the result of sin. Blessing deserts the sinner. All kinds of suffering come upon him. The speakers of the psalms of lament conceive of their suffering in terms of God's hand being upon them to punish them for their sins: "For day and night thy hand was upon me" (Ps. 32:4a). We read in Psalm 38:4-6 (Eng. 38:3-5):

> There is no soundness in my flesh
> because of thy indignation;
> There is no health in my bones
> because of my sin.
> For my iniquities have gone over my head;
> they weigh like a burden too heavy for me.
> My wounds grow foul and fester
> because of my foolishness.

When Job suffers, his friends conclude from his calamity that he has sinned (especially in chapters 4, 15, and 18), for example:

> Yea, the light of the wicked is put out,
> and the flame of his fire does not shine.
> . . . .
> His strength is hunger-bitten,
> and calamity is ready for his stumbling. (Job 18:5, 12)

Psalm 37:38 expresses the same idea:

> But transgressors shall be altogether destroyed;
> the posterity of the wicked shall be cut off.

In the Israelite view, then, there is an inexorable connection between a man's actions and the state of his life,[56] a connection interpreted in most cases as the consequence of divine retribution:

> . . . for I Yahweh your God am a jealous God, visiting the iniquity of the fathers upon the children to the third and the

---

[54] Cf. the analysis by Pedersen, *ibid.,* pp. 140 ff.

[55] Ringgren, *Faith of the Psalmists,* pp. 32 f.

[56] This expression comes from Koch, *op. cit.,* pp. 6, 25; cf. H. Gese, *Lehre und Wirklichkeit in der alten Weisheit* (Tübingen: Mohr, 1958), pp. 33 ff.

fourth generation of those who hate me, but showing steadfast love to thousands of those who love me and keep my commandments.[57] (Exod. 20:5 f.)

The introductions to the blessings and curses in Deuteronomy 28 proclaim the same principle:

> And if you obey the voice of Yahweh your God, being careful to do all his commandments which I command you this day, Yahweh your God will set you high above all the nations of the earth. . . . But if you will not obey the voice of Yahweh your God or be careful to do all his commandments and his statutes which I command you this day, then all these curses shall come upon you and overtake you. (Deut. 28:1, 15)

The righteous man is like a tree that has plenty of water and always remains green, we read in Psalm 1:3 and Jeremiah 17:8, a simile also encountered in Egyptian literature.[58] The wicked man, on the other hand, is like a shrub in the desert or in the parched places of the wilderness (Jer. 17:6). The writer of Job summarizes this entire conception:

> For according to the work of a man he will requite him,
> and according to his ways he will make it befall him.
>
> (Job 34:11)

Psalm 103:10 presupposes the same basic principle. When the poet says that Yahweh does not deal with men according to their sins, it means that Yahweh is expected to take vengeance upon them for their sins. The fact that he does not do so, but rather forgives them, is the result of his mercy. In the proverbial literature the connection between a man's actions and the state of his life appears most strongly as a manifestation of the order that informs the world; there is no express mention of God at all.[59] In Proverbs 12:14, for example, we read:

> From the fruit of his words a man is satisfied with good,
> and the work of a man's hands comes back to him.

Even here, though, God ultimately stands behind the order of the world.[60]

The theory of a connection between a man's actions and the state of his life is also a source of difficulty. The realities of human life cannot always be reduced to these categories. The success of the

---

[57] Or: ". . . showing steadfast love to the thousandth generation of those who love me. . . ."

[58] "The Instruction of Amen-em-opet," chap. iv., *ANET,* p. 422.

[59] Gese, *op. cit.,* pp. 33 ff.

[60] H. Skladny, *Die ältesten Spruchsammlungen in Israel* (Göttingen: Vandenhoeck & Ruprecht, 1962), pp. 7 ff., 21 ff., 29 ff., 58 f.

wicked becomes a problem for faith. Persecuted by his enemies, Jeremiah asks his God:

> Why does the way of the wicked prosper?
>> Why do all who are treacherous thrive?
> Thou plantest them, and they take root;
>> they grow and bring forth fruit. (Jer. 12:1b-2a)

This question grows out of the personal experience of the prophet: he knows that he is commissioned to speak by Yahweh; but still success comes not to him, but to his enemies.

Psalm 73 deals with the same problem.[61] The psalmist is enraged at the boasting of the godless; he is beside himself when he sees how they live without pain and suffering.

> They are not in trouble as other men are;
>> they are not stricken like other men.
> Therefore pride is their necklace;
>> violence covers them as a garment.
>
> . . . .
>
> Behold, these are the wicked;
>> always at ease, they increase in riches.
> All in vain have I kept my heart clean
>> and washed my hands in innocence.
> For all the day long 1 have been stricken,
>> and chastened every morning. (Ps. 73:5 f., 12-14)

A cultic experience provides a solution for the poet:

> . . . until I went into the sanctuary of God;[62]
>> then I perceived their end. (Ps. 73:17)

In the Temple he saw how the enemies of God—and that is what the wicked of this psalm are—ultimately perish. We may have here a reference to a cultic drama. The poet nevertheless does not rejoice in the final defeat of the godless, but in his communion with God:

> Nevertheless I am continually with thee;
>> thou dost hold my right hand.
>
> . . . .
>
> Whom have I in heaven but thee?
>> And there is nothing upon earth that I desire besides thee. (Ps. 73:23, 25)

---

[61] H. Ringgren, "Einige Bemerkungen zum lxxiii. Psalm," *VT,* III (1953), 265 ff.; idem, *Faith of the Psalmists,* pp. 72 f.

[62] The translation "until I understood God's holy mysteries" (R. Kittel, M. Buber, and others) is impossible; cf. the material mentioned in the preceding note.

God is everything to him, and worth more than any kind of success. Thus the problem is solved in striking fashion, for this communion with God remains basically undisturbed by the success or failure of the wicked.

An entire book, the Book of Job,[63] focuses on this theme. Its date is disputed—it is usually considered postexilic—but the problem as such surely was already present in pre-exilic times, and actually there are no really compelling reasons for assigning a late date to the entire book.

From the purely formal point of view, the book comprises a narrative prologue in prose, a poetic central section containing a conversation between Job and his friends, and a concluding narrative in prose. Closer observation shows that a certain ideological difference exists between the prose narratives and the dialogue. This difference is presumably due to the fact that the author of the dialogue used an earlier narrative as a framework. This original Job narrative probably told how, at the suggestion of the heavenly accuser (Heb. $śāṭān$), God put the righteous and successful Job to the test, in order to see whether he served God only because "it paid." Job is subjected to all kinds of misfortune; he loses his property and his children, and finally is afflicted with a terrible skin disease. He laments his fate, but maintains his righteousness. In the present form of the book, the dialogue follows next; but the original continuation must have told how Job humbled himself before Yahweh and finally was restored to his original condition.[64] In any case, the conclusion of the book tells how he was restored to health, and how renewed prosperity and more children were granted to him. This original Job legend may not even have originated in Israel; the action takes place in Edom[65] or Transjordan.[66] The legend obviously belongs to a literary type of which we have many examples from Sumerian literature: the answered lament. A man is afflicted with suffering, he humbles himself, prays for mercy, and is restored.[67]

The author of the book of Job, however, used this legend for his own special purposes. He is concerned to show how, on the basis of his experiences, Job comes to question the righteousness of God and finally learns that man, a creature, has no legal claim on God, the creator. The dialogue begins with Job's lament:

---

[63] Among the more recent literature are: C. Kuhl, "Vom Hiobbuche und seinen Problemen," *ThR*, XXII (1954), 261 ff.; Gese, *op. cit.*, pp. 51 ff.; H. H. Rowley, "The Book of Job and its Meaning," *BJRL*, XLI (1958), 167 ff.; M. Crook, *The Cruel God* (Boston: Beacon, 1959); cf. also Pedersen, *op. cit.*, pp. 363 ff.

[64] Gese, *op. cit.*, p. 73.

[65] Cf. J. Lindblom, *La composition du livre de Job* (Lund: Gleerup, 1944/45).

[66] Cf. F. Horst, *Hiob* (Neukirchen: Erziehungsverein, 1960), pp. 7 f.

[67] Gese, *op. cit.*, pp. 63 ff., 74 ff.

> Let the day perish wherein I was born,
>   and the night which said,
>   'A man-child is conceived.'
>
> ....
>
> Why did I not die at birth,
>   come forth from the womb and expire? (Job. 3:3, 11)

"Why was I born, since my life is nothing but suffering?" asks Job. At this point his three friends, Eliphaz, Bildad, and Zophar, come to "comfort" him. With minor variations, they all represent the "orthodox" doctrine of retribution: whoever suffers has sinned; his suffering is his punishment. Job must only recognize his sin and confess it; then he will be restored. Before God, no man is pure, no mortal righteous. The right is on Yahweh's side when he is angry with man. When Job acknowledges his sin, Yahweh will forgive him. Job, however, maintains his righteousness. He is unaware of any serious sin that could justify so cruel a torment. In other words, he casts doubt on the righteousness of God. He suggests that God is punishing him without any reason. In the course of the dialogue, he demands an accounting of God and the justice due him:

> How many are my iniquities and my sins?
>   Make me know my transgression and my sin.
> Why dost thou hide thy face,
>   and count me as thy enemy? (Job 13:23 f.)
> Know then that God has put me in the wrong,
>   and closed his net about me.
> Behold, I cry out, 'Violence!' but I am not answered;
>   I call aloud, but there is no justice. (Job 19:6 f.)

He points out that God by no means requites the wicked for their sin:

> Why do the wicked live,
>   reach old age, and grow mighty in power?
>
> ....
>
> How often is it that the lamp of the wicked is put out?
>   That their calamity comes upon them? (Job 21:7, 17)

The wicked continue their sport, they achieve success, God does not punish them, he does not seem to worry about them.

In a concluding speech Job looks back upon his earlier prosperity and compares it to his present misfortune (chapters 29-30). With an oath of purgation (chapter 31) he affirms his innocence and demands to hear God's defense:

> Oh, that I had one to hear me!
>   Here is my signature! let the Almighty answer me!
>   (Job 31:35)

At this point in the present book we have the speech of a fourth friend, Elihu. Probably it is an interpolation. It merely repeats the arguments of the other friends, with the single exception of emphasizing the disciplinary value of suffering. Then follows God's answer. He speaks to Job out of a whirlwind, i.e., in a theophany. But strangely he does not discuss Job's questions at all. Instead, he reproves Job for having rebelled against his creator.

> Where were you when I laid the foundation of the earth?
>   Tell me, if you have understanding.
> Who determined its measurements—surely you know!
>   Or who stretched the line upon it?
> . . . .
> Have you commanded the morning since your days began,
>   and caused the dawn to know its place? (Job 38:4, 5, 12)

By means of several examples taken from nature and the animal world, God demonstrates his incomparable power, greatness, and wisdom. There is perhaps also another idea in the background, the idea that God cares for all creatures, even those that seem to serve no useful purpose; for the examples chosen (mountain goat, wild ass, wild ox, ostrich, etc.) are not exactly the animals most important to man.

Although God's answer obviously fails to provide any real solution to the problem, Job's response implies that he no longer has any questions:

> I know that thou canst do all things,
>   and that no purpose of thine can be thwarted. . . .
> Therefore I have uttered what I did not understand,
>   things too wonderful for me, which I did not know.
> . . . .
> I had heard of thee by the hearing of the ear,
>   but now my eye sees thee;
> therefore I despise myself,
>   and repent in dust and ashes.   (Job 42:2 f., 5 f.)

The only solution of the problem seems therefore to be that man must submit to God's omnipotence. God is greater and wiser than man; no one understands his ways, no one can question his righteousness. Any man who claims to be able to pass judgment upon God's ways shows himself guilty of scandalous presumption. Man's proper course is rather to cease from all questioning and accept whatever comes from God's hand.

On the surface, the author seems to forego any real solution. Possibly, though, he may have ventured somewhat beyond this point, if only by way of suggestion. Occasionally he emphasizes God's wisdom and the purposeful design of creation. Does this not suggest that God knows better than his creatures and cares for everything, even if man is unable to comprehend his ways in detail? We may note, furthermore, that God appears to Job in his suffering. This might mean that man's suffering does not separate him from God—since it is not necessarily *punishment*—that communion with God is possible even in suffering.[68] This theory is consonant with the observation that only later is Job's previous good fortune restored.

This discussion should make it clear that the book of Job is unique, both literarily and ideologically. The Sumerian and Akkadian texts that are often quoted for comparison are only parallels in the sense that they deal with the suffering of a righteous man; their solution of the problem is completely different.[69] The so-called Sumerian Job ("Man and his God") tells of a man who had been rich and happy and was then afflicted with disease and suffering. In his misery he turned to his god, who saved and restored the sufferer.[70] As Gese has shown, what we have here is a "paradigm of the answered lament," in which the sufferer humbles himself before his god and is saved.[71] The Babylonian poem *Ludlul bēl nēmēqi* ("I will Praise the Lord of Wisdom"),[72] frequently called the Babylonian Job, belongs to the same type). It is actually the thanksgiving of a righteous sufferer, who was informed through dreams that he was about to be delivered.[73] An Old Babylonian poem, first published in 1952, follows the same pattern.[74] In many respects, the "Babylonian Theodicy"[75] is closest to Job. This text presents a conversation between a man struck by misfortune, who states that the gods do not reward righteousness and devotion, and his friend, who defends the gods. No actual solution is provided; at the end, the two friends have only decided that the gods have created man in such a way that he does evil.

All this shows that the problem discussed by the Book of Job must sooner or later come up wherever the idea of divine retribution is dominant, for the theory does not agree with the facts of human life. The problem is all the more aggravated in Israel because it coincides with the disintegration of the primitive Israelite concept of *ṣᵉdāqâ*.[76]

---

[68] This opinion is supported by Rowley, *op. cit.*, pp. 201 ff.

[69] See Gese's discussion, *op. cit.*, pp. 51 ff.

[70] S. N. Kramer, "Man and his God," *SVT*, III (1955), 170 ff.; Gese, *op. cit.*, pp. 61 ff.

[71] Gese, *op. cit.*, pp. 51 ff.

[72] Most recently translated and discussed by W. G. Lambert, *Babylonian Wisdom Literature* (Oxford: Clarendon, 1960), pp. 21 ff.

[73] It is therefore not a royal passion psalm, as suggested by I. Engnell, *Studies in Divine Kingship* (Uppsala: Almqvist & Wiksell, 1943), p. 48. The figure of the king is quite distinct from the "I" of this poem (I, 55 f.).

[74] *RB*, LIX (1952), 239 ff.; Gese, *op. cit.*, p. 58.

[75] Lambert, *op. cit.*, pp. 63 ff.

[76] Pedersen, *op. cit.*, pp. 292 f.

8.

THE CULT

a. Source-problems

Since the historical books give us only incidental information about ritual matters, two groups of texts are of primary importance as sources for our knowledge of the Israelite cult: the laws regulating the cult, and the psalms. The problems posed by each group are completely different.

Most of the cultic laws assumed their present form only in the exilic or postexilic period. Extreme caution is therefore necessary when they are used to reconstruct the pre-exilic cult. Many of them definitely contain very ancient material, but their final redaction is late. In particular, much seems to have been omitted of what the psalms and occasionally also the historical books indicate was pre-exilic practice. Furthermore, these laws by no means provide exhaustive descriptions of all cultic actions. They do not even present a complete, detailed account of the sacrifices which they represent as the basis of the Israelite cult.

The psalms come from diverse periods, and fixing the date of a particular psalm is frequently very complicated. In recent decades, there has been a swing away from the former tendency to ascribe most psalms to the postexilic period, or even the Maccabean period. Today most of the psalms are dated in the pre-exilic period. But even if we have a great number of psalms to draw on for our discussion of the pre-exilic cult, another difficulty still remains. The psalms do not contain any regulations for the conduct of the ritual; they simply assume a knowledge of the cultic ceremonies. As a result, these ceremonies can be determined only indirectly.

The most interesting question in the interpretation of the psalms concerns the possibility of reconstructing cultic practices for which we have no evidence except those psalms that cannot be immediately assigned to the usual *Gattungen*[1] (see below) or else constitute par-

---

[1] [This term, introduced by Gunkel some sixty years ago, refers to the various "types" or "categories" into which the psalms and other Old Testa-

ticular subgroups within these *Gattungen.* There is every reason to call certain psalms (e.g., Ps. 24) liturgies, since they were obviously recited by several speakers in the course of worship. Others contain clear references to cultic ceremonies, even though they do not permit a complete reconstruction of the ritual. Anyone convinced that the psalms must basically be taken as cultic poetry must ask continually what cultic ceremonies the psalms accompanied. When the psalms are interpreted as outpourings of individual piety, many expressions in them must be understood figuratively. If taken literally, these same expressions can furnish valuable hints as to cultic ceremonies. References to the Temple, to sacrifices or purification rites, to seeing God or his mighty works—these can be interpreted either literally or figuratively. When a psalmist says, "[I was bitter] until I went into the sanctuary of God" (Ps. 73:17), there is no need to make his statement refer to comprehension of God's holy counsels or his "holy governance."[2] The words can be understood quite literally to refer to visiting the Temple. When another psalmist prays, "Wash me thoroughly from my iniquity, and cleanse me from my sin. . . . Fill me with [literally: let me hear] joy and gladness" (Ps. 51:3, 9 [Eng. 51:2, 8]), he is quite possibly referring to purification rites and a divine oracle. Another psalmist extols those who have "ways" in their heart (Ps. 84:6 [Eng. 84:5]). This expression has long been thought to refer to the love of the ways (i.e., the works) of God, although the Hebrew word means very concretely "highway" or "processional way." A statement like: "We shall be satisfied with the goodness of thy house" (Ps. 65:5 [Eng. 65:4]) points quite specifically to a sacrificial meal; it is quite out of place in this context to think of emotional experiences in the course of worship in the Temple.

Unfortunately, however, such hints are frequently ambiguous or can at least refer to various situations. They can be placed in their proper cultic setting only when comparative material from outside the Bible is adduced. Such comparison must be made with extreme caution so as to avoid reading into the psalms ideas and cultic ceremonies alien to the Israelite religion. The prevailing disagreement as to the cultic interpretation of the psalms is due in large measure to differing estimations of the extrabiblical material.[3]

As for the historical books, they refer to the cult more or less only in passing, and consequently provide in most cases a very fragmentary

---

ment literature fall. Since it has become a technical term referring to this particular type of interpretation, it is here left untranslated.—TRANS.]

[2] These are the translations of the Swedish Bible and the *Zürcher Bibel,* respectively.

[3] Cf. A. R. Johnson, "The Psalms," in H. H. Rowley (ed.), *The Old Testament and Modern Study* (London: Oxford, 1951), pp. 162 ff.; J. J. Stamm, "Ein Vierteljahrhundert Psalmenforschung," *ThR,* XXIII (1955), 1 ff.

picture. Even when all three sources are combined and compared with extrabiblical material, it is impossible to give a complete description of the Israelite cult. This state of affairs has naturally led to many hypotheses. In discussing these questions, therefore, we must always distinguish carefully between demonstrable facts and more or less probable hypotheses.

b. Cult and Piety

What is the significance of the cult for the religion of Israel in general, and for individual piety in particular?[4] The psalms provide abundant answer to this question. They project a vivid picture of Israelite piety and its relationship to the cult. Quell has pursued this problem,[5] but his study suffers from an exaggerated dichotomy between cult and individual piety. He looks upon the cult as something basically distinct from piety, presupposing a concept of piety represented by certain modern tendencies. In reality, however, the cult is an expression of piety; conversely, the cult nourishes and encourages the piety of the individual. There is by no means a basic dichotomy between cult and piety; what we have is rather a productive mutual interaction between the two. It is therefore impossible to follow Quell in singling out certain elements of the psalms as cultic and even detrimental to piety, at the same time judging other elements to be expressions of "pure" (i.e., noncultic) piety.[6] The Israelite piety that we meet in the psalms and occasionally also in other texts is by its very nature cultic piety, and must be understood in this light.[7]

The Temple plays a basic role in the psalms. "Yahweh is in his holy temple" (Ps. 11:4); there is his dwelling place (Ps. 26:8; 46:5 [Eng. 46:4]; 74:2; 132:13 f.). In his sanctuary he reveals himself to the assembled worshipers:

Out of Zion, the perfection of beauty,
God shines forth.
Our God comes, he does not keep silence,
before him is a devouring fire,
round about him a mighty tempest. (Ps. 50:2-3)
Honor and majesty are before him;
strength and beauty are in his sanctuary. (Ps. 96:6)

Therefore another psalmist can say:

So I have looked upon thee in the sanctuary,
beholding thy power and glory. (Ps. 63:3 [Eng. 63:2])

---

[4] For a discussion of this question, see H. Ringgren, *The Faith of the Psalmists* (Philadelphia: Fortress, 1963), pp. xviii ff.
[5] G. Quell, *Das kultische Problem der Psalmen* (Stuttgart: Kohlhammer, 1926).
[6] See Ringgren, *op. cit.*, for a full discussion of this point.
[7] The following remarks are a summary of the first chapter of Ringgren, *op. cit.*

In other words, Yahweh is present in the Temple with his glory (*kābôd*). Significantly, the Temple is also the location of Isaiah's vision and call; here he perceives the glory of Yahweh. This idea of "glory" may be connected with a particular theophany rite; the important thing, however, is that Yahweh's presence plays a supremely important role.

The author of Psalm 84 says:

> My soul longs, yea, faints
> for the courts of Yahweh;
> my heart and flesh sing for joy
> to the living God. (Ps. 84:3 [Eng. 84:2])

It is noteworthy that the "courts of Yahweh" and the "living God" are put in parallel: the psalmist makes no essential distinction between the two. He longs for the courts of the Temple because his God is there. The courts themselves are not important by virtue of their objective holiness, but as the place of the divine presence. Similarly, the author of Psalm 42—43 prays:

> Oh send out thy light and thy truth;
> let them lead me,
> let them bring me to thy holy hill
> and to thy dwelling!
> Then I will go to the altar of God,
> to God my exceeding joy. (Ps. 43:3 f.)

Once again, "altar" and "God" are used almost synonymously: the altar is the place of God's presence, the place of sacrificial worship.

These observations immediately help us to understand the many expressions of love for the Temple and joy in it, for example:

> Yahweh, I love the habitation of thy house,
> and the place where thy glory dwells. (Ps. 26:8)
> I was glad when they said to me,
> "Let us go to the house of Yahweh!" (Ps. 122:1)
> One thing have I asked of Yahweh,
> that will I seek after;
> that I may dwell in the house of Yahweh
> all the days of my life,
> to behold the beauty of Yahweh,
> and to inquire [?] in his temple. (Ps. 27:4)

Unfortunately, we no longer know the concrete meaning of "beholding the beauty [*nō'am*] of Yahweh," and the precise significance of "inquire" (*baqqēr*) remains obscure.[8] One thing, however, is

---

[8] A. Haldar, *Associations of Cult Prophets among the Ancient Semites* (Uppsala: Almqvist & Wiksell, 1945), p. 102, interprets the verse as referring to receiving oracles.

certain: what the worshiper experienced in the Temple filled him with joy and strength. Consequently he yearned for the Temple and its worship. Therefore we also read:

> Blessed is he whom thou dost choose and bring near,
> to dwell in thy courts!
> We shall be satisfied with the goodness of thy house,
> thy holy temple! (Ps. 65:5 [Eng. 65:4])

Here we may have a reference to sacrificial meals ("be satisfied"), just as in Psalm 36:9 (Eng. 36:8):

> They feast on the abundance of thy house,
> and thou givest them drink from the river of thy delights.

In the sacrificial meal, the nearness of God is experienced as a reality. God himself shares in the meal, entering into the most intimate association with those who offer the sacrifice.

In one prayer, the psalmist first proclaims his assurance that the evildoers and the boastful shall not stand before Yahweh; he then continues:

> But I through the abundance of thy steadfast love
> will enter thy house,
> I will worship toward thy holy temple
> in the fear of thee. (Ps. 5:8 [Eng. 5:7])

In other words, God rejects the evildoers, but in his steadfast love gives to the pious worshiper in the Temple the treasure denied to those whom he "abhors" (vs. 7 [Eng. vs. 6]).

Psalm 84 also expresses love for the Temple: "How lovely is thy dwelling place, O Yahweh of hosts! My soul longs, yea, faints for the courts of Yahweh." The same psalmist goes on to describe the sense of security he feels in God's house:

> Even the sparrow finds a home,
> and the swallow a nest for herself,
> where she may lay her young,
> at thy altars, O Yahweh of hosts,
> my king and my God,
> Blessed are those who dwell in thy house,
> ever singing thy praise! (Ps. 84:4 f. [Eng. 84:3 f.])

Therefore, says the psalmist, "A day in thy courts is better than a thousand elsewhere." He would rather be a doorkeeper in the house of God than "in the tents of wickedness." The basic mood of the cult is joy. This joy finds expression in music:

> Sing aloud to God our strength;
> shout for joy to the God of Jacob!
> Raise a song, sound the timbrel,
> the sweet lyre with the harp.

Blow the trumpet at the new moon,
    at the full moon, on our feast day.
For it is a statute for Israel,
    an ordinance of the God of Jacob.

(Ps. 81:2-5 [Eng. 81:1-4])

The day of festival is "the day which Yahweh has made; let us rejoice and be glad in it," we read in another psalm (Ps. 118:24). This joyful mood of praise and worship dominates most of the festal hymns:

O come, let us sing to Yahweh,
    let us make a joyful noise to the rock of our salvation!
Let us come into his presence with thanksgiving;
    let us make a joyful noise to him with songs of praise!

(Ps. 95:1 f.)

Serve Yahweh with gladness!
Come into his presence with singing!
. . . .

Enter his gates with thanksgiving,
    and his courts with praise!   (Ps. 100:2, 4)

The prophet Isaiah alludes to this mood of joy when he speaks of the coming time of salvation, describing it as a joyous feast:[9] "You shall have a song as in the night when a holy feast is kept; and gladness of heart, as when one sets out to the sound of the flute to go to the mountain of Yahweh, to the Rock of Israel" (Isa. 30:29). Significantly, the next verse describes how God causes his voice to be heard (cf. Ps. 29) and appears for judgment—all motifs belonging to the festival of Yahweh's kingship.

c. The Cultic Sites

As we have seen,[10] the older traditions of Israel know of a number of places where cultic worship was offered to Yahweh. Many narratives, especially in the patriarchal stories, are intended to explain and justify the holiness of these sites. Because Abraham or Jacob offered sacrifice in a certain place, that place is appropriate for cultic ceremonial in Yahweh's honor. At Beer-sheba in southern Palestine Abraham planted a tamarisk and called on the name of Yahweh (Gen. 21:33); at Bethel Jacob had a remarkable dream and set up a stone pillar as a holy symbol (Gen. 28:10 ff.); etc. There is evidence, including Amos 5:5, that these two cities were cultic sites in the

---

[9] Despite the hesitation of many scholars, this passage is probably genuine; see G. Fohrer, *Das Buch Jesaja* (Göttingen: Vandenhoeck & Ruprecht, 1962), II, 106 f.

[10] See above, pp. 49 f., with a bibliography on the history of the various cultic sites.

period of the monarchy; Amos, in fact, censures the cult practiced there in the strongest terms. Amos also mentions Gilgal, in the Jordan Valley, where, according to Joshua 4, twelve stones were set up when the Israelites crossed the Jordan. These stones obviously served some cultic function. Other holy sites included Shiloh, where the ark was located for a while. In all probability, the Philistines destroyed this site around the end of the period of the Judges (I Sam. 1—3; cf. Jer. 7:12). In the Canaanite period, Shechem already possessed a shrine of Baal-berith ("Baal of the Covenant"), according to Judges 9:4. Later on, it sheltered the ark for a while. Deuteronomy still bears witness to its being a Yahwistic cultic site. During the time of Saul and David, an important shrine was located at Nob, in the tribe of Benjamin. David several times obtained oracles there; later, however, it was destroyed by Saul (I Sam. 21—22). Even Solomon, who built the Jerusalem Temple, still offered sacrifice at Gibeon (I Kings 3:4).

These cultic sites are the large and important ones. There were many others besides, about which we have no detailed information. There can be no doubt that the Israelites very often took over Canaanite shrines and worshiped Yahweh at them. The Old Testament calls such sites "high places" (Heb. *bāmâ*, pl. *bāmôt*). The basic meaning of this word is probably "back," "ridge," or "elevation." It was applied to what had once been Canaanite shrines, laid out in the open air upon hills or knolls. In a few cases, the word seems to mean "funerary mound"; and it is possible that ancestor worship was occasionally practiced at these sites.[11]

A high place consisted primarily of three things: an altar for sacrifice; a stone pillar (*maṣṣēbâ*), which in the Canaanite religion served as a symbol of the masculine divinity; and a wooden post (*ăšērâ*), symbol of the mother-goddess of fertility. The latter word corresponds linguistically to the name of the Amorite and Canaanite goddess Ashirtu or Athirat.[12]

The findings of archaeology confirm the picture reconstructed from the literary sources: altars and massebahs have been unearthed at several sites, while the asherahs have naturally decayed. When several stone pillars stand in a row, as at Gezer, we may be dealing with funerary shrines. There are examples illustrating the use of a massebah as a funerary monument (II Sam. 18:18).

The Old Testament, especially the prophets and the Deuteronomistic history, witnesses to the presence of high places with asherahs and massebahs throughout the entire period of the monarchy, con-

[11] W. F. Albright, "The High Place in Ancient Palestine," *SVT*, IV (1957), 242 ff.; cf. also R. Amiran, "The Tumuli West of Jerusalem," *IEJ*, VIII (1958), 205 ff.

[12] R. de Vaux, *Ancient Israel*, trans. John McHugh (New York: McGraw-Hill, 1961), pp. 284 ff.; for a discussion of the Asherah, see W. L. Reed, *The Ashera in the Old Testament*, 1949.

demning them as symptoms of a corrupt, syncretistic cult. To the extent that the cultic objects in question are of Canaanite origin, this judgment is correct. Presumably, however, the worship at these sites was not directed to Canaanite divinities, or at least not exclusively to them, but also to Yahweh. In any case, the high places suggest a syncretistic pattern of thought.

The Canaanite shrines also included trees. In a land like Palestine, almost completely without trees, a green tree was an obvious symbol of life and fertility. The shrine was therefore located in a grove, or else a tree grew upon the high place. This tree often had an oracular function. The cultic background of such trees is the point of departure for the accusation frequently made by the prophets in their polemic, that the Israelites worshiped idols "under every green tree." Obviously the prophets saw in these trees symbols of the Canaanite fertility cult.

Buildings serving specifically as temples probably existed only in a few exceptional instances. There was a temple at Bethel in the Northern Kingdom, known as "the king's sanctuary" (I Kings 12:31; Amos 7:13). I Samuel 9:22 mentions a "hall" (liškâ) for sacrificial meals. For the period of Samuel, I Samuel 1:9 and 3:3 mention a temple at Shiloh; but this may be an anachronism.

Only through the efforts of Solomon did Israel come to have a real temple as a central sanctuary. David had set up a tent in Jerusalem for the ark (II Sam. 6); but, if we can believe the biblical tradition, Nathan the prophet prevented him from carrying out his plan to build a temple (II Sam. 7). Solomon, the great builder, transformed this plan into reality.

The ground on which the Temple was erected had been purchased by David from Araunah the Jebusite; it had previously served as a threshing floor (II Sam. 24:15-25). Now threshing floors have had a cultic function since time immemorial; it is therefore possible that this area had long been considered holy.[13] A late tradition (II Chron. 3:1) equates the mountain on which the Temple was built with Mount Moriah, where, according to Genesis 22, Abraham was prepared to sacrifice his son Isaac. This tradition cannot be proved correct, however, particularly since Genesis 22 gives an explanation, not of "Moriah," but of some other name.

The Temple of Solomon[14] was built by Phoenician workmen. It

---

[13] G. Ahlström, "Nathan und der Tempelbau," *VT*, XI (1961), 115 ff.
[14] De Vaux, *op. cit.*, pp. 312 ff.; E. L. Ehrlich, *Kultsymbolik im Alten Testament und im nachbiblischen Judentum* (Stuttgart: Hiersemann, 1959), pp. 24 ff.; see also K. Möhlenbrink, *Der Tempel Salomos* (Stuttgart: Kohlhammer, 1932); W. F. Albright, *Archeology and the Religion of Israel* (4th ed.; Baltimore: Johns Hopkins, 1956), pp. 142 ff.; A. Parrot, *The Temple of Jesusalem*, trans. B. E. Hooke (London: SCM, 1957); G. E. Wright, *Biblical Archaeology* (2nd ed.; Philadelphia: Westminster, 1962), pp. 137 ff.

seems appropriate, therefore, to consider Phoenician prototypes.[15] This conjecture may be correct for a few details, but in general the dominant characteristics seem to be those of Canaan and the ancient Near East in general.

The Temple of Solomon (I Kings 6) was a rectangular building consisting of a vestibule (ûlām or êlām) and two rooms, one behind the other. The first of the two rooms was called hêkāl or qōdeš ("the holy place"); the second was called dᵉbîr ("the back room") or qōdeš haqqŏdāšîm ("the most holy place" or "the Holy of Holies"). The word hêkāl, which sometimes also refers to the entire Temple, is of Sumerian origin: e gal means literally "great house," and can refer either to a palace or a temple. The closest parallel to the floor plan of the Jerusalem Temple is provided by a ninth century temple at Tell Tainat in northern Syria, and in part by the recently discovered temple at Hazor, a Canaanite city in Galilee.[16]

In front of the entrance to the vestibule there stood two bronze pillars, bearing the names Jachin and Boaz. The significance of these pillars unfortunately remains unknown. The capitals were decorated in the form of lilies or lotus blossoms, which are encountered elsewhere as religious symbols. The bodies of the pillars were decorated with garlands of pomegranates, which recalls the role of pomegranates in the fertility cult. Some scholars see in these pillars the two cosmic pillars,[17] others take them as symbols of the two mountains between which the sun rises,[18] and still others as symbols of fertility, e.g., stylized massebahs or sacred trees.[19] All such conjectures are of course very precarious, since not a single word in our sources touches on the significance of the pillars. Three facts only are more or less definite. First, we are dealing with free-standing pillars at the entrance to the Temple; such pillars are relatively common in Syria, Phoenicia, and Cyprus in the first millennium B.C.[20] Second, the symbolism of the ornamentation is rooted in the fertility cults—although it is of course quite possible that their connection with these cults had been forgotten

---

[15] See, e.g., H. G. May, "Some Aspects of Solar Worship at Jerusalem," ZAW, LV (1937), 269.

[16] Y. Yadin, "Excavations at Hazor," IEJ, VIII (1958), 11 f.; idem, "The Fourth Season of Excavations at Hazor," SEÅ, XXIV (1959), 24 ff. [See also idem, "Excavations at Hazor." in D. N. Freedman and E. F. Campbell, Jr. (ed.), The Biblical Archaeologist Reader, 2 (Garden City: Doubleday, 1964), pp. 215 ff.—TRANS.] According to a communication from Professor G. Ernest Wright, this Middle Bronze Temple at Hazor had originally only two rooms; the impression of a third room is created by a tower that was added in the Late Bronze Age.

[17] Ehrlich, op. cit., p. 25.

[18] Albright, op. cit., p. 144.

[19] I. Engnell, The Call of Isaiah (Uppsala: Lundeqvist, 1949), pp. 35, 50, following R. B. Y. Scott, "The Pillars of Jachin and Boaz," JBL, LVIII (1939), 143 ff.

[20] Albright, op. cit., p. 144.

in Israel and at the time of Solomon. Third, there must have been some special meaning attached to the names of the pillars; here, however, we must rely once more on conjecture. In my opinion, a suggestion made by R. B. Y. Scott deserves special consideration.[21] He sees in the names the first words of two dynastic oracles written upon the pillars. The wording would be something like "Yahweh will establish [yākîn] your throne forever" and "In the strength [be'ôz] of Yahweh shall the king rejoice." Since the Temple of Solomon was a royal chapel connected with the palace, this suggestion seems quite likely. Admittedly, though, our sources never mention any inscription on the pillars; and for Boaz this interpretation requires the revocalization of the name. According to the book of Ruth, furthermore, one of David's ancestors was also named Boaz.

In the hêkāl, which measured approximately ten by twenty meters, stood a golden altar for incense offerings, a table for the bread of the Presence, and ten lampstands. (The bread of the Presence or "showbread" consisted of twelve loaves of unleavened bread, which were placed on the table "before the face of Yahweh" every Sabbath; hence the name leḥem pānîm, "bread of the face." After a week, it was eaten by the priests. It was probably considered a kind of sacrifice. Babylonian ritual tablets mention placing twelve, twenty-four, or thirty-six loaves of unleavened bread before the images of the gods.)[22]

The inner chamber had the form of a windowless cube ten meters on each side. In it stood the ark of the covenant, flanked by two cherubim with their wings outstretched to guard it.[23] Other temples of the ancient Near East had a cella containing the image of a god corresponding to this inner chamber. Since images of God were unknown in the religion of Israel, the ark represented the presence of God.

Traditionally the ark has been accorded a dual significance: it has been interpreted either as the empty throne of Yahweh or as a chest in which the tables of the law were preserved. According to De Vaux, both ideas could be right: Egyptian documents show that treaty documents were preserved at the foot of a divine image.[24] It is probable, however, that two theories have been combined here.

---

[21] Op. cit. A similar theory is represented by W. Kornfeld, "Der Symbolismus der Tempelsäulen," ZAW, LXXIV (1962), 50 ff. (". . . are intended . . . to express symbolically . . . the permanence of both the Temple and the dynasty," p. 57).

[22] H. Zimmern, Beiträge zur Kenntnis der babylonischen Religion, 1901, pp. 94 f.

[23] G. von Rad, "Zelt und Lade," NKZ, XLII (1931), 476 ff., reprinted in idem, Gesammelte Studien (Munich: Kaiser, 1957), pp. 109 ff.; M. Haran, "The Ark and the Cherubim," IEJ, IX (1959), 30 ff.

[24] Op. cit., p. 301.

In the courtyard of the Temple was located a bronze altar for burnt offerings, consisting of three square tiers. It rested on a base called, according to Ezekiel 43:14, the "bosom of the earth [or underworld]" (*ḥêq hā'āreṣ*), a term that seems to suggest some kind of cosmic symbolism.[25] This assumption is further confirmed by the name given to the top of the altar, supplied with four horns, one at each corner. It is called *ărî'ēl* (Ezek. 43:15 f.; cf. Isa. 29:1 f., 7), a word usually explained as meaning "hearth of God," and perhaps so understood by the Israelites. Albright suggests that the word is derived from the Akkadian *Arallu,* which, as we know, refers to the underworld which is conceived of as a mountain. The Hebrew variant *har'ēl* (Ezek. 43:15) can also be understood as meaning "mountain of God."[26] However, this combination is somewhat uncertain. Albright also suggests that the platform on which the officiating king or priest stood before the altar, the *kîyôr* (II Chron. 6:12-13), derives its name from the Sumerian, *ki-ur,* "foundation of the earth,"[27] which is another doubtful supposition.[28] It is not certain, therefore, that the altar of burnt offering was intended, as Albright suggests, to represent the world symbolically in the form of a mountain.

The same kind of symbolism, however, probably is found in the so-called molten sea, a great water container resting on twelve oxen, used by the priests for their ablutions. This sea was clearly a symbol of the fresh water ocean beneath the earth, which has its counterpart in the Akkadian *apsû.* In the Babylonian cult there was also a connection between the *apsû* and the portable containers for holy water used in the temples.[29]

Another item of cosmic symbolism probably lies behind Ezekiel's use of "navel of the earth" (Ezek. 38:12) to refer to Jerusalem or the mountain of the Temple.[30] This term means that the sanctuary was looked upon as the center of the world (cf. Ezek. 5:5: "in the center of the nations").[31] Similar ideas are found among many other peoples; there was a stone at Delphi, for instance, that was considered the *omphalos* or navel of the world.

In Israel, in the so-called Zion hymns, we meet the idea of Mount Zion as the mountain of God in the north (Ps. 48:3 [Eng. 48:2]). This is quite striking, since Jerusalem is not located in the north.

[25] Albright, *op. cit.,* p. 152.
[26] *Ibid.,* p. 151.
[27] *Ibid.,* pp. 153 f.
[28] See Å. Sjöberg, *SEÅ,* XXVIII-XXIX (1964), 147 f.
[29] *Ibid.,* pp. 148 f. For a discussion of the entire question, see also G. Widengren, "Aspetti simbolici dei templi e luoghi di culto del vicino Oriente antico," *Numen,* VII (1960), 1 ff., esp. 15 ff.
[30] Judg. 9:37 refers to Gerizim in the same way.
[31] A. J. Wensinck, "The Idea of the Western Semites concerning the Navel of the Earth," *Verhandel. d. kon. Akad. d. Wetensch.,* Amsterdam, Afd. Letterkunde, N.R. 19:2 (1917); Widengren, *op. cit.,* p. 14.

There is, however, a mythological conception found in the Ras Shamra texts and elsewhere that the gods live on Mount Zaphon; since *ṣāpôn* also means "north," we probably have here an ancient Canaanite myth reinterpreted.[32]

Now the mountain of God is also paradise. Ezekiel 28 describes the king of Tyre as the primordial king in the garden of Eden, upon the holy mountain of God (Ezek. 28:13-14). Another fact may be connected with this conception: flowing from the slope of the hill on which the Temple was built there was a spring named Gihon, a name borne by one of the four rivers flowing out of paradise (Gen. 2:13). Now the four rivers of paradise correspond to the four points of the compass; symbolically, they water and fructify the whole world. Since they flow out of paradise, paradise must be located at the center of the world. Both ideas also hold true symbolically for the Temple. The Old Testament contains several references to the spring near the Temple. In Psalm 46:5 (Eng. 46:4), for example, we read, "There is a river whose streams make glad the city of God," a clear reference to this spring. In a vision of the future, the prophet Ezekiel sees how the Temple spring brings fertility to the entire region between Jerusalem and the Dead Sea (Ezek. 47). A late oracle (Zech. 14:8) reflects a similar idea: water flows east and west from Jerusalem.[33] Similarly, an anonymous oracle, probably relatively early, that is preserved in the books of Isaiah and Micah (Isa. 2:1 ff.; Mic. 4:1 ff.) predicts that all nations will some day "flow" to Jerusalem in order to learn the word of Yahweh. Here again Jerusalem is the center of the world.

Another conception connected with the Temple is mentioned expressly only in late sources, but may be found already in Isaiah 28:16. Here the prophet speaks of a foundation stone laid by Yahweh in Zion, which gives security to him who believes. In the inner chamber of the postexilic Temple, instead of the ark, there was only a block of stone known as the *eben šetîyâ* ("foundation stone"). According to tradition, this stone rested on the rock of the original threshing floor. Later Jewish legend recounts that when "God created heaven and earth, he also created the stone over the deep . . . in order to keep down its waters. . . . But when the generation of the deluge sinned, he removed the stone, and immediately all the sources of the great deep sprang up." Thus the foundation stone of the Temple holds the chaos waters in check, and the continued existence of the Temple

---

[32] O. Eissfeldt, *Ba'al Zaphon* (Halle: Niemeyer, 1932), pp. 14 ff.; A. Kapelrud, *Joel Studies* (Uppsala: Lundeqvist, 1948), pp. 101 f., 104 f.

[33] G. Widengren, *The King and the Tree of Life* (Uppsala: Lundeqvist, 1951), pp. 5-41; *idem, Sakrales Königtum* (Stuttgart: Kohlhammer, 1955), p. 48; P. Reymond, *L'eau, sa vie, et sa signification dans l'Ancien Testament* (*SVT*, VI [1958]), pp. 182 ff.

guarantees the existence of the ordered and inhabited world.[34] Lucian preserves a similar ancient tradition concerning the temple at Hierapolis in Syria: there was a fissure in the rock there into which the waters of the deluge were said to have drained; this fissure was the focal point for certain rites. There was also a similar cleft in the rock in the temple of Zeus Olympios at Athens.

Several psalms and other passages illuminate the religious significance of the Temple. It is the house (*bayit*) of Yahweh or his habitation (*mā'ôn*, Ps. 26:8; *miškān*, Ps. 46:5 [Eng. 46:4]). At the dedication of the Temple, for example, Solomon says, "Yahweh has said that he would dwell in thick darkness. I have built thee an exalted house, a place for thee to dwell for ever" (I Kings 8:12 f.). The Temple is the place where his glory (*kābôd*) dwells (Ps. 26:8)— and, as we have seen, "*kābôd*" refers to the presence of God in the Temple. When Ezekiel sees Yahweh's *kābôd* depart from the Temple (Ezek. 11:22 ff.), this means that Yahweh is no longer present in the midst of his people as formerly. Likewise in another vision the same prophet sees Yahweh's *kābôd* return to the Temple after the restoration of Jerusalem; this means that Yahweh is once more present in Israel (Ezek. 43:4). In Psalm 132:13 f., we read:

> For Yahweh has chosen Zion;
>> he has desired it for his habitation:
> "This is my resting place for ever;
>> here I will dwell, for I have desired it."

The worshiper goes to the Temple "to behold the face of Yahweh"; this phrase even becomes the standard term for visiting the Temple.[35] What it originally meant to behold Yahweh's face—there was certainly no image in his Temple!—we do not know. Later Judaism took offense at the expression, and, by changing the vocalization of the verb, transformed the beholding of Yahweh into a beholding of the worshiper by Yahweh (i.e., an appearance before Yahweh). Other passages mention beholding the power and glory of God in the sanctuary (Ps. 63:3 [Eng. 63:2])—for his "strength and beauty" are there (Ps. 96:6)—or beholding his beauty (*nō'am*, Ps. 27:4). In another psalm (11:4), we read:

> Yahweh is in his holy temple,
>> Yahweh's throne is in heaven.

This verse immediately raises a question. Is Yahweh both in heaven and in the Temple, or was there a conception of a heavenly temple as the prototype of the earthly one? The latter idea was suggested in

---

[34] J. Jeremias, *Golgotha* (Leipzig: Pfeiffer, 1926), p. 73; R. Patai, *Man and Temple* (London: Nelson, 1947), pp. 57 f.

[35] F. Nötscher, *Das Angesicht Gottes schauen*, 1924.

later Judaism, but it is questionable whether it was considered in ancient Israel. Probably the psalmist is only trying to say that the same Yahweh who has his throne in heaven is also present in the earthly Temple. The Deuteronomistic historian puts a similar conviction into Solomon's mouth at the dedication of the Temple:

> Behold, heaven and the highest heaven cannot contain thee; how much less this house which I have built! Yet have regard to the prayer of thy servant . . . hearken to the cry . . . that thy eyes may be open night and day toward this house, the place of which thou has said, "My name shall be there." (I Kings 8:27 ff.)

In other words, Yahweh is actually so great that the entire universe cannot contain him; on the other hand, he has promised to be near his people in the Temple.

This presence of Yahweh of course means to the people of Israel a constant source of strength and security. After referring to God's presence in the Temple, one of the Zion hymns says:

> Yahweh of hosts is with us;
> the God of Jacob is our refuge.   (Ps. 46:8 [Eng. 46:7])

On the other hand, the prophet Jeremiah attacks any magical conception of God's presence. He censures the people for believing that the Temple in itself guarantees the presence of Yahweh. "This is the Temple of Yahweh," say the people, thinking to find here a guarantee of security. On the contrary, says the prophet, only if the people amend their ways will Yahweh protect Israel (Jer. 7:4 f.).

The Temple of Solomon was a royal chapel connected structurally with the palace; it was also a religious center for the entire nation. When the king installed the ark in the inner chamber, the old traditions of the amphictyonic sanctuary were transferred to the Temple. From then on it was the natural place for all Israel to assemble for cultic ceremonies. There was no opposition, however, to the local sanctuaries, which continued to exist. The altar law of the so-called Book of the Covenant (Exod. 20:24-26) presupposes that sacrifice can be offered everywhere that Yahweh "causes his name to be remembered."

The division of the kingdom provided the occasion for a new development. In order to prevent the inhabitants of the Northern Kingdom from continuing to conduct their worship at Jerusalem, King Jeroboam created two royal sanctuaries—at Bethel and at Dan—and placed in each the image of a calf or ox. These were intended to represent the presence of Yahweh, not that of some other god! It is possible, however, that they should not be thought of as images of Yahweh in animal form; more likely, the oxen should be seen as supporting the divinity. It is common among other peoples for a god to appear, not in the form of an animal, but mounted upon one.[36] The Deuteronomists, it is true, take the oxen as images of God. In addition to these two major shrines, the old local sanctuaries of course continued to function until the end of the Northern Kingdom.

King Hezekiah tried to carry out a reform in the Southern Kingdom. According to II Kings 18:4, 22, he destroyed the high places with their massebahs and asherahs, and decreed that Israel should worship Yahweh only at the altar in Jerusalem. This account may quite well be historically accurate. We may also trust the statement that he destroyed the bronze serpent (*neḥuštān*) that had been set up in the Temple. An old tradition told how Moses had made this serpent in the desert in order to protect the people against a plague of serpents (Num. 21:6-9). This account is clearly intended to explain the presence of a serpent image in the Temple and legitimize it by the reference to Moses. This serpent gives the impression of having been a means of magical protection. Since the serpent was a widespread religious and cultic symbol in Canaan, it is not impossible that what we actually are dealing with here is a cultic symbol of Canaanite origin, set up in the Temple for reasons unknown.[37] This would mean that Hezekiah's action in destroying the serpent as an alien symbol was instinctively correct.

Hezekiah's attempted centralization of the cult was decreed without success. His own successor, Manasseh, revived the cult of the high places and introduced syncretistic practices.

A new attempt at purification of the cult was undertaken by Josiah in 621 B.C. According to the account of the Deuteronomistic History, the discovery of an ancient law book in the Temple provided the impetus for his action. Following the statutes of this book, Josiah destroyed the high places and prohibited all cultic practices outside the Jerusalem Temple (II Kings 23). The newly-discovered law is usually presumed to have been the book of Deuteronomy. In fact, it looks as though the historian wanted to present the events in such a way that his readers would be compelled to think at once of Deuteronomy.[38] This assumption, however, involves many difficulties. Deuteronomy contains a reworking of ancient material from the Northern Kingdom.[39] If it mentions one central cultic site, it is

[36] H. T. Obbink, "Jahwebilder," *ZAW*, XLVII (1929), 264 ff.; W. F. Albright, *From the Stone Age to Christianity* (2nd ed.; Garden City: Doubleday, 1957), pp. 299 f.

[37] Cf. H. H. Rowley, "Zadok and Nehushtan," *JBL*, LVIII (1939), 113 ff.

[38] I. Engnell, *Orientalia Suecana*, I (1952), 42, note.

[39] G. von Rad, *Studies in Deuteronomy*, trans. D. Stalker (London: SCM, 1953), p. 68; A. Alt, "Die Heimat des Deuteronomiums," *Kleine Schriften* (Munich: Beck, 1953), II, 250 ff.; H. W. Wolff, "Hoseas geistige Heimat," *TLZ*, LXXXI (1956), cols. 83 f.; E. Nielsen, *Shechem* (Copenhagen: Gad, 1955), pp. 339, 345.

Shechem, not Jerusalem. The actual law referring to the centralization of the cult is found in chapter 12; but, surprisingly, even this section does not mention Jerusalem. Even if the principle enunciated there, that, just as Israel has only one God, it must also have only one Temple and one altar, is in full accord with the measures taken by Josiah, conclusive proof that the Josianic law book was identical with Deuteronomy remains impossible.[40] Apart from this question, there arise two others. Was the discovery of the book a *pia fraus?* If not, how did the book come to be in the Temple? Was there some connection between it and the earlier reform of Hezekiah? If there really is some connection with Deuteronomy, then we must follow von Rad in thinking of Levitical circles, "that must have been the representatives of a passionate movement for national and military rehabilitation."[41] Unfortunately, on this point we must be content with conjectures. It remains an indisputable fact that Josiah carried out a complete centralization of the cult in the Temple at Jerusalem and that the historian saw in this reform a fulfillment of the statutes of Deuteronomy.

The Josianic reform, too, seems to have failed to produce any lasting effect. Both Jeremiah and Ezekiel mention the cult of the high places and syncretistic practices in the Temple during the last years of the Kingdom of Judah (Jer. 13:27; Ezek. 6:1-6; 8:5-17).

d. Sacrifice

The sacrificial offerings[42] occupy a special place among the cultic ceremonies, inasmuch as quite detailed regulations regarding them are known to us. There is much, however, that remains obscure. In particular, we have no theory of sacrifice, no theological interpretation or justification of the sacrificial cult. The primary reason for this, of course, is that the priestly editors of the Pentateuch considered the sacrifices self-evident; they did not need any explanation. The laws regulating sacrifice actually constitute a sort of handbook for priests;

---

[40] I. Engnell, *Gamla Testamentet* (Stockholm: Svenska kyrkans diakonistyrelses bokförlag, 1945), I, 176 f., together with n. 3.

[41] Von Rad, *op. cit.*, p. 67.

[42] General studies: G. B. Gray, *Sacrifice in the Old Testament* (Oxford: Clarendon, 1925); A. Wendel, *Das Opfer in der altisraelitischen Religion* (Leipzig: Pfeiffer, 1927); A. Lods, "Israelitische Opfervorstellungen und –bräuche," *ThR*, N.F. III (1931), 347 ff.; W. O. E. Oesterley, *Sacrifices in Ancient Israel* (New York: Macmillan, 1937); D. M. L. Urie, "Sacrifice among the Western Semites," *PEQ*, LXXXI (1949), 67 ff.; H. H. Rowley, "The Meaning of Sacrifice in the Old Testament," *BJRL*, XXXIII (1950), 74 ff.; N. H. Snaith, "Sacrifices in the Old Testament," *VT*, VII (1957), 308 ff.; R. de Vaux, *Les sacrifices de l'Ancien Testament* (Paris: Gabalda, 1964); H. Ringgren, *Sacrifice in the Bible* (London: Lutterworth, 1962); H. J. Kraus, *Gottesdienst in Israel* (2nd ed.; Munich: Kaiser, 1962), pp. 134 ff.

they deal with certain technical questions, showing no interest in the theoretical basis of sacrifice.[43]

Furthermore, the sacrificial practice of Israel obviously did not remain constant through the centuries. The sacrificial laws that have been preserved were edited in the postexilic period and therefore reflect relatively late conditions; we cannot use them directly to elucidate the pre-exilic sacrificial system. For this earlier period, we actually have at our disposal only occasional references in historical, prophetical, and cultic texts. Traditio-historical analysis of the sacrificial laws in Leviticus 1—7 fortunately shows that they go back to ritual-like prototypes that are considerably older; they therefore contain material that is essentially pre-exilic.[44] It remains a surprising fact, however, that there is very little evidence from the early period for one whole class of sacrifice, namely, the so-called sin and guilt offerings. Outside of the laws, Ezekiel is the first to mention them explicitly.

A further question concerns the possible non-Israelite roots of the Israelite sacrifices, in other words, the use of foreign material for comparison. In 1921, Dussaud asserted the Canaanite origin of the Israelite sacrificial system on the basis of Punic sacrifice lists.[45] Since then, other material has come to light, especially in the Ras Shamra texts. It is preferable, however, to scrutinize the non-Israelite data only after a careful examination of the Israelite evidence.

Comparative religion distinguishes three basic ways of looking at sacrifice: the sacrifice is a gift, it effects communion with the divinity, it atones for guilt. These three aspects seem also to be represented in the Israelite sacrificial system.

It is quite clear that the sacrifices were gifts. Two of the general terms for sacrifice have the basic meaning of "gift," or the like. One is *minḥâ*, which in the earliest strata of the Old Testament refers to sacrifice in general, though on occasion it can also mean an ordinary "present offered to express reverence, thanks, homage, friendship, allegiance,"[46] e.g., Genesis 32:14; I Samuel 10:27; Judges 3:15. Later, when *"minḥâ"* came to be used in the sense of "cereal offering" or grain offering, another word was used to emphasize the aspect of giving: *qorbān*, which is connected with the verb *hiqrîb* (from the root *qrb*, "be near"), "bring near," "present," and thus means "that which is presented," i.e., a gift.

---

[43] Ringgren, *Sacrifice in the Bible,* pp. 13 f.

[44] K. Koch, *Die Priesterschrift von Ex. 25 bis Lev. 16* (Göttingen: Vandenhoeck & Ruprecht, 1959), pp. 46 ff.

[45] R. Dussaud, *Les origines cananéennes du sacrifice israélite* (2nd ed.; Paris: Leroux, 1921).

[46] L. Köhler, *Lexicon, s.v.*

In this category belongs first of all the offering of firstlings,[47] which in a certain sense is perhaps not a true offering at all. The Old Testament frequently enunciates the principle that every first-born of the herd and the first fruits of the field belong to Yahweh, and must be surrendered to him as a sacred gift (Exod. 13:2; 22:29; 23:19; 34:26; etc.). Human beings are the only exception: first-born children are to be "redeemed," i.e., a young animal is to be substituted for them (Exod. 13:13). The offering of firstlings is based on the conviction that everything is given by Yahweh and therefore really belongs to him. By dedicating the first fruits to him, man recognizes God's claim of ownership and guarantees himself the right to use the rest. The Old Testament does not state expressly that the firstlings are a sign of thankfulness, but there is evidence that they were felt to be so. A regulation concerning the offering of first fruits begins, for example, with the words, "When you come into the land . . . and when you eat of the food of the land, you shall present an offering to Yahweh. . . . You shall present a cake as an offering" (Num. 15:18 ff.). And the ritual for the offering of first fruits in Deuteronomy 26 speaks of "the fruit of the ground, which you harvest from your land that Yahweh your God gives you" (Deut. 26:2), and prescribes the recitation of a confession of faith that recounts the blessings bestowed by Yahweh in Israel's history. The passage continues: "And you shall set it [the first fruits of the land] down before Yahweh your God, and worship before Yahweh your God; and you shall rejoice in all the good which Yahweh your God has given to you and to your house" (Deut. 26:10b-11a).

The regulations for the cereal offering (*minḥâ*) are found in Leviticus 2. The offering consists of flour, cakes, or crushed grain (this restriction is late; at an earlier stage of the language, *"minḥâ"* meant any kind of offering; cf. Gen. 4:3 ff.; I Sam. 2:17; 3:14); it is presented along with oil and incense and laid on the altar. Then a part of it, the so-called *azkārâ*,[48] is burned. This word may contain a hint at the meaning of the *minḥâ* offering; it is derived from *zākar*, "remember," and may therefore mean that the offering was intended to bring the worshiper to the remembrance of Yahweh and make him "accepted" (cf. Lev. 1:3).

A third kind of sacrifice, presumably also to be interpreted as a gift, is the burnt offering (*'ôlâ*, etymologically "that which goes up").[49]

---

[47] O. Eissfeldt, *Erstlinge und Zehnten im Alten Testament* (Leipzig: Hinrichs, 1917); S. Herner, *Vegetabilische Erstlingsopfer im Pentateuch,* 1918.

[48] Cf. G. R. Driver, "Three Technical Terms in the Pentateuch," *JSS,* I (1956), 97 ff.

[49] L. Rost, "Erwägungen zum israelitischen Brandopfer," in J. Hempel and L. Rost (ed.), *Von Ugarit nach Qumran* (Berlin: Töpelmann, 1958), pp. 177 ff.; W. B. Stevenson, "Hebrew 'olah and zebach Sacrifices," in *Festschrift für Alfred Bertholet* (Tübingen: Mohr, 1950), pp. 488 ff.

Occasionally it is also called a *kālîl*, "whole burnt offering." The regulations of Leviticus 1 (cf. also Exod. 29:15-18), however, ascribe to it an atoning virtue, which may correspond to a later stage of development. A bull, a goat, a ram, or a dove might be used for this sacrifice. In the case of the first three, the person presenting the sacrifice had first to lay his hand upon its head, a ceremony that has been variously interpreted. We may have here a transfer of the worshiper's sins to the animal, as Leviticus 16:21 seems to suggest; this explanation is not very probable, however, since the passage quoted does not deal with sacrifice offered to Yahweh. Otherwise the imposition of hands may be intended merely to establish a close association between the worshiper and the animal, so that the animal is really made the personal offering of the worshiper. This second interpretation raises the least difficulties and is therefore preferable. After this ceremony, the animal is killed "before Yahweh," i.e., before the altar, and its blood poured on the altar; the flesh is cut in pieces and burned on the altar. This is "an offering by fire [*iššeh*], a pleasing odor [*rêaḥ nîḥōaḥ*] to Yahweh" (Lev. 1:9b). This latter expression shows that Yahweh was thought to smell the smoke and thereby be appeased. There are, it is true, a few passages suggesting rather that this sacrifice was intended to provide food for Yahweh. In Numbers 28:2, for example, he calls these offerings "my food for my offerings by fire, my pleasing odor." Of course this expression can be understood figuratively; the association with *rêaḥ nîḥōaḥ* even supports this view. But it must be conceded at the same time that this very expression "bread of God" or "food of God" (also found in Lev. 21:6, 8, 17; 22:25) must go back to extremely ancient conceptions presupposing that food was really provided for God. It is also worthy of notice that an expression comparable to "pleasing odor" is found in Babylonia,[50] where the prevalent view was that sacrifice provided food for the gods.

The primary motivation for these sacrifices looked upon as gifts is thanksgiving. Within this class, the so-called freewill offerings (*nedābâ*), the votive offerings (*neder*), and the thank offerings (*tôdâ*) represent a special category. They can be either burnt offerings or "peace offerings" (Lev. 7:12-17; 22:18-30; Num. 15:1-10). A votive offering was presented in consequence of a vow: in a dangerous situation a man might vow to offer a sacrifice to God if he were delivered; the offering should then be considered an expression of thanksgiving. The thank offering had a similar function. The freewill offering is not defined more precisely in the laws.

The psalms occasionally mention offerings of this kind, illustrating at the same time the mood in which they were presented:

---

[50] E.g., the Gilgamesh Epic, XI, 1. 160.

With a free-will offering I will sacrifice to thee;
  I will give thanks to thy name, O Yahweh, for it is good.
For thou hast delivered me from every trouble. . . .
                    (Ps. 54:8 f. [Eng. 54:6 f.])

My vows to thee I must perform, O God;
  I will render thank offerings to thee.
For thou hast delivered my soul from death. . . .
                    (Ps. 56:13 f. [Eng. 56:12 f.])

The idea that a sacrifice is a gift is occasionally called into question on the grounds that actually everything belongs to God; how could man give him anything? Thus the author of Psalm 50, for example, has Yahweh say:

I will accept no bull from your house,
  nor he-goat from your folds.
For every beast of the forest is mine,
  the cattle on a thousand hills.
I know all the birds of the air,
  and all that moves in the field is mine.
If I were hungry, I would not tell you;
  for the world and all that is in it is mine.
Do I eat the flesh of bulls,
  or drink the blood of goats?   (Ps. 50:9-13)

This almost looks like a total rejection of sacrifice; but the psalm as a whole does not seem to justify this impression, for the psalmist speaks approvingly of thank offerings and votive offerings (vs. 14) and of a covenant that is made by sacrifice (vs. 5). What we have here is probably an admonition to those who offer sacrifice not to forget that what they present to Yahweh has in fact always belonged to him, and therefore not to misconstrue their sacrifice as a purely human performance.[51] A similar attitude lies behind the words of David in I Chronicles 29:14, although here we are not actually dealing with sacrifice in the strict sense: "All things come from thee, and of thy own have we given thee." It would be tempting to assume that we hear in this passage a late stage of development with a tendency to theologize. Since, however, Psalm 50 cannot possibly be dated in the postexilic period, we must conclude that people were already thinking along these lines in pre-exilic Israel.

The idea of communion is represented by the so-called šᵉlāmîm offerings (Lev. 3). The Hebrew word is very difficult to translate. The usual rendering, "peace offering," fails to do justice to the full meaning of the word. It is true that the word šālôm, derived from the same root, means peace; but this word by no means exhausts the nuances of the term. The term Abschlussopfer ("final offerings")

___
[51] Cf. also Ringgren, *Faith of the Psalmists*, pp. 10 f.

suggested by Köhler[52] is linguistically unobjectionable, but does not really seem to be to the point. It might be better to take a cue from the use of the adjective šālēm in such an expression as "his heart was šālēm, i.e., in complete harmony, with God."[53] We would then have here a sacrifice for the purpose of establishing communion with God. This interpretation can also be defended on other pertinent grounds.

When a peace offering is made, only the blood and fat of the sacrificial animal are presented to Yahweh; the former is poured on the altar, the latter burned. The flesh, however, is eaten by all those present at the sacrifice. In all probability this meal was felt to be the purpose and culmination of the peace offering. We read that guests were invited to the meal (Zeph. 1:7; Deut. 12:18; I Sam. 9:12 f.; 16:3 ff.) in order to eat and drink before Yahweh (Deut. 12:18). At the sacrificial meal, the dominant mood was joy occasioned by the awareness that Yahweh, too, shared the meal. The earlier sources usually use the word zebaḥ for this kind of sacrifice.[54] Because the corresponding verb also means "slaughter," this term is usually connected with sacrificial slaughter (note the German translation Schlachtopfer, "slaughter-sacrifice"); but it can also be used to mean sacrifice or offering in general. In the earliest period of Israel's history, sacrificial slaughtering of animals was obviously the most common kind of sacrifice. It could be performed everywhere at the sanctuaries on the high places, and every time an animal was slaughtered, it was considered more or less a sacral act. Josiah's centralization of the cult created a new situation: sacrifice could be offered only in Jerusalem, and special rules were promulgated for the secular slaughter of animals (Deut. 12, especially vss. 15 f.).[55]

The ritual in Leviticus 3 does not specify the occasions at which peace offerings were performed. A supplement (Lev. 7:11-21) distinguishes three kinds of peace offering: thank offering, votive offering, and freewill offering. This list probably does not exhaust all the possibilities.

According to Leviticus 4 and 5, there are two kinds of sacrifice intended to make atonement:[56] sin offerings (ḥaṭṭā't) and guilt offerings (āšām). The precise distinction between them is never clearly defined. Sin offering is provided for transgression of a commandment, particularly a ritual commandment, as 5:1-3 shows. According to Leviticus 5:15, the guilt offering seems to presuppose primarily an offense against one of God's privileges. The laws also mention both

---

[52] L. Köhler, Lexicon, s.v.
[53] Ringgren, Sacrifice in the Bible, p. 27, following Gray.
[54] Cf. Stevenson, op. cit., pp. 492 ff.; Snaith, op. cit.
[55] Cf. also Ehrlich, op. cit., p. 42, n. 102.
[56] D. Schötz, Schuld- und Sündopfer im Alten Testament, 1930; L. Moraldi, Espiazione sacrificiale e riti espiatori nell'ambiente biblico e nell'AT, 1956.

sin and guilt offerings in cases not mentioned in Leviticus 4 and 5, e.g., at the ordination of priests (Exod. 29:14), at the annual purification of the altar (Exod. 30:10; Lev. 16:16), and in connection with purification of the people (Num. 6:10 f.; Lev. 12:6) or of lepers (Lev. 14:10), as well as for sexual sins (Lev. 19:20-22), etc. The present form of the law probably represents a later systematization and simplification of an earlier practice no longer completely understood. Since, furthermore, the two terms seem occasionally interchangeable, it is best to forego precise definition, the more so because no special regulations are provided for the guilt offering, and the supplement (Lev. 7:1-7) shows that the procedure in both cases was essentially the same.

The ritual is reminiscent of the burnt offering, but differs in that the blood is treated differently and the flesh is burned outside the Temple. This is probably done because the flesh has been contaminated with uncleanness and sin, and therefore does not belong in the holy Temple. It also becomes clear that it is the blood, sprinkled on the "horns" of the altar, that makes atonement, and not the flesh. Another important similarity to the burnt offering is the fact that the person offering the sacrifice must lay his hand upon the sacrificial animal (cf. above, p. 169).

The result of sin and guilt offerings is called atonement. The priest "makes atonement for" the person concerned (*kippēr 'al*). The exact meaning of this term cannot be determined precisely. Etymologically it could mean either "cover" or "erase."[57] Unfortunately, comparison with the corresponding Babylonian word *kuppuru* is not much help.[58] This word refers to a ceremony of atonement in which dough or similar material was applied to the person in question and then washed off, or at least removed. The expression, however, refers to the ceremony as a whole and therefore can scarcely have preserved its original meaning. Consequently we must restrict our study to the Old Testament material exclusively.

The first fact to note is that the earliest sources mention a few occasions on which sacrifice was offered in order to appease the wrath of Yahweh (I Sam. 26:19; II Sam. 24:25; probably also Job 1:5; 42:7 f.). (These passages admittedly do not use the term sin or guilt offering, just as in general there are few references to this kind of sacrifice in sources antedating Ezekiel [44:24 ff.; 40:39; 45:21 ff.] and P; cf. Mic. 6:7 and perhaps also II Kings 12:17 [Eng. 12:16]). In

[57] J. J. Stamm, *Erlösen und Vergeben im Alten Testament*, 1940, pp. 59 ff., supports the former; G. R. Driver, "Studies in the Vocabulary of the Old Testament: V," *JTS*, XXXIV (1933), 34 ff., supports the latter.

[58] The relevant passages are listed in an article by S. Langdon, *ET*, XXII (1900-01), 320 ff., 380. W. von Soden seems to favor the rendering "wipe off"; see the article "Kapāru" in *Akkadisches Handwörterbuch* (Wiesbaden: Harrassowitz, 1959-).

addition, Leviticus 17:11 says that an animal's blood contains its life
and therefore must not be eaten (cf. Gen. 9:4); the blood has actually been given man in order to make atonement upon the altar.[59]
Finally, Deuteronomy 21 prescribes a sacrifice for the case when a
murder has been committed by an unknown person; the prayer to
be recited runs, "Make atonement, O Yahweh, for thy people . . .
and set not the guilt of innocent blood in the midst of thy people
Israel . . ." (Deut. 21:8).[60] The crime that has been committed has
obviously violated a divine command and destroyed the equilibrium
of society, so that guilt falls upon the people or the city. Now this
guilt is removed through the slaying of a sacrificial animal in place of
the murderer. The death of the animal atones vicariously for the guilt.
It is important to note in this connection that neither the people nor
the sacrifice is the subject of the verb *kippēr*, but rather God; it is he
who accepts the sacrifice and removes the guilt. In the priestly laws,
on the other hand, we read that the priest "makes atonement" for the
person offering the sacrifice when he sprinkles the blood on the horns
of the altar. In this case, however, the priest evidently is commissioned
by Yahweh.

Leviticus 16 describes a special ceremony used annually on the
Day of Atonement.[61] After the High Priest has sacrificed a bull as a
sin offering for himself, he takes two goats and assigns them by lot,
one to Yahweh—as a sin offering for the Temple—and the other "for
Azazel." He lays his hands on the head of the latter and confesses
over it all the iniquities of Israel. Then the goat is sent away into the
wilderness; "the goat shall bear all their iniquities upon him to a
solitary land." We do not know what Azazel is. The word is usually
interpreted as the name of a desert demon, but it is quite possible
that originally it was a term referring to the trackless desert or a
steep declivity.[62] In any case, we have here an extremely ancient
ceremony, which vividly symbolizes, or rather effects, the removal of
sins. A similar rite is also found in the Babylonian New Year's Festival: a ram is slain, used to purify the temple, and then thrown into
the river.[63] A rite of purification occurring in the Greek festival of
Thargelia provides another striking parallel: two men decked in figs

---

[59] With regard to the following discussion, see G. von Rad, *Old Testament Theology*, trans. D. M. G. Stalker (Edinburgh and London: Oliver
and Boyd, 1962), pp. 269 f.

[60] RSV: Forgive thy people; the Hebrew expression is *kappēr lᵉ*.

[61] S. Landesdorfer, *Studien zum biblischen Versöhnungstag* (Münster.
Aschendorff, 1924); M. Löhr, *Das Ritual von Lev. 16*, 1925; R. Schur,
Versöhnungstag und Sündenbock, 1934; E. Auerbach, "Neujahrs- und
Versöhnungs-Fest," *VT*, VIII (1958), 337 ff.

[62] See above, pp. 102 f. The KJV connected *'azāzel* with *'ēz*, "goat," and
read: "for a scapegoat."

[63] For a translation of the ritual, see *ANET*, pp. 331 ff.; the passage in
question is found at 11. 353 ff.

were whipped with branches, then led about the town, and finally driven out, in order to remove all evil from the town.[64]

The sacrifices made for atonement obviously presuppose a very primitive, almost physical conception of guilt and an equally primitive conception of the atoning power of the life of the sacrificial animal sacrificed vicariously. This fact is much more important than the observation that the regulations are contained in a late collection of laws and that the early sources mention this kind of sacrifice rarely if at all.

There existed other sacrifices besides those described in detail in the laws. The story of Jacob at Bethel, for example, presupposes an offering of oil (Gen. 28:18), and Exodus 29:40 bears witness to an offering of wine, probably borrowed from the Canaanite religion. An offering of incense is frequently mentioned.[65] The aromatic ingredients came for the most part from southern Arabia, but the burning of incense was also customary in all the other cults of the ancient Near East. Exodus 30:7-8 contains a law prescribing an incense offering every morning and every evening. In addition, incense was burned in connection with the cereal offering.

Finally, the question of human sacrifice presents a special problem. Such sacrifice is occasionally found in the religions of the ancient Near East,[66] and attempts have been made to find traces of it in Israel, also. In I Kings 16:34, for example, we read that during the reign of Ahab a certain Hiel rebuilt Jericho "at the cost of" his two sons. Since there is archaeological evidence for so-called foundation sacrifice, this passage has been so interpreted. The expression, however, is quite ambiguous. In addition, the narrative in Genesis 22 (telling how Abraham was commanded to sacrifice his son Isaac, but, having demonstrated his obedience, was allowed to substitute a ram for the boy) has been viewed as a tradition intended to explain why the Israelites no longer followed the Canaanites in practicing human sacrifice. It must be emphasized, however, that the story in its present form is primarily concerned with Abraham's obedience, and that, even if an interest in human sacrifice can be shown to be present, this interest is in opposition to the practice, not in support of it. Finally, the Book of Judges tells how Jephthah sacrificed his daughter (Judg. 11:30-

---

[64] M. P. Nilsson, *Griechische Feste*, 1906, pp. 186 f.; L. Deubner, *Attische Feste*, 1932, pp. 179 ff. [For a discussion in English of the Thargelia, including most of the relevant texts, see J. E. Harrison, *Prolegomena to the Study of Greek Religion* (London: Merlin, 1961 [reprint of the 1921 edition]), pp. 77 ff., esp. pp. 95 ff.—TRANS.]

[65] M. Löhr, *Das Räucheropfer im Alten Testament*, 1927; M. Haran, "The Use of Incense in the Ancient Israelite Ritual," *VT*, X (1960), 113 ff.

[66] Cf. F. M. T. de L. Böhl, "Das Menschenopfer bei den alten Sumerern," in *idem, Opera Minora* (Groningen: Wolters, 1953), pp. 162 ff.; J. Henninger, "Menschenopfer bei den Arabern," *Anthropos*, LIII (1958), 721 ff., 776 f.

40).[67] Now in the first place we are here dealing with a common fairy tale motif: Jephthah vows to sacrifice the first thing he meets upon his return home. Furthermore, the particular aim of the story is to explain a specific cultic practice: the young women of Gilead engage in ritual lamentation upon the mountains, a custom obviously connected with the Canaanite fertility cult. If we really do have human sacrifice here, it is probably not to be seen as a custom genuinely at home in Israel.

The real references to human sacrifice in the Old Testament all refer to a specific cultic practice borrowed from the Canaanites, which is usually characterized by the word *mōlek* (in the Holiness Code, Lev. 18:21; 20:2-5; also II Kings 23:10; Jer. 32:35). The passages speak of the sacrifice of a child, who is "caused to pass through the fire" (cf. also II Kings 16:3; 17:31; 21:6; Jer. 7:31; 19:5; Deut. 12:31). This sacrifice appears for the first time during the reign of Ahab, and is clearly felt to be an alien element. The traditional view is that *mōlek* is a bowdlerized form of the name of the god Melek or Malik ("King"), and that these sacrifices were offered *to* Melek. Eissfeldt and others have recently challenged this view.[68] This challenge is based on the evidence that in Punic the word *molk* refers to a particular kind of sacrifice, not to a god. If, then, we are dealing with a *molk* of human beings, there is good reason to connect this with a statement made by Diodorus to the effect that in 310 B.C. the Carthaginians sacrificed a great number of children to Kronos. They were laid upon the arms of the statue of the god and cast into the fire. Archaeological discoveries support this statement.[69] This kind of sacrifice probably also existed in Phoenicia proper; the custom was then borrowed by Israel under certain circumstances. In a few passages of the Bible, though, *"mōlek"* must undoubtedly be considered the name of an idol (compare Ezek. 23:39 with Jer. 19:5; 32:35). Either the Phoenician sacrificial term was misunderstood in Israel from the beginning, or else there was secondary confusion between it and the divine name Melek.[70] However the case may be, this sacrifice of children was definitely never considered a part of the genuine Israelite religion. As among the Moabites (II Kings 3:27), it was probably performed only in especially critical situations.

---

[67] Cf. above, p. 50.

[68] O. Eissfeldt, *Molok als Opferbegriff im Punischen und Hebräischen und das Ende des Gottes Moloch* (Halle: Niemeyer, 1935).

[69] On this point, cf. J. G. Février, *RHR*, CXLIII (1953), 8 ff.; *Journal asiatique*, CCXLIII (1955), 49 ff.; R. Charlier, *Karthago*, VI (1953), 3 ff.; J. Hoftijzer, "Eine Notiz zum Punischen Kinderopfer," *VT*, VIII (1958), 288 ff.

[70] For a discussion of the entire question see H. Cazelles, "Molok," in *Dictionnaire biblique*, Supplement V, 1957, pp. 1337 ff.; E. Dhorme, "Le dieu Baal et le dieu Moloch dans la tradition biblique," *Anatolian Studies,* VI (1956), 57 ff.

Now we can and must discuss the question of the extent to which the Israelite sacrificial system is dependent in other respects on the Canaanite system. The data contained in the Old Testament itself seem to presuppose no basic difference between Canaanite and Israelite sacrifices: Naaman offers burnt offerings and sacrifices (II Kings 5:17), the prophets of Baal sacrifice a burnt offering upon Carmel (I Kings 18:23 f.), Jehu pretends that he wants to offer burnt offerings and sacrifices to Baal (II Kings 10:18-27). But these accounts might have been influenced by Israelite terminology. It is therefore best to look for other sources from which to reconstruct the Canaanite sacrificial system. Two groups of material are particularly relevant: two Punic sacrificial tariffs from Marseille and Carthage, and the Ras Shamra texts.[71] The former mention three primary kinds of sacrifice: *galil*, *ṣewa'at*, and *šelem kalil*. *Kalil* and *šelem* occur also in Hebrew. In all probability the Punic sacrifices do not correspond to the Israelite sacrifices with the same name; *kalil* seems to be a sacrifice for atonement, *ṣewa'at* a peace offering, and *šelem kalil* a burnt offering or whole burnt offering. Two other Punic sacrificial terms are known, *'olat* and *minḥat*; but we are unable to say whether they refer to the same thing as the Israelite terms.

The Ras Shamra texts contain four words of special importance as parallels to Israelite terminology: *ḏbḥ*, "sacrifice," corresponds to Hebrew *zebaḥ*; *šlmm*, "peace offering (?)," corresponds to *šelāmîm*; *šrp*, "burnt offering," has no etymological counterpart in Israel, though the same kind of sacrifice existed there; and *kll* corresponds to Hebrew *kālîl*, "whole (burnt) offering." Other correspondences are doubtful. The descriptions in the narrative texts presuppose burnt offerings or animal sacrifices. The blood, on the other hand, seems to have no special significance.[72]

These data suggest two conclusions: first, the Israelite sacrificial system was very similar to the Canaanite system; second, in view of the differences in terminology, the Israelite system cannot have been "borrowed" unchanged from the Canaanites. The close relationship between the two languages is probably insufficient to explain all the points of agreement; on the other hand, many differences can be accounted for by a long period of parallel development.

If we examine the Israelite sacrificial system in an even broader milieu, an additional fact stands out. The Canaanite and Israelite systems share the practice of completely or partially burning the offerings; this practice is unknown in Mesopotamia and Arabia, and there-

---

[71] See especially R. Dussaud, *op. cit.;* cf. also J. G. Février, "Le vocabulaire sacrificiel punique," *Journal asiatique,* CCXLIII (1955), 49 ff.

[72] J. Gray, "Cultic Affinities between Israel and Ras Shamra," *ZAW,* LXII (1949), 207 ff.; A. De Guglielmo, "Sacrifice in the Ugaritic Texts," *CBQ,* XVII (1955), 76 ff.; J. Gray, *The Legacy of Canaan (SVT,* V [1957]), pp. 143 ff.

fore cannot be considered a general Semitic phenomenon. The Greeks, however, did burn their sacrifices. The Hebrew *šelāmîm* and *'ôlâ* correspond to the Greek *thusia* and *holokauston*. In addition, the Greek word *bōmos*, "platform," "altar," is reminiscent of the Canaanite *bāmâ*, "high place." It is not impossible that these points of agreement go back to a pre-Hellenic and pre-Canaanite population living at the eastern end of the Mediterranean.[73]

The great importance of the sacrificial blood, however, has its closest parallels among the pre-Islamic Arabs. It may represent a nomadic trait preserved by Israel from its very earliest history.

The theological estimation of sacrifice in Israel was subject to many variations. The writing prophets leave the impression that sacrifice was considered an *opus operatum* that was effective without any inward participation on the part of the worshiper. Hosea, for example, says:

> For I desire steadfast love and not sacrifice,
> the knowledge of God, rather than burnt offerings. (6:6)

These lines obviously presuppose that love and knowledge no longer accompany the offering of sacrifice. A similar idea is placed in Samuel's mouth: "Behold, to obey is better than to sacrifice, and to hearken than the fat of rams" (I Sam. 15:22). Obviously this does not mean that the sacrifices are without value; it means that their effect is not mechanical. There were doubtless proponents of the *opus operatum* theory, but it is questionable whether this theory really corresponds to the view lying behind the sacrificial laws. In fact, the laws regulating atonement sacrifices presuppose both confession of sins and reparation.[74] It is now generally admitted that the laws of the Priestly Code do not conceive of sacrifice as something enabling man to exercise control over the will of Yahweh. They are rather a means provided by Yahweh in order that man may enter into communion with him.[75]

The prophets, too, by no means demanded a religion without sacrifice; they primarily censured the cult that had come under Canaanite influence, bitterly attacking a mechanical view of sacrifice. Thus when Yahweh says through Amos, "Even though you offer me your burnt offerings, I will not accept them, and the peace offerings

---

[73] R. K. Yerkes, *Sacrifices in Greek and Roman Religions and Early Judaism* (New York: Scribner, 1952); cf. L. Rost, "Erwägungen zum israelitischen Brandopfer," in J. Hempel and L. Rost (ed.), *Von Ugarit nach Qumran* (Berlin: Töpelmann, 1958), pp. 177 ff.; De Vaux, *Ancient Israel, op. cit.*, pp. 440 f.

[74] On this question, see especially H. H. Rowley, "The Meaning of Sacrifice in the Old Testament," *BJRL*, XXXIII (1950/51), 87 ff.

[75] Von Rad, *Old Testament Theology*, p. 260; Ringgren, *Sacrifice in the Bible*, p. 42.

of your fatted beasts I will not look upon" (Amos 5:22), the prophet is not condemning the sacrifices as such, but rather the opinion that sacrifice alone is sufficient. On the contrary, he emphasizes that justice and righteousness are essential. And when Isaiah has Yahweh say, "Bring no more vain offerings; incense is an abomination to me" (Isa. 1:13), the context demonstrates that he is not thinking of the abolition of sacrifice; in the following verses he even condemns prayer, because the hands of the worshiper are full of blood (Isa. 1:15). What the prophet censures is the erroneous opinion that sacrifice is effective per se, without the corresponding deeds.[76, 77]

e. The Worship of the Temple and the Poetry of the Cult

The ritual regulations of the laws give the impression that the sacrifices constituted the framework of the Temple cult. Twice a day the sacrifice of a lamb (the so-called *tāmîd*) was prescribed, in the morning and in the evening (Exod. 29:38-42; Num. 28:1-8). On every Sabbath, additional burnt offerings were to be presented (Num. 28:9 f.). In addition, of course, there were special sacrifices at festivals and sacrifices on particular occasions.

The Israelite Temple cult consisted of more than sacrifice, however, although the other practices were not codified in the laws. The historical books occasionally mention other rites; the evidence of the psalms, in particular, helps supplement this information. In addition to sacrifice, processions played an important role. We hear of an altar procession (Ps. 26:6), a procession about the walls of Jerusalem (Ps. 48:13 [Eng. 48:12]), a procession to the Temple (Ps. 42:5 [Eng. 42:4]), etc. Psalm 68:25 f. (Eng. 68:24 f.) gives us a detailed description of a procession:

> Thy solemn processions are seen, O God,
>> the processions of my God, my King, into the sanctuary—
> the singers in front, the minstrels last,
>> between them maidens playing timbrels.

This passage also shows us the importance of music. Psalm 81, already quoted above, mentions singing, playing on the harp and lyre, blowing the trumpet, and sounding the timbrel in its description of a festival at the Temple (Ps. 81:2-4 [Eng. 81:1-3]). In one passage

---

[76] H. H. Rowley, *The Unity of the Bible* (London: Kingsgate, 1953), pp. 30 ff.; H. W. Hertzberg, "Die prophetische Kritik am Kult," *TLZ*, LXXV (1950), cols. 219 ff.; an oversimplified view is presented by R. Hentschke, *Die Stellung der vorexilischen Schriftpropheten zum Kultus* (Berlin: Töpelmann, 1957); cf. the review by H. Ringgren in *SEA*, XXV (1960), 165 f.

[77] [For a thorough study of the nonlegal material bearing on sacrifice, see R. J. Thompson, *Penitence and Sacrifice in Early Israel outside the Levitical Law* (Leiden: Brill, 1963).—TRANS.]

Isaiah refers to a night in which a festival is kept, with "gladness of heart, as when one sets out to the sound of the flute to go to the mountain of Yahweh" (Isa. 30:29). Psalm 98:4-6 speaks in similar fashion of rejoicing and singing to the accompaniment of lyres, trumpets, and horns before Yahweh the King. The basic mood of most cultic activities is joy and enthusiasm. But there were also days of mourning and penance, characterized by the recitation of penitential psalms and fasting (Joel 1:13 f.; Jer. 36:6, 9; Zech. 7:2 ff.; Lev. 16:29).

We obviously do not know in detail at what occasions the psalms collected in the Psalter were recited. Recent research on the psalms is inclined to date the majority of them in the pre-exilic period. It views them almost exclusively as cultic poetry, not as expressions of individual piety or as documents of the religious experience of particular writers. Comparative studies have shown that the psalms are strikingly similar to Babylonian psalms in language, style, and structure; there are also some similarities to Egyptian psalms.[78] There is frequent stylistic agreement with Canaanite cultic poetry.[79] This means that the poetry of Israel's cult does not stand in isolation, but is rooted in the general tradition of the ancient Near East.

Ever since the work of H. Gunkel, the psalms have been classified into several *Gattungen*, each of which had its own *Sitz im Leben*, i.e., its own special place and special function in the religious and cultic life of Israel. The following are the three major *Gattungen*:

1. The Hymn. These psalms praise the greatness of God and his mighty acts. They could also be called "descriptive praise,"[80] since their major emphasis is upon description of God's glorious attributes. These attributes are never thought of statically, however; they are always manifested in acts of history and creation.[81] A hymn usually begins with a summons to praise God (e.g., *hallelû-yah*, "Praise Yahweh!" or "Sing to the Lord!"). Then follows a statement of motivation, which is either introduced by *kî*, "for," or given the form of a series of participles; this constitutes the body of the hymn. A renewed summons to praise concludes the form. The Temple worship

---

[78] See, for example, F. Stummer, *Sumerisch-akkadische Parallelen zum Aufbau alttestamentlicher Psalmen*, 1922; D. C. Simpson (ed.), *The Psalmists* (London: Oxford, 1926), pp. 109 ff., 177 ff.; C. G. Cumming, *The Assyrian and Hebrew Hymns of Praise* (New York: Columbia, 1934); G. Widengren, *The Accadian and Hebrew Psalms of Lamentation* (Stockholm: Thule, 1937); E. R. Dalglish, *Psalm Fifty-one* (Leiden: Brill, 1962), chaps. i—iii.

[79] J. H. Patton, *Canaanite Parallels to the Book of Psalms* (Baltimore: Johns Hopkins, 1944).

[80] *"Beschreibendes Lob";* this expression is taken from C. Westermann, *Das Loben Gottes in den Psalmen* (Göttingen: Vandenhoeck & Ruprecht, 1954), p. 21.

[81] Cf. Ringgren, *Faith of the Psalmists,* pp. 56, 82 ff.

is obviously the *Sitz im Leben* of the hymn. It is impossible, however, in most cases to define the cultic situation precisely, since a hymn could be used on various occasions. Only isolated psalms can be connected with specific festivals. Typical hymns are Psalms 8; 103; 104; 135; 146—150.

Two specific types of hymns are the enthronement psalm [82] (Pss. 47; 93; 95—99), which praises the kingship of God, and the Zion hymn (e.g., Pss. 48; 84), which praises the beauty and majesty of the sanctuary or the holy city. Interesting parallels to this latter type are found both in Egypt and in Mesopotamia.[83] We shall discuss below the *Sitz im Leben* of the enthronement psalms. The Zion hymns are obviously connected with special ceremonies of the Temple, e.g., pilgrimages to the Temple, or processions in it or in the city.

2. The Thanksgiving Psalm. Originally these psalms probably accompanied the presentation of thank offerings. A person who had experienced divine intervention in his life would offer a sacrifice in thanksgiving, at the same time reciting a thanksgiving psalm. The structure of these psalms clearly indicates this function: an introductory formula such as "I will bless the Lord" is followed by an account of the particular favor granted by God that has occasioned the thank offering. Reference is frequently made to the preceding distress and the lament that has now been answered. Thus the thanksgiving psalm has also been called a "narrative praise."[84] Typical thanksgiving psalms are Psalms 30 and 34.

3. The Lament. These psalms were recited in situations of distress or suffering in order to pray for Yahweh's aid. They can refer either to an individual or the community (the worshiping congregation). The structure of the Israelite lament is in remarkable agreement with that of the Babylonian *šu'illa*, the "prayer of incantation." The following motifs are generally common to both: address to the god (often expanded by clauses expressing praise), lament, description of distress, plea for aid, confession of sins, vow to present a thank offering. Some of these elements can be missing, and the order is not absolutely fixed; but on the whole the similarity of form is remarkable.[85]

[82] There is some confusion as to the use of this term. W. Harrelson uses it with reference to psalms dealing with the enthronement of kings, e.g., Psalms 2 and 110 (see his *Interpreting the Old Testament* [New York: Holt, Rinehart & Winston, 1964], pp. 409, 419 f.). In this book we use it, following Mowinckel, for those psalms which Harrelson calls "hymns to Yahweh as king."

[83] E.g., A. Erman, *The Literature of the Ancient Egyptians*, trans. A. M. Blackman (London: Methuen, 1927), pp. 270 ff.; A. Falkenstein and W. von Soden, *Sumerische und akkadische Hymnen und Gebete* (Zürich: Artemis, 1953), pp. 131 ff.

[84] Westermann, *loc. cit.*

[85] See especially Widengren, *op. cit.*; C. Westermann, "Struktur und Geschichte der Klage im Alten Testament," *ZAW*, LXVI (1954), 44 ff.; Dalglish, *op. cit.*, chap. iii, especially pp. 43 ff.

The description of distress is especially interesting.[86] The bulk of the material consists not of details of a particular situation but of certain general expressions and standard images, most of which are equally common in the Babylonian prayers. The speaker says, for example, that he is sinking in water or in mire (Ps. 18:5 [Eng. 18:4]; 69:2 f. [Eng. 69:1 f.]; 69:15 f. [Eng. 69:14 f.]; 88:8 [Eng. 88:7]), or that he is in Sheol or in the power of death (Ps. 18:6 [Eng. 18:5]; 88:4-7 [Eng. 88:3-6]). The waters are a symbol of the forces of chaos that are hostile to life; sinking in water is an image of death. But death can also stand for almost any form of distress. Every kind of disease and suffering threatens man's life, and is conceived of as a potential death. In addition, there are references to suffering brought about by enemies. In a few cases, disease and enemies are even mentioned together (e.g., Ps. 38; 41:3 f. [Eng. 41:2 f.]; 102:6, 9 [Eng. 102:5, 8]). Various explanations have been given of this phenomenon.[87] It has been suggested, for example, that the enemies are sorcerers who cause sickness,[88] or demons who harm the speaker.[89] In many cases, perhaps even in most, they are clearly political enemies.[90] Their occasional representation as wild animals or demons is probably connected with the religious interpretation of events: everything that threatens man, whether the attacks of enemies, sickness, or other kinds of misfortune, represents the forces in life that are hostile to God and to life; they are felt and depicted as being opposed to God, and therefore demonic.[91]

It follows from what has been said that the laments do not allow us to reconstruct the life history of the individual worshiper; what they express is typical and universal. Their purpose is not to describe a particular event, but to assign it to familiar categories. To characterize a form of suffering by means of standard expressions means at the same time to interpret it religiously: it is a work of forces hostile to God, and can be escaped only if the worshiper turns to God. This classification helps the individual to understand his suffering and shows him the way to obtain aid.[92]

A special problem attaches to the thanksgiving that stands at the conclusion of many laments (e.g., Ps. 22:23 ff. [Eng. 22:22 ff.]). This circumstance is perhaps best explained by the assumption of a divine

---

[86] See Widengren, op. cit.; H. J. Franken, *The Mystical Communion with Jhwh in the Book of Psalms* (Leiden: Brill, 1954), pp. 59 ff.; Ringgren, *Faith of the Psalmists*, pp. 61 f.

[87] See Widengren's discussion, op. cit., pp. 202 ff.

[88] S. Mowinckel, *Psalmenstudien* (2nd ed.; Amsterdam: Schippers, 1961), I, 121.

[89] Cf. Widengren, op. cit., pp. 197 ff.

[90] H. Birkeland, *The Evildoers in the Psalms* (Oslo: Dybvad, 1955), has developed this point of view to its extreme limit.

[91] Ringgren, *Faith of the Psalmists*, pp. 44 ff., 62 ff.

[92] Franken, op. cit.

oracle, now usually omitted: a priest or "cult prophet" announced that the prayer had been heard, at which point the worshiper gave thanks that his request had been granted. The psychological interpretation, to the effect that the worshiper, while he was praying, became confident that his request would be granted, is of course possible, but less satisfactory. Divine oracles are occasionally contained in the psalms (e.g., 91:14 ff.) or mentioned in them (e.g., 85:9 [Eng. 85:8]; perhaps also 51:10 [Eng. 51:8]), though not in the canonical laments.

The generalized descriptions of distress also make it difficult to determine the precise *Sitz im Leben* of certain laments. In a few psalms, in which the change of mood just described takes place and the passing of the speaker from death to life is depicted, Scandinavian scholars have found echoes of ritual suffering on the part of the king. A symbolic humiliation of the king does indeed take place at the Babylonian New Year's Festival. The king is stripped of his royal insignia, recites a negative confession before the high priest of Marduk, receives a box on the cheek from the priest, and is finally restored to his office. Many think that the Tammuz cult was concerned with a ritual death and resurrection, and that the king "played" the role of the god. It is uncertain to what extent similar ceremonies may have taken place in Israel; this question will be discussed in more detail below.[93] The strict formality of the laments makes it impossible to determine whether the suffering they refer to is real or ritual and typical. The decision must be based on other arguments. Other criteria must be studied to determine whether there existed a symbolic suffering and death of the king.

Probably even in the monarchy the psalms were sung by professional Temple singers and choirs.[94] Unfortunately, all our information on this point comes from late sources, especially the Chronicles, which naturally paint a picture of postexilic conditions, even though they place the institution of the guilds of singers in the time of David (I Chron. 15:16 ff.; 16:4 ff.). For the period of the monarchy, we have only the hints from the psalms mentioned above. At the conclusion of a psalm, the people could answer "Amen" ("truly") (Neh. 8:6) or "Hallelujah" (Ezra 3:11; I Chron. 16:36); such responses also come down to us in the Book of Psalms, and should therefore be considered early. Some psalms contain a refrain (Ps. 136; 118:1-4; 46:8, 12 [Eng. 46:7, 11]; 42:6, 12 [Eng. 42:5, 11]; 43:5), which may have been sung by the people or by special choirs.

Cultic dancing is mentioned several times.[95] When the ark was brought up to Jerusalem, "David and all the house of Israel were making merry before Yahweh with all their might, with songs and lyres

---

[93] Pp. 234 ff.

[94] De Vaux, *Ancient Israel*, pp. 382 ff., 391 f.

[95] Ehrlich, *op. cit.*, pp. 34 ff.

and harps and tambourines and castanets and cymbals" (II Sam. 6:5). In Psalm 149:3, we read, "Let them [the sons of Israel] praise his name with dancing, making melody to him with timbrel and lyre!" The dance performed around the golden calf (Exod. 32:6, 19) and the limping dance of the prophets of Baal on Mount Carmel (I Kings 18:26) are condemned as syncretistic and illegitimate. The very words ḥag, "feast," and pesaḥ, "Passover," however, probably contain a reminiscence of cultic dancing; the former actually means "circle" or "ring," the latter "hopping" or "limping," probably best understood as a ritual mimetic dance.

Finally, the existence of certain symbolic dramas in the Israelite cult has been suggested.[96] Such a suggestion admittedly rests primarily on comparative evidence; the psalms, however, do contain a few hints to support it. In Psalm 66:5, for example, we read:

> Come and see what God has done:
> he is terrible in his deeds among men.

The following verse states expressly that these deeds refer to the deliverance from Egypt, in other words, an historical event, or at least an event thought to be historical. Nevertheless, it is "seen." The question arises whether this event was somehow represented dramatically or symbolically. Psalm 46:9 (Eng. 46:8) suggests something similar:

> Come, behold the works of Yahweh,
> how he has wrought desolations in the earth.

This passage admittedly is not speaking of a specific historical occurrence, but of victory over the enemy in general; the context, however, does suggest a representation taking place in the Temple of the deeds of Yahweh "in the earth." In another psalm, also a Zion hymn, we read:

> As we have heard, so have we seen
> in the city of Yahweh of hosts. (Ps. 48:9 [Eng. 48:8])

In other words, something that has been told is also seen in Zion (the subject is victory over the enemy). However these passages are to be understood in detail, one thing can be stated with assurance: on the great festivals, something took place in the Temple that could be described as seeing the deeds of Yahweh.[97] Comparative evidence suggests a cultic drama, which would, so to speak, renew the event that took place in the past, so that its effects would be actualized once more and made productive for the people participating in the cult.

---

[96] Mowinckel, op. cit., II, 126 ff.; Ringgren, Faith of the Psalmists, pp. 15 ff.

[97] Ringgren, Faith of the Psalmists, p. 17; cf. also A. R. Johnson, Sacral Kingship in Ancient Israel (Cardiff: University of Wales, 1955), pp. 78 ff.

Psalm 48, just quoted, provides another interesting statement. We read in verse ten (Eng. vs. 9):

> We have thought on thy steadfast love, O God,
> in the midst of thy temple.

Now to "think of" something in Hebrew means more or less to experience it once more, to conjure up the events once more.[98] In addition, the Hebrew word used here could even mean "reproduce." This would cast new light on a statement contained in the Passover law in Exodus 12: the Passover is to be celebrated as a "memorial." The word *pesaḥ* seems originally to have referred to a limping dance, probably intended to imitate the hurried flight from Egypt; it is even prescribed that the Passover lamb is to be eaten in readiness for departure (Exod. 12:11). The Passover festival consequently means a re-experiencing of the events connected with the exodus. Even today the ritual for the Passover states that every Jew is to celebrate the feast as though he had himself been delivered out of Egypt. We are obviously dealing with a re-experiencing of the exodus, which is to be accomplished through certain symbolic actions.

In Deuteronomy we have further evidence for this view. In Deuteronomy 5:2-4, Moses says to the Israelites:

> Yahweh our God made a covenant with us in Horeb. Not with our fathers did Yahweh make this covenant, but with us, who are all of us here alive this day. Yahweh spoke with you face to face at the mountain, out of the midst of the fire.

Here Israelites of a later generation are really addressed as contemporaries of a past event. In chapter 29, Moses speaks once more to the people:

> You stand this day all of you before Yahweh your God . . . that you may enter into the sworn covenant of Yahweh your God, which Yahweh your God makes with you this day. (vss. 9, 11 [Eng. 10, 12])

The making of the covenant is re-experienced, so to speak, and renewed. A covenant renewal probably took place regularly in Israel.

It must be admitted that all of this comes very near to the idea of cultic drama. But it does not in itself justify us in suggesting other dramatic performances in the Israelite cult, such as a counterpart to the cultic battle at the Babylonian New Year's festival, which ends with the victory of the creator god over the forces of chaos, as long as there is no other basis for such an assumption.

---

[98] J. Pedersen, *Israel* (London: Oxford, 1959), I-II, 106 f. Cf. also B. Childs, *Memory and Tradition* (Naperville: Allenson, 1962).

f. The Festivals

As we have seen, sacrifices and other cultic ceremonies took place daily in the Temple. But certain days were considered particularly holy; they were observed in special ways.[99] The sacrificial laws prescribed special offerings for them. On the Sabbath, for instance, two lambs were sacrificed in addition to the daily sacrifices (Num. 28:9-10). The first day of the lunar month, the "new moon," was considered a feast day (Isa. 1:13 f.; Hos. 2:13 [Eng. 2:11]; Amos 8:5; cf. also I Sam. 20:5, 18, 26) and was observed with additional sacrifices (Num. 28:11-15). Psalm 81:4 (Eng. 81:3) also mentions the full moon as a feast day.

The general term for the great religious festivals is *ḥag*, which, as has already been noted, actually means movement in a circle or a round dance. It is etymologically identical with the Arabic *ḥaǧǧ*, which designates the pilgrimage to Mecca.

The laws of the Pentateuch contain no less than five lists of the great annual feasts. These lists differ widely in age; since they have preserved their individuality, the development and history of the Israelite festivals can be derived from them. The earliest calendar of feasts is found in the Book of the Covenant, Exodus 23:14-17. It is quite brief:

> Three times in the year you shall keep a feast [*ḥag*] to me. You shall keep the feast of unleavened bread; as I commanded you, you shall eat unleavened bread [*maṣṣôt*] for seven days at the appointed time in the month of Abib, for in it you came out of Egypt. . . . You shall keep the feast of harvest [*ḥag haqqāṣîr*] of the first fruits of your labor, of what you sow in the field. You shall keep the feast of ingathering [*ḥag hā'āsîp*] at the end of the year, when you gather in from the field the fruit of your labor. Three times in the year shall all your males appear before Yahweh, the Lord.

The first point to note is that all these feasts are agricultural, although the exodus from Egypt is referred to in connection with the feast of unleavened bread. This shows that the calendar reflects the situation of Israel when it was settled in Canaan. Probably the Israelites borrowed the names of the feasts and also many of the festival observances from the Canaanites.

Another calendar of feasts is contained in the "J" account of the covenant on Sinai, Exodus 34:18-23. It agrees for the most part with the calendar just quoted, mentioning the same series of three feasts.

[99] For general discussion of the festivals, see Ehrlich, *op. cit.,* pp. 52 ff.; E. Kutsch, "Feste und Feiern," *RGG,* II, cols. 910 ff.; De Vaux, *op. cit.,* chaps. xv and xvii; H. J. Kraus, *Gottesdienst in Israel* (2nd ed.; Munich: Kaiser, 1962), pp. 40 ff.

The second of them, however, is here called the feast of weeks (*ḥag šābū'ôt*).

The calendar of Deuteronomy (16:1-17) is somewhat more detailed. It differs from the other two in the fact that the first feast represents a combination of passover (*pesaḥ*) and the feast of unleavened bread. The former is the exodus feast, at which a lamb is slaughtered; the latter remains the feast of unleavened bread. The two other feasts are called the feast of weeks and the feast of booths (*ḥag hassukkôt*); no explanation is given of the latter name.

Within the so-called Holiness Code, Leviticus 23 contains a fourth calendar of feasts. Since it has taken over the Babylonian system of reckoning the months, it must represent a somewhat later stage of development than Deuteronomy 16. In addition to the three great feasts, this calendar lists a few other feast days: a passover lasting one day followed immediately by a seven-day feast of unleavened bread, a feast of first fruits, the feast of weeks, the first day of the seventh month (the old New Year's Day), the day of atonement on the tenth day of the seventh month, and, finally, the feast of booths. The same order of feasts is presupposed by the sacrificial regulations in Numbers 28—29, which specify precisely the sacrifices to be offered on each particular feast.

The Passover and Feast of Unleavened Bread.[100] As we have seen, the later calendars consider the Passover and feast of unleavened bread to be so closely connected that they seem almost one common feast. On the evening of the fourteenth day of the first month of the year (according to the postexilic calendar), a lamb is slaughtered, its blood smeared on the doorposts of the house, its flesh roasted and eaten with unleavened bread and bitter herbs. On the following day there begins a seven-day festival during which only unleavened bread (*maṣṣôt*) may be eaten (Lev. 23:5-8; Num. 28:16-25; Exod. 12:1-20, 40-51; similarly in Deut. 16:1-8, though here a distinction is made between the Passover and the feast of unleavened bread[101]). The earlier calendars, strangely enough, mention only the feast of unleavened bread as one of the three major festivals (Exod. 23:15; 34:18), mentioning the Passover separately (Exod. 34:25; perhaps also 23:18). We must assume that two originally independent

---

[100] Discussions of the passover include: F. Horst, *Das Privilegrecht Jahwes* (Göttingen: Vandenhoeck & Ruprecht, 1930), pp. 81 ff., reprinted in *idem, Gottes Recht* (Munich: Kaiser, 1961), pp. 106 ff.; J. Pedersen, "Passahfest und Passahlegende," *ZAW*, LII (1934), 161 ff.; *idem, Israel*, III-IV, 728 ff.; H. J. Kraus, "Zur Geschichte des Passah-Massot-Festes im Alten Testament," *ETh*, XVIII (1958), 47 ff.; E. Kutsch, "Erwägungen zur Geschichte der Passahfeier und des Massotfestes," *ZThK*, LV (1958), 1 ff. [Now see also J. B. Segal, *The Hebrew Passover* (London: Oxford, 1963).—TRANS.]

[101] Vss. 1, 2, 4b-7 refer to the Passover; vss. 3, 4a, 8 to the feast of unleavened bread.

religious observances have here coalesced, although the historical circumstances under which this happened can no longer be ascertained.

There is every reason to think that the feast of unleavened bread is rooted in an agricultural civilization and connected with the beginning of the barley harvest. The loaves of unleavened bread represent the first fruits of the field, and they are eaten in order to release the entire harvest for profane use. None of the old bread from the previous year may be kept; the new loaves mean a new beginning. Probably we have here a feast that was originally Canaanite and was borrowed by the Israelites.

The Passover, on the other hand, seems to fit best with a pastoral civilization. We may have here a feast originating among the nomadic Israelites, observed in the spring, at the time of transhumance, in order to protect the herds during the coming trek and promote the fertility of the animals.[102] The fact that the passover lamb was to be eaten in great haste and in complete readiness to depart might be connected with a readiness to depart in order to seek new places of pasturage. The smearing of blood on the doorposts would then be an apotropaic rite intended to provide protection against the "destroyer"—obviously a demonic figure (Exod. 12:23). The regulation against breaking any of the lamb's legs is familiar from many civilizations based on hunting. Its purpose may have been to assure the continued life of the animal. It must be pointed out, of course, that such ideas are not found at work anywhere in the Old Testament. The texts are ignorant of any other motivation for the Passover than reference to the exodus from Egypt. The same is true of the feast of unleavened bread (Exod. 23:15). This phenomenon could be considered proof that the connection between the two feasts is very ancient.

Whatever answer is given to the question of what these two feasts originally meant, it is a definite fact that, to the Israelite mind, they were inextricably linked with the deliverance from Egypt and were understood as memorial festivals. This is especially true for the Passover, of course; but the feast of unleavened bread seems to have had no independent significance, and is connected expressly with the exodus even in the earlier sources.

In this connection, it is significant that the word zikkārôn ("memorial," "remembrance") does not mean mental recall, but rather the re-evoking of events so that they are made "real" to the participants, whose life and actions they can influence (p. 184). Certain dramatic elements can even be found in the observance of Passover: the readiness to depart already mentioned; and the limping dance, perhaps alluded to in the name pesaḥ, which was probably intended to symbolize hurried flight. It is an open question whether we can

---

[102] L. Rost, "Weidewechsel und altisraelitische Festkalender," *ZDPV*, LVI (1943), 205 ff.

assume the existence of further elements of this sort; our answer will depend on how we take the institution legend Exodus 1—15. Engnell believes that he has discovered traces of a cultic sham fight in which the evil Pharaoh is conquered and of a nocturnal celebration (*lêl šimmûrîm*, "night of watching," Exod. 12:42) that concluded with the victory hymn Exodus 15:1-12.[103] Except for the psalm passages already mentioned, however, there is no real evidence to support the dramatic character of the Passover celebration. The Song of Songs is read in the synagogue on the eighth day of the feast of Passover, or rather the feast of unleavened bread; Engnell sees in this fact evidence for the celebration of a sacred marriage.[104] It must be said, however, that all evidence for reading the Song of Songs as part of the passover celebration is late (6th century C.E.) and that the traces of a *hieros gamos* in the Old Testament are disputed and precarious. It should be noted, though, that Judaism (e.g., in the Targum) interpreted the Song of Songs allegorically as referring to the covenant between Yahweh and Israel. Obviously it is difficult to do more than present hypotheses in this area.

Engnell has also pointed out interesting similarities between the structure of the Passover and the Babylonian *akītu* festival.[105] Both were celebrated in the spring, in the month of Nisan. If the Passover is reckoned as extending from the first day of preparation on the 10th of Abib (Nisan) to the 21st, the total length of the feast is eleven (or twelve) days, which corresponds exactly to the duration of the *akītu* festival. The cultic drama of the *akītu* re-enacts the victory over Tiamat, the primeval sea, and her consort Kingu; in the Passover, we have the Reed Sea and Pharaoh. It is also noteworthy that the passage through the sea is often depicted by means of the categories of the creation myth, that is, a myth that was one of the focal points of the *akītu* festival. Furthermore, the wilderness wandering is reminiscent of the Babylonian custom of celebrating a portion of the festival in a special sanctuary "in the open country" (*ina ṣēri*). There could well be some connection here. Possibly we should think of it in terms of a structural peculiarity of the ancient Near Eastern cults. The key element of the Israelite festival, however, has no parallel: the focal point of the Passover is an event thought to be historical, understood in "mythological" categories as an act of God.

The feast of weeks or harvest festival was celebrated seven weeks after the feast of unleavened bread.[106] In Numbers 28:26, it is also

---

[103] I. Engnell, "Paesaḥ-Maṣṣōt and the Problem of 'Patternism,'" *Orientalia Suecana*, I (1952), 39 ff., esp. 47.

[104] *Ibid.*, pp. 46 f.

[105] *Ibid.*

[106] E. Brögelmann, "Pfingsten in Altisrael," *MGKK*, XLIV (1939), 119 ff.; K. H. Rengstorf, "Christliches und jüdisches Pfingstfest," *ibid.*,

called "the day of the first fruits" (*bikkûrîm*). It was a joyous festival (Deut. 16:11; cf. also Isa. 9:2 [Eng. 9:3]) at the conclusion of the wheat harvest, at which, according to Leviticus 23:16 f., two loaves of bread were presented as an offering of first fruits. Here we unquestionably have an agricultural festival; the Old Testament gives no other explanation of the feast at all. Only later do we come upon an historicizing interpretation: the Book of Jubilees designates the feast of weeks as the time when the covenant was made between God and Noah, and also between God and Abraham (Jub. 6:17 f.; 15:1 f.); and in the Mishna and Talmud the feast of weeks is connected with the revelation of the ten commandments, which constitute the basis of the covenant. In this connection, one might point to Exodus 19:1, which states that the Israelites arrived at Sinai in the third month and there received the promise of the covenant; according to II Chronicles 15:10 ff., a covenant renewal was celebrated in the third month during the reign of Asa.[107] Whether the annual renewal of the covenant at Qumran took place at the feast of weeks cannot definitely be determined, but seems probable.[108]

The earliest sources (Exod. 23:16; 34:22) call the feast of booths the feast of harvest (*ḥag hā'āsîp*), and consider it also a feast of agricultural origin. It took place at the conclusion of the fruit harvest and vintage, and lasted seven days. It is characterized by joy and thanksgiving.[109] Judges 9:27 mentions a festival banquet with drinking at the time of the vintage, I Samuel 1:14 f. seems to suggest the possibility of excessive drinking, and Judges 21:19-21 speaks of dancing in the vineyards. It was, then, a typical joyous harvest festival that included partaking of the fruit of the vine.

The later calendars of feasts introduce a new explanation. In them the feast is called the feast of booths (*sukkôt*), supposedly because Israel dwelt in booths in the desert. This "dwelling in booths" was very possibly part of an ancient vintage festival. There is even evi-

---

XLV (1940), 75 ff.; cf. also G. Kretschmar, "Himmelfahrt und Pfingsten," *ZK*, LXVI (1954/55), 209 ff., esp. 222 ff.

[107] H. Wildberger, *Jahwes Eigentumsvolk* (Zürich: Zwingli, 1961), pp. 40 ff., connects the election with the feast of unleavened bread.

[108] M. Burrows, *More Light on the Dead Sea Scrolls* (New York: Viking, 1958), pp. 377 f.; for the contrary view, see S. Talmon, "The 'Manual of Benedictions,'" *RQ*, II (1960), 498 f.

[109] General discussions: A. Wensinck, "Arabic New Year and the Feast of Tabernacles," *Verhandel. d. kon. Akad. v. Wetensch.*, Letterk., N.R. 25:2 (1925); G. von Rad, *Das formgeschichtliche Problem des Hexateuchs* (Stuttgart: Kohlhammer, 1938), pp. 30 ff., reprinted in *idem, Gesammelte Studien* (Munich: Kaiser, 1958), pp. 41 ff.; A. Alt, "Zelte und Hütten," in H. Junker and J. Botterweck (ed.), *Alttestamentliche Studien, Fr. Nötscher zum 60. Geburtstag* (Bonn: Hanstein, 1950), pp. 16 ff., reprinted in *idem, Kleine Schriften* (Munich: Beck, 1953), pp. 233 ff.; H. J. Kraus, *Gottesdienst in Israel, Studien zur Geschichte des Laubhüttenfestes* (Munich: Kaiser, 1954).

dence suggesting that the booths were originally associated with the celebration of a sacred marriage.[110] Later, though, Israel reinterpreted the feast, giving it an historical basis. Here the same process is at work that we observed earlier in the case of the passover: transformation of a seasonal agricultural festival into a memorial of an historical event.

Apart from the regulations governing dwelling in booths, the only information given by the laws concerns the sacrifices to be offered. The Talmudic sources, on the other hand, provide a detailed description of the ritual in the late period of Judaism. Now this ritual is not built on the material in the Old Testament. Since the ceremonies are most reminiscent of the old fertility cult, this festival may quite possibly preserve extremely ancient practice. The worshipers, carrying various kinds of branches, marched in procession about the altar, which was decked with green willows. Lamps were lit and a dance was performed with torches. At dawn on the last day water was brought from the pool of Siloam and poured upon the altar as a drink offering. Offerings of wine were also made. The Mishna (Suk. V, 4) apparently still connects the light symbolism with the old sun cult. The water is poured out in order to produce rain; the fruits and branches obviously are explained by the old fertility cult. The booths were of course also originally connected with this cult.

The question remains, though, whether we have thus exhausted the significance of the festival. According to the earliest sources, we have here a feast celebrated at the turn of the year (Exod. 34:22 says "at the year's end," Exod. 23:16 says "at the beginning of the year"[111]); according to the later calendar, the beginning of the year came in the spring, and the feast of booths consequently fell in the seventh month. We must therefore see whether and to what extent the feast of booths possessed the character of a New Year's festival and was connected with other New Year's festivals of the ancient Near East, e.g., the Babylonian akītu. Unfortunately, our sources fail us almost completely at this point, at least if we are looking for direct evidence expressed in so many words. The suggested connection can be determined only indirectly and hypothetically.

Two theories in particular occupy the field: Mowinckel's theory of an enthronement festival of Yahweh, and the theory of a covenant festival supported by von Rad and Weiser. Both theories are based

---

[110] G. Widengren, *Sakrales Königtum* (Stuttgart: Kohlhammer, 1955), pp. 78 f.; H. Ringgren, in S. Linder, *Palästinische Volksgesänge*, I, (1952) 94 f.

[111] The statements are not precise, and probably cannot be reconciled. [The RSV translates the latter phrase as "at the end of the year" also; the Hebrew word, ṣēʾt, is the infinitive of the verb meaning "go out" or "come forth," and so could refer either to the "going out" of the old year or the "coming forth" of the new year.—TRANS.]

primarily on the cultic interpretation of certain psalms, and both have been vigorously challenged by other scholars.

Mowinckel takes as his point of departure[112] a group of psalms (primarily 47, 93, and 95—99) containing the phrase *yahweh mālak*, "Yahweh is king" or "Yahweh has become king."[113] Apart from Yahweh's kingship, these psalms deal primarily with the creation of the world, victory over enemies, and judgment of the nations. Since several other psalms contain one or more of these motifs even though they do not contain the formula "Yahweh is king," Mowinckel has also drawn upon them in his study.

The statement *yahweh mālak* corresponds precisely to a formula used at the enthronement of an earthly king, e.g., *mālak yēhû'*, "Jehu has become king" (II Kings 9:13).[114] Furthermore, the word *terû'â*, which occurs frequently in these psalms, is also used to refer to the shouts of joy that greet the accession of a new king.[115] Mowinckel rejects the eschatological and historical interpretation of these psalms, defending instead a cultic interpretation. He points out that both in Egypt and in Babylonia a god could be worshiped as king during a festival. He therefore concludes that Yahweh's enthronement was celebrated annually in Israel and that in the course of this celebration Yahweh was worshiped not only as king of the universe, but also as creator, victor, and judge. Then, having discovered the presence of a cultic drama, Mowinckel attempts to determine the legend and ritual of the Israelite "enthronement festival" on the basis of the psalms and the references in the Mishna. The legend contains three major components: the battle with the dragon and the creation of the world; victory over the enemies of Yahweh and Israel; and the judgment of the nations. The latter two elements probably express different aspects of the same idea. These motifs were probably dramatized through symbolic actions. The ritual also involved the light and water ceremonies known from the Mishna, which have already been described, as well as a procession in which Yahweh was felt to be present through the ark. Psalm 24 provides a description of this procession. The people making up the procession sing a brief hymn to Yahweh as creator (Ps. 24:1-2). When they come to the gates of the Temple, they ask, "Who shall stand in Yahweh's holy place?" (vs. 3). In re-

---

[112] Especially in *Psalmenstudien* (Amsterdam: Schippers, 1961), II; also in *Zum israelitischen Neujahr und zur Deutung der Thronbesteigungspsalmen* (Oslo: Dybwad, 1952).

[113] For a discussion of the translation, see D. Michel, "Studien zu den sog. Thronbesteigungspsalmen," *VT*, VI (1956), 40 ff. Michel defends the translation "Yahweh is king"; Mowinckel defends "Yahweh has become king," which, according to Michel, would demand the word order *mālak yahweh*. See, however, A. S. Kapelrud, "Nochmals *Jahwä mālak*," *VT*, XIII (1963), 299: ". . . has become king and is now active as king."

[114] Cf. below, p. 222.

[115] P. Humbert, *La terou'a, analyse d'un rite biblique*, 1946.

sponse, a priest names the conditions (vss. 4-6). Then the gates of the Temple are addressed: "Lift up your heads . . . that the King of glory may come in." The doorkeepers ask, "Who is the King of glory?" and are answered, "Yahweh, strong and mighty." Obviously Yahweh is thought to be present in the procession; probably only the ark could symbolize this presence. It is significant that Yahweh is here hailed as the victorious king. Psalm 47 obviously refers to the same procession:

> God has gone up with a shout,
> Yahweh with the sound of a trumpet.
>
> . . . .
>
> God reigns over the nations;
> God sits on his holy throne. (Ps. 47:6, 9 [Eng. 47:5, 8])

In Psalm 68:25 (Eng. 68:24), we read, "Thy solemn processions are seen, O God, the processions of my God, my King, into the sanctuary." The next verse mentions the accompanying music. Here we have a demonstrably cultic element. We are probably justified in assuming that the other psalms glorifying Yahweh as king are likewise connected with this procession. Schmidt speaks of "Yahweh's enthronement procession at the feast of the turn of the year."[116] The texts give no direct information on the extent to which creation, the battle with the nations, and the judgment of the nations were also represented by ritual actions. We do, however, have references to seeing the mighty acts of Yahweh; these references may refer to representation in symbolic drama.[117]

The most important argument against this theory is the fact that neither the laws nor the historical books show any knowledge of such a festival, at least of an independent festival of this nature. But if we are merely dealing with one aspect of the feast of booths, we cannot expect to find all its details treated in the laws; for the laws also fail to mention many other features known from the Mishna.

The other theory, defended by Weiser and von Rad,[118] argues for the existence of a covenant festival. Unlike Mowinckel's theory, this theory is supported by specific facts mentioned in the biblical texts. Deuteronomy provides for a public recitation of the law at the feast of booths every seven years (Deut. 31:10 ff.). This ceremony was probably also thought of as a renewal of the covenant based on the law. Joshua 24 bears witness to a covenant renewal at Shechem:

---

[116] H. Schmidt, *Die Thronfahrt Jahwes am Fest der Jahreswende im alten Israel* (Tübingen: Mohr, 1927).

[117] See above, p. 183.

[118] Von Rad, *Das formgeschichtliche Problem des Hexateuchs*, pp. 30 ff.; A. Weiser, *The Psalms*, trans. H. Hartwell (Philadelphia: Westminster, 1962), Introduction.

Joshua assembles the people and addresses them, reminding them of Yahweh's gracious acts in the past (the deliverance from Egypt, the desert wandering, the occupation of Canaan; vss. 2-13); he then exhorts the assembly to put away all foreign gods and serve Yahweh alone (vss. 14-23). The people express their willingness to fulfill these conditions, and the covenant between Yahweh and Israel is renewed (vs. 25).

Now in Deuteronomy 26 a confession of Yahweh's mighty acts in history, similar to Joshua's address, forms a part of the ritual connected with the presentation of first fruits (Deut. 26:5-9). Then, as was suggested above, some words follow that in reality imply a renewal of the covenant (vss. 16-19): "This day Yahweh your God commands you to do these statutes and ordinances . . . he is your God . . . you shall be a people holy to Yahweh your God. . . ." Furthermore, Deuteronomy 27 and 28 describe a ceremony connected with Shechem; this ceremony involves the pronunciation of blessings and curses upon those who keep the law and those who disobey it. It is legitimate to conclude that a regularly recurring renewal of the covenant took place at Shechem. Such a celebration must have appealed to the Sinai event, and in fact the Sinai pericope in Exodus contains several features that point to a cultic celebration: the people are to consecrate themselves (Exod. 19:14 f.), trumpets are sounded (Exod. 19:13, 16, 19), etc. This tradition must therefore have attained its present form in a cultic environment. Such a celebration may also be reflected in Psalms 50 and 81. The composition of the entire book of Deuteronomy also seems to suggest a definite series of ceremonies that corresponds rather closely to the Sinai narrative in Exodus:

1. Parenesis and historical account of the events at Sinai (Deut. 1—11; Exod. 19 f.).
2. Recitation of the law (Deut. 12—26:15; Exod. 20—23).
3. Statement of obligation (Deut. 26:16-19); conclusion of the covenant (Exod. 24).
4. Blessings and curses (Deut. 27 ff.); promise of blessing (Exod. 23:20 ff.).

This ceremony may represent the cultic *Sitz im Leben* of the Decalogue in Exodus 20 and Deuteronomy 5.

"In the cultic celebration Israel gave expression to the fact that the event which took place at Sinai had an undiminished importance for each age: it was renewed upon each succeeding generation: it was for all of them 'contemporary.' "[119] Or, in the terminology of comparative religion: the Sinai event here became the myth behind a cultic

---

[119] Von Rad, *Old Testament Theology*, p. 193.

drama, "in the course of which the fundamental events in the history of man's salvation were re-enacted; that is, at the performance of the sacral act, the cultic 'representation' . . . became a new 'event.' The congregation attending the feast experienced this as something which happened in its presence, and thereby participated in the assurance and realization of salvation which was the real purpose of the festival."[120]

According to Weiser, it is still possible to reconstruct some elements of this covenant festival on the basis of the psalms.[121] In fact, Yahweh's theophany, the self-revelation of God, which Weiser puts in first place, is described several times, e.g., Psalm 50:2-3:

> Out of Zion, the perfection of beauty,
>   God shines forth.
> Our God comes, he does not keep silence,
>   before him is a devouring fire,
>   round about him a mighty tempest.

This description fits both the Sinai event (Exod. 19 f.) and also the description of Yahweh's appearance given, for instance, by the Song of Deborah, the well-known victory song from the period of the Judges (Judg. 5), which sings of how Yahweh comes from Sinai to aid his people. Similar descriptions of theophanies are found in Psalm 18:8 ff. (Eng. 18:7 ff.); 68:8 f. (Eng. 68:7 f.); Deuteronomy 33:2; and Habakkuk 3:3 ff. Psalm 50 states, significantly, that Yahweh does not come from Sinai but from the Temple ("Zion"). It is no longer possible to determine how this theophany was visualized in the cult. It should be noted that the biblical writers are especially fond of connecting it with the concept of *kābôd*, "glory," "radiance." Possibly a ritual involving light or fire was performed.[122] Weiser goes on to suggest that a cloud of smoke (Lev. 16:12 f.; Isa. 6:4) and the sound of trumpets (Exod. 19:16, 19; Isa. 30:29 ff.; Ps. 47:6 [Eng. 47:5]; 98:6) must have formed part of the ritual.[123]

As a further constituent of the covenant festival, Weiser mentions the cultic recapitulation of God's work in history (Josh. 24:2 ff.; I. Sam. 12:8 ff.; cf. also Judg. 5:11).[124] Here we are dealing more or less with the same material discussed above, called a Credo by von Rad. There was also a proclamation of God's will (the law, the Decalogue) and a renewal of the covenant. The idea of judgment, which Mowinckel had found in the enthronement psalms, Weiser con-

---

[120] Weiser, *op. cit.*, p. 28.

[121] A. Weiser, "Theophanie in den Psalmen und im Festkult," in *Festschrift für Alfred Bertholet* (Tübingen: Mohr, 1950), pp. 513 ff.; *idem, The Psalms*, pp. 29, 35 ff.

[122] See above, pp. 90 f.

[123] *The Psalms*, p. 375.

[124] *Ibid.*, pp. 31, 42.

nects with the proclamation of God's will, together with the blessings and curses and the renunciation of foreign gods (Josh. 24:14 f., 23; Gen. 35:2 ff.). Psalm 50, for example, contains these elements: the theophany (vss. 2 f.), a reference to the covenant (vs. 5), the proclamation of Yahweh's will (vss. 7 ff.), and a pronouncement of judgment, which may perhaps be considered the counterpart of the curses.

In addition, Weiser would like to introduce here the idea of Yahweh's kingship and the concept of creation.[125] We are familiar with these ideas as essential elements of Mowinckel's enthronement festival. It is not quite clear, however, how we are to conceive the organic connection between these motifs and the covenant festival in the strict sense.

Obviously we are here dealing with two divergent interpretations of what are by and large the same data. The basic difference between them is that Mowinckel would like to place the Israelite data in the context of the New Year's festival found throughout the ancient Near East, but especially in Babylonia, while von Rad and Weiser work almost exclusively with the Israelite material contained in the Old Testament. Perhaps the two interpretations are not mutually exclusive. In all probability, the celebration of Yahweh's kingship is of Canaanite origin; in this context we find the motifs of creation and battle, which cannot be harmonized easily with the theory of a covenant festival, have good parallels elsewhere in the ancient Near East. The renewal of the covenant, on the other hand, is specifically Israelite; in this context we find the theophany and the motif of blessing and cursing —for these there are no parallels in the ancient Near East. From these two roots, then, the Israelite New Year's festival arose, as it can be reconstructed from the psalms as one aspect of the feast of booths.

All this raises a further question. If the Israelite New Year's festival of the pre-exilic period contains important elements common to the New Year's festival throughout the Near East (Babylonia, Canaan), are we justified in assuming the presence, in Israel, of those elements of this feast for which there is no express evidence? Even though this question has not hitherto been asked in quite such pointed form, in practice many scholars have nevertheless given an affirmative answer. It must be stated emphatically, however, that such a procedure is methodologically very suspect, even if one is inclined to follow a few British and Scandinavian scholars in defending the existence of a common cultural "pattern" in the ancient Near East.[126]

---

[125] *Ibid.*, pp. 33 f.

[126] In particular, S. H. Hooke (ed.), *Myth and Ritual* (London: Oxford, 1933); *Myth, Ritual and Kingship* (Oxford: Clarendon, 1958). Among the Scandinavians, special mention should be made of I. Engnell, G. Widengren, A. Kapelrud, A. Haldar, G. Ahlström. Cf. C. Westermann, "Kultgeschichtliche Schule," *RGG*, IV, cols. 93 f.

The evidence must nevertheless be examined to see whether traces of such mythological conceptions and cultic ceremonies cannot be found in some biblical texts. Two motifs are especially important in this regard: the dying and rising of the divinity, and the sacred marriage. The latter plays an important role in the Babylonian New Year's festival, and the Ras Shamra texts together with other material provide abundant evidence for the existence of both motifs in Canaan.

It is also disputed whether the motif of the dying and rising god is found in the Babylonian *akītu* festival. Certain texts tell how Bel (Marduk) is imprisoned in a "mountain" and then set free; these texts have been understood as evidence for the dying and rising of Marduk in the course of the cultic celebration of the festival. Recently, however, they have been interpreted differently.[127] There is abundant evidence of this motif, however, in the Tammuz cult and especially in the Canaanite Baal cult.[128] The Baal myth from Ras Shamra connects the return of the god with his kingship. Was there a similar conception in Israel? Widengren, for example, thinks this question must be answered affirmatively.[129] He connects the triumphal shout *ḥay yahweh*, "Yahweh lives," of Psalm 18:47 (Eng. 18:46) with the Ugaritic cry "Aliyan Baal lives," which announces the return to life of the divinity. Widengren finds in Hosea 4:15 ("Swear not, 'As Yahweh lives'") evidence that the prophet felt this formula to be Canaanite and consequently prohibited (cf. also Amos 8:14). In his view, furthermore, the summons to Yahweh to wake from his "sleep" (i.e., his failure to act; Isa. 51:9; Ps. 35:23; 59:5 f. [Eng. 59:4 f.]; 44:24 [Eng. 44:23]; cf. Ps. 7:7 [Eng. 7:6]; 78:65) is based on a vestige of the idea that Yahweh had been asleep, i.e., dead, and then awoke to attack his enemies and conquer them. In I Kings 18:27, a similar expression is applied to Baal.

These observations are undoubtedly important. It is certainly possible that some syncretistic circles in Israel made use of this Canaanite motif. On the other hand, the expressions quoted may quite well have been meant metaphorically; obviously they were so taken by the redactors of the psalter. The conception of a dying God seems irreconcilable with the genuine religion of Yahweh. Yahweh is the living God (*ēl ḥay*), who has power even over death (Ps. 48:15 [Eng. 48:14]).[130] His inactivity prior to the battle and victory makes

---

127 W. von Soden, *ZA*, N. F. XVII (1955), 130 ff.; cf. also A. Falkenstein in *Festschrift Friedrich*, 1959, pp. 147 ff.

128 [For a discussion of Tammuz, see T. Jacobsen, "Toward the Image of Tammuz," *HR*, I (1962), 189 ff.; *idem*, *Proceedings of the American Philosophical Society*, CVII (1963), 474 ff.; S. N. Kramer, *ibid.*, pp. 485 ff.—TRANS.]

129 *Sakrales Königtum*, pp. 68 ff.; cf. above, p. 87.

130 Cf. Johnson, *op. cit.*, p. 81.

an effective contrast with the triumph to come, but it does not necessarily mean that he has died.

Another fact deserves attention in this context. Hvidberg has pointed out several instances of cultic "weeping and laughter," which he understands as vestiges of the rites connected with the death and resurrection of the fertility god.[131] Now most of these passages (e.g., Hos. 7:14; Mic. 1:10; Jer. 5:7; Ezek. 8:14 f.; Zech. 12:11; Mal. 2:13) deal with practices that are syncretistic or even totally foreign to Israel, which the prophets are censuring. But Hosea 10:5 speaks of mourning and rejoicing "for the calf of Beth-aven," i.e., Bethel, where Yahweh was certainly worshiped in the "royal sanctuary." Judges 21:2 ff. tells how the people "lifted up their voices and wept bitterly" before God at Bethel, which, according to Hvidberg, could mean not only an isolated event, but also a rite performed annually. Furthermore, he points out that the people wept when Ezra read the law (Neh. 8:9), and he interprets this weeping as a reinterpreted vestige of ancient rites of mourning at the New Year's festival. It is certainly possible for ancient rites to live on with new meaning; but it must also be emphasized that the weeping in these instances is not connected with the death of a god. Mourning seems usually to have been taken as a penitential rite; when this was not the case, it was criticized as something alien. It is impossible to determine the extent to which syncretistic circles thought of Yahweh as a dying and rising god. There was hardly any recognition of this view in the official cult at Jerusalem.

We are in a much better position with regard to the sacred marriage.[132] In particular, we have the Song of Songs, which can hardly be understood as anything other than a garbled collection of songs for use at the sacred marriage.[133] Numerous stylistic similarities between the Song of Songs and Sumerian, Babylonian, and Ugaritic songs used at the sacred marriage point to a close connection. The fact that the bride retains the initiative excludes any interpretation of the text as secular marriage poetry.[134] Taken literally, i.e., without allegorical interpretations, the Song of Songs tells of the union at night between the (divine) bride and the (royal) bridegroom in a garden or bower. The time is spring, which of course excludes any connection with the feast of booths. We might think instead of a

---

[131] F. F. Hvidberg, *Weeping and Laughter in the Old Testament* (Leiden: Brill, 1962), esp. pp. 98 ff.

[132] Widengren, *Sakrales Königtum,* pp. 76 ff.; H. Ringgren, "Hieros gamos i Egypten, Sumer och Israel," *Religion och Bibel,* XVIII (1959), 23 ff., esp. 45 ff.

[133] H. Ringgren, *Das Hohe Lied* (Göttingen: Vandenhoeck & Ruprecht, 1958), Introduction.

[134] This point is emphasized particularly by H. Schmökel, *Heilige Hochzeit und Hohes Lied* (Wiesbaden: Steiner, 1956), p. 119.

vernal equivalent to the New Year's festival. Obviously we are dealing here with practices that are primarily Canaanite, but were engaged in by certain circles in Israel—the numerous references to cultic prostitution and rites performed under green trees in the prophetic books are proof enough. These rites became a popular custom, lost their original significance, and, reinterpreted allegorically as referring to the covenant between Yahweh and Israel, were taken into the Canon.

The Old Testament employs the marriage motif metaphorically in several ways. For instance, the relationship between Yahweh and Israel is often described as a marriage relationship (Hos. 2, esp. vss. 16-18 [Eng. vss. 14-16]; Jer. 2:2; Ezek. 23; 16:8; Isa. 62:4 f.). Did this image develop without any connection with the sacred marriage?[135] Was the sacred marriage in Israel reinterpreted as a symbol of the covenant even prior to the prophets, and did this interpretation arise in connection with the covenant festival? Our sources are not sufficient for a definite answer, but it is impossible a priori to deny the possibility that the prophets were not the first to use this image.

We come upon another use of the marriage metaphor in the wisdom literature.[136] There the relationship between (personified) Wisdom and her students is frequently described as a relationship of love (Prov. 4:6, 8; 7:4 f.; Sir. 14:23 ff.; 51:19 f.). In Proverbs 7:4-23 there even appears Wisdom's antagonist, "the loose woman," many of whose features are reminiscent of the cultic prostitutes of the Canaanite fertility cult. Here the image of Wisdom has obviously been embellished in deliberate polemic against pagan or syncretistic cults: the author wants to point to something comparable and at the same time better within his own religion.[137]

Since the pure cult of Yahweh knew nothing of any female divinity, it had no place for a sacred marriage. Nevertheless, the syncretistic practices of certain circles in Israel influenced the imagery of the Old Testament along these lines. The Song of Songs preserves allegorically interpreted popular songs used at the sacred marriage.

We can now sum up. The New Year's festival of the ancient Near East, as we know it primarily through the Babylonian *akītu* festival, comprised the following motifs: the creation of the world (the battle and victory of the creator-god), Marduk's kingship, the death and resurrection of the god (?), the humiliation and restoration of the king, the sacred marriage, and the determination of good fortune for the coming year. Of these, the enthronement psalms in Israel

---

[135] Cf. G. Widengren, "Early Hebrew Myths and their Interpretation," in S. Hooke (ed.), *Myth, Ritual and Kingship,* pp. 180 ff.; A. Neher, "Le symbolisme conjugal," *RHPR,* XXXIV (1954), 30 ff.; cf. below, p. 269.

[136] H. Ringgren, *Word and Wisdom* (Lund: Ohlsson, 1947), pp. 133 ff.

[137] Cf. also von Rad, *Old Testament Theology,* p. 444.

mention the creation of the world, together with the battle and victory of God and his kingship. But in Israel the royal motif plays a more important role than it does in Babylon: it has, in fact, become the leitmotif of this group of psalms. Of two other motifs, death-resurrection and the sacred marriage, we find only traces in the Old Testament. At most, they may have had a place in syncretistic forms of the Israelite religion.

Certain royal psalms and a few prophetical texts, whose interpretation is still debated, may contain hints of the humiliation of the king. We shall later return to this point.[138] Here we shall only point out that the ceremonies of the day of atonement may represent the vestiges of such a ritual of atonement in the New Year's festival, although in the postexilic period this day is the tenth day of the first month. In these ceremonies the High Priest obviously takes the place of the king, so that the sacrifice offered by him continues what had been a royal atonement ceremony.[139]

The psalms do not expressly mention the determination of destiny. The expression šûb šᵉbût, however, meaning "to turn the turn (of fortune)," which designates the sudden change from humiliation and defeat to victory and triumph (Ps. 14:7; 53:7 [Eng. 53:6]; 85:2 [Eng. 85:1]; 126:4), probably presupposes some such ritual.[140] There may be an allusion to this practice in Zephaniah 2:2, which uses the phrase "before a decree [ḥōq] is born" (RSV margin; presumably a divine decree) in connection with the day of Yahweh. Since the day of Yahweh was originally a festival in his honor, or, more precisely, his New Year's festival (as suggested by parallels elsewhere in the ancient Near East), we may have here a connection between the New Year's festival and a divine decree determining the fortune of Israel. As Largement and Lemaitre point out, it is also significant that Leviticus 23:36 calls the eighth day of the feast of booths an 'ăṣeret. This word is usually translated "solemn assembly," but these two scholars think it may possibly be connected with the Akkadian uṣurāti.[141]

In making these remarks, we must never lose sight of the fact that the only evidence for this feast is found in the psalms and in non-Israelite parallels; the laws and the historical books do not mention it explicitly. Furthermore, the psalms mentioned provide no evidence to connect it with the feast of booths. Zechariah 14:16 reads, "Then every one that survives of all the nations that have come against

138 See below, pp. 234 ff.
139 Widengren, Sakrales Königtum, pp. 22 f.
140 Mowinckel, Psalmenstudien, II, 75 f., 287 f.; E. L. Dietrich, Šûb šᵉbût: die endzeitliche Wiederherstellung bei den Propheten (Giessen: Töpelmann, 1925); E. Baumann, "Šûb šᵉbût," ZAW, XLVII (1929), 17 ff.
141 R. Largement and A. Lemaitre, "Le jour de Yahweh dans le contexte original," SP, I (1959), 259 ff.

Jerusalem shall go up year after year to worship the King, Yahweh of hosts, and to keep the feast of booths." This passage would be of decisive significance, since it connects the kingship of Yahweh with the feast of booths, and since the following verse makes the coming of the rain depend on the celebration of this feast, which sounds like an ancient feature of the fertility religion. Unfortunately, however, the text of Zechariah 14 is so late that considerable reservations must attend any conclusions drawn from it with regard to the pre-exilic period.

Perhaps we may state our conclusions as follows: a group of Israelite psalms contains evidence that certain motifs indigenous to ancient Canaan occur also in Israel; but the sources know nothing of a special feast associated with these motifs, nor can a connection between these motifs and the feast of booths be proved conclusively. The fact that the Babylonian *akītu* was celebrated in the spring does not contradict the theory of an Israelite New Year's festival in autumn; as is well-known, any new beginning in the annual cycle can be observed as a New Year's festival. In Egypt there were at least two yearly feasts with the character of New Year's festivals. The question arises whether the simplest way to explain this whole complex of motifs in the psalms is not to assume that it was based on a cultic observance, the more so because good parallels can be found among the neighboring peoples.

Opinions can still differ as to details, but on the whole it seems probable that pre-exilic Israel at the feast of booths celebrated Yahweh's kingship and creation of the world, and also renewed the covenant with him. The former motif, found throughout the Near East, Israel probably borrowed from Canaan; the latter is the historical reinterpretation of an ancient festival, so characteristic of Israel. The covenant festival, probably originally independent of the New Year's festival, seems to have been most intimately associated with Shechem, while the festival of Yahweh's kingship presumably originated at Jerusalem or was borrowed there from the Canaanite cult.[142] In the postexilic period, the components of the festival were distributed over three different days: the feast of booths, New Year's Day, and the Day of Atonement. At Qumran, however, the Essenes still combined renewal of the covenant with the rite of atonement.

g. The Sabbath

The fourth commandment of the Decalogue (or the third, by a different enumeration) contains the following law:

---

[142] Cf. G. Mendenhall, *Law and Covenant* (Pittsburgh: Biblical Colloquium, 1955), p. 46; R. Marshall, *LQR,* XIV (1962), 33 ff.; H. Ringgren, "Enthronement Festival or Covenant Renewal?" *BR,* VII (1962), 45 ff.

Remember the sabbath day, to keep it holy. Six days you shall labor, and do all your work; but the seventh day is a sabbath to Yahweh your God; in it you shall **not do any work**. . . . (Exod. 20:8-10)

In other words, every seventh day is to be a day of rest, on which no work must be done.[143] Strangely, the two versions of the Decalogue give different reasons for the Sabbath commandment. In Deuteronomy 5:14 f., the criterion is humanitarian: Israel's slavery in Egypt and subsequent deliverance are mentioned, and the conclusion is drawn that sympathy should lead the Israelites to grant rest to their servants (slaves) and domestic animals. In Exodus 20:11, on the other hand, reference is made to the (Priestly) creation account: in six days Yahweh created the world, but he rested on the seventh day. Therefore the Israelites should also rest on the seventh day. Now, as we have seen, the creation account in Genesis 1 has been adjusted to fit the seven-day scheme.[144] The basis for the Sabbath given in Exodus must therefore be considered secondary. Of course this does not mean that the basis given in Deuteronomy is original; in all probability, it is also secondary. All that remains is the fact that the Sabbath was observed.

The origin of the institution of the Sabbath is obscure. Genesis 2:3 at least hints at a connection between the word šabbāt and the verb šābat, "rest." It is doubtful, however, whether this derivation is correct; for, according to general Hebrew usage, the nominal form šabbāt would refer to a person who engages in the "activity" of resting. The question arises therefore whether we may be dealing with a loan word. If so, the only possibility is the Akkadian šapattu, the name of the day of the full moon, which falls in the middle of the month. This day was considered a "day for quieting the heart [of the gods]" and a day of good fortune generally. But as far as we know the šapattu is not a day of rest, nor does it have anything to do with the seven-day interval of the Israelite Sabbath. The Babylonian hemerologies do provide another parallel: the 7th, 14th, 19th, 21st, and 28th days of the month were looked upon as "evil" days. Here we have the seven-day interval; but the function and significance of these days are completely different from the function and significance of the Sabbath. In

---

[143] Literature on the problem of the Sabbath: J. Meinhold, *Sabbat und Woche* (Göttingen: Vandenhoeck & Ruprecht, 1905); J. Hehn, *Siebenzahl und Sabbat bei den Babyloniern und im Alten Testament* (Leipzig: Hinrichs, 1907); E. G. Kraeling, "The Present Status of the Sabbath Question," *AJSL*, XLIX (1932/33), 218 ff.; G. J. Botterweck, "Der Sabbat im Alten Testament," *TQ*, CXXXIV (1954), 134 ff., 448 ff.; E. Jenni, *Die theologische Begründung des Sabbatgebotes* (Zollikon-Zürich: Evangelischer Verlag, 1956); H. J. Kraus, *Gottesdienst in Israel* (2nd ed.; Munich: Kaiser, 1962), pp. 98 ff. [For a recent discussion in English, see R. North, "The Derivation of Sabbath," *Biblica*, XXXVI (1955), 182 ff.—TRANS.]

[144] See above, p. 106.

addition, they are not called *šapattu*.[145] This exhausts the possibilities for elucidating the background of the Sabbath. Periods of seven days or seven years are occasionally mentioned in the Ugaritic texts,[146] but this does not prove that the Canaanites had a seven-day week, nor is there any indication of an institution like the Sabbath. The theory of Kenite origin[147] is merely an attempt to explain one unknown by means of another.

Only this much can be stated with some assurance: the Israelite Sabbath is an ancient institution; it is mentioned not only in the Decalogue, but also in the Book of the Covenant (Exod. 23:21) and in the cultic dodecalogue of the "Yahwist" (Exod. 34:12). It may have originated outside Israel, but detailed evidence is lacking. Furthermore, observance of a particular day as a feast day or a day of rest is found among a number of peoples; but this does not enable us to exhibit a genetic relationship.[148]

The earliest references outside the laws mention the Sabbath as a festival together with the day of the new moon and solemn assemblies (Isa. 1:13; Hos. 2:13 [Eng. 2:11]; cf. II Kings 4:23—does this indicate that the Sabbath was originally the day of the full moon?). We also learn that it was a day on which no trade could be carried on (Amos 8:5). Such passages as II Kings 4:23 and 11:5-8, however, show that the Sabbath was not yet a day of strict abstinence from all work: a journey could be undertaken, the palace guard was relieved. The strict observance of later times was still unknown. As we shall see, this strictness developed during the exile.[149] The important point is that the Sabbath was primarily a day specially dedicated or "holy" to the Lord (Exod. 31:15); it was "the sabbath of Yahweh" or "a sabbath for Yahweh" (Lev. 23:38).[150] Although these passages are presumably postexilic, the idea that the Sabbath belongs to the Lord is surely ancient.

We are otherwise poorly informed about the observance of the Sabbath in pre-exilic Israel. The laws prescribe special sacrifices for the Sabbath (Num. 28:9 f.), but we do not know how old this ordinance is. An equally late text calls the Sabbath a day of "holy convocation" (Lev. 23:3), which definitely suggests special cultic observances.

---

145 For a discussion of the various theories, see E. Kutsch, "Sabbat," *RGG*, V, cols. 1258 f.

146 C. Gordon, *Or*, NS XXII (1953), 79 ff.; E. Kutsch, "Erwägungen zur Geschichte der Passafeier und des Massotfestes," *ZThK*, LV (1958), 25 ff., contains a good discussion.

147 K. Budde, "The Sabbath and the Week," *JTS*, XXX (1929), 1 ff.

148 Ehrlich, *op. cit.*, p. 77.

149 See below, p. 298.

150 Cf. von Rad, *Old Testament Theology*, p. 241.

h. Circumcision

In obedience to the law, every male child had to be circumcised (Lev. 12:3). During and after the exile, this rite of initiation acquired the special significance of being a mark of the Israelites; in reality, however, it is by no means an exclusively Israelite practice. It was performed in Egypt, for example, at the consecration of children (despite some interpretations of Josh. 5:9), although it was necessary only in the case of priests.[151] There appears to be no mention of circumcision at Ugarit, but Herodotus seems to witness to the custom among the Phoenicians.[152] Similarly, the Ammonites (despite Jth. 14:10, a late passage), Moabites, and Edomites were familiar with circumcision (Jer. 9:25 f.). The term "uncircumcised" is applied by the Old Testament primarily to the Philistines (Judg. 15:18; I Sam. 14:6; 18:25-27; 31:4). This term is not applied to the Canaanites; a carving from Megiddo corroborates the existence of circumcision.[153]

There are two traditions concerning the origin of circumcision. On the one hand, Exodus 4:25, a passage obscure in many respects, tells of the circumcision of Moses. This account must probably be understood as an etiological legend. On the other hand, the custom is traced back to Abraham (Gen. 17:9-14). The latter tradition is obviously more recent. The Abraham passage also presupposes that young children were circumcised, while the earlier sources obviously connect it with adolescence (Gen. 34; Exod. 4:25; and Josh. 5:2 f., which tells how the practice was reinstituted upon the soil of Palestine).

Originally circumcision may have signified readiness for marriage, or at least a rite of puberty. Genesis 34:14-16 demands the circumcision of the Shechemites before they may marry Israelite women. In Exodus 4:25, Moses is called a "bridegroom of blood" (ḥatan dāmîm) after his circumcision. The Hebrew word ḥātān, which designates a relationship through marriage, is derived from a root that in Arabic refers to circumcision. Only later did it become customary to circumcise children. Then the rite took on the meaning presupposed in Genesis 17: it expresses membership in the chosen people and participation in the covenant between Yahweh and Israel. As a consequence, only the circumcised may participate in the Israelite cult (Exod. 12:47-48).[154]

---

[151] H. Bonnet, *Reallexikon der ägyptischen Religionsgeschichte* (Berlin: De Gruyter, 1952), pp. 109 ff.

[152] E. Meyer, "Zur Beschneidung der Phöniker," *ZAW*, XXIX (1909), 152, despite Ezek. 32:30.

[153] *ANEP*, fig. 332.

[154] [For a discussion of Exod. 4:25, see B. S. Childs, *Myth and Reality in the Old Testament* (Naperville: Allenson, 1960), pp. 58 ff.—TRANS.]

9.

THE CULTIC FUNCTIONARIES

The earliest traditions of the Old Testament presuppose that there was no regular priesthood. As the heads of families, the patriarchs perform cultic acts, e.g., sacrifices (Gen. 22; 31:54; 46:1). As late as Judges 13 the father of Samson personally offers sacrifice to Yahweh. But priests are also mentioned as early as the period of the Judges (Judg. 17).

The Hebrew word for priest is *kōhēn*.[1] This word occurs with the same meaning in Ugaritic, Phoenician, and Nabataean. The Arabic *kāhin* has the primary meaning of soothsayer, although a *kāhin* does appear occasionally as a sanctuary attendant.[2] Another word, *kmr*, plural *kᵉmārîm*, is applied by the Old Testament only to priests of foreign gods (II Kings 23:5; Hos. 10:5; Zeph. 1:4); it is found also among the Assyrians in Cappadocia, in Old Aramaic, in Palmyrene, and in Syriac.[3]

The derivation of the word *kōhēn* is not definitely known. Two suggestions have been made: the root *kwn*, "stand" (the priest stands before God as his servant), or the Akkadian *kānu* (root *k'n*), "bow."[4] Both suggestions require the assumption of a comparatively uncommon phonetic change (*w* or ' to *h*). Since all the languages in which the word occurs witness to the root *khn*, these derivations are

---

[1] Literature on the priesthood: W. W. von Baudissin, *Die Geschichte des alttestamentlichen Priestertums* (Leipzig: Hinrichs, 1889); G. B. Gray, *Sacrifice in the Old Testament* (Oxford: Clarendon, 1925), pp. 179-270; G. R. Berry, "Priests and Levites," *JBL*, XLII (1923), 227 ff.; S. H. Hooke, *Prophets and Priests* (London: Oxford, 1938); O. Plöger, "Priester und Prophet," *ZAW*, LXIII (1951), 157 ff.; M. Noth, *Amt und Berufung im Alten Testament* (Bonn: Hanstein, 1958), reprinted in *idem, Gesammelte Studien* (Munich: Kaiser, 1960), pp. 309 ff.

[2] A. Haldar, *Associations of Cult Prophets among the Ancient Semites* (Uppsala: Almqvist & Wiksell, 1945), pp. 163 ff.

[3] C.-F. Jean and J. Hoftijzer, *Dictionnaire des inscriptions sémitiques de l'ouest* (Leiden: Brill, 1962), *s. v.*; cf. J. Février, *La religion des Palmyréniens*, p. 167; Haldar, *op. cit.*, p. 77.

[4] Cf. Haldar, *op. cit.*, p. 84.

204

quite unlikely. The etymology can cast little light on the original meaning of the word.

In the pre-monarchic period, the priest appears as the attendant of a sanctuary and a giver of oracles. Micah builds a shrine in Ephraim, installing as priest first his son and then a Levite, to care for the shrine and its image (Judg. 17). At Shiloh, Eli serves as guardian of the ark and Temple (I Sam. 1—4). I Samuel 2:28 mentions in addition the offering of sacrifice and the use of the ephod, i.e., supervision of the oracle, as duties of the Elide priesthood. Verse thirty summarizes all these functions as "going in and out before Yahweh." According to I Samuel 7:1, as soon as the ark was recovered from the Philistines, a guardian was appointed for it. Joshua 3 speaks of priests carrying the ark during the crossing of the Jordan; since we are here dealing with a tradition associated with Gilgal, we may probably assume that priests guarded the sanctuary there, also.

In the earliest period, the giving of oracles was obviously one of the most important priestly functions.[5] In the Blessing of Moses (Deut. 33), the first thing said about the priestly tribe of Levi is that it has charge of the oracle; only afterwards are instruction in the law and offering of sacrifice mentioned (vss. 8-10). Exodus 33:7-11 preserves an ancient tradition: the Israelites come to the tent sanctuary, here called the tent of meeting, in order to "seek" (*dāraš*) Yahweh, i.e., in order to obtain an oracle. Yahweh, whose presence is symbolized by a pillar of cloud that descends upon the tent, speaks to Moses, who in turn repeats the divine oracle to the inquirer. At the conclusion of the pericope, Joshua appears as guardian of the tent (vs. 11). This direct intercourse with Yahweh is reserved to Moses, however; the priests must make use of mechanical aids. The most important aids mentioned in the Old Testament are the ephod and the Urim and Thummim.

The word ephod has many meanings, and has therefore occasioned many hypotheses.[6] In a few early passages, it seems to refer to a cult object (Judg. 8:27; 17:5; 18:14, 17, 20; I Sam. 2:28; 14:3; 21:10 [Eng. 21:9]; 23:6, 9; 30:7). In two cases it is clear that the ephod was used to make inquiry of Yahweh. In addition, the word can also mean a linen garment worn by the priests (I Sam. 2:18; 22:18; II

---

[5] General studies include: J. Döller, *Die Wahrsagerei im Alten Testament* (Münster, 1923); A. Guillaume, *Prophecy and Divination among the Hebrews and other Semites* (New York: Harper, 1938); F. Küchler, "Das priesterliche Orakel in Israel und Juda," in W. Frankenberg (ed.), *Abhandlungen zur semitischen Religionskunde und Sprachwissenschaft W. W. von Baudissin dargebracht* (Giessen: Töpelmann, 1918), pp. 285 ff.

[6] H. Thiersch, *Ependytes und Ephod* (Stuttgart: Kohlhammer, 1936); E. Sellin, "Noch einmal der alttestamentliche Efod," *JPOS*, XVII (1937), 236 ff.; *idem*, "Zu Efod und Terafim," *ZAW*, LV (1937), 296 ff.; H. G. May, "Ephod and Ariel," *AJSL*, LVI (1939), 44 ff.; K. Elliger, "Ephod und Choschen," *VT*, VIII (1958), 19 ff.

Sam. 6:14), and in the later laws a special vestment of the high priest (Exod. 28:6-14; 29:5; 39:2-7; Lev. 8:7) which had a pocket (or breast piece, *ḥōšen*), to contain the Urim and Thummim.[7]

How the word came to have these various meanings remains obscure. The etymology suggests that it originally referred to a garment: in the Ugaritic texts, *ipd* is the garment worn by the goddess Anat; the Akkadian *ēpattu* (plural *ēpadātu*) is the name of a costly garment. Possibly such a garment served to dress a divine image or the like, used for obtaining oracles, and the name came to be applied to the image. Since images were prohibited in the worship of Yahweh, only the garment remained as a priestly vestment. The original association with oracles was preserved, however.

The Urim and Thummim were employed to obtain an oracle by lot.[8] According to Numbers 27:21, they were entrusted to Eleazar the priest. Deuteronomy 33:8 (an early passage), however, states that the tribe of Levi was in charge of them. I Samuel 14:41 f. (LXX) shows that we are dealing with two lots that allow a choice between two alternatives: Are Saul and his son Jonathan guilty, or are the people guilty? Is it Saul himself, or Jonathan? If Urim appears, the one alternative is correct; if Thummim, the other. In this connection, the usual suggestion is stones kept in a pocket; but small sticks of wood would also be a possibility: the ancient Arabs had an oracle called *istiqsām*, for which arrows were used,[9] and the Old Testament contains a similar word (*qesem*), which refers to a kind of divination that is usually prohibited (Prov. 16:10 is an exception). Hosea 4:12 also mentions divination with articles of wood and staffs. The actual meaning of the words *ûrîm* and *tummîm* is obscure. At first glance, we seem to have here words for "light" and "perfection." Perhaps, however, originally only the first and last letters of the Hebrew alphabet, aleph and tau, were inscribed on the stones, and these were later interpreted as abbreviations for *ûrîm* and *tummîm*.[10]

Strangely enough, neither the ephod nor Urim and Thummim are mentioned after the time of David. In cases where we might expect divination by these means, the later practice was to have recourse to prophets (I Kings 20:13 f.; 22:6; II Kings 3:11). It is not unlikely that this state of affairs points to a differentiation of the priestly

---

[7] [This variation of meaning is partially obscured by the RSV, which follows the traditional KJV rendering of the Hebrew phrase *nāśā' ēpôd:* "to wear an ephod" (I Sam. 2:28; 14:3). The verb *nāśā'*, "lift," "bear," is never used to mean "wear"; the meaning of the two passages in question must be simply "carry an ephod."—TRANS.]

[8] R. Press, "Das Ordal im Alten Testament," *ZAW*, LI (1933), 227 ff.; J. Lindblom, "Lot-casting in the Old Testament," *VT*, XII (1962), 164 ff.

[9] J. Wellhausen, *Reste arabischen Heidentums* (2nd ed.; Berlin: Reimer, 1897), pp. 132 f.

[10] Lindblom, *op. cit.*, p. 170.

functions, and that during the monarchy divination was primarily the job of prophets, who made use of other techniques.

Another duty of the priests was to give instruction.[11] Ezekiel shows that the priests were supposed to instruct the people in the distinction between what was holy and what was common, what was clean and what was unclean (Ezek. 22:26; 44:23; cf. the unique instance in Hag. 2:11-13). Micah denounces the priests because they teach (*hôrâ*) for hire (Mic. 3:11). This instruction is called *tôrâ*, "law" (Deut. 31:9, 26; 33:10; Hos. 4:6; Jer. 18:18; Ezek. 7:26), a word that is connected with the verb *hôrâ*, and corresponds etymologically to the Akkadian *tērtu*, "oracle."[12] Probably priestly instruction also covered more areas than the distinction between clean and unclean, etc. The later semantic development of the word shows that legal decisions were also arrived at by the priests in this fashion. As we have seen, *tôrâ*, which originally referred to any decision or instruction, later became the ordinary word for "law." This means that the priests were the expert administrators of God's law.

Form-critical analysis shows that the priests frequently used so-called declaratory formulas,[13] e.g., in rendering decisions concerning leprosy: "It is leprosy" (*ṣāraʿat hûʾ*), "He is clean" (*ṭāhor hûʾ*) (Lev. 13:15, 17); or in legal decisions: "He is righteous, he shall surely live" (*ṣaddîq hûʾ, ḥāyô yiḥyeh*); "He shall surely die" (*môt yûmāt*) (forms preserved in Ezek. 18:9, 13); etc.[14]

The way in which instruction in the sacral law was given can perhaps be determined from certain literary *Gattungen*. First of all, we have the so-called entrance liturgy, which summarized briefly for those visiting the Temple the demands that were made of them. In Psalm 15, for example, the psalmist asks, "Yahweh, who shall sojourn in thy tent? Who shall dwell on thy holy hill?" A voice, probably belonging to a priest, answers, "He who walks blamelessly, and does what is right, and speaks truth from his heart," etc.[15] The concise formulas of so-called apodictic law probably also belong in this category.[16]

---

[11] J. Begrich, "Die Priesterliche Tora," in J. Hempel (ed.), *Werden und Wesen des AT* (Berlin: Töpelmann, 1936), pp. 63 ff.; G. Östborn, *Tora in the Old Testament* (Lund: Ohlsson, 1945), pp. 89 ff.; O. Plöger, "Priester und Prophet," *ZAW*, LXIII (1951), 157 ff.

[12] I. Engnell, *Israel and the Law* (Uppsala: Wretmans, 1946), pp. 1 ff.

[13] R. Rendtorff, *Die Gesetze in der Priesterschrift* (Göttingen: Vandenhoeck & Ruprecht, 1954), pp. 74 ff.; G. von Rad, "Die Anrechnung des Glaubens zur Gerechtigkeit," *TLZ*, LXXVI (1951), cols. 129 ff.; *idem*, *Old Testament Theology*, trans. D. M. G. Stalker (Edinburgh & London: Oliver & Boyd, 1962), I, 246 f., 259 ff.; W. Zimmerli, "Die Eigenart der prophetischen Rede des Ezechiel," *ZAW*, LXVI (1954), 23 f., reprinted in *idem, Gottes Offenbarung* (Munich: Kaiser, 1963), pp. 173 ff.

[14] W. Zimmerli, "'Leben' und 'Tod' im Buche des Propheten Ezechiel," *ThZ*, XIII (1957), 494 ff., reprinted in *idem, Gottes Offenbarung* (Munich: Kaiser, 1963), pp. 178 ff.

[15] Cf. above, pp. 134 f., 191 f.

[16] Cf. above, p. 135.

Those series of short commandments setting out God's will in terms of a simple "You shall" or "You shall not" were recited at the great festivals in order to impress the divine law upon the people participating in the feast. In the course of time, however, they were expanded through all kinds of supplements and motivation clauses. What we find in Deuteronomy would be better termed preaching about the law than regular proclamation of the law. The short commandments are here embedded in longer discourses and can only tentatively be isolated. According to von Rad, this preaching of the law was the task of the Levites.[17]

Finally, the priest had sacrificial duties.[18] The idea that he alone had the privilege of offering sacrifice, however, belongs to a later era. In the earliest period, any head of a family clearly could offer sacrifice. Even in later periods, the sacrificial animal had to be killed by the person offering it (Lev. 1:5; 3:2, 8; 4:24 f.; etc.); the duties of the priest were limited to sprinkling the altar with blood and burning the sacrifice. In other words, the priest performed his sacrificial duties at the altar (I Sam. 2:28; cf. II Kings 23:9).[19] When offering sacrifice, the priest had certain declaratory formulas to recite: "It is a burnt offering" (*'ôlâ hû'*; Exod. 29:18; Lev. 1:9, 12, 17), "It is a cereal offering" (*minḥâ hû'*; Lev. 2:6, 15). The priest speaks here as the commissioned representative of God. It seems likely that only the divine word pronounced by the priest can make the sacrifice valid and effective. There may also have been a formula of acceptance, "It is accepted"; all the examples, however, are negative: "It is not accepted" (*lō' yērāṣeh*; Lev. 19:7; 22:23, 25). Although God is ultimately the one who accepts or rejects the sacrifice, it was incumbent upon the priest to declare God's rejection (or, probably, acceptance). "Only the addition of the divine word made the material observance what it was meant to be, a real saving event between Jahweh and his people. Only in virtue of the declaratory word of the priest did the sacral event become a gracious act of God."[20]

As a man endowed with divine authority, the priest also appears at the blessing of the people. On certain occasions, he has formulas of blessing to pronounce, thereby securing blessing (*berākâ*) for the worshiping community. The psalms contain such formulas of blessing, e.g., "Blessed be he who enters in the name of Yahweh!" (Ps.

---

[17] G. von Rad, *Studies in Deuteronomy*, trans. D. Stalker (London: SCM, 1953), pp. 66 f.

[18] L. Gautier, "Prétre ou sacrificateur?" *Études sur la religion d'Israel*, 1927, pp. 247 ff.; A. E. J. Rawlinson, "Priesthood and Sacrifice," *ET*, LX (1949), 115 ff.

[19] R. de Vaux, *Ancient Israel*, trans. J. McHugh (New York: McGraw-Hill, 1961), pp. 355 f.

[20] Von Rad, *Old Testament Theology*, p. 262.

118:26),[21] "Yahweh bless you from Zion!" (Ps. 128:5). Numbers 6:24 ff. provides a longer formula:

Yahweh bless you and keep you:
Yahweh make his face to shine upon you, and be gracious to you:
Yahweh lift up his countenance upon you, and give you peace.

In this fashion, says Yahweh, the priests "shall put my name upon the people of Israel, and I will bless them." A similar formula of blessing, likewise consisting of three elements, is known from Babylonia, although it names three different deities.[22]

From the point of view of comparative religion, we have here a special development of magically effective blessings: once they are pronounced, their fulfillment is automatic. The Old Testament, too, is familiar with the magical efficacy of a blessing: the aged Isaac blesses Jacob instead of his first-born, Esau, and cannot retract the blessing; the word has been spoken and must be fulfilled. Pedersen has described this transmission of blessing (or *berākâ*) as the communication of magical power (akin to *mana*).[23] It is noteworthy, though, that in Israel blessing was always conceived of as the gift of Yahweh, not as an independent entity or power. Therefore the formula of blessing is either a promise of blessing spoken on divine authority or an expression of the desire that Yahweh should give his blessing.[24]

Curses, too, were pronounced by priests in the course of sacral actions; they have not left many traces in the literature, however. Curses uttered by priests appear primarily in the context of the covenant festival; we find them in Deuteronomy 27 f. There, however, they are not unconditional curses called forth by specific situations, but rather curses that will come to pass if the commandments are not obeyed. In other words, the curse is thought of as a divine punishment following upon any transgression. In similar fashion, some of the psalms assimilated ancient curse formulas, so that they appear in the form of prayers that God take vengeance upon the godless (e.g., Ps. 58:7-10 [Eng. 58:6-9]).[25]

---

[21] [This is the rendering of the RSV; the author's punctuation ("Blessed be he who enters, in the name of Yahweh") connects the name of Yahweh with the blessing, and is much more likely than the traditional English translation.—TRANS.]

[22] H. Ringgren, "Den aronitiska välsignelsen," *Talenta quinque* (Helsinki, 1953), pp. 35 ff.; G. Widengren, *Sakrales Königtum* (Stuttgart: Kohlhammer, 1955), p. 19.

[23] J. Pedersen, *Israel* (London: Oxford, 1959), I-II, 200.

[24] H. Ringgren, *The Faith of the Psalmists* (Philadelphia: Fortress, 1963), pp. 32 f.; cf. also S. Mowinckel, *Segen und Fluch in Israels Kult und Psalmdichtung*, Vol. V: *Psalmenstudien* (Amsterdam: Schippers, 1961); J. Hempel, "Die israelitischen Anschauungen von Segen und Fluch im Lichte altorientalischer Parallelen," *ZDMG*, 1925, pp. 120 ff., reprinted in *idem, Apoxysmata* (Berlin: Töpelmann, 1961), pp. 30 ff.; S. Gevirtz, "Semitic Curses," *VT*, XI (1961), 137 ff.

[25] Ringgren, *Faith of the Psalmists*, pp. 31 f.; cf. the other works mentioned in the preceding note.

The curse spoken in the course of rendering divine judgment (Num. 5:11-28) is of a different sort.[26] A woman suspected of unfaithfulness is brought before the priest. He "sets her before Yahweh," takes "holy water," and recites the formula, "If . . . some man other than your husband has lain with you, then . . . may Yahweh make you an execration and an oath among your people, when Yahweh makes your thigh fall away and your body swell; may this water that brings the curse pass into your bowels . . ." (vss. 20 f.). Then the words of the curse are written down and washed off into the water, and the woman drinks the water. If the woman is guilty, the curse is expected to take effect; if not, she will remain unharmed. Here a magical view of the curse is indisputable; it is noteworthy, however, that the whole ceremony takes place "before Yahweh."

We have evidence that, in the pre-monarchic period, the priestly office was occasionally hereditary. In particular, we learn that the house of Eli (Eli and his sons) constituted a priestly family at Shiloh (I Sam. 1—4). A descendant of Eli, Ahimelech, was a priest at Nob during the reign of Saul; his son Abiathar appears during the reign of David as one of the most distinguished priests. Of the priests at other sanctuaries we know very little; of the priesthood at such an important sanctuary as Shechem we know nothing at all.

The rule that the priests had to be descendants of Levi seems to be early. The prehistory of this regulation is obscure; in particular, opinions differ as to whether Levi was a tribe entrusted with the priestly office from the beginning, or whether it was a tribe like all the others, becoming a distinct priestly tribe only in the course of time.[27] It is an established fact that priests who actually did not belong to the tribe of Levi were later provided with a Levitic genealogy.

With the appearance of the monarchy, the king takes over the management of the priesthood, at least in Jerusalem, and the organization of the priests becomes more rigid. During the reign of David, the most important priests were Abiathar, already mentioned, and a certain Zadok, who, strangely, is introduced without any genealogy. This fact has occasioned much speculation. The most probable assumption seems to be that he was a member of the Canaanite priesthood in Jerusalem; for the names Melchizedek and Adonizedek shows that ṣdq was a divine name current in Jerusalem, and ṣādôq is derived from the same root.[28] If this interpretation is true, we would have here an example of deliberate religious compromise by the first kings for which there is also other evidence. After the palace intrigues at

---

26 Cf. R. Press, "Das Ordal im AT," *ZAW,* LI (1933), 121 ff., 227 ff.

27 See above, pp. 37 f., 42. Cf. E. Nielsen, "The Levites in Ancient Israel," *Annual of the Swedish Theological Institute,* III (1964), pp. 16 ff.

28 Cf. most recently G. W. Ahlström, "Nathan und der Tempelbau," *VT,* XI (1961), 122; with references.

the accession of Solomon, Abiathar was removed because of his support of Adonijah, the other claimant to the throne, and Zadok became the chief priest in Jerusalem.

During the period of the monarchy the Zadokite priesthood grew more and more powerful. Perhaps the prophecy at the end of the story of Eli (I Sam. 2:27-36) still contains hints of the struggles of the Zadokites against other priestly families, especially the house of Eli: "And I will raise up for myself a faithful priest [i.e., Zadok], who shall do according to what is in my heart and in my mind . . . and he shall go in and out before my anointed for ever" (vs. 35). In the course of time, the Zadokites claim to have descended from Levi through Aaron; all priests are now considered descendants of Aaron (Ps. 115:10, 12; 118:3; 135:19). Ezekiel goes so far as to demand that all priests must be Zadokites (Ezek. 44:15).[29]

Since the Temple at Jerusalem was a royal chapel, the priests naturally were royal officials. They were appointed and removed by the king (I Kings 2:27, 35); occasionally the king even intervenes in the priestly administration of the Temple (II Kings 12:5 ff. [Eng. 12:4 ff.]; 16:10 ff.; 22:3 ff.). The priests probably endeavored to restrict the influence of the king so that they, as specialists, might have sole charge of the Temple worship; but we hear of this conflict only occasionally.

As head of the Jerusalem priesthood we find a priest who is called simply "the priest" (I Kings 4:2; II Kings 11:9 f.; 12:8 f. [Eng. 12:7 f.]; 16:10 f.; 22:12, 14; Isa. 8:2); only once in the books of Kings is he called the "chief priest" (kōhēn hārō'š; II Kings 25:18). The later title "high priest (kōhēn gādôl; literally "great priest") is probably a later addition to the accounts of the monarchy (II Kings 12:11 [Eng. 12:10]; 22:4, 8; 23:4).[30] Under the chief priest stood a "second priest" (kōhēn mišneh; II Kings 23:4; 25:18; Jer. 52:24).

On the evidence given by the Deuteronomistic writers, the priests at the other cultic sites, especially in the Northern Kingdom, were called "Levitical priests" or simply "Levites." They seem to have been faithful guardians of the old local sanctuaries. During the later monarchy, their primary function was probably preaching: in the view of many recent scholars, Deuteronomy is the outgrowth of their activity as preachers.[31] This probably explains why Deuteronomy is concerned to represent the Levites as having equal rights with the priests. As a result of the Josianic reformation, these country priests could not longer be considered guardians of legitimate sanctuaries;

---

[29] A. Bentzen, *Studier over det Zadokidiske Praesteskabs historie* (Copenhagen: Gad, 1931); cf. *idem*, "Zur Geschichte der Zadokiden," *ZAW*, LI (1933), 173 ff.

[30] J. Gabriel, *Untersuchungen über das alt-testamentliche Hohepriestertums*, Vienna, 1933; N. B. Barrow, *The High Priest*, 1947.

[31] See, for example, von Rad, *Studies in Deuteronomy*, pp. 66 f.

the program of Deuteronomy was therefore to obtain for them the right to serve at the Jerusalem Temple alongside the resident priests. In reality, of course, the resident priesthood of Jerusalem carried the day, and the Levites were subordinated to them as priests of lower rank.[32]

Obviously there were also other cultic functionaries attached to the Temple, although in most cases our only data are late. Joshua 9 contains an etiological narrative about the Gibeonites and their position as hewers of wood and drawers of water. Its purpose is probably to explain a situation that really existed in the pre-exilic period. It has been suggested that the word *nōqēd,* applied to Amos in Amos 1:1 (and probably also 7:14), which obviously means "herdsman," refers to a Temple official, in other words, a guardian of the Temple flocks.[33] The psalms assume the existence of Temple musicians and singers; Psalm 68:26 (Eng. 68:25) specifically mentions maidens playing timbrels in a procession at the Temple. The Chronicler provides detailed information about the Temple singers. They are said to have been organized by David (I Chron. 25)—obviously an anachronism. Although the organization described undoubtedly reflects postexilic conditions, it is probably based on the facts of the pre-exilic situation, by and large. According to this setup, the singers and musicians were divided into guilds, each of which traced its descent back to one of the Levitic patriarchs. (According to I Chron. 25:1-7, these were Asaph, Jeduthun, and Heman; cf. I Chron. 6:31-40, where the division is somewhat more complex. The "Sons of Korah" mentioned in several psalm superscriptions are probably another family of singers.)

The cult prophets are not specifically mentioned in the laws, because they did not exist as an institution in the postexilic period. Their existence during the period of the monarchy may be considered established, since they are mentioned in several passages.[34]

The word *nabî'* (etymologically connected with the Akkadian *nabū,* "call") has various meanings in the Old Testament. At times it refers to ecstatic "men of God," at times to professional diviners in the service of the king, at times to the great writing prophets. The fact that the same word is used in all these cases suggests that the three

---

[32] [This is the generally accepted view of the position of the Levites in Deuteronomy; recently, however, certain reservations have been stated. Cf. R. Abba, "Priests and Levites," *IDB* (Nashville: Abingdon, 1962), II, 876 ff., esp. 886 ff.—TRANS.]

[33] See below, p. 262.

[34] General studies: Mowinckel, *Kultprophetie und prophetische Psalmen,* Vol. III: *Psalmenstudien;* A. R. Johnson, *The Cultic Prophet in Ancient Israel* (Cardiff: University of Wales, 1944); A. Haldar, *Associations of Cult Prophets among the Ancient Semites* (Uppsala: Almqvist & Wiksell, 1945); O. Plöger, *op. cit.;* J. Lindblom, *Prophecy in Ancient Israel* (Philadelphia: Fortress; 1962).

groups have something in common. We shall return later to the writing prophets, here discussing only the first two categories.

The ecstatic prophets lived in groups or associations; they seem for the most part to have been connected with the local sanctuaries (see especially I Sam. 3:19-21). The first book of Samuel mentions the seer (rō'eh; I Sam. 9:9) as an early kind of prophet; but it is not certain that we have here a genuine ancient tradition. Seers are also mentioned in other passages, frequently with ḥōzeh substituted for the basically synonymous rō'eh (II Sam. 24:11; II Kings 17:13; Amos 7:12—in this last passage the name "seer" is a contemptuous term for a prophet). Isaiah equates both kinds of seer (Isa. 30:10);[35] the two terms may be identical.[36] It is not clear whether these terms refer to visionary experiences or to extispicy.

The ecstatic prophets used music and dancing (I Sam. 10:5; II Kings 3:15) to induce in themselves a state of ecstasy and inspiration that is called "prophesying" (hitnabbē' or nibbā'; I Sam. 10:5-13; 19:18-24).[37] This ecstatic behavior is ascribed to the influence of the divine spirit (rûaḥ; I Sam. 10:6, 10; 19:20, 23). The passages cited say nothing about the purpose and function of the ecstatic condition. Other passages, however, show that the prophets acted as givers of oracles. According to I Kings 22, for example, Ahab assembles about four hundred prophets in order to inquire for Yahweh's word (dābār; vs. 5). The word hitnabbē' is used throughout this account to describe the behavior of the prophets.

Ancient sources demonstrate the existence of similar phenomena among the west Semitic population of Mari in the 18th and 19th centuries B.C., as well as among the Phoenicians and Canaanites. The Mari letters contain divine messages transmitted through cult prophets called maḥḥū;[38] the Akkadians used the same word to refer to an ecstatic oracle priest.[39] In the 11th century B.C., the Egyptian ambassador Wen-amun saw at Sidon a young man who fell into a prophetic ecstasy and transmitted to the king the message that he should

---

[35] [The author translates Heb. rō'eh as "Seher," ḥōzeh as "Schauer." The RSV, lacking two equivalent words, translates both as "seer" except in the Isaiah passage, where it translates rō'eh as "seer" and ḥōzeh as "prophet."—TRANS.]

[36] Johnson, op. cit. p. 11; cf. I. Engnell, Religion och Bibel, VIII (1949), 8 ff., citing R. Kraetzschmar, Prophet und Seher im alten Israel (Tübingen: Mohr, 1901), pp. 19 ff.

[37] The verb can mean either "act as a prophet" or "be in a state of ecstasy."

[38] W. von Soden, in E. Michel (ed.), Die Welt des Orients (Wuppertal: Putty, 1947), I, 397 ff.; M. Noth, "Geschichte und Gotteswort im AT," in idem, Gesammelte Studien (Munich: Kaiser, 1957), pp. 230 ff.; H. Schmökel, "Gottes Wort in Mari und Israel," TLZ, LXXVI (1951), cols. 53 ff.; C. Westermann, Grundformen prophetischer Rede (Munich: Kaiser, 1960), pp. 82 ff.

[39] Haldar, op. cit., pp. 21 ff.

pay tribute to the Egyptians.[40] Later, in the Old Testament itself, we hear of a great number of prophets of Baal who assemble on Mount Carmel in order to compete with Elijah (I Kings 18:21 ff.). The narrative mentions dancing, crying out, and prophetic frenzy, during which these prophets lacerated themselves with swords and lances (vss. 28 f.). Among the pre-Islamic Arabs we also find soothsayers possessed by a spirit.[41] Thus we are dealing here with a phenomenon common to all the Semitic peoples, in all probability borrowed by Israel from the Canaanites.

In the period of the monarchy, we meet these prophets as advisers to the king. Prophecy has become an institution, and the kings do not undertake anything important without making inquiry of the prophets. This is particularly true in the case of military undertakings. I Kings 22, already cited, is especially instructive. King Ahab, in league with Jehoshaphat, the king of Judah, is about to attack the Aramaeans; he assembles the prophets in order to discover Yahweh's will. He asks, "Shall I go to battle against Ramoth-gilead, or shall I forbear?" The prophets answer, "Go up; for Yahweh will give it into the hand of the king" (vs. 6). But this does not completely convince the king. While the assembled prophets are "prophesying" before the two kings, one of them makes horns of iron and says, "Thus says Yahweh, 'With these you shall push the Syrians until they are destroyed.' " Finally, however, Micaiah the son of Imlah appears; he obviously is not a member of the prophetic guild. He announces the complete defeat of the two kings. The favorable oracle of the four hundred prophets was inspired by a lying spirit, and they turn out to be false prophets.

Two observations of primary importance can be made on the basis of this narrative. First, the prophets use the traditional formula, "Thus says Yahweh." As we can see from Genesis 32:4-6 (Eng. 32:3-5), 45:9, and II Kings 18:29, such a formula was generally customary when a message was delivered: "Thus says your servant Jacob," "Thus says the king." In other words, the prophets are identified as Yahweh's messengers, whose duty it is to transmit Yahweh's word to the inquirer. Similar forms of speech are already found among the cult prophets in the Mari texts.[42] Second, these prophets make use of symbolic actions to emphasize their message. Such actions should not be considered merely illustrative; originally they were thought to be magically efficacious: just as God's word is per se efficacious, creating reality, so also is the symbolic action, but to a far greater degree. The sound-

---

[40] Papyrus Golénischeff; cf. A. Erman, *The Literature of the Ancient Egyptians,* trans. A. M. Blackman (London: Methuen, 1927), pp. 177 f.

[41] G. Hölscher, *Die Profeten* (Leipzig: Hinrichs, 1914), pp. 93 ff.; J. Pedersen, "The Role Played by Inspired Persons Among the Israelites and the Arabs," in H. H. Rowley (ed.), *Studies in Old Testament Prophecy* (Edinburgh: Clark, 1950), pp. 127 ff., esp. pp. 132 f.

[42] See above, note 38.

ing of trumpets, for example, not only signifies victory, it brings about victory.[43]

In addition, this narrative shows how strongly these professional prophets felt themselves obligated to announce good fortune and success; since they were royal officials, it was very tempting to humor the king. This fact forms the background for the numerous complaints raised by the writing prophets against the professionals, whom they called false prophets. Micah has this to say of them:

> Thus says Yahweh concerning the prophets
>> who lead my people astray,
> who cry "Peace"
>> when they have something to eat,
> but declare war against him
>> who puts nothing into their mouths.
>
> . . . .
>
>> Its priests teach for hire,
>> its prophets divine for money;
> yet they lean upon Yahweh. . . . (Mic. 3:5, 11)

Jeremiah says:

> For from the least to the greatest of them,
>> every one is greedy for unjust gain;
> and from prophet to priest,
>> every one deals falsely.
> They have healed the wound of my people lightly,
>> saying, "Peace, peace,"
>> when there is no peace. (Jer. 6:13 f.)

And:

> The prophets say to them, "You shall not see the sword, nor shall you have famine, but I will give you assured peace in this place." (Jer. 14:13)

And:

> Do not listen to the words of the prophets who prophesy to you, filling you with vain hopes; they speak visions of their own minds, not from the mouth of Yahweh. They say continually to those who despise the word of Yahweh, "It shall be well with you"; and to everyone who stubbornly follows his own heart, they say, "No evil shall come upon you". . . . I have heard what the prophets have said who prophesy lies in my name, saying, "I have dreamed, I have dreamed!" . . . Let the prophet who has a dream tell the dream, but let him who has my word speak my word faithfully. (Jer. 23:16 f., 25, 28)

---

[43] See W. Robinson, "Prophetic Symbolism," *Old Testament Essays*, 1924, pp. 1 ff.; G. Fohrer, *Die symbolischen Handlungen der Propheten* (Zürich: Zwingli, 1953); cf. also G. Widengren, *The Accadian and Hebrew Psalms of Lamentation* (Stockholm: Thule, 1937), pp. 258 f.

These passages show that, in the opinion of the writing prophets, the professional prophets had conjured up false hopes in the people through their prophecies of peace. They also show that visions and dreams had an important role to play as vehicles of revelation. An ancient tradition in the Pentateuch states the same basic principle: "Hear my words: If there is a prophet among you, I Yahweh make myself known to him in a vision, I speak with him in a dream. Not so with my servant Moses . . ." (Num. 12:6).

The sources from the period of the monarchy do not tell us how closely these professional prophets were connected with the Temple or with local sanctuaries. We read once that a priest has authority over the prophets (Jer. 29:26); but the point is primarily negative: the priest is to put those "madmen" into the stocks and collar. It is significant, however, that the Chronicler uses the word "prophecy" (*nibbā'*) for the singing of the Levites (I Chron. 25:1-3) and that in one passage he has one of the Levites give a prophetical answer to the prayer of the congregation (II Chron. 20:14 ff.). This indicates that, in the post-exilic period, the professional prophets were absorbed into the ranks of the Levites.[44]

This conclusion confronts us with another question. The term "cult prophet" is also applied by modern Old Testament study to certain cult officials whose duty it was to reply in God's name to prayers and laments of the community.[45] A few such replies are contained in the psalms. In Psalm 12:6 (Eng. 12:5), for example, the following words come in reply to a prayer of the worshiping community for aid against the godless:

> "Because the poor are despoiled, because the needy groan,
> I will now arise," says Yahweh;
> "I will place him in the safety for which he longs."

Significantly, this is followed by a statement of confident assurance:

> The promises of Yahweh are promises that are pure,
> silver refined in a furnace on the ground,
> purified seven times. (vs. 7 [Eng. vs. 6])

Here, then, a divine answer is given to the prayer of the congregation, and this answer is extolled because it is pure. In Psalm 91, a meditation on the security of the man who trusts in God is followed by a divine promise (vss. 14 ff.):

> Because he cleaves to me in love, I will deliver him;
> I will protect him, because he knows my name.
> When he calls to me, I will answer him.

---

[44] Cf. S. Mowinckel, *The Psalms in Israel's Worship*, trans. D. R. Ap-Thomas (Oxford: Blackwell, 1962), II, 92.

[45] S. Mowinckel, *Psalmenstudien*, III ("Kultprophetie und prophetische Psalmen"); A. R. Johnson, *op. cit.*; O. Plöger, *op. cit.*; G. Quell, "Der Kultprophet," *TLZ*, LXXXI (1956), cols. 401 ff.

In Psalm 60, a prayer of the nation is followed by the statement, "God has spoken in his sanctuary"; then follows an oracle that refers to Yahweh's dominion over the nations. Psalm 108 contains the same oracle in a different context; this fact means that the same divine answer could be applied to various situations. In Psalm 21:9 (Eng. 21:8), God addresses a king:

> Your hand will find out all your enemies;
> your right hand will find out those who hate you.

In other cases, the divine answer is only alluded to. In Psalm 51, a confession of sins, the psalmist says, for example, "Make me to hear joy and gladness" (vs. 10 [Eng. vs. 8]), which could refer to a promise of forgiveness.[46] In Psalm 85:9 (Eng. 85:8), the psalmist says:

> Let me hear what God Yahweh will speak,
> for he will speak peace to his people,
> to his saints, to those who turn to him in their hearts.

Other passages bear witness to the confidence of the believer after he receives an answer, e.g., Psalm 20:7 (Eng. 20:6):

> Now I know that Yahweh will help his anointed;
> he will answer him from his holy heaven.

It was probably a cult official who gave divine answers of this sort; he must have spoken with the authority of God's divine commission. Of course we do not know whether these officials were called priests or prophets. The essential point is that they were considered mediators of God's decisions. In the light of our discussion of the professional prophets, it might be more proper to speak in this case of a *priestly* salvation oracle.[47]

Something can be said about the form of such oracles, partially on the basis of the few actually preserved, partially on the basis of imitations employed by the prophets, especially Deutero-Isaiah.[48] They seem usually to have been quite short. In the overwhelming number of instances they were spoken directly to the worshiper: "I am your deliverance" (Ps. 35:3); "Be strong, and let your heart take courage; yea, wait for Yahweh" (Ps. 27:14). But answers in the third person also occur (Ps. 12:6 [Eng. 12:5]; 91:14-16). A standard introductory formula is "Do not fear!" (Lam. 3:57, and frequently in Deutero-Isaiah). Then follows the assurance that Yahweh has heard the prayer, and a promise of divine assistance: "I am with you," "I will deliver

---

[46] [This is the rendering of the Hebrew followed by the author and the RSV margin; the RSV text reads, "Fill me with . . ."—TRANS.]

[47] This is the term used by J. Begrich, "Das priesterliche Heilsorakel," *ZAW*, LII (1934), 81 ff. The *Heilsorakel* is simply a "positive" or "favorable" oracle.

[48] Cf. *ibid.*

you," "You shall not be harmed," "I will answer when you call," etc. Such statements as, "You are my servant," "I will not forsake you," and "I am your redeemer," found with great frequency in Deutero-Isaiah, also probably belong to the style of the salvation oracle. Babylonian psalms and rituals contain corresponding formulaic elements.[49]

Did these "cult prophets," or, better, prophetical priests, use special means to determine the will of Yahweh? Or was mere free, "ecstatic," inspiration the decisive element? The answer to this question depends on how we define the relationship of the "cult prophets" involved here to the professional prophets mentioned above on the one hand and to the writing prophets on the other. A priori, it is probable that mechanical means were employed for divination; in certain cases, like that of the Urim and Thummim, their use can be proved. But on the whole we can do no more than make conjectures in this area.[50]

Some scholars have seen in the word *biqqēr* a reference to extispicy. Psalm 27:4 speaks of beholding the beauty of Yahweh and "inquiring" (?), *biqqēr*, in his Temple. This might be interpreted as referring to omens appearing in the Temple, especially since II Kings 16:15 mentions a bronze altar that is to serve for "inquiry." It is possible that extispicy is meant.[51] A related word, which resembles the ordinary word for morning, occurs in Psalm 5:4 (Eng. 5:3):

> O Yahweh, in the morning thou dost hear my voice;
> *bōqer* I prepare for thee, and watch.[52]

Here *bōqer* can mean either "in the morning," "early," or "a *bōqer* sacrifice," i.e., a sacrifice performed for divination.[53] Significantly, the verb *ṣapâ*, "look out," "keep watch," is also used in connection with the activity of the prophets.[54] Thus we read in Habakkuk 2:1:

> I will take my stand to watch,
> and station myself on the tower,
> and look forth to see what he will say to me,
> and what I will answer concerning my complaint.

The next verse contains Yahweh's answer: "And Yahweh answered me . . . ." Obviously we are dealing here with a special kind of

---

[49] See, for example, B. Meissner, *Babylonien und Assyrien* (1925), II, 245 f.; Mowinckel, *Psalmenstudien*, III, 114 f.; H. Gunkel and J. Begrich, *Einleitung in die Psalmen* (Göttingen: Vandenhoeck & Ruprecht, 1933), pp. 100 f.

[50] For a discussion of this question, see especially Haldar, *op. cit.*, pp. 99 ff.

[51] *Ibid.*, p. 102; Ringgren, *Faith of the Psalmists*, pp. 3 f.

[52] [The RSV conflates the two possible meanings, and reads, "In the morning I prepare a sacrifice for thee.—TRANS.]

[53] Haldar, *op. cit.*, p. 102.

[54] *Ibid.*, p. 104.

"watching" engaged in by the prophet in order to receive a vision or audition.

Isaiah 21:6 ff. is interesting in this regard. There we read:

> For thus Yahweh said to me:
>   "Go set a watchman;
>   let him announce what he sees."
>
> . . . .
>
> Then he who saw (?) cried:
> "Upon a watchtower I stand, O Lord,
>   continually by day,
> and at my post I am stationed
>   whole nights.
> And, behold, here come riders,
>   horsemen in pairs!"

According to the usual interpretation, the "watchman" here is the prophet himself, speaking of himself in the third person: he is watching for a revelation and receives a vision.[55] But the concrete process cannot be determined in detail.

In connection with this discussion, however, we must not forget that the general attitude elsewhere in the Old Testament is very unfavorable toward all kinds of soothsaying and haruspication. The law contained in Deuteronomy 18:10 f. prohibits a whole series of magical and divinatory practices, whose exact nature is unfortunately unknown to us. Certain kinds of soothsaying and necromancy (cf. I Sam. 28) are mentioned specifically. Here we are obviously dealing with practices felt at the time of Deuteronomy to be pagan and foreign. The same book goes on to say in the very same chapter that every prophet who really speaks Yahweh's word can claim absolute obedience (vss. 18 ff.).[56] The difference lies in the fact that the prophet speaks in the name of Yahweh, and what he says really comes to pass (vs. 22). Perhaps Deuteronomy here represents a later reaction against practices to which there was no objection during the early monarchy.

---

[55] *Ibid.*, pp. 104 ff.

[56] This passage was understood formerly as the promise of a particular prophet, a new Moses; von Rad is now inclined to accept this view (cf. his *Theologie des Alten Testaments* [Munich: Kaiser, 1960], p. 274; also his *Deuteronomium* [Göttingen: Vandenhoeck & Ruprecht, 1964], *ad loc.*).

10.

THE KINGSHIP

When, about 1020 B.C., Saul became Israel's first king, there obviously was a general awareness that something new had been introduced into Israel from without. The somewhat hostile account in I Samuel 8 tells how the Israelites begged Samuel to give them a king, "like all the other nations" (vs. 5). Samuel at first refused, but finally allowed himself to be persuaded, since Yahweh gave his consent.

Israel, therefore, was well aware that the kingship was actually a foreign institution; and throughout the entire period of the monarchy, there existed circles hostile to the kingship, or at least critical of it, on the grounds that Yahweh was the true king of Israel. On the other hand, circles loyal to the king gave a theological and religious interpretation to the kingship, viewing it as a god-given institution. Unfortunately, scholars have not paid sufficient attention to this dichotomy. As a result, some scholars, who consider primarily the historical (Deuteronomistic) books and the prophets hostile to particular kings, deny the existence of any "sacral kingship," viewing the kingship as a secular institution and the king as "an ordinary man,"[1] while others, who base their views primarily on the psalms and the prophecies looking forward to a coming ideal king (the Messiah), emphasize the sacral character of Israelite kingship, comparing the king of Israel to the "divine" kings of the great empires of the ancient Near East.[2]

---

[1] M. Noth, "Gott, König, Volk im Alten Testament," *ZThK*, XLVII (1950), 157 ff., reprinted in *idem, Gesammelte Studien* (Munich: Kaiser, 1960), pp. 188 ff.; A. Lauha, "Några randanmärkingar till diskussionen om kungaideologien," *SEÅ*, XII (1947), 182 ff.; J. de Fraine, *L'aspect religieux de la royauté israélite* (Rome: Pontifical Biblical Institute, 1954); K. H. Bernhardt, *Das Problem der altorientalischen Königsideologie im Alten Testament* (*SVT*, VIII [1961]).

[2] I. Engnell, *Studies in Divine Kingship* (Uppsala: Almqvist & Wiksell, 1943); G. Widengren, *Sakrales Königtum* (Stuttgart: Kohlhammer, 1955); A. R. Johnson, *Sacral Kingship in Ancient Israel* (Cardiff: University of Wales, 1955); S. Mowinckel, *He That Cometh*, trans. G. W. Anderson (Nashville: Abingdon, 1954); also H. Ringgren, *The Messiah in the Old Testament* (London: SCM, 1956); G. W. Ahlström, *Psalm 89* (Lund: Gleerup, 1959).

In addition, the difference between the Northern Kingdom and the Southern Kingdom must not be overlooked. In the latter, the Davidic dynasty continued throughout the entire period of the monarchy, a fact given a religious interpretation in terms of a divine "covenant" with David. In the Northern Kingdom, on the other hand, the kingship probably was charismatic; no real dynasty ever took root on this soil. Prophets seem to have exerted considerable influence in the choosing and appointing of kings (e.g., Jeroboam in I Kings 11:29 ff.; Jehu in II Kings 9:1 ff.; cf. also I Kings 14:7 ff.; 10:1 ff.).[3]

On the basis of what has been said, any talk of *an* Israelite royal ideology must be considered extremely questionable. Since, however, we have very few records from the Northern Kingdom, and since hostility to the kingship can hardly be called a royal ideology, it seems justifiable to base our presentation on the witness of the (Jerusalemite) royal psalms, supplementing them only occasionally with information drawn from the historical books. A second group of sources must also be taken into account: the so-called Messianic prophecies. For when the prophets express their hope for a coming ideal ruler, they depend for all their details upon the ancient royal ideal: the Messiah will completely fulfill all the expectations shared by the people with respect to the king. As a consequence, these prophecies can be drawn upon—though only with caution—in reconstructing the ancient Israelite ideal of kingship.

The special position occupied by the king appears as soon as he ascends the throne. The historical books preserve several accounts of accessions, each of which contributes a few details to the total picture; further information is given by Psalms 2 and 110, and to some extent by Psalm 45.

The very earliest accounts mention the anointing of the king: Samuel pours oil on Saul's head and says, "Has not Yahweh anointed you to be prince over his people Israel? And you shall reign over the people of Yahweh and you will save them from the hand of their enemies round about" (I Sam. 10:1).[4] Soon afterwards, the spirit of Yahweh (i.e., the divine power that makes it possible to perform wonders) comes upon Saul (I Sam. 10:6). Later we read how Samuel anoints David (I Sam. 16); here, too, there is a gift of the spirit (vs. 13). Solomon is anointed king of Israel by Zadok the priest and Nathan the prophet. At the same time, the trumpet is blown and the people shout, "Long live King Solomon!" (I Kings 1:34 f., 39; cf. also I Kings 1:25; II Kings 11:12). Elisha anoints Jehu king of the Northern

---

[3] A. Alt, "Das Königtum in den Reichen Israels und Juda," *VT*, I (1951), 2 ff.

[4] This version follows the LXX, which preserves a longer form than the MT; cf. the commentaries. The phraseology of the LXX is in better agreement with the formula used by Elisha (see below), especially in proclaiming the duties of the king after the formula of anointing.

Kingdom, saying, "Thus says Yahweh, the God of Israel, I anoint you king over the people of Yahweh, over Israel." Then the people shout, "Jehu is king" (*mālāk yēhû'*, II Kings 9:6, 13; a similar formula is found at II Sam. 15:10, with reference to Absalom, David's rebellious son, who orders his followers to sound the trumpet and proclaim him king: "Absalom is king at Hebron"). The connection between anointing and the gift of the spirit is also confirmed by Isaiah 61:1, an oracle that is in many respects obscure:

> The Spirit of Lord Yahweh is upon me,
> because Yahweh has anointed me . . .[5]

Isaiah 11:2, a Messianic prophecy, also expresses the spiritual endowment of the king:

> And the Spirit of Yahweh shall rest upon him,
> the spirit of wisdom and understanding,
> the spirit of counsel and might,
> the spirit of knowledge and the fear of Yahweh.

This passage, however, does not mention anointing.

It would be logical to assume that anointing was borrowed from the Canaanites. But the relevant evidence from Canaan is scarce and precarious.[6] One of the Amarna letters presupposes the anointing of a prince. In this case, however, we may be dealing with an Egyptian rite at the investiture of vassals. Judges 9:8, 15, however, seems to witness to this rite for pre-Israelite Canaan; this note might, of course, be an anachronism. The Assyrian and Babylonian kings were probably not anointed; this was the practice, though, among the Hittites.[7]

The Israelite king was therefore called "the anointed" (*māšíaḥ*) or "the anointed of Yahweh" (I Sam. 24:7, 11 [Eng. 24:6, 10]; 26:9, 11, 16, 23; II Sam. 1:14, 16; 19:22 [Eng. 19:21]; Lam. 4:20).[8] As such, he was considered inviolable (I Sam. 24:7, 11 [Eng. 24:6, 10]; 26:9; etc.; cf. II Sam. 1:14 ff.). This term was used later to designate the ideal eschatalogical king. The New Testament uses the Greek form

---

[5] To whom this text refers is not made clear by the context. Widengren, *op. cit.,* p. 57, calls it a royal hymn of self-glorification. Most commentators, however, think the words refer to the prophet.

[6] *UM* 76 (IV AB) II, 22 f. (Baal anointing the horn of Anat) is not relevant.

[7] R. de Vaux, *Ancient Israel,* trans. J. McHugh (New York: McGraw-Hill, 1961), p. 104; cf. Mowinckel, *op. cit.,* pp. 5 f., 63 ff. Sumerian priests were anointed; see T. Jacobsen, *Proceedings of the American Philosophical Society,* CVII (1963), 477, n. 11. For an exhaustive discussion of all relevant problems see E. Kutsch, *Salbung als Rechtsakt* (Berlin: Töpelmann, 1963), pp. 33 ff.

[8] In the usage of the Old Testament, therefore, "Messiah" is a royal title, not an eschatological *terminus technicus.* Engnell (*op. cit.,* p. 43, n. 3) and von Rad (*Old Testament Theology,* trans. D. M. G. Stalker [Edinburgh & London: Oliver & Boyd, 1962], p. 316, n. 13) are therefore correct when they apply the word "messianic" to the Israelite king. The word acquired its eschatological meaning only in later Judaism.

Messias interchangeably with the Greek word *Christos,* which also means "anointed."

If we can make a general statement on the basis of I Kings 1:38, the anointing of the king was performed at the Gihon, a spring in the valley of Kidron. Psalm 110:7 ("He will drink from the brook by the way") may allude to this ceremony. Then followed a joyous procession up to the palace, where the king took his place on the throne (I Kings 1:35). In the case of Joash, a ceremony in the Temple is mentioned instead; this may possibly correspond to later practice (II Kings 11). The young king stands upon a platform. He is crowned with the crown (*nēzer*) and handed the "testimony" (*'ēdût*). The crown or diadem is widespread as a royal symbol; it is referred to elsewhere in the Old Testament (II Sam. 1:10; Jer. 13:18; Ezek. 21:30 f. [Eng. 21:25 f.]; Ps. 89:40 [Eng. 89:39]; 132:18). The "testimony," on the other hand, presents certain difficulties. The usual solution has been to read *ṣeʿādôt,* "armlets," instead of *'ēdût*—as a matter of fact, after the death of Saul a messenger brings David the crown and an armlet of the king (II Sam. 1:10), although the latter is not expressly described as part of the royal insignia. On the other hand, *'ēdût* can also refer to a solemn decree. Now Psalm 89:40 (Eng. 89:39) mentions a "covenant" (*berît*) in connection with the crown, and the meaning of *berît* is very close to that of *'ēdût.* Psalm 2:6 f. employs a similar, more or less synonymous expression in connection with the enthronement of the king, namely, *ḥōq,* "decree," "statute." These three expressions have been compared to the Egyptian royal protocol, which was handed to the king at his coronation; it contained, among other things, the royal title with the five throne names and the recognition of the king as son of God. Thut-mose III, for example, says, "He [Amon] set my crown upon me and wrote my protocol himself." Von Rad and Wildberger have recently compared the names of the messianic king in Isaiah 9:5 with this protocol:[9] this text does indeed call the Messiah a child and son (of God?), setting forth his names (in this case four, not five): "Wonderful Counselor, Mighty God, Everlasting Father, Prince of Peace" (Isa. 9:5 [Eng. 9:6]).

Widengren has proposed another explanation.[10] He starts from the fact that *'ēdût* can also mean "law," and assumes that the "testimony" refers to the two tables of the law. In this connection, he cites Deuteronomy's law governing the king (Deut. 17:18 f.), which states that the king is to have a copy of the law, which he is to study all the days of his life. Widengren's hypothesis has much to commend it. It receives additional support from Psalm 132:12, where we read:

---

[9] G. von Rad, "Das judäische Krönungsritual," *TLZ,* LXXII (1947), cols. 211 ff., reprinted in *idem, Gesammelte Studien* (Munich: Kaiser, 1958), pp. 205 ff.; H. Wildberger, "Die Thronnamen des Messias, Jes. 9, 5b," *TZ,* XVI (1960), 314 ff.; cf. also Johnson, *op. cit.,* p. 21.

[10] *Op. cit.,* p. 29; *idem,* "King and Covenant," *JSS,* II (1957), pp. 5 ff.

If your sons keep my covenant
and my testimonies which I shall teach them,
their sons also for ever
shall sit upon your throne.[11]

Here the continuity of the royal dynasty depends on obedience to the covenant and the law. Widengren then goes on to equate, or at least compare, the tables of the law with the Urim and Thummim and also with the Babylonian tablets of destiny; when he does so, however, we must ask whether he is not juxtaposing things that are basically not comparable.

A third element of the royal insignia is mentioned in a few psalms: the rod or scepter. In Psalm 2:9, an oracle addressed to the king reads, "You shall break[12] them [the enemy nations] with a rod of iron, and dash them in pieces like a potter's vessel." Psalm 110, which also refers to the coronation, says, "Yahweh sends forth from Zion your mighty scepter. Rule in the midst of your foes!" Psalm 45, which actually deals with a royal marriage, also mentions the scepter; there it is the "scepter of equity." All this evidence points to the scepter as a symbol of power and dominion. The texts do not state expressly that it was given to the king at his coronation, but such a ceremony seems quite probable. But the symbolism of the scepter may have gone even further. Widengren has attempted to show that it actually was thought to represent a branch from the tree of life.[13] Unfortunately, however, he can find support for this hypothesis only in late Jewish sources, whose relevance for the earlier period is disputed.

Psalms 2 and 110 definitely refer to the coronation and enthronement of the king. The former begins by painting a picture of the world in rebellion "against Yahweh and his anointed." Yahweh, however, merely laughs in derision, and speaks to the rebels in wrath, "I have set my king on Zion, my holy hill." In other words, the king of Israel has been appointed byYahweh to preserve order in the world. The king is obviously the next to speak. He refers to his appointment by Yahweh:

I will tell of the decree [$ḥōq$] of Yahweh:
He said to me, "You are my son,
today I have begotten you.
Ask of me, and I will make the nations your heritage,
and the ends of the earth your possession.
You shall break them. . . ."

[11] Cf. Johnson, *op. cit.*, p. 10.

[12] [This is the MT, followed by the RSV; the author follows the LXX, Syriac, and many commentators in repointing the text to read "tend" (*rāʿâ*) rather than "break" (*rāʿaʿ*).—TRANS.]

[13] G. Widengren, *The King and the Tree of Life* (Uppsala: Lundeqvist, 1951), pp. 37 ff.

Two important ideas appear in this oracle, here called a *ḥōq*. The king is the son of God; he is given dominion over the world. The former conviction is also contained in the prophecy uttered by Nathan with reference to Solomon: "I [i.e., Yahweh] will be his father, and he shall be my son" (II Sam. 7:14; Ps. 89:27 f. [Eng. 89:26 f.] refers to this passage). We are not told how to picture this divine sonship. In the two passages quoted, the idea of physical generation is probably excluded. In all probability, we have here a formula of adoption.[14] This means that the relationship was primarily one of protection: the king is under the special care of Yahweh.

It should be pointed out, furthermore, that both divine sonship and world dominion are indispensable elements of the sacral kingship found in the ancient Near East. These two motifs reappear in Psalm 110:

> Yahweh says to my lord [i.e., the king]:
>> "Sit at my right hand,
> till I make your enemies
>> your footstool."
> Yahweh sends forth from Zion
>> your mighty scepter.
>> Rule in the midst of your foes!
> To you belongs honor
>> on the day of your power
>> upon the holy mountains.
> From the womb of the morning
>> like dew I have begotten you.[15]

The king is seated on his throne symbolically beside Yahweh—the Chronicler says expressly that he sits upon the throne of Yahweh (I Chron. 28:5; 29:23; II Chron. 9:8). He is begotten by Yahweh. If we have interpreted the difficult text correctly at this point, the manner of expression is semi-mythological; for both the dew and the dawn (*šaḥar*) are familiar figures in Canaanite mythology.[16] A further divine oracle in Psalm 110 terms the king "a priest for ever after the order of Melchizedek," i.e., the legitimate successor to the priest-king of Jerusalem from the time of Abraham (Gen. 14:18).[17] Then the king is once more promised victory over all his

---

[14] S. Ahlström, *op. cit.*, pp. 111 f.; cf. the comments by Å. Sjöberg, *SEÅ*, XXV (1960), 102 f. On the formula of adoption in the Code of Hammurabi, see De Vaux, *op. cit.*, pp. 111 ff.; for similar formulas in Israel, see I Sam. 18:21; Hos. 2:4 [Eng. 2:2]; Tob. 7:11.

[15] The Hebrew text is corrupt; the translation suggested here represents only one of several possible reconstructions. For a recent discussion of this psalm, see J. Coppens, "Les apports du Ps. CX à l'idéologie royale israélite," in *La regalitá sacra* (Leiden: Brill, 1959), pp. 353 ff.

[16] Widengren, *Sakrales Königtum*, p. 46; Ahlström, *op. cit.*, pp. 137 f.

[17] See above, pp. 60 f.

enemies. To this is appended an obscure statement about a ritual of drinking from a brook (the Temple spring?).

A third psalm mentioning among other things the election of David refers to the same ceremonies and the same promises:

> I have found David, my servant;
>> with my holy oil I have anointed him.
>
> . . . .
>
> The enemy shall not outwit him,
>> the wicked shall not humble him.
> I will crush his foes before him
>> and strike down those who hate him.
>
> . . . .
>
> I will set his hand on the sea
>> and his right hand on the rivers.[18]
> He shall cry to me, "Thou art my Father,
>> my God, and the Rock of my salvation."
> And I will make him the first-born,
>> the highest of the kings of the earth.
>
> . . . .
>
> I will establish his line for ever
>> and his throne as the days of the heavens.
>>> (Ps. 89:21-30 [Eng. 89:20-29])[19]

It is impossible to reconstruct the coronation ritual in detail. A late passage in the Testament of Levi (chap. 8), however, may provide additional material. Here Levi is installed as a priest-king and receives the insignia of his office: the priestly garment, the crown of righteousness, etc. He is anointed and receives a staff of judgment, he is washed (i.e., purified) and given bread and wine, he is clothed with a sacred garment and also with an ephod and a girdle. He is handed a branch from the green olive tree (as a scepter?), together with the crown and diadem of the priesthood. Finally, incense is placed in his hands. Obviously components of priestly ordination have here been combined with features of the old enthronement ritual. It is possible, though, to distinguish with some assurance those major features that are basically royal: washing, anointing, bread and wine, sacred garments, the crown and scepter, the royal proclamation, the enthronement proper.[20] Most of these elements are also found in the early texts.

What we have learned about the coronation ritual gives us infor-

---

[18] This statement implies world dominion; or it may even go so far as to equate David with God, as victor over the waters of chaos.

[19] For a discussion of this psalm, see Ahlström, *op. cit.*

[20] Widengren, *Sakrales Königtum*, pp. 49 f.; H. Ludin Jansen, "The Consecration in the Eighth Chapter of the Testament of Levi," in *La regalitá sacra*, pp. 356 ff.

mation about some elements of the royal ideology. As we have seen, the king is considered Yahweh's son; he is enthroned at Yahweh's side. Since he was chosen and installed as king by Yahweh, he exercises his dominion on Yahweh's behalf (cf. the description of the messianic king in Mic. 5:3 [Eng. 5:4]). He is Yahweh's representative, so to speak. Therefore he can claim dominion over the world, an idea that appears in Psalm 72:

> May he have dominion from sea to sea
>> and from the River to the ends of the earth.[21]
> May his foes bow down before him,
>> and his enemies lick the dust!
> . . . .
> May all kings fall down before him,
>> all nations serve him! (vss. 8 f., 11)

As is well-known, the Assyrian and Babylonian kings make similar claims.[22] The messianic prophecies express the same ideal in almost identical words (especially Zech. 9:10; cf. also Mic. 5:3 [Eng. 5:4]; 7:12).[23]

Psalm 2 probably also implies that the king is to maintain the world order as Yahweh's representative: the enemies who have rebelled against Yahweh and his anointed should take warning and serve Yahweh with fear and trembling (vss. 10-12). Above all, however, the king is responsible for preserving "righteousness" in his land.[24] In Psalm 72, for example, we read:

> Give the king thy justice, O God,
>> and thy righteousness to the royal son!
> May he judge thy people with righteousness,
>> and thy poor with justice!
> . . . .
> May he defend the cause of the poor of the people,
>> give deliverance to the needy,
>> and crush the oppressor!
> . . . .
> For he delivers the needy when he calls,
>> the poor and him who has no helper.
> He has pity on the weak and the needy,
>> and saves the lives of the needy. (vss. 1 f., 4, 12 f.)

---

[21] I.e., either from the Mediterranean to the Persian Gulf and from the Euphrates to the ends of the known world, or, if "sea" refers to the world ocean and "river" is a synonym of it, simply, "throughout the entire world."

[22] H. Frankfort, *Kingship and the Gods* (Chicago: University of Chicago, 1948), pp. 227 f.

[23] Ringgren, *op. cit.,* pp. 34, 37.

[24] See especially Johnson, *op. cit.,* pp. 3 ff.

Here we see reflected the ideal king of the ancient Near East: he is to espouse the cause of the weak, especially widows and orphans; and he is to be a righteous judge. But to this conception is coupled a totally different idea, which the Israelites also included in the word *ṣedeq*, "righteousness": the proper order of nature somehow depends on the proper government of the king. In Psalm 72, statements concerning righteousness and world dominion alternate with statements concerning the fertility of the land:

> Let the mountains bear prosperity for the people,
>   and the hills, in righteousness!
>
> . . . .
>
> May he [the king] be like rain that falls on the mown grass,
>   like showers that water the earth!
> In his days may righteousness flourish,
>   and peace abound, till the moon be no more!
>
> . . . .
>
> May there be abundance of grain in the land;
>   on the tops of the mountains may it wave;
>   may its fruit be like Lebanon;
> and may men blossom forth from the cities
>   like the grass of the field!   (vss. 3, 6 f., 16)

Obviously the total well-being of the land is intimately connected with the righteousness of the king. The language vacillates in typical fashion between fertility and success in general. Words like "bear," "blossom forth," etc., are applied both to the people and to prosperity; and the king himself is compared with the rain.

The so-called last words of David are another characteristic expression of the royal ideology:

> The Spirit of Yahweh speaks by me,
>   his word is upon my tongue.
>
> . . . .
>
> When one rules justly over men
>   ruling in the fear of God,
> he dawns on them like the morning light,
>   like the sun shining forth upon a cloudless morning,
>   like rain that makes grass to sprout from the earth.
> Yea, does not my house stand so with God?
>   For he has made with me an everlasting covenant,
>   ordered in all things and secure.
> For will he not cause to prosper
>   all my help and my desire? (II Sam. 23:2-5)

David, "the anointed of the God of Jacob" (vs. 1), is the mouthpiece of Yahweh; he knows that Yahweh will grant him success as long as

228

he rules righteously and in the fear of God. This conception is expressed once again through metaphors taken from the plant world ("sprout").

Special significance attaches to the covenant between God and David, which is also referred to by Psalm 89:20 ff. (Eng. 89:19 ff.):

> Of old thou didst speak in a vision
>> to thy faithful one, and say:
> "I have set a young man over the mighty ones,
>> I have exalted one chosen over the people.[25]
> I have found David, my servant;
>> with my holy oil I have anointed him;
>
> . . . .
>
> And I will make him the first-born,
>> the highest of the kings of the earth,
> My steadfast love I will keep for him for ever,
>> and my covenant will stand firm for him.
> I will establish his line for ever
>> and his throne as the days of the heavens.

Then Yahweh goes on to guarantee that even if David's children forsake the law he will not violate his covenant or alter his word. The children will be punished on account of their sins, but the stability of the dynasty is grounded upon the promise of Yahweh:

> His line shall endure for ever,
>> his throne as long as the sun before me.
> Like the moon it shall be established for ever;
>> it shall stand firm while the skies endure."
>
> (vss. 37 f. [Eng. 36 f.])

These words refer to the story contained in II Samuel 7, where Nathan the prophet announces Yahweh's promise to David and states the terms of the covenant:

> I will be his father, and he shall be my son. When he commits iniquity, I will chasten him with the rod of men, with the stripes of the sons of men; but I will not take my steadfast love from him. . . . And your house and your kingdom shall be made sure for ever before me; your throne shall be established for ever. (vss. 14-16)

Psalm 132 also recalls this promise, but places somewhat more stress on the conditions necessary if the dynasty is to endure eternally: its endurance is dependent upon the keeping of the covenant (vs. 12).

---

[25] This is the translation of A. Weiser, *The Psalms,* trans. H. Hartwell (Philadelphia: Westminster, 1962), p. 588, following W. F. Albright; for a different translation, see Ahlström, *op. cit.,* p. 98.

This shows that the Israelite royal ideology was not completely homogeneous: some placed more emphasis on the king's responsibility, others on Yahweh's irrevocable promise.

An interesting image is found in Psalm 89:15 (Eng. 89:14), where we read:

> Righteousness and justice are the foundation of thy throne;
> steadfast love and faithfulness go before thee.

Similar statements occur also in some of the proverbs (Prov. 16:12; 25:5). At first glance, this looks like a metaphorical expression. But Brunner has pointed out that the throne of the Egyptian king is represented as resting upon the hieroglyphic symbol for $m^3't$ ("rightness," "order," "truth"), and that Assyrian and Babylonian thrones were borne by spirits. It is not impossible that similar pictorial representations were also found in Israel. Righteousness and justice, grace and truth, are personified qualities "bearing" the throne of the Israelite king.[26] However the case may be, this passage clearly expresses the responsibility of the king for maintaining justice. The stability of the kingship depends on the righteousness of the king. An ambiguous passage in Psalm 45 also refers to the eternal stability of the throne and the righteousness of the king. In verse seven (Eng. vs. 6) of this royal marriage song, we read:

> Your throne, O God, endures for ever and ever.
> Your royal scepter is a scepter of equity.[27]

In the first line, the word *ĕlōhîm*, "god," is used. This seems to indicate that the king was looked upon as a god, or at least thought to be divine. This was the case among the Egyptians and (at least occasionally) among the Sumerians. Since such a conception is rather strange in the context of the Yahwistic religion, many attempts have been made to interpret this verse in a different way, for example, "Your throne is divine" or "Your throne is like God's."[28] It seems inadvisable to alter the text; the more difficult reading is preferable. It is perhaps unlikely that the king could be called "god" without any qualifications; but the fact remains that he holds a special position: as the representative of Yahweh, he belongs to the sphere of the divine and rules with divine authority. Precisely for this reason he must represent the righteousness of God.

Verse three (Eng. vs. 2) of the same psalm also emphasizes the special position occupied by the king:

---

[26] H. Brunner, "Gerechtigkeit als Fundament des Thrones," *VT,* VIII (1958), 426 ff.

[27] [RSV margin; RSV text reads "your divine throne."—Trans.]

[28] See the commentaries, e.g., H. J. Kraus, *Die Psalmen* (Neukirchen: Erziehungsverein, 1961), I, 334 f.

You are the fairest of the sons of men;
    grace is poured upon your lips;
        therefore God has blessed your for ever.

Even if we are here dealing with the extravagance of a court poet, one thing is certain: the king owes his special position to God's blessing. God has chosen him, God has given him everything.

Somewhat more problematical is another passage, which speaks of a man or "son of man":[29]

Yet thou hast made him little less than God,
    and dost crown him with glory and honor.
Thou hast given him dominion over the works of thy hands;
    thou hast put all things under his feet.

                       (Ps. 8:6 f. [Eng. 8:5 f.])

The continuation unquestionably refers to the creation account in Genesis 1. It seems reasonable, therefore, to assume that the verses quoted refer to man in general. The words "crown" and "honor" (*hādār*), however, suggest the office of king; and "glory" (*kābôd*) is usually an attribute of God. If we could assume that the creation story was somehow represented dramatically in the cult and that the king played the role of the first man, representing all mankind, this difficulty would be solved.[30] This would also tie in with the messianic interpretation of this passage (Heb. 2:6 f.). Ezekiel 28:12 ff. could also support this view: here the king of Tyre is depicted as the first man in the garden of God. Of course this does not necessarily apply to the *Israelite* king. Conclusive proof is probably impossible.

The extraordinary wisdom of the king is frequently mentioned. "My lord has wisdom," says a woman of Tekoa to David, "like the wisdom of the angel of God to know all things that are on the earth" (II Sam. 14:20). Solomon's wisdom was famous and even became proverbial (I Kings 4:29-34; 10:1-9, 24). It was looked upon as a gift he had received from God in answer to his prayers (I Kings 3:4-15); it manifested itself particularly as judicial wisdom (I Kings 3:16-28). In similar fashion, the judicial wisdom of the messianic king is also emphasized:

And the Spirit of Yahweh shall rest upon him,
    the spirit of wisdom and understanding.

. . . .

He shall not judge by what his eyes see,
    or decide by what his ears hear;
but with righteousness he shall judge the poor. (Isa. 11:2-4)

---

[29] I.e., according to the Hebrew idiom, "man."

[30] Ringgren, *op. cit.,* pp. 19 f.; I. Engnell, "Die Urmenschvorstellung und das Alte Testament," *SEÅ,* XXII/XXIII (1958), 277 ff.; E. Larsson, *Christus als Vorbild* (Uppsala: Almqvist & Wiksell, 1962), pp. 119 f.

Ezekiel 28:12 says of the king that he is "the signet of perfection, full of wisdom and perfect in beauty." But here we are dealing once more with the king of Tyre, and the passage is not immediately relevant for Israel.

In addition, the king is in a special way the servant (*'ebed*) of Yahweh.[31] David especially has this term applied to him (sixty times, e.g., II Sam. 3:18; 7:5, 8; Ps. 89:4, 21 [Eng. 89:3, 20]). But "servant of Yahweh" is by no means an exclusively royal title (as Engnell has sometimes argued): it is applied to Abraham (Ps. 105:6, 42), Moses (forty times, e.g., Num. 12:7 f.; Josh. 1:7, 13, 15; Ps. 105:26), and various prophets (e.g., I Kings 18:36; Jer. 26:5; Isa. 20:3). All these passages cannot possibly derive from the royal ideology. The situation is actually this: anyone who stands in right relationship with Yahweh is the servant of Yahweh, although this applies in its fullest sense to the king. In any case, it is very significant that, whenever Deutero-Isaiah speaks of Israel as the servant of Yahweh, he employs numerous elements of the royal ideology.[32] It should also be pointed out that the king (and probably other worshipers) refers to himself as "thy servant," a custom frequently found also in Babylonian psalms.[33]

At this point we must at least ask to what extent the extravagant statements about the king, which we have been discussing, are really intended to be taken seriously. Are we merely dealing, as has often been asserted, with the language of a "court style" prone to flattery and exaggeration? The general opinion is that "divine" kingship, such as would take these expressions at their face value, is to be found in Egypt and in ancient Mesopotamia, but that in Israel the kingship is a completely secular office, and the evidence here cited is merely the remnants of the common court style of the ancient Near East and was not meant to be taken seriously. The king of Israel, in this view, is definitely a man, not a god.[34]

Admittedly there is no infallible criterion by which to tell whether a statement about the Israelite king is really meant the way it sounds or merely represents an accommodation to the court style of the ancient Near East. The fact that criticism of the kings and of kingship also existed in Israel proves only that certain circles had a critical attitude toward the kingship, while others—as the psalms show quite conclusively—accepted and approved many elements of the oriental royal ideology. There is also a further consideration: we know that

---

[31] C. Lindhagen, *The Servant Motif in the Old Testament* (Uppsala: Lundeqvist, 1950), pp. 280 ff.

[32] See below, pp. 293 f.

[33] B. Landsberger, *Mitteilungen der Altorientalischen Gesellschaft,* IV, 308 f.; G. Widengren, *The Accadian and Hebrew Psalms of Lamentation* (Stockholm: Thule, 1937), p. 36; Lindhagen, *op. cit.,* pp. 263 f.

[34] Bernhardt, *op. cit.,* pp. 262 f.

even in those states that had "divine" kingship opposition was possible, that the authority of the king was occasionally questioned, that rebellions took place, etc. Even if the royal ideology stated that the king was divine, the people knew very well that he was a human being, mortal and imperfect and even removable.[35] It must also be kept in mind that the Israelite king was definitely not looked upon as a god,[36] but rather as the representative of God upon earth, appointed by Yahweh and responsible to him. It might be better, therefore, to avoid the term "divine kingship"[37] and speak instead of "sacral kingship." The Israelite king is not divine, but he does have sacral duties and functions.

In the first place, from the time of David and Solomon on, it is his duty to take charge of the Temple and its cult.[38] David plans to build a temple and Solomon carries out this intention. Throughout the entire period of the monarchy, the king appears as head of the official cult. David and Solomon appoint priests, Jeroboam establishes two new sanctuaries in the Northern Kingdom and issues regulations concerning the cult to be practiced there (I Kings 12:31 ff.). The Deuteronomistic historian imputes to the kings responsibility for guarding the purity of the official cult. Cultic innovations are introduced or abolished by the kings (e.g., II Kings 21:3 ff.); Hezekiah and Josiah in particular work as reformers (II Kings 18:4; 23:1 ff.). In his blueprint for the organization of the cult and the state, Ezekiel makes the prince responsible for the cult (Ezek. 45 f.).[39]

Somewhat more dubious is the priestly office of the king. Psalm 110:4 says, "You are a priest for ever after the order of Melchizedek." But there are only scattered accounts of the king performing priestly functions. When the ark is brought up to Jerusalem, David officiates as a priest, dancing before the ark, offering burnt offerings, and blessing the people in the name of Yahweh (II Sam. 6:16-18). At the dedication of the Temple, Solomon leads the ceremonies (I Kings 8); he also blesses the entire assembly (8:14). The blessing of Aaron (as high priest) in Numbers 6:24-26 may preserve the text of this blessing.[40] Jeroboam goes up to the altar (I Kings 12:33). There are other occasions, however, when kings are censured for exercising priestly functions. Saul offers sacrifice without waiting for Samuel to arrive, for which Samuel reproves him (I Sam. 13:8-15). According to the

---

[35] See, for example, G. Posener, *De la divinité du Pharaon,* 1960; H. Goedecke, *Die Stellung des Königs im Alten Reich,* 1960.

[36] Despite Ps. 45:7 (Eng. 45:6).

[37] As used by Engnell, for instance.

[38] Widengren, *Sakrales Königtum,* pp. 14 ff.

[39] Cf. E. Hammershaimb, "Ezekiel's View of the Monarchy," *Studia Orientalia Joanni Pedersen dicata* (Hauniae: Munksgaard), pp. 130 ff., esp. p. 139.

[40] Widengren, *Sakrales Königtum,* p. 19.

Chronicler, Uzziah offers incense in the Temple and is punished for doing so (II Chron. 26:16 ff.). This account probably represents a defense of later priestly interest. Ezekiel, however, though himself a priest, assigns certain cultic duties to the prince in his plan for the new Israel. In particular, the prince is to offer sacrifice on the great festivals. Especially noteworthy is the regulation that, on the Day of Atonement, the prince is to offer a bullock on behalf of all the people (Ezek. 45:22 f.); the ritual outlined in Leviticus 16 makes this the duty of the high priest (Lev. 16:11, 16, 24). In the postexilic period, the high priest obviously took over the function of the king. We are probably justified in assuming that the king officiated at certain atonement ceremonies in the context of the New Year's festival.[41] It is no longer possible to discover the nature of these ceremonies. It should not be forgotten, however, that the ritual of the Day of Atonement (Lev. 16) bears a very primitive stamp—we may recall in particular the sending forth of the scapegoat—and that a similar ceremony is also attested for the Babylonian New Year's festival.[42]

It should be pointed out further in this connection that the description of the vestments of the high priest in Exodus 28 and 29 is strikingly reminiscent of the royal apparel in Ezekiel 28:13. Even if Ezekiel is discussing the king of Tyre, some connection must exist. In all probability, the high priest took over at least portions of the official vesture of the king. Royal vesture outside of Israel furnishes good parallels to the cosmic symbolism of the vesture of the high priest in the Book of Wisdom (18:24—"For upon his long robe the whole world was [depicted]").[43]

Any conjectures we might make as to other functions of the king at the New Year's festival are even more precarious. It has often been suggested that, following the pattern of the other ancient Near Eastern religions, the king "played" the role of the deity in the cultic drama at the festival.[44] Now the very existence of this pattern has not been proved conclusively in all particulars. In fact, the instances in which the king definitely plays the role of a god are very few: e.g., the creation drama of the Babylonian New Year's festival and the Osiris drama of ancient Egypt. On the other hand, the king does represent his people before the gods. In fact, it is very questionable methodologically to ask how much evidence there is for elements of a foreign cult in Israel. It is preferable to examine the documents themselves to see what they say about the Israelite cult and the role

---

[41] *Ibid.,* pp. 22 f.

[42] See above, p. 172.

[43] Ringgren, *op. cit.,* pp. 13 f.

[44] S. H. Hooke, *Myth and Ritual* (London: Oxford, 1933), p. 8; Engnell, *Studies in Divine Kingship,* pp. 175 f.; Widengren, *Sakrales Königtum,* p. 75; Bernhardt, *op. cit.,* pp. 80 f., 255 f.

of the king in it. But it is precisely these documents, especially the psalms, whose interpretation is disputed today.

One group of psalms, dealing with the theme "Through Death to Life," is of particular interest in this regard. This group includes Psalms 18, 22, 69, 71, 86, 88, 116, 118, and the psalm of Hezekiah in Isaiah 38.[45] Of the motifs appearing in these psalms, the following are the most important.[46]

1. The suppliant is in the power of death or Sheol, which is often expressed through the traditional images of deep waters, waves, breakers, or the like, e.g.:

> The cords of death encompassed me,
>> the torrents of perdition assailed me;
> the cords of Sheol entangled me,
>> the snares of death confronted me.
>
> (Ps. 18:5 f. [Eng. 18:4 f.])

(Cf. also Ps. 49:15 [Eng. 49:14]; 88:4-8 [Eng. 88:3-7]; 116:3; Isa. 38:10, 17.)

2. The suppliant is surrounded by enemies, sometimes described as wild beasts (demons),[47] e.g.:

> Many bulls encompass me,
>> strong bulls of Bashan surround me;
> they open wide their mouths at me,
>> like a ravening and roaring lion.
>
> ....
>
> Yea, dogs are round about me;
>> a company of evildoers encircle me.
>
> (Ps. 22:13 f., 17 [Eng. 22:12 f., 16])

(Cf. also Ps. 18:18 [Eng. 18:17]; 22:21 f. [Eng. 22:20 f.]; 86:14; 118:10-12.)

3. The suppliant is despised and reviled: "But I am a worm and no man; scorned by men, and despised by the people" (Ps. 22:7 [Eng. 22:6]; cf. 71:10 f.; 88:9, 19 [Eng. 88:8, 18]).

4. God saves him and gives him life: "I shall not die, but I shall live" (Ps. 118:17), "I walk before Yahweh in the land of the living" (Ps. 116:9; cf. Isa. 38:11).

5. He shall proclaim his salvation to the "great congregation" (Ps. 22:23, 26 [Eng. 22:22, 25]; 116:14; 118:17), or it shall be told to coming generations (Ps. 22:31 f. [Eng. 22:30 f.]; 71:18; Isa. 38:19).

6. The suppliant is called "servant" ('ebed) (Ps. 86:2, 4, 16; 116:16; cf. 22:1 [Eng. 22, heading]).

---

[45] Engnell, *Studies in Divine Kingship,* p. 176, n. 4, calls them Ebed-Yahweh psalms.

[46] This summary is taken from Ringgren, *op. cit.,* pp. 63 f.

[47] See above, pp. 101 f.

7. There are several allusions to themes that are otherwise connected with the New Year, or enthronement, festival (e.g., the theophany in Ps. 18:8 ff. [Eng. 18:7 ff.], the uniqueness of God and the worship of the nations in Ps. 86:8-10, and probably also references to certain ceremonies in Ps. 118:24, 27).

8. The aid comes in the morning (Ps. 49:15 [Eng. 49:14];[48] this fact is also alluded to in several other psalms, especially New Year psalms, e.g., 46:6 [Eng. 46:5]; 143:8).[49]

It would be reasonable to assume that a ritual lies behind all this: after the king has ritually "died" and spent a night (symbolically) in Sheol, he returns to life in the morning. If we may follow Johnson in assuming that in the course of the Israelite New Year's festival a nocturnal ceremony represented the triumph of darkness and the powers of chaos, followed in the morning by the victory of Yahweh, it would be possible to interpret these psalms as referring to the participation of the king in this ritual: he goes through the peril of night with the triumph of death and in the morning experiences the victory of God. He proclaims his deliverance and triumph: "I shall not die, but I shall live."[50] But even if this assumption should be right, this would not prove that the king played the role of the deity in the cult. In reality, there is no proof that in the official cult—and that is what we are dealing with here—Yahweh was viewed as a dying and rising god.[51] But then it is meaningless to speak of a cultic identification of the king with God.[52]

The question still remains, however, whether some kind of humiliation of the king did not take place, followed by his restoration. The primary evidence for this conclusion is the fact that in Psalm 89 the king is deprived of his crown, while his enemies mock him and his days are cut short (vss. 40-52 [Eng. vss. 39-51]). This description is strongly reminiscent of the humiliation of the king in the Babylonian New Year's festival.[53] It is noteworthy that the same psalm contains so many allusions to motifs of the New Year's festival (the creation myth, vss. 10-13 [Eng. 9-12]; Yahweh as the only God, vss. 7-9 [Eng. 6-8]). It should be noted also that the Ebed-Yahweh songs in Deutero-Isaiah are reminiscent in many ways of these psalms; they are found in a book whose form is permeated with motifs of the New Year's festival.

---

[48] [Note the RSV margin, which preserves the MT.—TRANS.]

[49] Cf. J. Ziegler, "Die Hilfe Gottes 'am Morgen,'" in H. Junker and J. Botterweck (ed.), *Alttestamentliche Studien Fr. Nötscher* (Bonn: Hanstein, 1950), pp. 281 ff.

[50] Johnson, *op. cit.*, pp. 103 ff.; cf. Ahlström, *op. cit.*, pp. 143 ff.

[51] See above, pp. 87 f., 196 f.

[52] As is done, for example, by Widengren, *Sakrales Königtum*, p. 75.

[53] There are also other Sumerian and Akkadian parallels; see Ahlström, *op. cit.*, p. 147.

The really vital question is this: does Psalm 89 really contain the ritual of a regularly recurring observance, or was it written for a specific historical situation? It is admittedly difficult to think of an historical situation that fits the content of this psalm. The king has been deposed and the walls of the city destroyed. The destruction of Jerusalem is a possible suggestion; but it is hardly reasonable to assume that Zedekiah had the opportunity to recite such a psalm in a liturgy. The possibility remains open that, in the course of the New Year's festival, the king went through a night of humiliation, followed by triumph the next morning. This may also have been thought of as experiencing the triumph of the powers of chaos and the victory of Yahweh. Conclusive proof is, of course, hardly possible. For the time being, we must make do with conjectures. There are two facts about which there can be no doubt: (1) certain psalms, which describe the death and restoration to life of the suppliant, were either spoken by the king or placed in his mouth; (2) these psalms also contain motifs of the New Year's festival. There must therefore have been some connection between a New Year's celebration and the pangs of death followed by triumph. The same motifs are associated in Deutero-Isaiah and the Ebed-Yahweh songs.

It is obvious that numerous elements can be detected in the Israelite royal ideology that derive from ancient Near Eastern conceptions and rites. Since kingship was not indigenous to Israel, this is to be expected. If we go on to inquire into the uniqueness of the Israelite royal ideology, we must direct our attention primarily to the idea of the covenant. Yahweh chose David and his seed and made a covenant with them.[54] The parallel with the Sinai covenant is immediately evident. Here we obviously see the feature peculiar to Israel. Elements of non-Israelite royal ideology became fused with the Israelite covenant concept. The Davidic covenant was thought of as a continuation or particularization of the Sinai covenant, as a new event in *Heilsgeschichte*. We are by no means dealing here with a completely secular institution[55]—so much is clear. The Israelite king was chosen and appointed by Yahweh and responsible to Yahweh. We have seen, in addition, that, as Yahweh's anointed, he was considered inviolable. He was called Yahweh's adopted son, and consequently belonged in part to the sphere of the divine. Never, though, was he thought of as a god, not even in theory.

The Israelite royal ideology achieved significance because in the course of time it gave rise to the expectation of a coming ideal king. This ideal king is usually referred to in modern writing as the Messiah, a usage taken over from late Judaism. It was hoped that he would

---

[54] L. Rost, "Sinaibund und Davidbund," *TLZ*, 1947, cols. 129 ff.; von Rad, *Old Testament Theology*, p. 310.

[55] As suggested by Noth, *op. cit.*

accomplish all that men had originally expected of the king. The earliest messianic oracles are found in the pre-exilic prophets; we have already used some of them in our reconstruction of the Israelite royal ideology. Strangely enough, the term "Messiah" does not occur in them. In the Old Testament, this word is applied only to the king; it first appears as a technical term of eschatology in the late Jewish apocalyptic writings, to which we shall return later.

11.

DEATH AND THE AFTERLIFE

The attitude of the majority of the Old Testament texts toward death is relatively neutral.[1] It is an acknowledged fact that every man must die (Ps. 39:5-7 [Eng. 39:4-6]). Man is mortal, his life is brief:

> The years of our life are threescore and ten,
>   or even by reason of strength fourscore;
> yet their span is but toil and trouble. (Ps. 90:10)

Man came from dust, and to dust he shall return (Gen. 3:19). Ecclesiastes—writing considerably later—says in his characteristic fashion, "For the fate of the sons of men and the fate of the beasts is the same; as one dies, so dies the other" (Eccles. 3:19). Most of these passages seem to have pessimistic overtones. In general, however, a man's death is merely mentioned as part of the natural order.

Long life is a great boon, and is mentioned frequently by Deuteronomy, for example, as a reward for keeping the commandments (Exod. 20:12 [=Deut. 5:16]; also Deut. 4:4; 6:2; 11:9; probably also Ezek. 18:9, 19, 21). Death at a great age is even described in positive terms (Gen. 25:7 f.; Num. 23:10). Sudden death, on the other hand, is a terrible misfortune, and is usually interpreted as a divine punishment. The wicked and godless come to a sudden end (Prov. 10:21; 11:9; etc.; Ps. 73:18 f.; Job 20:6 ff.).

The ideas and customs associated with death frequently bear a very "primitive" stamp. The dead body is unclean, and whoever touches a corpse becomes unclean (Num. 19:11 ff.). This rule is probably based on extremely ancient taboo regulations no longer completely understood. Originally, they may have codified the natural

---

[1] O. J. Baab, *Theology of the Old Testament* (Nashville: Abingdon, 1949), pp. 198 ff. General discussions: G. Quell, *Die Auffassung des Todes im Alten Testament* (Leipzig: Hinrichs, 1925); G. von Rad, "Alttestamentliche Glaubensaussagen von Leben und Tod," *AELK*, 1938, pp. 826 ff.

reaction to the unknown and sinister. No explanation or motivation of any sort is ever given in the Old Testament laws regulating matters of cleanness and uncleanness.

The mourning rites[2] basically provide a means for the survivors to express their grief and despair; to a great extent, however, they have been stylized and conventionalized. The mourners rend their garments (Gen. 37:34; Lev. 10:6; I Sam. 4:12), a practice found elsewhere as a general means of expressing violent emotion (Mt. 26:65). A garment made of dark, coarse cloth is put on; this is usually called "sackcloth" (Gen. 37:34; II Sam. 3:31; 21:10; Isa. 3:24; 15:3; etc.). The head is covered with earth or ashes (I Sam. 4:12; II Sam. 1:2; Job 2:12; Ezek. 27:30). The mourners sit or lie upon the ground (Isa. 3:26; 47:1; "roll in ashes," Jer. 6:26; Lam. 2:10). This last practice may of course be intended to communicate some kind of feeling of solidarity with the dead person, now lying in the dust or returned to the dust; there is no express statement to this effect, however.

Other expressions of pain and grief include beating the breast (Isa. 32:12; cf. Jer. 31:19); self-injury ("cuttings"), which was considered a pagan custom and therefore prohibited (Lev. 19:28; 21:5; Deut. 14:1; Jer. 16:6; 41:5; 47:5; 48:37); and the shaving of a bald spot (Deut. 14:1; Job 1:20; Isa. 22:12; Jer. 7:29; Amos 8:10; Mic. 1:16). The latter practice has been explained, albeit not convincingly, as a vestige of what had originally been an offering of hair to the dead.

The lament (*mispēd*)[3] consisted in loud wailing, performed either by the relatives or by professional female mourners. Probably at first a spontaneous expression of grief, it was very early reduced to fixed forms. Like proper burial, it was considered an obligation; it was very important, even for the deceased. We hear of expressions like "Alas, my brother!" "Ah sister!" and "Alas, lord!" in this context (I Kings 13:30; Jer. 22:18; 34:5). Identical laments also occurred in the mourning ritual of the Tammuz cult. In addition, however, we find real literary laments, such as David's lament over Saul and Jonathan in II Samuel 1:19-27. In many ways it can be considered typical.

> Thy glory, O Israel, is slain upon thy high places!
> How are the mighty fallen!
>
> . . . .
>
> Ye daughters of Israel, weep over Saul.
>
> . . . .

---

[2] H. J. Elhorst, *Die israelitischen Trauerriten* (Giessen: Töpelmann, 1914); P. Heinisch, *Die Trauergebräuche bei den Israeliten* (Münster: Aschendorff, 1931).

[3] P. Heinisch, *Die Totenklage im Alten Testament* (Münster: Aschendorff, 1931); cf. also H. Jahnow, *Das hebräische Leichenlied* (Giessen: Töpelmann, 1923).

How are the mighty fallen,
in the midst of the battle!
Jonathan lies slain upon thy high places.
I am distressed for you, my brother Jonathan.

Many scholars have tried to find in the Old Testament vestiges of worship of the dead.[4] In the book of Jeremiah, a "cup of consolation" is mentioned (Jer. 16:7); Hosea speaks of "mourners' bread," which is considered unclean (Hos. 9:4; cf. also Ezek. 24:17, 22). These passages remain obscure, however. They could quite as easily be dealing with a memorial meal or gifts for consolation and as evidence of sympathy as with the uncomprehending continuance of a sacrificial meal. The only passage to mention food placed upon a grave is very late (Ecclus. 30:18). The other texts cited as evidence for a cult of the dead are even more precarious (e.g., Deut. 26:14, where assurance is given at the presentation of first fruits that none of the food presented has been offered to the dead, which might be interpreted as a disavowal of the cult of the dead; or Ps. 106:28, which obviously refers to a pagan cult).

The Israelites shared most of these mourning customs with the Canaanites and other peoples of the ancient Near East.[5] The Aqhat text from Ras Shamra, for example, describes the weeping of the mourners and the self-injury of the "men that gashed their flesh"[6] (I Aqht IV, 9-17 [= 171 ff.]); and one of the Baal texts expresses the grief over the death of Baal as follows:

Straightway Kindly El Benign
Descends from the throne,
Sits on the footstool;
From the footstool,
And sits on the ground;
Pours dust of mourning on his head,
Earth of mortification on his pate;
And puts on *sackcloth and loincloth.*
He *cuts a gash* with a stone
Incisions with . . .
He *gashes* his cheeks and his chin,
He *harrows* the *roll* of his *arm.*

---

[4] For example, F. Schwally, *Das Leben nach dem Tode nach den Vorstellungen des alten Israels und des Judentums* (Giessen: Töpelmann, 1892); A. Lods, *La croyance à la vie future et le culte des morts dans l'antiquité israélite* (Paris: Fischbacher, 1906).

[5] E. L. Ehrlich, *Die Kultsymbolik im Alten Testament und im nachbiblischen Judentum* (Stuttgart: Hiersemann, 1959), pp. 116 f.

[6] [This is the author's translation of *pẓġm ġr*, following G. R. Driver, *Canaanite Myths and Legends* (Edinburgh: Clark, 1956), p. 65; this translation is generally accepted, e.g., by Aistleitner. H. L. Ginsberg, however, in *ANET*, p. 155, leaves the phrase untranslated and suggests that it is the proper name of Daniel's court.—TRANS.]

He plows his chest like a garden,
>   *Harrows* his back like a plain.
He lifts up his voice and cries:
>   "Baal's dead! . . ."[7]

Here, then, we find the same customs as in Israel.

Even though the Old Testament tradition never once states in so many words why it is necessary to bury the body, many passages make it unambiguously clear that a proper burial was considered very important. After Jezebel's death, enough of her body could not be found for her to be buried; this was felt to be exceptionally dreadful (II Kings 9:30-37). David's action in ordering the burial of the bones of Saul and Jonathan is singled out for special praise (II Sam. 21:13 f.). Interment far from home (II Sam. 19:38 [Eng. 19:37]; I Kings 13:22) or in the burial place of the common people (Jer. 26:23) was considered a terrible misfortune. As a divine punishment upon Jehoiakim, Jeremiah prophesies that he will be buried in disgrace and without mourners (Jer. 22:18 f.—"the burial of an ass"). The same prophet considers it the height of misfortune to die without burial and the usual mourning rites (Jer. 16:5-7). All this obviously presupposes that man somehow continues his existence after death, and that the nature of this afterlife depends on burial. Similar thoughts expressed in the Gilgamesh Epic suggest the belief that those who were not buried had to wander the earth as ghosts.

Belief in an afterlife is also indicated by the practice of necromancy, or divination with the aid of the dead. When caught in a desperate situation, Saul visits a medium at Endor with the request that she conjure up the spirit of the dead Samuel. Samuel appears to her as an *ĕlōhîm* or divine being in the form of a man, so that Saul recognizes him at the description of the woman. Samuel asks, "Why have you disturbed me by bringing me up?" In all probability, this practice was not uncommon in Israel; it was felt, however, to be alien to the religion of Yahweh. Deuteronomy 18:11 forbids necromancy along with all other kinds of magic; and Isaiah heaps scorn on those who "consult the spirits of the dead (*yiddĕʿōnîm*), asking 'Should the people not consult their gods, the dead on behalf of the living?'" (Isa. 8:19).[8] Here the spirits of the dead are called divine and "knowing" (*yiddĕʿōnî*, from *yādaʿ*, "know"); they are able to give the living important information. Isaiah, of course, did not approve of this practice.

---

[7] *UM* 67 (I* AB) VI, 11-13. [The translation given is that of H. L. Ginsberg in *ANET*, p. 139; it differs from that of the author only in detail.—Trans.]

[8] The verse can also be translated differently by taking the last question as a negative answer: "Should not a people consult their God? Should they consult the dead on behalf of the living?" [This latter translation is followed by the RSV.—Trans.]

The way in which the continued existence of the dead is conceived is not precisely formulated.[9] The frequent expression, "He was gathered to his fathers," seems to indicate that the departed spirits of the family somehow lived together. One might follow Pedersen in think-ing in terms of a family grave, which becomes the site of the after-life.[10] On the other hand, Sheol ($\check{s}e'\hat{o}l$) is mentioned as the place to which all the dead go. No clear spatial distinction is made between Sheol and the grave, however; and on occasion both are used almost synonymously.[11]

The actual meaning of the word $\check{s}e'\hat{o}l$ is uncertain. Neither the derivation from $\check{s}\bar{a}'al$, "ask," nor the comparison with $\check{s}\bar{o}'al$, "hollow hand," really fits. The derivation from Akkadian also carries little conviction.[12] There may be some connection with $\check{s}\bar{a}'\hat{a}$, "be desolate."[13]

In the last analysis, however, it is not the etymology but the actual usage that determines the meaning of a word. The first thing to note is that Sheol is the abode of the dead. "To go down into Sheol" means the same as "to die." Such words as $\check{s}aḥat$, "pit," and '$\bar{a}p\bar{a}r$, "dust," are more or less synonymous with Sheol; this indicates the close association with the grave. Sheol is clearly located in the depths of the earth (Deut. 32:22). It is also associated, however, with water, waves, and torrents. In II Samuel 22:5 f., for instance, the waves of death, the torrents of perdition, the cords of Sheol, and the snares of death are all juxtaposed with approximately the same meaning in order to describe a deadly danger. And the psalm incorporated in the book of Jonah says:

> Out of the belly of Sheol I cried,
> and thou didst hear my voice.
> For thou didst cast me into the deep,
> into the heart of the seas,
> and the flood was round about me;
> all thy waves and thy billows
> passed over me. (Jon. 2:3 f. [Eng. 2:2 f.])

Doubtless the ancient Near Eastern conception of the universe lies in the background here: if the earth is a flat disc floating on the ocean,

---

[9] In addition to the works mentioned in notes 1 and 4 above, see: A. Bertholet, *Die israelitischen Vorstellungen vom Zustande nach dem Tode* (2nd ed.; Tübingen: Mohr, 1914); E. J. Sutcliffe, *The Old Testament and the Future Life* (Burns, Oates & Washburn, 1946); O. Schilling, *Der Jenseitsgedanke im Alten Testament* (Mainz, 1951); R. Martin-Achard, *From Death to Life*, trans. J. P. Smith (Edinburgh & London: Oliver & Boyd, 1960).

[10] J. Pedersen, *Israel* (London: Oxford, 1959), I-II, 462.

[11] *Ibid.*

[12] W. Baumgartner, "Zur Etymologie von sche'ol," *TZ*, II (1946), 233 ff.

[13] L. Köhler, "Sche'ol," *ibid.*, pp. 71 ff.

there must be water under the surface of the earth; but that is also the abode of the dead.[14]

The realm of the dead is a place of darkness and desolation. It is a land of deep shadows and disorder, black as night (Job 10:21 f.), a place where the worm is addressed as father, mother, and sister (Job 17:13 f.). Hither all men must someday come, rich and poor, wise and foolish, kings and princes, slaves and masters, great and humble (Job 3:13-19; Ps. 49:7-15 [Eng. 49:6-14]; Ezek. 32:18, 32). Sheol is like a monster that opens its insatiable jaws to swallow up all men and their splendor (Isa. 5:14; cf. Hab. 2:5; Prov. 30:15 f.). Like the Babylonian realm of the dead, it is a land of no return: "He who goes down to Sheol does not come up" (Job 7:9; cf. also 10:21; 16:22). The man who goes down into Sheol is forgotten by all (Job 24:20). And even more: he is cut off from communion with God.

> Dost thou work wonders for the dead?
>> Do the shades rise up to praise thee?
> Is thy steadfast love declared in the grave,
>> or thy faithfulness in Abaddon?
> Are thy wonders known in the darkness,
>> or thy saving help in the land of forgetfulness?
>>> (Ps. 88:11-13 [Eng. 88:10-12])

Sheol is not part of the realm of Yahweh; he is the God of the living. This probably does not mean that Sheol originally stood under the sovereignty of another god, but only that the man who is there no longer can be in communion with Yahweh. Other passages, on the contrary, assert that Yahweh is present even in Sheol.

> If I ascend to heaven, thou art there!
> If I make my bed in Sheol, thou art there! (Ps. 139:8)

But here, as in Amos 9:2, the point of the passage is that there is no escape from Yahweh.

Isaiah 14, a taunt song against Babylon, provides an interesting description of Sheol. Here we see depicted how the king of Babylon enters Sheol after his defeat:

> Sheol beneath is stirred up
>> to meet you when you come,
> it rouses the shades to greet you,
>> all who were leaders of the earth;
> it raises from their thrones
>> all who were kings of the nations.
> All of them will speak
>> and say to you:

---

[14] [For a discussion of the liquid aspects of Sheol connected with the word šaḥat, see M. H. Pope, "The Word šaḥat in Job 9:31," *JBL*, LXXXIII (1964), 269 ff.—TRANS.]

"You too have become as weak as we!
   You have become like us!"
Your pomp is brought down to Sheol,
   the sound of your harps;
maggots are the bed beneath you,
   and worms are your covering. (Isa. 14:9-11)

Here we learn in the first place from the connection with worms and maggots how closely the concept of Sheol is associated with the grave. In the second place, we discover that the dead live as feeble shades, but nevertheless somehow retain something of their earthly dignity: they still possess thrones. Like a few other passages in the Old Testament (Isa. 26:14; Ps. 88:11 [Eng. 88:10]; Job 26:5), this song refers to the spirits of the dead in Sheol as $r^e p\bar{a}'\hat{i}m$, a word connected either with $r\bar{a}p\hat{a}$, "be weak," or with $r\bar{a}p\bar{a}'$, "heal." It is uncertain whether there is any connection between this word and the $r^e p\bar{a}'\hat{i}m$ that inhabited Palestine before the Israelites. The word probably is connected with the $rp\grave{u}m$ of the Ras Shamra texts, which perhaps should be thought of as chthonic deities that bring fertility. A derivation from rp', "bind up," would then suggest that the shades were "a massed community leading a common life in the netherworld."[15]

The thought of the realm of the dead thus produces a feeling of hopelessness. That Yahweh's power ultimately does extend to Sheol is no comfort; it means only that man cannot escape him. A ray of hope is seen in those passages that characterize Yahweh as the one who will not deliver a man over to Sheol, but will save him from death. "For thou hast delivered my soul from death," we read in Psalm 116:8, for example, after the preceding verses have spoken of Sheol. And the author of Psalm 30 says:

Yahweh, thou hast brought up my soul from Sheol,
   restored me to life from among those gone down to the
      Pit. (vs. 4 [Eng. vs. 3])

Another psalmist, confident of victory, cries out, "I shall not die, but I shall live. . . . Yahweh has chastened me sorely but he has not given me over to death" (Ps. 118:17 f.). What is the concrete meaning of these statements? There is no other evidence in ancient Israel for belief in a resurrection of the dead. Babylonian gods are given the title *muballiṭ mītē*, "giving life to the dead"; this could indicate that we are here dealing with expressions meant to be taken figuratively, since the Akkadian term seems to refer primarily to healing the sick. Since Israel also thinks of sickness as potential death, the words might be taken to refer to God's healing power. It is also possible, of course, that the primary thought is of deliverance from mortal danger and granting of long life.

---

[15] Ginsberg's suggestion; see Driver, *op. cit.*, p. 10, n. 2.

Despite all this, it is impossible to escape the impression that these words express the conviction that God is somehow stronger than death and Sheol, that he is able to give life. In his hand he holds life and death, and he can preserve the life of the man that is threatened by death.

> For thou dost not give me up to Sheol,
>> or let thy godly one see the Pit. (Ps. 16:10)

> But God will ransom my soul from the powers of Sheol,
>> for he will receive me. (Ps. 49:16 [Eng. 49:15])

It is not said *how* this deliverance from death takes place; but it is stated, clearly and unambiguously, that Yahweh will not deliver the psalmist over to death or Sheol. We hear nothing of any resurrection of the dead, but we do encounter the assurance that Yahweh is mightier than death and Sheol.[16]

The last passage quoted uses the verb *lāqaḥ*, "take," in the statement, "he will receive me." Psalm 73:24 uses the same word in a similar context: "I am continually with thee. . . . Thou dost guide me with thy counsel, and afterward thou wilt receive me to glory." Unfortunately, the Massoretic Text of the last line is obscure; the words could equally well be translated, "And after glory thou wilt receive me." In Genesis 5:24, the same word is applied to Enoch: "And he was not, for God took him"; this obviously means that he was carried off. II Kings 2:9 ff. uses this verb in the same meaning to describe the ascension of Elijah. Of course this does not prove that such an idea formed a part of the normal hope for the afterlife entertained by a religious Israelite. In the first place, *lāqaḥ* is the ordinary word for "take"; in the second place, the cases of Enoch and Elijah are clearly exceptional. The precise meaning of the two passages from the psalms cannot be determined at present.

A real doctrine of resurrection appeared in Israel only much later, in the postexilic period, probably at least to some extent under Persian influence. But the basis for this doctrine was already present in ancient Israel. One contributing factor was the conviction, already mentioned, that Yahweh is mightier than death and Sheol. Another is probably to be found in certain Canaanite ideas associated with the dying and rising fertility god. Hosea is probably referring to such ideas when he puts the following words into the mouths of optimistic Israelites in the course of a penitential liturgy:

> Come, let us return to Yahweh;
>> for he has torn, that he may heal us;
>> he has stricken, and he will bind us up.

---

16 A. Weiser, *The Psalms*, trans. H. Hartwell (Philadelphia: Westminster, 1962), pp. 176 ff., 388 f.; H. Ringgren, *The Faith of the Psalmists* (Philadelphia: Fortress, 1963), pp. 74 f.

> After two days he will revive us;
> on the third day he will raise us up,
> that we may live before him. (Hos. 6:1-2)[17]

The people clearly hope to be brought back to life, just like the god. "On the third day" is an interesting phrase. The book of Jonah states that Jonah spent a similar length of time in the fish's belly, a period described by the psalm in Jonah 2 as a stay in Sheol, i.e., death. This three-day period is apparently based on an ancient tradition, probably cultic, and may well derive ultimately from a Canaanite ritual.

It is also noteworthy that one of the passages that speaks of resurrection in the most unambiguous terms, Isaiah 26:19 (definitely postexilic), associates the resurrection of the dead with the dew:

> Thy dead shall live, their bodies shall rise.
> O dwellers in the dust, awake and sing for joy!
> For thy dew is a dew of light,
> and on the land of the shades thou wilt let it fall.

This is reminiscent of the ancient conception that the dew is a life-giving force, a conception appearing occasionally in the Ras Shamra texts.[18] Although this passage must be dated somewhat later, it, too, suggests a Canaanite background for the Israelite doctrine of resurrection. Certain aspects of the New Year's festival probably served as the connecting link.[19] Other sections of the Isaiah apocalypse also contain a wealth of motifs connected with this festival, a fact which makes a connection between the idea of resurrection and these Canaanite conceptions seem quite probable.

Detailed discussion of the doctrine of resurrection must be reserved for a later chapter.

---

[17] W. W. von Baudissin, *Adonis und Eschmun* (Leipzig: Hinrichs, 1911), pp. 403 ff.; H. G. May, "The Fertility Cult in Hosea," *AJSL*, XLVIII (1931), 73 ff.; W. Baumgartner, *Zeitschrift für Missionskunde und Religion-Wissenschaft*, XLVIII (1933), 193 ff.

[18] Cf. above, p. 225; H. Riesenfeld, *The Resurrection in Ez. XXXVII and in the Dura-Europas Paintings*, 1948, p. 10; G. Widengren, *Sakrales Königtum* (Stuttgart: Kohlhammer, 1955), p. 46.

[19] Cf. Riesenfeld, *op. cit.*, pp. 5 ff.

12.

THE WRITING PROPHETS

It is an astonishing fact that a large part of the Old Testament consists of writings that in many ways represent a point of view quite different from that of the "official" religion of their period. The prophetic books, at least those belonging to the pre-exilic period, are the literary precipitate of a movement that was highly critical of form generally assumed by the religion of Yahweh.[1]

The prophets viewed themselves as the champions of the original religion of Yahweh in its pure form, censuring the popular religion of the day as being syncretistic and corrupt. In reality, though, matters are not quite so simple. Doubtless the Israelite religion was threatened in the eighth century B.C. with the danger of becoming Canaanized. This tendency could be observed in all aspects of the religion. But the prophets themselves were unconsciously indebted to ideas and practices that were Canaanite, at least in origin. Pedersen in particular has emphasized that the process of Canaanization had already gone so far in Israel that the prophets were no longer capable of distinguishing precisely between what was Canaanite and what was genuinely Israelite.[2] The messianic hope of the prophets, for example, has its roots in the royal ideology, which itself shows Canaanite influence. Literary forms and individual mythological conceptions utilized by

---

[1] The literature dealing with the prophetic movement in Israel is vast. The following represent only a few basic studies: G. Hölscher, *Die Profeten* (Leipzig: Hinrichs, 1914); T. H. Robinson, *Prophecy and the Prophets in Ancient Israel* (2nd ed.; London: Duckworth, 1953); G. Widengren, *Literary and Psychological Aspects of the Hebrew Prophets* (Uppsala: Lundeqvist, 1948); G. von Rad, *Theologie des alten Testaments* (Munich: Kaiser, 1957-1960), II; C. Westermann, *Grundformen prophetischer Rede* (Munich: Kaiser, 1960); J. Lindblom, *Prophecy in Ancient Israel* (Philadelphia: Fortress, 1962). For bibliographical surveys, see O. Eissfeldt, "The Prophetic Literature," in H. H. Rowley (ed.), *The Old Testament and Modern Study* (London: Oxford, 1951), pp. 115 ff.; G. Fohrer, "Neuere Literatur zur alttestamentlichen Prophetie," *ThR*, N.F. XIX (1951), 277 ff., XX (1952), 193 ff., 295 ff.; *idem*, "Zehn Jahre Literatur zur alttestamentlichen Prophetie," *ibid.*, XXVIII (1962), 1 ff., 235 ff.

[2] J. Pedersen, *Israel* (London: Oxford, 1959), I-II, 25.

the prophets are frequently of Canaanite origin, although the prophets clearly considered them part of the true heritage of Israel.

The relationship of the writing prophets to the earlier "ecstatic" $n^eb\hat{i}$'$\hat{i}m$ and the "cult prophets" is still a matter of considerable debate. The traditional view, which looks upon the writing prophets as unique, is today gradually being replaced by a view that admits more continuity. The very fact that the same word, $nab\hat{i}$', is used for the ecstatic prophets as well as for the writing prophets suggests a connection, or at least a certain similarity. The fragmentary nature of our sources makes it very difficult to determine precisely the relationship existing between the two classes. Our information about the message of the early ecstatic prophets is insufficient. The fact that ecstatic prophets ($mahh\bar{u}$) in Mari made use of the same messenger formula used by the writing prophets in Israel suggests that this formula was no innovation in Israel.[3] Only scattered passages illuminate the psychological processes of the writing prophets; what evidence there is leaves the impression that ecstatic phenomena were less frequent in their case than was true of the earlier $n^eb\hat{i}$'$\hat{i}m$. This is not to deny that in certain cases and for certain prophets ecstatic phenomena are to be noted. Our sources are simply insufficient to allow a satisfactory psychological evaluation of Old Testament prophecy.[4]

The early $n^eb\hat{i}$'$\hat{i}m$ lived in groups under the direction of a leader or master. The members of such a company were called $b^en\hat{e}$ $n^eb\hat{i}$'$\hat{i}m$, "sons of the prophets." Amos denies that he is such a "son" or disciple (Amos 7:14). Isaiah, in contrast, was surrounded by a number of disciples (Isa. 8:16-18). In most cases, however, we are told nothing about the presence or absence of any adherents or disciples. A prophet like Jeremiah probably always remained an individualist, even though he had a scribe or secretary. The same is probably true of Ezekiel. Therefore we should probably not think in terms of a direct continuation of the prophetic guilds, but should speak instead of their further development.

How close was the connection, if indeed one existed at all, between the institutional cult prophets and the writing prophets? This question is violently debated.[5] Our insufficient sources do not permit an unambiguous answer. We know that Ezekiel was a priest and that Jeremiah came from a priestly family, but priest and cult prophet are not necessarily the same thing. Isaiah seems to have had some connection with the Temple, but details are hard to supply. Amos was a $n\bar{o}q\bar{e}d$; this word apparently refers to a particular kind of herds-

---

[3] Westermann, op. cit., pp. 82 ff.

[4] Cf. W. C. Klein, The Psychological Pattern of Old Testament Prophecy (Evanston: Seabury-Western, 1956).

[5] I. Engnell, "Profetismens ursprung och uppkomst," Religion och Bibel, VIII (1949), 1 ff.; H. H. Rowley, "Ritual and the Hebrew Prophets," JSS, I (1956), 338 ff.

man: in certain instances, at least, a guardian of herds belonging to the Temple. But even if this should be true in Amos' case, it certainly does not mean that he was a Temple or cult prophet.[6]

It is not easy, therefore, to determine the connection or difference between ecstatic and cultic prophetism on the one hand and the writing prophets on the other, and reduce it to a formula. The fact that the latter left written documents is not a determining factor. If championship of a purified Yawhism is taken as the criterion, then Elijah, for example, belongs among the "classic" prophets. In a few other cases (for instance, that of Nathan, in II Sam. 12), the nature of the source material does not permit us to arrive at definite conclusions; either the account is too brief, or it has attained its present form only after revision by the Deuteronomist. It is probably also an oversimplification to take as a criterion the ethical content of the prophet's message; for in the first place we find the same ethical intensity in Nathan, and in the second place there is nothing to indicate that the earlier $n^e b\hat{i}'\hat{i}m$ were not concerned with ethical questions. Perhaps we can approach a solution to the problem by saying that in reality no sharp distinction can be drawn. There are $n^e b\hat{i}'\hat{i}m$ with intense ethical concern, and there are writing prophets with ecstatic experiences. We do not know what led to the writing down of the prophets' words. It has been suggested that the fall of Samaria hastened the process of written codification: the people wanted to preserve all that was left to preserve.

The nature of the sources makes study of the prophets difficult. It is practically certain that the prophetical books as we know them do not simply represent the collected works of the prophets whose names are attached to them. On the one hand, various sections clearly reflect the situation of a much later period and must therefore be looked upon as additions; on the other hand, there is considerable evidence that many words of the prophets have come down to us much revised.

There are two divergent opinions on this question.[7] In the view of the earlier literary critics, the prophets are authors whose works have been subjected to later revision and amplification. All that is necessary to arrive at the original words of the prophets is a thorough literary analysis of their books.

According to the other view, the prophets were primarily preachers, who wrote very little themselves. What we possess are discourses that were handed down orally in a circle of disciples; in the course of this process, they were subject to more or less radical transformation.[8] Only exceptionally can we assume that the words were reduced to written form soon after they were spoken. Only for Jeremiah do we have specific evidence for a written collection of oracles (Jer. 36). This is obviously a unique instance, nor is there any evidence that this collection is preserved, either in whole or in part, in the present book of Jeremiah. Isaiah mentions the existence of certain oracles in a written form (Isa. 8:16), but we know nothing of the scope of this collection. Yahweh commands Habakkuk to write down his vision (Hab. 2:2), but here we have a special situation.

According to this view, the oral transmission of the prophets' words proves that the message of the prophets was thought to remain relevant for later periods. This means, however, that the words must have been changed to accommodate them to new situations, although we are often unable to determine in detail how far-reaching this revision and transformation was.[9] Supporters of this opinion must of necessity renounce any recovery of the *ipsissima verba* of the prophets.[10]

When we attempt to discover the common characteristics of the writing prophets on the basis of the preserved material, the first thing to strike our attention in the case of most of them is a pronounced awareness of being called.[11] Amos knows that Yahweh has taken him from following the flock, saying, "Go, prophesy to my people Israel" (Amos 7:15). In other cases, the call takes the form of a vision. Worshiping in the Temple on a feast day, Isaiah sees Yahweh the king upon his throne, surrounded by heavenly beings. He hears Yahweh's voice: "Whom shall I send, and who will go for us?" "Here I am! Send me," he replies (Isa. 6:8). Jeremiah hears the word of Yahweh that announces his appointment as a prophet. He refuses, on the grounds that he is too young; but Yahweh replies, "Do not say, 'I am only a youth'; for to all to whom I send you you shall go, and whatever I command you you shall speak" (Jer. 1:7). In Ezekiel's case, the inaugural vision assumes fantastic proportions (chapters 1—3); the essential element, however, is still the sending: "Son of man, I send you to the people of Israel . . . and you shall say to them, 'Thus says Lord Yahweh' " (Ezek. 2:3a, 4b).

The description of the inaugural vision has become stereotyped to a certain extent: Ezekiel has much in common with Isaiah, and

---

[8] S. Mowinckel, *Prophecy and Tradition* (Oslo: Dybvad, 1946); a more extreme form of the same thesis is represented by I. Engnell, "Profetia och tradition," *SEÅ*, XII (1947), 110 ff.; *idem, The Call of Isaiah* (Uppsala: Lundeqvist, 1949), pp. 55 ff.

[9] Cf. H. W. Hertzberg, *Die Nachgeschichte alttestamentlicher Texte innerhalb des Alten Testaments* (Berlin: Töpelmann, 1936), pp. 110 ff.; von Rad, *op. cit.,* pp. 51 ff.; D. Jones, "The Traditio of the Oracles of Isaiah of Jerusalem," *ZAW*, LXVII (1955), 226 ff.

[10] Engnell, "Profetia och tradition," p. 134, and elsewhere.

[11] See, for example, Lindblom, *op. cit.,* pp. 182 ff.

Isaiah's vision is remarkably similar to the prophetic vision of Micaiah, as preserved in I Kings 22. There is no reason, however, to doubt that these experiences were genuine. The experience itself and the stylized form in which it is portrayed are two different things. Unfortunately, the accounts that have been preserved are too brief to make a thorough psychological interpretation possible. One must be very careful not to base one's conclusions on the argument from silence.[12]

This awareness of his vocation gives rise to a second characteristic: the prophet's assurance that he is not speaking his own words, but God's. "Behold, I have put my words in your mouth" (Jer. 1:9b). In the case of Ezekiel, we read, "Son of man, all my words that I shall speak to you receive in your heart. . . . Go, get you to the exiles, to your people, and say to them, 'Thus says Lord Yahweh' " (Ezek. 3:10 f.).

The language used by the prophets also expresses this conviction. As has already been suggested, one of the most common formulas used to introduce a prophet's words is the messenger formula, "Thus says Yahweh" (*kōh āmar yahweh*). By using this formula, the prophet makes it clear from the very outset that he is not speaking on his own initiative, but on behalf of Yahweh.[13] The other formula frequently used, "oracle of Yahweh" (*ne'ūm yahweh*), also indicates the divine origin of the prophet's message. Here we are dealing with an ancient formula traditionally used with oracles.

The prophet's word possesses divine authority (cf. also Deut. 18:18 f.). More than this, it is efficacious and powerful, like a hammer which breaks the rock in pieces (Jer. 23:29); whatever it declares, it accomplishes: "It shall not return to me empty, but it shall accomplish that which I purpose, and prosper in the thing for which I sent it" (Isa. 55:11).[14]

Thirdly, we find that the prophets feel constrained by an inner necessity to prophesy.[15] "The lion has roared; who will not fear? Lord Yahweh has spoken; who can but prophesy?" asks Amos (3:8). In other words, the prophet cannot get around the necessity to proclaim the word of Yahweh. Jeremiah expresses this idea with particular clarity:

> If I say, "I will not mention him,
>   or speak any more in his name,"
> there is in my heart as it were a burning fire
>   shut up in my bones.
> I am weary with holding it in,
>   and I cannot. (Jer. 20:9)

---

[12] As is done by I. Seierstad, *Die Offenbarungserlebnisse der Propheten Amos, Jesaja, und Jeremia* (Oslo: Dybvad, 1946).

[13] See above, pp. 214 f.

[14] Cf. L. Dürr, *Die Wertung des göttlichen Wortes* (Leipzig: Hinrichs, 1938); O. Grether, *Name und Wort Gottes im Alten Testament* (Giessen: Töpelmann, 1934), pp. 59 ff.; von Rad, *op. cit.*, pp. 93 ff.

[15] Lindblom, *op. cit.*, pp. 194 ff.

He has tried to keep silent, to avoid persecution; but it was no use: Yahweh compels him to speak.

But how does the prophet receive the word of Yahweh? The commonest expressions suggest auditory and visual experiences. The frequent formula "The word of Yahweh came to me"[16] is too general to permit definite conclusions. Only sporadically do we encounter other, more precise, expressions, such as "Yahweh of hosts [has sworn] in my hearing" (Isa. 5:9). Much more frequently, the prophets refer to visual experiences. "Yahweh caused me to see" is a common formula. "Vision" (ḥāzôn) becomes the technical term for a prophetical revelation. We even read of "The words of Amos . . . which he saw" (Amos 1:1). This demonstrates that the terminology is not always very precise, and that the manner in which the revelation is received is not considered important.

Descriptions of visions do occur, however, and not infrequently, from Amos to Zechariah and the apocalyptists. Presumably most of these represent hallucinations of the sort familiar to us from mystics and religious ecstatics. But occasionally we come upon the phenomenon that Lindblom has called "symbolic perception."[17] The prophet sees something real, something belonging to the everyday world; but for him it acquires a deeper significance. Jeremiah sees a rod of almond; the similarity between šāqēd, "almond," and šōqēd, "watching," inspires in him the thought that Yahweh is "watching" over his word (Jer. 1:11 f.). The sight of a potter suggests to him the idea that Yahweh is the potter who does with Israel as he pleases in order to realize his purpose (Jer. 18:1 ff.). Even today such associations of ideas are found in personalities with a particularly religious bent: the most ordinary objects take on symbolic meaning.

The prophets themselves have two favorite expressions by which to characterize their inspiration.[18] First, we read that the hand of Yahweh falls or rests upon them. This expression is applied to Elijah and Elisha (I Kings 18:46; II Kings 3:15), and very frequently to Ezekiel (1:3; 3:14; 8:1; 37:1; 40:1); but it is also used of Isaiah (8:11) and Jeremiah (15:17). In this fashion, God's coercion, his claim upon the prophet, is described. Second, the spirit (rûaḥ) of God is represented as the motivating force of the prophet's activity. This expression is also ancient. We even encounter it in the case of the early nᵉbî'îm, as the term for the divine force that excites them. Hosea, for instance, calls a prophet a "man of the spirit" (Hos. 9:27), and Micah states that he is filled with power and the spirit of Yahweh

---

[16] Von Rad, op. cit., p. 80, n. 20; p. 100, n. 12.

[17] Op. cit., pp. 137 ff.

[18] Cf. S. Mowinckel, "The 'Spirit' and the 'Word' in the Preexilic Reforming Prophets," JBL, LIII (1934), 199 ff.; A. Haldar, Associations of Cult Prophets among the Ancient Semites (Uppsala: Almqvist & Wiksell, 1945), pp. 115 f.

(Mic. 3:8). Ezekiel says of himself, "And the Spirit of Yahweh fell upon me, and he said to me, 'Say, Thus says Yahweh . . .'" (Ezek. 11:5). It has frequently been stated that the great pre-exilic prophets spoke less of being possessed by the spirit than of receiving the word; it is doubtful, however, whether such a distinction is feasible.

To what extent can the inspiration of the prophets be thought of as ecstasy? This question has been much debated.[19] The visions clearly presuppose an abnormal state of consciousness; there are also references to other sorts of conduct that can be classed as ecstatic. The verb *hiṭṭîp*, which means "drip" or "prophesy," is frequently cited as evidence of concurrent ecstatic phenomena; it may, however, be nothing more than a fossilized expression from the earlier period of the *nebî'îm*. Neither do the words *ṣaw lāṣāw qaw lāqāw*, quoted sarcastically in Isaiah 28:13, necessarily reproduce the stammering speech of an ecstatic. It is equally possible that they are the old names of the letters *qôp* and *ṣādê*, and that the people are accusing the prophet of treating them like children who are taught to read.[20] When we reach Ezekiel, though, we find experiences that do betray an abnormal psychical state: the prophet lies for an extended period without moving (Ezek. 4:4 ff.), becomes dumb (3:26), feels himself lifted by the spirit and transported to distant places (8:3; 11:1), has a vision in which he is given a scroll to eat, which leaves a sweet taste in his mouth (3:1-3). These are all experiences found among ecstatic mystics.[21] But Ezekiel actually seems to be an exception in this regard; ecstatic traits are not so apparent in the other prophets.

In any case, it is hardly possible to detect signs of ecstatic experiences in the agitated style the prophets give their message. It has been shown that the formulas used by the prophets depend on the poetry and language of the cult; this naturally does not exclude individual poetic inspiration. Even the great importance attached by the prophets to having received their message does not necessarily suggest ecstatic experiences. Perhaps exceptionally striking poetic inspiration may be suggested as the closest comparable phenomenon. Ever certain visions, such as Jeremiah 25 and the night visions of Zechariah, and passages cast in the form of a vision, like Jeremiah 6:22-26, do not give the impression of being genuine visionary experiences; they could well be

---

[19] J. Lindblom, "Einige Grundfragen der alttestamentlicher Wissenschaft," in *Festschrift für Alfred Bertholet* (Tübingen: Mohr, 1950), pp. 325 ff.; *idem*, "Die Religion der Propheten und die Mystik," *ZAW*, LVII (1939), 65 ff.; *idem, Prophecy in Ancient Israel*, pp. 47 ff., 122 ff.; F. Maas, "Zur psychologischen Sonderung der Ekstase," *WZKMU*, III (1953/54), 167 ff.; von Rad, *op. cit.*, pp. 73 f. Cf. also G. Widengren, *Literary and Psychological Aspects of the Hebrew Prophets* (Uppsala: Lundeqvist, 1948), pp. 94 ff.

[20] G. Fohrer, *Das Buch Jesaja* (Göttingen: Vandenhoeck & Ruprecht, 1962), II, 51 f.

[21] Widengren, *op. cit.*, pp. 94 ff.

based on poetic imitation of a vision or inspiration with a strong visual component. Parallels to all the gradations of prophetical inspiration can be found among mystics and inspired religious personalities; but this does not mean that we can undertake to give an exact psychological description of the phenomenon in all its details. Lindblom finds interesting comparative material among the shamans and dervishes, among the medieval mystics, and among the Finnish trance-preachers.[22]

Considered as a psychological phenomenon, Israelite prophecy is obviously not unique. What makes it unique is the religious environment in which it developed.

The presupposition behind Israelite prophecy is the conviction that Israel is the people of Yahweh and Yahweh the God of Israel, in other words, the idea of election or the covenant. Yahweh chose the people of Israel and made them his own. For this reason he makes special demands of the people. He expects of them exclusive and proper worship and complete obedience. To be elected means to be responsible. "You only have I known of all the families of the earth," says Yahweh through Amos. "Therefore I will punish you for all your iniquities" (Amos 3:2). Different metaphors are used to express the same thought over and over again: "Sons have I reared and brought up, but they have rebelled against me" (Isa. 1:2).

> When Israel was a child, I loved him,
> and out of Egypt I called my son.
> The more I called them,
> the more they went from me.
> . . . .
> Yet it was I who taught Ephraim to walk,
> I took them up in my arms;
> but they did not know that I healed them. (Hos. 11:1-3)
>
> I remember the devotion of your youth,
> your love as a bride,
> how you followed me in the wilderness,
> in a land not sown.
> . . . .
> And I brought you into a plentiful land
> to enjoy its fruits and its good things.
> But when you came in you defiled my land,
> and made my heritage an abomination.
> . . . .
> Therefore I still contend with you, says Yahweh. (Jer. 2:2, 7, 9)

Strangely enough, the pre-exilic prophets make little direct mention of the covenant. Hosea refers to it twice (6:7; 8:1), but only in

---

[22] Lindblom, *Prophecy in Ancient Israel*, pp. 6 ff.

Jeremiah does it occur in significant contexts (11:1 ff.; 31:31 ff.). It has been suggested[23] that this is due to the fact that, had they stressed the idea of the covenant, the prophets might have aroused false hopes in the people, who could think that the covenant obligated Yahweh to help Israel in spite of everything. However, as we shall see, the covenant idea is implicit in the lawsuit form of prophetic preaching, so it is doubtful if this is the real reason.

In this situation, the primary message of the pre-exilic prophets is judgment. Yahweh, the lord of history, will summon mighty nations to attack Israel; they shall utterly destroy the people and the land. Yahweh will use the great powers of the period as instruments of judgment against his people.

The formal structure of the prophecies of judgment is especially interesting.[24] Naturally the messenger formula is employed, with the addition of other material in varying amounts. The prophet typically begins with a motivation, in which he outlines the sin of the people. Then follows the messenger formula, "Therefore thus says Yahweh," and, finally, the decree of what punishment is to follow (Amos 7:16 f.; Mic. 2:1-4; Jer. 5:10-14; 7:16-20). The prophets also use many other forms and idioms, however.[25] The language of the law court is frequently used: "Yahweh has a lawsuit with the inhabitants of the land" (Hos. 4:1); "Come now, let us state our case" (Isa. 1:18).[26] But many other *Gattungen* are also represented: laments and songs of mourning (such as Amos 5:2; Jer. 9:17-22), love songs (such as Isa. 5:1 ff.), hymns of thanksgiving, parables, allegories, priestly formulas (such as "He is righteous, he shall surely live," Ezek. 18:9), etc. The prophets are masters in the art of using traditional literary forms for their own purposes. Sometimes several *Gattungen* are combined in a larger composition of liturgical character (e.g., Joel, Habakkuk). We find imitations of liturgical forms in Deutero-Isaiah. Many similar instances could be given.

In addition, the writing prophets, too, perform symbolic actions, through which their message is made vivid and efficacious.[27] Isaiah goes naked and barefoot to illustrate the fate of the Egyptians, to

---

[23] *Ibid.*, pp. 329 ff.

[24] Westermann, *op. cit.*, pp. 94 ff., 120 ff.

[25] See the Introductions, e.g., O. Eissfeldt, *Einleitung in das Alte Testament* (3rd ed.; Tübingen: Mohr, 1964), pp. 87 ff.; A. Bentzen, *Introduction to the Old Testament* (3rd ed.; Copenhagen: Gad, 1957), pp. 191 ff., esp. p. 202; C. Kuhl, *The Prophets of Israel,* trans. R. Ehrlich and J. P. Smith (Edinburgh & London: Oliver & Boyd; 1960), Introduction.

[26] [The RSV consistently replaces the legal language of the OT with more general terms. These two verses are good examples: in the first, the technical term meaning "lawsuit" (Heb. *rîb*) is translated "controversy"; in the second, the technical term meaning "state one's case" (Heb. *niwwākehâ;* cf, its use in Job 23:7) is translated "reason."—TRANS.]

[27] G. Fohrer, *Die symbolischen Handlungen der Propheten* (Zürich: Zwingli, 1953).

whom Israel had turned for help (Isa. 20:2 ff.). Jeremiah breaks an earthen flask to symbolize the downfall of Israel (Jer. 19:1, 10 f.); he bears a yoke as a sign of his demand that the people submit to Babylon (Jer. 27; cf. also 28:1 f., 12 ff.). We learn of several such symbolic actions performed by Ezekiel (see below). Originally, these actions were thought to be magically efficacious: if a word is powerful and effective, an action is even more so. This view probably still influences the writing prophets, although it is nowhere expressly stated.

The positive statements in the writings of the pre-exilic "prophets of judgment" present a special problem. Is it conceivable (so the question runs) that these men, whose message was primarily one of judgment, could have lessened the effectiveness of their preaching by promising salvation? Most scholars have answered No, and viewed the positive statements as secondary additions. Recently, however, a reaction against this view has made itself heard.[28] It has been pointed out that alternation between periods of disaster and well-being is a kind of fixed schema in the ancient Near Eastern understanding of history, and the conclusion drawn that the positive statements formed a part of this schema and should be considered original and genuine.

It is probably impossible to reach a conclusion that will be generally valid on this point. The psychological arguments against the genuineness of the prophecies of salvation are not in themselves decisive. When calling people to repentance, a preacher can entice with promises as well as threaten with punishment. On the other hand, the reference to the cyclic schema does not hold for all cases. The situation of the prophets is not completely identical with the suggested parallels. The Egyptian prophecy of Neferti (formerly read Neferrohu) is a *vaticinium ex eventu,* the purpose of which is to present the present period as the period of well-being: the Babylonian texts are best classified as interpretations of history,[29] comparable to the Deuteronomistic History. But the pre-exilic prophets are not preaching *vaticinia ex eventu;* neither are they historians or philosophers of history. They are preachers proclaiming the word of God in a particular situation, not prognosticators shaping the future according to a fixed historical schema. Of course their message is based on a particular understanding of history, the conception that history is the realm of God's action; but this conception by no means makes them slaves of an immutable schema.

---

[28] I. Engnell, "Profetia och tradition," pp. 123 f.; cf. E. Hammershaimb, *Amos* (Copenhagen: Busck, 1946), pp. 136 f.; Widengren, *Literary and Psychological Aspects of the Hebrew Prophets,* pp. 88 ff.; for different reasons, H. Reventlow, *Das Amt des Propheten bei Amos* (Göttingen: Vandenhoeck & Ruprecht, 1962), pp. 90 ff.

[29] See A. K. Grayson and W. G. Lambert, "Akkadian Prophecies," *JCS,* XVIII (1964), 7 ff.

Finally, even if this schema can be shown to be present in a prophetic book, it can owe its presence to the collector or redactor. In fact, two of the three longest prophetic books, Jeremiah and Ezekiel, are arranged according to the following schema: prophecies of judgment, oracles against foreign nations, oracles of salvation. It is possible that the preservation of the prophetic word was made easier by the positive interpretation of certain prophecies and by the addition of later prophecies of salvation.

Speaking generally, then, a positive statement can in theory be either genuine or not. Each case must be decided on its merits. The decisive considerations are style and content. Prophecies that foresee the return of Israel from the dispersion presuppose the exile, or at least the fall of Samaria. Some of the messianic prophecies, however (i.e., promises of a coming ideal king), definitely do not presuppose the end of the Davidic dynasty.

The prophecies dealing with the remnant to be spared are unquestionably genuine: even if the nation as a whole perishes in consequence of its sins, a small remnant will be converted and saved.[30] Whether this idea was familiar to Amos is doubtful (the clear passages, 3:12 and 9:8 f., may be secondary); Amos 5:14 ff. does suggest, however, that he thought in terms of the deliverance of certain penitent individuals:

> Hate evil, and love good,
> and establish justice in the gate;
> it may be that Yahweh, the God of hosts,
> will be gracious to the remnant of Joseph.

Isaiah names his son Shear-jashub, "a remnant shall return" (Isa. 7:3), and says:

> In that day the remnant of Israel and the survivors of the house of Jacob will no more lean upon him that smote them, but will lean upon Yahweh, the Holy One of Israel, in truth. A remnant will return, the remnant of Jacob, to the mighty God. (Isa. 10:20 f.)

We find the same idea in Zephaniah:

> For I will leave in the midst of you
> a people humble and lowly.
> They shall seek refuge in the name of Yahweh,
> those who are left in Israel. (Zeph. 3:12 f.)

Hosea expresses his hopes in a somewhat different form. He knows that Yahweh is a merciful and loving God; therefore wrath cannot be his final word:

---

30 W. Müller, *Die Vorstellung vom Rest im Alten Testament* (Borsdorf-Leipzig: Hoppe, 1939); E. W. Heaton, "The Root š'r and the Doctrine of the Remnant," *JTS*, NS III (1952), 27 ff.; von Rad, *op. cit.*, pp. 34 f.; Lindblom, *Prophecy in Ancient Israel*, pp. 357 ff.

How can I give you up, O Ephraim!
    How can I hand you over, O Israel!
How can I make you like Admah!
    How can I treat you like Zeboiim!
My heart recoils within me,
    my compassion grows warm and tender.
I will not execute my fierce anger,
    I will not again destroy Ephraim;
    for I am God and not man. (Hos. 11:8 f.)

Yahweh's aim is to grant the people a new opportunity for repentance: "I will allure her, and bring her into the wilderness, and speak tenderly to her" (Hos. 2:16 [Eng. 2:14]). This means a new beginning, a new covenant and renewed obedience.

Jeremiah, too, speaks of a new covenant (31:31 f.); but, as we shall see, this prophecy may presuppose the fall of Jerusalem. In any case, this is a different situation.

Is it possible to speak of eschatology in the pre-exilic prophets? This problem has been much discussed, but no consensus has been reached.[31] The answer seems to depend on two things: how one defines eschatology and what parts of the prophetic books one considers genuine. If eschatology is taken in the sense it has in dogmatic theology, as a doctrine of the last things, the end of the world and the end of history, the coming into being of a completely new and different world, then naturally no eschatology is found in the prophets. Their message, however, does contain a novel element, something that can be called eschatological in a wider sense. As von Rad emphasizes, even when the events expected by the prophets seem to our way of thinking to be completely within the realm of history there is something about them so final and absolute that they transcend all prevailing ideas of history. The discontinuity with what has gone before is so extreme "that the new age that is coming can no longer be understood as the continuation of previous history."[32] J. Grønbaek makes the same point when he speaks of the "conclusive aspect" of the prophetic view of the future and defines the eschatology of the prophets more precisely as an eschatology of judgment. The day of Yahweh, he says, is for Amos the absolute and final manifestation of Yahweh's wrath. The plagues that have gone before have been in vain, "the people have not repented; therefore Yahweh will exterminate his people" (Amos 4:6 ff., esp. 4:12).[33]

---

[31] J. Lindblom, "Gibt es eine Eschatologie bei den alttestamentlichen Propheten?" *STh*, VI (1952), 79 ff.; T. C. Vriezen, "Prophecy and Eschatology," *SVT*, I (1953), 199 ff.

[32] Von Rad, *op. cit.*, p. 129.

[33] J. Grønbaek, "Zur Frage der Eschatologie in der Verkündigung der Gerichtspropheten," *SEÅ*, XXIV (1959), 10 f.

Many theories have been suggested to account for the origin of this eschatology. These suggestions include the influence of non-Israelite catastrophic conceptions,[34] the application of a cyclic schema of disaster and well-being, and the extension of certain motifs belonging to the enthronement festival.[35] Probably no single, one-sided explanation will suffice. The judgment eschatology of the pre-exilic prophets may well be based on a transformation of the judgment motif belonging to the New Year's festival[36] (involving, among other things, a reinterpretation of the way the day of Yahweh was conceived[37]). The messianic hope is clearly a product of the royal ideology, the idea of the new covenant is an extension of the idea of the covenant, etc.

The first aspect deserves special attention. It is sometimes asserted that eschatology developed out of the cult of the New Year's festival after the course of history had dashed all the hopes connected with the festival.[38] This opinion undoubtedly represents an oversimplification of the problem. In the first place, the cult means a re-experiencing of ancient events, an awareness of their effects here and now, and a corresponding shaping of the future; in other words, the cult is always oriented in part toward the future. In the second place, the eschatology of the prophets from the very beginning is an eschatology not of salvation but of judgment. We are dealing, therefore, not with a regular extension of the enthronement (or covenant) festival, but with the transformation of one single aspect of it, the motif of judgment.

G. E. Wright has recently stressed this last point, basing his argument on the use of the lawsuit (*rîb*) pattern in the prophets' preaching (e.g., Isa. 1:2 ff.; Jer. 2:4 ff. [notice v. 9]; Mic. 6:3-5). He thinks that this pattern has developed out of the covenant idea and as an extension of the yearly covenant renewal. As the lord of the suzerainty treaty Yahweh calls his vassal, the people, to task for their breaking the covenant. Heaven and earth are taken as witnesses just as in the Hittite treaties.[39] This theory certainly accounts for the occurrence of a certain form of prophetic preaching, but it is doubtful whether it

---

[34] H. Gressmann, *Der Ursprung der israelitisch-jüdischen Eschatologie* (Göttingen: Vandenhoeck & Ruprecht, 1905).

[35] S. Mowinckel, *Psalmenstudien* (Amsterdam: Schippers, 1961), II; see above.

[36] Cf. E. Würthwein, "Der Ursprung der prophetischen Gerichtsrede," *ZThK*, XLIX (1952), 1 ff.

[37] S. Mowinckel, "Jahwes dag," *Norsk teol. tidsskr.*, LIX (1958), 1 ff.; for a contrary view, see G. von Rad, "The Origin of the Concept of the Day of Jahwe," *JSS*, IV (1959), 97 ff.

[38] Mowinckel, *Psalmenstudien*, II; see above.

[39] See G. E. Wright, "The Lawsuit of God," *Israel's Prophetic Heritage*, ed. B. W. Anderson and W. Harrelson (New York: Harper, 1962), pp. 26 ff. Arriving at a similar result independently, E. von Waldow derives the form of the sermon of judgment from the secular lawsuit, while the contents are based on the covenant idea; see his *Der traditionsgeschichtliche Hintergrund der prophetischen Gerichtsreden* (Berlin: Töpelmann, 1963).

can be used as a general explanation of the origin of prophecy. The messenger formula is at least another essential element that should be taken into account.

If the judgment aspect of prophetic eschatology develops certain motifs derived from the cult, it is also possible that messianic prophecies were uttered while the monarchy still continued to exist. It is impossible to draw a well-defined boundary between the future-oriented aspects of the cult and an eschatology freed from the cult.

Having made these general remarks, we shall devote some discussion to the individual prophetic figures in their historical context. Elijah is included, because in many ways he lays the groundwork for classical prophecy.

When Ahab ruled the Northern Kingdom (869-850), there appeared a prophet named Elijah. The accounts of his activity are contained in I Kings 17—19, 21, and II Kings 1—2.[40] In large measure these narratives bear the stamp of legend, but they undoubtedly contain reliable historical reminiscences. Two points typify his activity: he attacks the syncretistic cult of the Tyrian Baal or Melkart,[41] which was introduced by the queen, Jezebel, who came from Tyre (or was at least promoted by her); and he opposes the king's arbitrary appropriation of the vineyard of a certain Naboth (I Kings 21). Both points are reminiscent of the program of the later writing prophets: the former suggests their struggle for the purity of the religion of Yahweh; the latter suggests the intense social concern of such prophets as Amos and Isaiah.

Elijah's struggle against Baal-Melkart reaches its climax in a unique duel, depicted very dramatically, between him and the prophets of Baal upon Mount Carmel, after thirty years of drought (I Kings 18). The prophets of Baal attempt to bring about the intervention of their god by dancing and by ecstatic exercises—in vain. In answer to Elijah's prayer, however, Yahweh sends fire from heaven to consume the sacrifices upon the altar, and soon afterwards brings rain to the land. This miracle results in general recognition of Yahweh's superiority.[42] Some details of this narrative may be legendary accretions;

---

[40] J. Steinmann, "La geste d'Elie dans l'Ancien Testament" in *Elie le prophète* ("Études carmelitaines" [Desclée de Brouwer, 1956]), I, 93 ff.; G. Fohrer, *Elia* (Zürich: Zwingli, 1957); H. H. Rowley, "Elijah on Mount Carmel," *BJRL*, XLIII (1960/61), 190 ff., reprinted in *idem, Men of God* (London: Nelson, 1963), pp. 37 ff.

[41] This identification is accepted by R. de Vaux, "Les prophètes de Baal sur le Mont Carmel," *Bull. du Musée de Beyrouth,* V (1941), 7 ff.; for a different view, see A. Alt, "Das Gottesurteil auf dem Karmel," in *Festschrift G. Beer* (Stuttgart: Kohlhammer, 1935), pp. 1 ff., reprinted in *idem, Kleine Schriften* (Munich: Beck, 1953), II, 135 ff.; O. Eissfeldt suggests Baalshamem in *Der Gott Karmel* (Berlin: Töpelmann, 1953), pp. 8, 41.

[42] Perhaps we should follow Eissfeldt (*Der Gott Karmel,* p. 41) in

but the fact remains that Elijah appeared as the champion of the religion of Yahweh against Phoenician and Canaanite syncretism. Another legend concludes the story of Elijah by telling how he was borne up to heaven in a fiery chariot (II Kings 2).

The "successor" of Elijah was Elisha. The legends concerning him (II Kings 2—8:15; 9:1-10; 13:14-21) are typified by a stress on the miraculous element. They do not permit us to draw any significant historical conclusions. The miracles performed by the prophet constitute the center of interest; of his religious message we hear almost nothing. A few narratives give the impression of trying to equal and better Elijah.

The first of the writing prophets is Amos.[43] He appeared in the Northern Kingdom during the reign of Jeroboam II (786-746), although his home was Tekoa, in Judah. According to Amos 1:1, his actual profession was that of a *nōqēd*, "shepherd." The same word is probably also intended in 7:14, where the text now has *bōqēr*, "herdsman" (?); this latter text also describes him as a dresser of sycamore trees. The precise meaning of *nōqēd* is disputed. An Akkadian word *nāqidu* refers to the supervisor of the flocks belonging to a temple;[44] in the Ras Shamra texts, a high priest (*rb khnm*) is also supervisor (*rb*) of the *nqdm*;[45] finally, Mesha, king of Moab, is a *nōqēd* (II Kings 3:4). It is clear, first of all, that the word has something to do with raising sheep. It is also clear that a certain relationship to temples and priests is frequently involved. Since we read that Amos was one of the *nōqᵉdîm* in Tekoa, he can hardly have been a high-ranking supervisor; in any case, Amos 7:15 emphasizes the actual care of the flock. Perhaps there were in Tekoa flocks of sheep belonging to the Jerusalem Temple, and the shepherds were *nōqᵉdîm*. Amos, then, was a shepherd; but his preaching shows that he was not an uneducated man: he was familiar with the rules of poetry and the stylistic forms of the language of the cult.[46]

Amos himself denies that he has any connection with the professional prophets (*nᵉbî'îm*). When attacked by Amaziah, a priest at Bethel, he replies, "I was no prophet, nor a prophet's son; I was a *nōqēd* (or *bōqēr;* see above], and a dresser of sycamore trees.[47] But,

---

assuming that Yahweh's victory on Mount Carmel was not final, but represents only a single episode.

[43] A. Kapelrud, *Central Ideas in Amos* (Oslo: Oslo University Press, 1956); J. D. W. Watts, *Vision and Prophecy in Amos* (Leiden: Brill, 1958); H. Reventlow, *op. cit.*

[44] M. San Nicolo, *Orientalia,* NS XVII (1948), 237 ff.; cf. Kapelrud, *op. cit.,* p. 8.

[45] *UM* 62, VI, 53 ff.; cf. also *UM* 113, 70 ff.; 300, 7-16.

[46] Kapelrud, *op. cit.,* p. 8.

[47] The RSV reads "I am no prophet, etc." For a discussion of the translation, cf. H. H. Rowley, "Was Amos a Nabi?" in J. Fück (ed.), *Festschrift O. Eissfeldt* (Halle: Niemeyer, 1947), pp. 191 ff.; I. Engnell, *Religion och Bibel,* VIII (1949), 14 ff.

Yahweh took me from following the flock, and Yahweh said to me, 'Go, prophesy to my people Israel' " (7:14 f.). In other words, he received his prophetic commission directly from Yahweh. This probably presupposes that he experienced a call, although no details are given. The five visions contained in 7:1-9; 8:1-3; and 9:1-4 may belong in this context.

We learn from the superscription that Amos made his appearance "two years before the earthquake." Obviously the earthquake—not mentioned in other sources—was thought to fulfill and confirm his words (e.g., 8:8; 9:1 ff.). Perhaps we are justified in concluding that the duration of his ministry was rather short, since it is dated as a whole "two years before the earthquake."[48] It cannot be demonstrated, however, as many have suggested, that Amos appeared only once, at a New Year's festival celebrated in Bethel.[49]

The first two chapters of the book contain a series of oracles of judgment against foreign nations, all with the same structure. These nations are said to have transgressed the general rules of ethics. At the climax, however, Israel (the Northern Kingdom) itself is named; it is censured primarily for social injustices and religious apostasy. The numerical structure of the oracles is noteworthy ("For three transgressions . . . and for four"); in addition, it is closely related to the Egyptian execration texts, in which curses are called down upon the foreign nations.[50] It is conceivable that a ceremony similar to the Egyptian execration ceremony formed part of the New Year's festival at Bethel; there is no positive proof of this, however. In any case, this section is a good example of the way the prophets used all kinds of stylistic forms for their own purposes. It is interesting that Amos here presupposes that the foreign nations are ethically answerable to Yahweh. He thinks of Yahweh not only as the God of Israel, but also as the God of the entire world. We also find this feature elsewhere in the book. It is Yahweh, says Amos, who brought the Philistines and Syrians from their original homes, just as he brought Israel out of Egypt (9:7). It remains true, however, that of all the nations of the earth Yahweh has especially chosen Israel (3:2).

Amos directs most of his preaching against two things: social injustice and false worship.

The time of Jeroboam II was for the Northern Kingdom a time of political and economic progress. One of the results of this prosperity was bitter oppression of the poor by the rich. The old tribal organization had begun to disintegrate, a class of large landowners had come into being, and those without property had to live as serfs or slaves.

---

[48] See Kapelrud, *op. cit.*, pp. 10, 12, 14 f.
[49] This theory is supported by J. Morgenstern, *Amos Studies* (Cincinnati: Hebrew Union College, 1941), pp. 173 f.
[50] A. Bentzen, "The Ritual Background of Amos i, 2—ii, 16," *OTS*, VIII (1950), 85 ff.; Kapelrud, *op. cit.*, pp. 17 ff.

Amos felt strongly the injustice of the new order. He bitterly attacked the luxurious life led by the rich at the expense of the poor (3:12, 15; 6:4-6); he assailed the venality of the judges and the general dishonesty in trade (2:6 f.; 5:7, 10, 12; 8:5). All these conditions meant not only the dissolution of that solidarity which formed the basis of Israelite society, but also a violation of the divine law that God had given Israel. It has been shown that for this latter point Amos is dependent upon the ancient traditions of the sacral law, especially the Book of the Covenant, although he never expressly cites any written or oral authority.[51]

Despite all this, these wealthy people worship Yahweh as though everything were fine. They offer sacrifice in abundance (4:4; 5:22), they visit the sanctuaries and celebrate the festivals (4:4; 5:5; 8:5). But they ask at the same time, "When will the festival be over, so that we can carry on our dishonest trade once more?" (8:5). Therefore Yahweh says through Amos:

> I hate, I despise your feasts,
>> and I take no delight in your solemn assemblies.
> Even though you offer me your burnt offerings and cereal offerings.
> I will not accept them,
> and the peace offerings of your fatted beasts
>> I will not look upon.
> Take away from me the noise of your songs;
>> to the melody of your harps I will not listen.
> But let justice roll down like waters,
>> and righteousness like an ever-flowing stream.
>> (Amos 5:21-24)

This does not mean, as has often been asserted, that Amos sought to do away with the sacrificial cult in its entirety. The object of his attack is the combination of outward observance and lack of righteousness. Yahweh demands not only sacrifice and the worship of the cult, but also righteousness and justice.[52]

During this period pagan elements had obviously gained a foothold in the Israelite cult. Amos mentions sacral prostitution (2:7b), which we know was an element of the Canaanite fertility religion; he mentions the goddess Ashimah of Samaria,[53] the god of Dan, and the *dôd* (young god) of Beer-sheba[54] (8:14; 5:5), he alludes to Sakkuth and

---

[51] Von Rad, *Theologie des Alten Testaments,* II, 146.

[52] Kapelrud, *op. cit.,* pp. 68 ff.; cf. Watts, *op. cit.,* pp. 18 ff.

[53] The MT vocalizes the name as *ašmat šōmᵉrôn,* "the guilt of Samaria." The same goddess is mentioned in II Kings 17:30.

[54] This is the case if we assume the commonly accepted reading *dôdᵉkâ* in place of *derek.* Or does *derek* here mean "dominion," "power" (cf. Ugaritic *drkt,* "dominion"), used as the epithet of a god? The LXX reads "your god."

Kaiwan, astral deities possibly of Babylonian origin (5:26).[55] All of these he counters with "Seek Yahweh and live" (5:6).

When Amos assails the various cultic sites ("Do not seek Bethel, and do not enter into Gilgal or cross over to Beer-sheba"; 5:5), this might mean that he, a Judean, is defending Jerusalem as the proper site for the cult. But although in 1:2 he mentions Jerusalem as the place where Yahweh appears, he never states that Yahweh is to be worshiped only in Jerusalem.[56] In Amos, we see Yahweh as the universal God who controls the history of the nations (9:7) and finds out his opponents everywhere, in heaven, on earth, and in Sheol (9:2). Amos is more concerned for the purity of worship than for the place where it is offered. What is missing in Israel, in his opinion, is primarily the proper way of thinking.

There can be only one consequence: judgment. If Yahweh has chosen Israel, then he will also hold Israel responsible to a higher degree (3:2). Enemies will ravage the land (3:11), the big houses will be destroyed (6:11), the people will be taken into captivity (5:27; 6:7); neither swiftness nor strength will avail, and no one will save his life (2:14 f.).

To depict the judgment, Amos makes use of the concept of the "day of Yahweh":[57]

> Woe to you who desire the day of Yahweh!
>   Why would you have the day of Yahweh?
> It is darkness, and not light. (Amos 5:18)

The day of Yahweh is the day on which, as the people thought, Yahweh will destroy all his enemies. In all probability the New Year's festival was thought of as the day of Yahweh, and all kinds of high hopes were associated with it. Amos says that the day will indeed come, but destruction will befall the sinful Israelite nation, because its apostasy has made it an enemy of Yahweh.

> "And on that day," says Lord Yahweh,
>   "I will make the sun go down at noon,
>   and darken the earth in broad daylight.
> I will turn your feasts into mourning,
>   and all your songs into lamentation." (Amos 8:9 f.)

Three quotations from a hymn praising Yahweh as creator and ruler of the universe belong to the motif of the New Year's festival (4:13; 5:8 f.; 9:5 f.).[58] These passages are usually thought to be later

---

[55] The Masoretes have garbled the vocalization; see the commentaries.
[56] Kapelrud, *op. cit.*, pp. 49 f.
[57] *Ibid.*, pp. 71 ff.; Watts, *op. cit.*, pp. 68 ff., 81 ff.
[58] Cf. J. D. W. Watts, "An Old Hymn Preserved in the Book of Amos," *JNES*, XV (1956), 33 ff.; idem, *Vision and Prophecy in Amos*, pp. 51 ff.; Kapelrud, *op. cit.*, pp. 38 f.

additions; but probably the hymn is earlier than Amos, and either he or an early traditionist inserted the quotations here. The way this hymn depicts God does not basically differ from the way the prophet depicts him.

Several oracles of salvation at the conclusion of the book represent a special problem (9:11-15). It cannot be denied that Amos reckoned with the possibility of deliverance: "Seek good, that you may live," he says; "Hate evil, and love good . . . it may be that Yahweh will be gracious to you" (5:14 f.). In the past, Yahweh has given the people an opportunity to repent (4:6-12); perhaps the opportunity still exists. But the oracles in 9:11 ff., which preach hope without qualification, appear so unexpectedly and harmonize so poorly with the rest of Amos' message that it is doubtful whether he really uttered these promises.[59]

It is quite understandable that Amos aroused the wrath of Israel's leaders through his preaching. It is reported that Amaziah, the high priest at Bethel, approached him with specific orders not to speak in the sanctuary. Amos answered fiercely that he was speaking in behalf of Yahweh, and that a terrible punishment would befall Amaziah (Amos 7:10-17). Unfortunately, we do not know whether this collision meant the end of Amos' activity. The book contains no further account of his life and activity.

Hosea was a younger contemporary of Amos;[60] like the latter, he appeared in the Northern Kingdom.[61] We know very little about his personal life. It has been suggested that his marital experiences played some part in his call to be a prophet, but the relevant sections of the book of Hosea (chaps. 1—3) allow more than one interpretation.[62] According to the usual view, his wife was unfaithful to him; the prophet saw her infidelity as a symbol of the religious infidelity of Israel. If we take the biblical narrative exactly as it stands, however, a rather different picture emerges. Hosea is commanded to marry a certain Gomer, who was probably not a "harlot" but a woman who participated in the Canaanite fertility rites. In other words, we are

---

[59] Kapelrud, *op. cit.*, pp. 56 f.; von Rad, however, thinks these oracles are genuine (*op. cit.*, pp. 148 f.).

[60] The dating in 1:1 is not consistent. Jeroboam II reigned 786-746; the reigns of Uzziah, Ahaz, and Hezekiah occupy the years 783-687; the shortest period of time that would include all three reigns is 742-715. Does this mean that Hosea began his ministry in the Northern Kingdom under Jeroboam II, and continued it in the Southern Kingdom until 715?

[61] H. S. Nyberg, *Studien zum Hoseabuche* (Uppsala: 1935); G. Östborn, *Yahwe and Baal* (Lund: Gleerup, 1956); of the commentaries, that of H. W. Wolff, *Dodekapropheton: Hosea* (Neukirchen: Erziehungsverein, 1961), deserves special mention.

[62] See the discussion by H. H. Rowley, "The Marriage of Hosea," *BJRL*, XXXIX (1956), 200 f., reprinted in *idem, Men of God*, pp. 66 ff.

dealing here with a symbolic action of the prophet.[63] The infidelity
of the woman symbolizes the religious infidelity of Israel. The children
of the prophet accordingly are given symbolic names: Lo-ruhamah,
"Not pitied"; and Lo-ammi, "Not my people." These names are intended to describe the situation of Israel. Once again Hosea is commanded to love the same (?) lascivious woman and to restrain her
from her activity. This action symbolizes God's disciplinary intentions:
after spending a period without a king and without national existence,
Israel will return to Yahweh.

These experiences leave their stamp upon Hosea's entire message.
Israel is the bride of Yahweh; but she has been untrue to him, and
must therefore prepare herself to be rejected. "She is not my wife,
and I am not her husband," says Yahweh (2:4 [Eng. 2:2]). Israel has
played the harlot.

> For she said, "I will go after my lovers,
>   who give me my bread and my water,
>   my wool and my flax, my oil and my drink."
>
> (Hos. 2:7 [Eng. 2:5])

This basic charge leveled by Hosea also provides the psychological
explanation for syncretism. The Israelites worshiped the fertility gods
of Canaan because thy thought these gods gave them the fruit of the
land. Yahweh says:

> And she did not know
>   that it was I who gave her
>   the grain, the wine, and the oil,
> and who lavished upon her silver
>   and gold which they used for Baal. (2:10 [Eng. 2:8])

The entire book of Hosea is a bitter polemic against the worship of
Baal. Two alternatives are presented: Yahweh or Baal. In reality,
Yahweh, the God of Israel, is also the giver of fertility, not, as the
Israelites thought, the Canaanite gods. Israel therefore has no need to
turn to other gods. Such apostasy will bring punishment:

> I will punish her for the feast days of the Baals
>   when she burned incense to them
> and decked herself with her ring and jewelry,
>   and went after her lovers,
>   and forgot me, says Yahweh. (2:15 [Eng. 2:13])

Again and again Hosea returns to the syncretistic practices.

> My people inquire of a thing of wood,
>   and their staff gives them oracles.
> For a spirit of harlotry has led them astray,
>   and they have left their God to play the harlot.
> They sacrifice on the tops of the mountains,
>   and make offerings upon the hills. (4:12 f.)

---

[63] This theory is suggested by von Rad, *Theologie des Alten Testaments*,
II, 149, 151 f.

The images of calves or bulls at Bethel also come under attack:

> I have spurned your calf, O Samaria.
> . . . .
> For what has Israel to do with it?[64]
> A workman made it;
>   it is not God. (8:5 f.)

Israel has forgotten Yahweh's acts of mercy. Yahweh loved Israel and delivered the people from Egypt, he brought them up and cared for them: "I led them with cords of compassion, with the bands of love" (11:1-4). But "the more I called them, the more they went from me" (11:2).

> It was I who knew you in the wilderness,
>   in the land of drought;
> but when they had fed to the full,
>   they were filled, and their heart was lifted up;
>   therefore they forgot me. (13:5 f.)

Here the prophet assails the self-sufficient attitude of the people that think they can get along without God. The truth remains, however: "Besides me there is no savior" (13:4).

Sacrifices cannot turn aside the wrath of Yahweh, "for I desire steadfast love and not sacrifice, the knowledge of God, rather than burnt offerings" (6:6). Destruction is at hand. "For they sow the wind, and they shall reap the whirlwind" (8:7). The days of punishment and recompense have come (9:7), the land will be destroyed and laid waste (2:13 f. [Eng. 2:11 f.]; 9:6).

> Samaria's king shall perish,
>   like a chip on the face of the waters.
> The high places of Aven, the sin of Israel,
>   shall be destroyed.
> Thorn and thistle shall grow up
>   on their altars. (10:7 f.)

The sanctuaries where syncretistic worship was practiced will be laid waste.

But wrath is not Yahweh's last word. Hosea takes back his faithless wife because he loves her (chap. 3); Yahweh's love for Israel compels him to find a way to save her.

> How can I give you up, O Ephraim!
>   How can I hand you over, O Israel!
> . . . .
> My heart recoils within me,
>   my compassion grows warm and tender.
> I will not execute my fierce anger,

---

[64] The translation here follows Nyberg, *op. cit.*, p. 62.

> I will not again destroy Ephraim;
> for I am God and not man,
> the Holy One in your midst. (11:8 f.)

He seeks to entice Israel once more into the desert, to the place where his history with his people began.[65] Here he seeks to renew the former love and faithfulness of the people (2:16 f. [Eng. 2:14 f.]); in other words, there is to be a new beginning.

> And I will betroth you to me for ever; I will betroth you to me in righteousness and in justice, in steadfast love and in mercy. I will betroth you to me in faithfulness; and you shall know Yahweh. (2:21 f. [Eng. 2:19 f.])

Here, as in 6:6 (already cited), the knowledge of Yahweh comes to the fore as an ideal. Hosea obviously is not thinking of theoretical knowledge, but of an intimate relationship of communion and trust, which also includes obedience and love.[66]

The marriage metaphor and the emphasis on God's love are characteristic of Hosea. This means, quite surprisingly, that the language and images used by Hosea depend on precisely the same fertility religion that he is attacking.[67] He compares the marriage relationship between Yahweh and Israel with the sacred marriage of the Canaanite cult. The oracle of salvation at the end of the book uses a whole series of images taken from the same sphere: Yahweh will love Israel, he will be to Israel like the luxuriant cypress, like the dew; Israel will blossom and strike root; its fragrance shall be like Lebanon (Hos. 14:5-8). Here, too, Yahweh takes the place of Baal.

Isaiah probably came from Jerusalem.[68] There is no basis for the Jewish tradition that makes him a member of the royal family. Neither can it be proved conclusively that he belonged to the upper class. The fact that he had access to the king, to high officials, and to priests (Isa. 7:3; 22:15; 8:2) could also be true of a cult prophet. In any case, he was a prophet (8:3), wore the garments of a prophet (20:2), and had a circle of disciples (8:16). A connection with the Temple is implied both by his inaugural vision and by his preaching. Of his private life we learn only that he was married (8:3) and had children (7:3; 8:3).

---

[65] Wolff, *op. cit.*, p. 78.

[66] See above, p. 130.

[67] H. Ringgren, "Hieros gamos," *Religion och Bibel*, XVIII (1959), 47 f.; Wolff, *op. cit.*, p. 60; idem, *Tidsskrift for teologi og kirke*, 1962, pp. 88 f.

[68] A bibliography on Isaiah is given by G. Fohrer, *ThR*, XIX (1951), 291 ff., XX (1952), 218 ff., XXVIII (1962), 57 ff. Commentaries include R. B. Y. Scott, *Interpreters' Bible* (Nashville: Abingdon, 1956), V, 151 ff.; O. Kaiser, *Jesaja* (Göttingen: Vandenhoeck & Ruprecht, 1960—); G. Fohrer, *Das Buch Jesaja* (Zürich: Zwingli, 1960-62). See also S. H. Blank, *Prophetic Faith in Isaiah* (New York: Harper, 1958).

Isaiah experienced his call in 742, in the Jerusalem Temple, perhaps on the occasion of a New Year's celebration (Isa. 6).[69] He saw Yahweh enthroned as king and heard the angels praise him as the thrice-holy one. His first reaction was an intense feeling of uncleanness. But after his sin had been taken away by a symbolic act, he was ready to go forth as a prophet: "Here I am! Send me." This experience obviously influenced Isaiah's entire preaching: "the Holy One of Israel" is one of his favorite terms for God, and he has a highly-developed sense that Jerusalem is the holy and inviolable city of Yahweh.

The message of Isaiah is reminiscent of that of Amos in many respects. Like Amos, he attacks social injustice. He assails the rich, "who join house to house, and add field to field, until there is no more room, and you are made to dwell alone in the midst of the land" (Isa. 5:8). He denounces the judges who "turn aside the needy from justice and rob the poor of my people of their right" (10:2). Like Amos, he speaks of a lack of righteousness (1:21; 5:7): "Woe to those," he says, "who call evil good and good evil" (5:20). In a poem in which he makes use of the forms of a love song,[70] he compares the people of Israel to a vineyard on which all conceivable care and attention has been lavished, but which has nevertheless failed to produce fruit (5:1-7).

In addition, Isaiah also attacks false worship.

> What to me is the multitude of your sacrifices?
>   says Yahweh;
> I have had enough of the burnt offerings of rams,
>   and the fat of fed beasts;
> I do not delight in the blood of bulls,
>
> . . . .
>
>   or of lambs, or of he-goats.
> Your new moons and your appointed feasts
>   my soul hates;
> they have become a burden to me,
>   I am weary of bearing them. (1:11, 14)

It is not the cult itself which Yahweh detests, but the false cult, the cult that the Israelites think is efficacious *ex opere operato*: "I cannot endure iniquity and solemn assembly" (1:13). Cult without righteousness is useless. Under these conditions, even prayer is reprehensible: "I will not listen; your hands are full of blood" (1:15).[71]

Isaiah therefore expects God's judgment to strike the sinful nation.

---

[69] Cf. I. Engnell, *The Call of Isaiah* (Uppsala: Lundeqvist, 1949).

[70] A. Bentzen, *AfO*, IV (1927), 209 f.

[71] H. H. Rowley, "The Meaning of Sacrifice in the Old Testament," *BJRL*, XXXIII (1950), 93, note.

He sees the Assyrians as Yahweh's agents in executing the punishment.

> Therefore the anger of Yahweh was kindled against his people,
> and he stretched out his hand against them and smote
> them.
>
> . . . .
>
> He will raise a signal for a nation afar off,
> and will whistle for it from the ends of the earth;
> and lo, swiftly, speedily it comes!
>
> . . . .
>
> Their arrows are sharp,
> all their bows bent,
> their horses' hoofs seem like flint,
> and their wheels like the whirlwind. (Isa. 5:25, 26, 28)

Like Amos, Isaiah speaks of the "day of Yahweh" on which the pride of men will be humbled and Yahweh alone will be exalted. Then all gods will turn out to be worthless idols, and men will take refuge in caves to avoid Yahweh's wrath (2:6-21). Only a small remnant will be saved (10:22; cf. 6:13).

Finally, Isaiah, like Amos, calls upon men to do what is good and just:

> Cease to do evil,
> learn to do good;
> seek justice,
> correct oppression;
> defend the fatherless,
> plead for the widow. (1:16 f.)

What is especially characteristic of Isaiah, however, appears primarily in his conflicts with the kings on account of the foreign policy of the nation. As von Rad has shown, we are dealing here with two ideas that belong to the Jerusalemite tradition: the inviolability of Zion and the messianic hope.[72]

The first conflict took place under Ahaz. The Northern Kingdom and the Syrians of Damascus had formed an alliance to throw off the yoke of Assyria. They tried to force Ahaz and the kingdom of Judah to join their coalition (735-733 B.C.). Ahaz was afraid, and wanted to ask the Assyrians for aid. Isaiah went to the king and told him to have faith and confidence, that Yahweh would protect Judah and its king, and that the two enemy powers would be destroyed. This was the occasion of the famous words, "If you will not believe, surely you shall not be established" (7:1-9).

But Ahaz remained in a state of indecision. When Isaiah promised

---

[72] Von Rad, *Theologie des Alten Testaments,* II, 166 ff.

him a sign to strengthen his faith, he refused the offer, on the grounds that he did not want to tempt God. Then Isaiah said:

> Yahweh himself will give you a sign. A[73] young woman ['almâ] shall conceive and bear a son, and shall call his name Immanu-el [i.e., God with us]. . . . Before the child knows how to refuse the evil and choose the good, the land before whose two kings you are in dread will be deserted. (7:14, 16)

No other Old Testament text has given rise to as many differences of opinion as this one.[74] This is partly due to the presence of a Christian messianic interpretation, partly to the later revision of the following verses. Formally, the oracle is similar to ancient Near Eastern (Egyptian and Ugaritic) birth oracles, which are customary at the birth of a royal child, though found also in other connections.[75] In addition, the word 'almâ, "young woman," appears to be some kind of technical term; and the statement "God [or Yahweh] is with us" is found in the psalms belonging to the New Year's festival (Ps. 46:8, 12 [Eng. 46:7, 11]). Thus Isaiah is saying to Ahaz, Take seriously the words spoken in the cult;[76] the Davidic dynasty and the election of Jerusalem guarantee divine aid. Another oracle makes the same point:

> Be broken, you peoples, and be dismayed;
> > give ear, all you far countries;
> > gird yourselves and be dismayed.
> Take counsel together, but it will come to nought;
> > speak a word, but it will not stand,
> > for God is with us. (8:9 f.)

As in many other passages that describe the failure of assaults upon Zion (Isa. 10:27b-34; 14:24-32; 17:12-14; 29:1-8; 30:27-33), the prophet is here drawing upon the Zion hymns (Pss. 46, 48, 76). Yahweh has chosen Mount Zion to be his holy mountain; he will protect it against the assaults of all its enemies.[77] The proper attitude of the people consists in faith (7:9), confidence, and quiet trust (7:4): "In quietness and in trust shall be your strength" (30:15).

Ahaz did not heed Isaiah's warnings. Soon afterwards, Isaiah seems to have withdrawn from public activity for a while (Isa. 8:16-

---

[73] [The Hebrew text has: "The young woman . . ."—TRANS.]

[74] J. J. Stamm, "La prophetie d'Emmanuel," *RTP*, 1944, pp. 97 ff.; idem, "Neuere Arbeiten zum Immanuel-Problem," *ZAW*, LXVIII (1956), 46 ff.; J. Lindblom, *A Study of the Immanuel Section in Isaiah* (Lund: Gleerup, 1958); W. Vischer, *Die Immanuelbotschaft im Rahmen des königlichen Zionsfestes* (Zollikon-Zürich: Evangelischer Verlag, 1955); E. Hammershaimb, "The Immanuel Sign," *STh*, III (1949), 124 ff.

[75] G. Widengren, *Religion och Bibel*, VII (1948), 28 f., 32 f.

[76] H. Ringgren, "König und Messias," *ZAW*, LXIV (1953), 132.

[77] H. Wildberger, "Die Völkerwallfahrt zum Zion," *VT*, VII (1957), 62 ff. [See also J. H. Hayes, "The Tradition of Zion's Inviolability," *JBL*, LXXXII (1963), 419 ff.—TRANS.]

18 probably belongs to this period; it shows Isaiah entrusting his message to his disciples). The messianic oracle 8:23—9:6 may also date from this period. The historical background is the campaign of Tiglath-Pileser in which he stripped the kingdom of Israel of many of its territories and incorporated them into the provincial system of Assyria.[78] In this moment of darkness, Isaiah, "speaking in the style of an objective ceremonial,"[79] gives promise of light and the accession (or birth) of a new king who will break the power of the enemy. The prophet gives his throne-names: Wonderful Counselor, Mighty God, Everlasting Father, Prince of Peace.[80]

If the peace that the new king brings is here equated with triumph over the enemies, 11:1-8 prophesies a kingdom of true peace under a new descendant of David, and the return of paradise. This Davidic king will be primarily a just judge, endowed will all the gifts of the spirit.

About twenty years after the Syro-Ephraimitic war, we find Isaiah active once more in the realm of national politics. The Philistine city of Ashdod, with the support of Egypt, is trying to revolt against the Assyrians, and urges Judah to participate (714-711). Isaiah argues energetically against revolt (Isa. 14:28-32; 18). Yahweh has founded Zion, he says, and therefore he will protect it (14:32); in his own time, he will himself destroy the Assyrians (18:3-6). Faith and confidence are once again demanded of the Israelites, not coalitions and political machinations.

After the death of Sargon (705), Judah was prepared to undertake a revolt with the help of Egypt. Isaiah protested bitterly (28:14-22; 30:1-7; 31:1-3). In his opinion, the alliance with Egypt was worthless, since it was made without the spirit of Yahweh (30:1). "The Egyptians are men, and not God; and their horses are flesh, and not spirit" (31:3). To rely on Egypt for help means distrust of Yahweh. While the Israelites are basing their plans on alliances, Isaiah asserts:

> Therefore thus says Lord Yahweh,
> "Behold, I am laying in Zion for a foundation
> a stone, a tested stone,
> a precious cornerstone, of a sure foundation:[81]
> 'He who believes will not be in haste.' " (28:16)

---

[78] A. Alt, "Jesaja 8, 23—9, 6. Befreiungsnacht und Krönungstag," in *Festschrift Alfred Bertholet* (Tübingen: Mohr, 1950), pp. 29 ff., reprinted in *idem, Kleine Schriften,* II, 206 ff.

[79] Von Rad, *Theologie des Alten Testaments,* II, 182.

[80] Von Rad, "Das judäische Krönungsritual," *TLZ,* LXXII (1947), cols. 214 ff., reprinted in *Gesammelte Studien* (Munich: Kaiser, 1958), pp. 212 ff.; H. Wildberger, "Die Thronnamen des Messias," *TZ,* XVI (1960), 314 ff.

[81] See above, p. 162.

Here we find once more the idea that Zion, the chosen city, is inviolable. Yahweh has founded Zion and he will protect it; human aid is not only worthless, it is a sign of distrust.

Isaiah preached to no avail. Isaiah 1:2-9 depicts the desolation of the land after Sargon's punitive expedition.

Later, when Hezekiah once more rebelled against Assyria and Sennacherib attacked Judah, Isaiah was again convinced that God would help Jerusalem.

> Yahweh of hosts has sworn:
> "As I have planned,
> so shall it be,
> and as I have purposed,
> so shall it stand,
> that I will break the Assyrian in my land,
> and upon my mountains trample him under foot;
> and his yoke shall depart from them,
> and his burden from their shoulder." (14:24 f.)

Once more we come upon the motif of the assault made by the nations in the Zion hymns:

> The nations roar like the roaring of many waters,
> but he will rebuke them, and they will flee far away,
> chased like chaff on the mountains before the wind. (17:13)

For now the Assyrian king has overstepped his authority. He was in fact the instrument of Yahweh, intended to carry out Yahweh's judgment of wrath against Israel. "But he does not so intend, and his mind does not so think" (10:7). "For he says: 'By the strength of my hand I have done it, and by my wisdom, for I have understanding' " (10:13). This is hybris, this is putting oneself in God's place. "Shall the ax vaunt itself over him who hews with it?" asks the prophet (10:15). Now Yahweh must proceed against the instrument he used: he will destroy Assyria.

Now we hear the sound of hope in the preaching of Isaiah: on that day the remnant of Israel will lean upon Yahweh in truth. "A remnant will return, the remnant of Jacob, to the mighty God" (10:20 f.). A purged remnant will be saved and will once more dwell secure upon Zion.

So we see that Isaiah combines the tradition of Amos, the prophet of judgment, with the ancient traditions of Jerusalem, which give the prophet confidence and hope in spite of everything. His political activity is not grounded upon realistic considerations, but grows out of his religious faith. Thus even beyond the catastrophe that must come he sees the salvation of a tiny remnant. It is quite consistent to ascribe to Isaiah the vision of the future preserved in Isaiah 2 (and also in Micah): the mountain of the house of Yahweh is established, and all the nations shall flow to it to learn the law (*tôrâ*) of Yahweh (2:1-4).[82] This is the logical conclusion of the ideas contained in the Zion hymns, which Isaiah obviously esteemed highly.

Micah of Moresheth in Judea was a younger contemporary of Isaiah.[83] According to a reference in Jeremiah 26:18, the bulk of his ministry came under the reign of Hezekiah. His message was primarily one of judgment, although not all the positive oracles in the book of Micah can be rejected as secondary.

Micah was not interested in questions of international politics. He was concerned primarily with the social and religious condition of the land. In both content and style he is less original than Isaiah. He attacks the rich who oppress the poor (2:1 f., 9), the priests and prophets who for a price tell the people what they want to hear (3:5, 11), and syncretistic cult practices (5:10-15).

The consequence must be judgment. The land will be destroyed and laid waste (5:10; 6:16). Even the holy city with the mountain of the Temple will be taken: "Zion shall be plowed as a field; Jerusalem shall become a heap of ruins, and the mountain of the house a wooded height" (3:12).

Chapter 6:1-8 contains an interesting description of Yahweh's lawsuit against his people. He challenges Israel to reply:

> O my people, what have I done to you?
> In what have I wearied you? Answer me!
> For I brought you up from the land of Egypt,
> and redeemed you from the house of bondage. (6:3 f.)

But the people have forgotten Yahweh's gracious acts, or else they think that the official cult is a sufficient expression of their thankfulness. The stylized question "With what shall I come before Yahweh?" is reminiscent of the entrance liturgies (Pss. 15 and 24); it is answered by an oracle that makes no mention of cultic requirements:

> He has showed you, O man, what is good;
> and what does Yahweh require of you
> but to do justice, and to love kindness,
> and to walk "humbly" with your God? (6:8)

The demands are formulated in the same general terms we found in Amos: "what is good," "justice," and "kindness"; but they are also set in the context of man's relationship with God, with whom man should walk circumspectly and carefully.[84]

---

[82] Wildberger, *op. cit.*, pp. 62 ff.

[83] W. Beyerlin, *Die Kulttraditionen Israels in der Verkündigung des Propheten Micha* (Göttingen: Vandenhoeck & Ruprecht, 1959).

[84] For a discussion of the translation, see H. J. Stoebe, *Wort und Dienst, Jahrbuch der theologischen Schule Bethel*, 1959, pp. 180 ff.

Occasionally, however, Micah also expresses hope, especially in 5:1-3 (Eng. 5:2-4), a messianic oracle: from Bethlehem, the city of David, "shall come forth one who is to be ruler in Israel." The land is to be given up, but only until the time when the royal child is born; then Assyria will be destroyed and the new king will rule the world. Here Micah obviously stands within the traditions of the Davidic covenant, although he avoids the term "king."[85] This conception associates him closely with Isaiah, although he is unable to share Isaiah's confidence in the election of Zion (3:11 f.).

＊　　＊　　＊　　＊　　＊

The reign of Manasseh (687-642) represents a period of pronounced syncretism. No prophetic writings from these decades have been preserved—we cannot say whether this fact is due to persecution of the prophets or to other reasons. From the last third of the seventh century, however, we have three small prophetic books: Zephaniah, Habakkuk, and Nahum. Of these three men, only the first actually stands in the tradition of the great prophets.

According to the superscription of the book, Zephaniah was active "in the days of Josiah" (640-609).[86] His references to idolatry (1:4-6) suggest that he appeared at the time before Josiah's reformation. The dominant theme of his message is the approach of the day of Yahweh.

> The great day of Yahweh is near,
> near and hastening fast;
> the sound of the day of Yahweh is bitter,
> the mighty man cries aloud there.
> A day of wrath is that day,
> a day of distress and anguish,
> a day of ruin and devastation,
> a day of darkness and gloom.
> . . . .
> I will bring distress on men,
> so that they shall walk like the blind,
> because they have sinned against Yahweh. (1:14, 15, 17)

Nahum seems to have been one of the cult prophets.[87] His words are not directed against the sins of Israel, but are exclusively threats uttered against Nineveh. The liturgical style of the book suggests execration texts like those lying behind Amos 1 and 2. Perhaps Nahum, a cult prophet, uttered his threats against the enemy city in the context of the cult. It is noteworthy, however, that almost the only section to refer to Yahweh is the introductory "psalm"; apart from it, the oracles are strikingly "secular." The fall of Nineveh, however, was

85 H. Ringgren, "König und Messias," pp. 135 f.

86 G. Gerleman, *Zephanja* (Lund: Gleerup, 1942).

87 Cf. A. Haldar, *Studies in the Book of Nahum* (Uppsala: Lundeqvist, 1946).

undoubtedly predicted as an act of judgment on the part of Yahweh. It took place in 612 B.C.

Habakkuk, who probably appeared between 609 and 597, bewails the havoc wrought by the Chaldeans (i.e., the Neo-Babylonians), and prophesies their downfall.[88] His prophecy consists of two sections. The first is an almost liturgical dialogue between the prophet and Yahweh, in which the prophet laments that "the wicked surround the righteous" and Yahweh promises to destroy the wicked. A superscription calls the second section "a prayer"; in fact, however, it is the hymnic description of a theophany. In Habakkuk we find the famous statement that was to be so significant for Paul and Luther: "The righteous shall live by his faith [faithfulness]" (2:4).

Jeremiah came from a priestly family of Anathoth, not far from Jerusalem.[89] In 627/626, while still quite young, he was called to be a prophet. He heard the voice of Yahweh, which announced to him that he had been chosen to speak for God. He refused the commission, since he considered himself too young, but finally had to admit defeat and accept his mission. The account of this call in Jeremiah 1 is followed by two "symbolic perceptions," the first of which stresses the reliability of God's word, and the second of which predicts a threatened invasion from the north.[90]

The disaster or, to put it more concretely, the foe from the north constitutes the basic theme of Jeremiah's early preaching. In a series of stirring poems (4:5—6:30) he depicts the onslaught of the enemy:

> Behold, a people is coming from the north country,
>> a great nation is stirring from the farthest parts of the
>> earth.
> They lay hold on bow and spear,
>> they are cruel and have no mercy,
>> the sound of them is like the roaring sea;
> They ride upon horses,
>> set in array as a man for battle,
>> against you, O daughter of Zion! (6:22 f.)

The result is destruction and devastation, the return of the chaos that ruled before the creation of the world:

---

[88] Cf. P. Humbert, *Problemes du livre d'Habacuc* (Neuchatel: Secretariat de l'université, 1944).

[89] For a bibliography on Jeremiah, see G. Fohrer, *ThR*, XIX (1951), 305 ff., XX (1952), 242 ff., XXVIII (1962), 250 ff.; also E. Vogt, "Jeremias-Literatur," *Biblica*, XXXV (1954), 357 ff. The following studies deserve special mention: J. Skinner, *Prophecy and Religion* (Cambridge: Cambridge University Press, 1926); A. C. Welch, *Jeremiah, his Time and his Work* (2nd ed.; London: Oxford, 1951); J. Steinmann, *Le prophete Jeremie* (Paris: Editions du cerf, 1952); J. P. Hyatt, *Jeremiah* (Nashville: Abingdon, 1958). Of the commentaries, those by W. Rudolph and A. Weiser should be mentioned.

[90] Cf. above, p. 253.

> I looked on the earth, and lo, it was waste and void;
>> and to the heavens, and they had no light.
> I looked on the mountains, and lo, they were quaking,
>> and all the hills moved to and fro.
> I looked, and lo, there was no man. (4:23-25)

These poems have been thought to refer to an invasion of Scythians from the north, and have accordingly been termed Scythian songs; most scholars now reject this theory, however.[91] The "foe from the north" seems to have been a more or less constant, semi-mythological concept.[92] Perhaps Jeremiah was thinking in particular of the Neo-Babylonian empire, then beginning to extend its power. Later on, at least, he almost surely identified the foe from the north with the Babylonians. The religious motivation is important: the disaster is Yahweh's punishment for Israel's apostasy.

The popularity of Baal worship is the second basic theme of Jeremiah in his early period. He does not speak of it in the cold and harsh manner of the earlier prophets of judgment. He stresses particularly that the behavior of God's people is incomprehensible. Israel was the bride of Yahweh's youth, but has broken the bands of love:

> Surely, as a faithless wife leaves her husband,
>> so have you been faithless to me, O house of Israel,
> says Yahweh. (3:20)

"They went far from me and went after worthlessness [i.e., Baal]" (2:5). No other nation has ever changed its gods, even if they are not gods at all; but Israel has changed its glory (Yahweh) for that which does not profit (2:11). The people have forsaken "the fountain of living waters, and hewed out cisterns for themselves, broken cisterns, that can hold no water" (2:13). Therefore the prophet calls upon the people to return to Yahweh:

> Return, O faithless sons,
>> I will heal your faithlessness. (3:22)
> If you return, O Israel, says Yahweh,
>> to me you should return.
> If you remove your abominations from my presence,
>> and do not waver. (4:1)

In all probability, this preaching of Jeremiah falls in the period before Josiah's reformation in 621. Jeremiah might be expected to have hailed this event; unfortunately, however, the collection of Jeremiah's words that has come down to us contains nothing about the reformation. Either he kept silent about it, or his words have been lost. Possibly

---

[91] O. Eissfeldt, "Das Skythenproblem," in T. H. Robinson and F. Horst, *Die zwölf kleinen Propheten* (Tübingen: Mohr, 1954), pp. 188 f.; W. Rudolph, *Jeremia* (Tübingen: Mohr, 1958), pp. 44 f.

[92] Cf. A. Kapelrud, *Joel Studies* (Uppsala: Lundeqvist, 1948), pp. 93 ff.

he first approved the measures taken by the king, but then, when he saw that the reformation of the cult occasioned a false confidence in the external performance of worship, changed his attitude.[93] We know for a fact that later, when Jehoiakim, Josiah's son and successor, was on the throne, Jeremiah looked back on Josiah as a good king (22:15 f.).

The basic stratum of the so-called Book of Comfort (Jer. 30—31) should probably also be assigned to the reign of Josiah. The background of these oracles is Josiah's annexation to Judah of certain territories that had formerly belonged to the Northern Kingdom. Jeremiah sees here the beginning of a reunion of the divided kingdom under the rule of the Davidic dynasty. Unfortunately, these statements were later expanded through the addition of new oracles of salvation, so that we can recover their original form only hypothetically. Of special interest are the words that the prophet addresses to Rachel, as the ancestress of the northern tribes: do not weep, he says, for your sons will return to their land. If Ephraim (i.e., the Northern Kingdom) repents and returns to Yahweh, Yahweh will have mercy on him; for Ephraim is Yahweh's "dear son" and "darling child," whom he cannot give up (Jer. 31:15-20; cf. also 3:6 ff.). These ideas are not irreconcilably opposed to the judgment preached by Jeremiah. Even in the oracles of judgment, we find the same sympathy, the same grief in the face of necessary disaster (see, for example, 4:19).

After the death of Josiah in 609, his son Jehoiakim soon acceded to the throne. He was in many respects the very opposite of his father, an oriental despot "who builds his house by unrighteousness and makes his neighbor serve him for nothing," who "sheds innocent blood and practices oppression and violence" (22:13, 17). Now Jeremiah comes forward once more. He rebukes the king and prophesies his downfall: he will be buried like an ass, i.e., without the proper ritual and mourning (22:19). In a sermon delivered in the courtyard of the Temple, he attacks false reliance on the Temple and its ritual (7:1-15; 26:1 ff.). "Do not trust in these deceptive words: 'This is the temple of Yahweh, the temple of Yahweh, the temple of Yahweh' . . . . Amend your ways and your doings . . ." (7:4 f.). "For a people that disregards the Decalogue (7:9), the Temple no longer offers protection."[94] As a consequence of this sermon, Jeremiah was arrested; he would probably have been put to death if several "princes" had not intervened on his behalf (26:10, 16 f.).

---

[93] For a discussion of this problem, see J. P. Hyatt, "Jeremiah and Deuteronomy," *JNES*, I (1942), 156 ff.; H. H. Rowley, "Jeremiah and the Book of Deuteronomy," in *idem* (ed.), *Studies in Old Testament Prophecy* (Edinburgh: Clark, 1946), pp. 157 ff.; H. Cazelles, "Jérémie et le Deutéronome," *RSR*, XXXIX (1951), 5 ff.

[94] Von Rad, *Theologie des Alten Testaments*, II, 208.

After this, Jeremiah could no longer appear or preach in public. Therefore at Yahweh's command he had his servant Baruch prepare a scroll with a collection of his prophecies of doom. When Baruch tried to read from the scroll in the Temple, however, he was brought before the king, who ordered the scroll burned. But Jeremiah saw to it that a new scroll was prepared, containing not only the earlier oracles, but also some new ones (chap. 36). It is generally suggested that this so-called Baruch scroll formed the nucleus of the present book of Jeremiah, but this cannot be demonstrated. In any case, it is erroneous to take these facts and draw from them general conclusions about how the words of the prophets were preserved and transmitted. In this case, the words were written down because Jeremiah was not allowed to preach in person. It does not follow that every prophet had his words written down in similar fashion.[95]

A third phase of Jeremiah's ministry begins with the year 597, when Nebuchadnezzar captured Jerusalem and deported a great number of its leaders. Zedekiah, the new king, was weak and vacillating, sometimes prepared to listen to Jeremiah (chap. 37), sometimes dependent on the new ruling class in Judah, composed of men friendly toward Egypt. When Zedekiah was planning a revolt with Egyptian assistance, Jeremiah admonished him to remain a loyal subject of Babylon. Jeremiah was finally arrested as a traitor, and only released by the Babylonian conqueror after the fall of Jerusalem (Jer. 38—39). Later he went to Egypt with some Judean fugitives. After a brief period of activity in Egypt (chap. 44), nothing more is heard of him.

Several very interesting features make their appearance in Jeremiah's preaching. First, he refers frequently to the traditions of the exodus, the covenant, and the occupation of Canaan, while there is no trace of the Zion tradition, which played such an important role for Isaiah.[96] This situation may be due to Jeremiah's descent from a priestly family with its home in the tribe of Benjamin. This family would be related to the northern, Rachel tribes, and might even trace its origins to the priesthood of the old amphictyonic shrine at Shiloh.

In addition, no other prophet furnishes so many expressions of personal emotion as does Jeremiah. He literally suffers from the message he must proclaim. His heart is filled with pity for his countrymen. In most of his oracles of judgment, we hear an undertone of personal concern and compassion. The very forms in which he speaks express this feeling. Whereas the earlier prophets preferred to distinguish between the motivation, spoken in their own name, and the actual message coming from God, these two components intermingle so

[95] E. Nielsen, *Oral Tradition* (London: SCM, 1954), pp. 64 ff.

[96] Von Rad, *Theologie des Alten Testaments,* II, 203 f.

freely in Jeremiah's oracles that his own personal feelings color the message he delivers.[97]

We can gain a deeper insight into Jeremiah's inner struggle from a series of poems usually referred to as his confessions (11:18-23; 12:1-6; 15:10-12, 15-21; 17:12-18; 18:18-23; 20:7-18).[98] It is impossible to date these compositions, though some of them at least must come from the time of his persecution under Jehoiakim. In any event, he constantly speaks of enemies lying in wait for him. But he is also tormented with inner uncertainty about his prophetic commission. With joyful readiness he received the word of God, he says, and only on account of this word he left the company of merrymakers and sat alone; "for thou hast filled me with indignation." But he has been unsuccessful. He asks why, and accuses God of having deceived him. God's answer is simply:

> If you return, I will restore you,
>   and you shall stand before me.
> If you utter what is precious, and not what is worthless,
>   you shall be as my mouth. (15:19)

In other words, the important thing is not outward success, but fidelity to God's commission. Only in absolute obedience can the prophet deliver God's message.

Another time Jeremiah speaks of his attempt to avoid the message. We have already heard that the inner necessity to preach overpowered him: "There is in my heart as it were a burning fire . . . I am weary with holding it in, and I cannot" (20:9). In bitter agony, he bursts out:

> Cursed be the day
>   on which I was born!
> The day when my mother bore me,
>   let it not be blessed!
> Why did I come forth from the womb
>   to see toil and sorrow,
>   to spend my days in shame? (20:14, 18)

The prophet receives no answer. Another question, reminiscent of Job, "Why does the way of the wicked prosper?" (12:1), is answered with these mysterious words: if you cannot stand up to these difficulties, how can you expect to endure to the end? (12:5). But despite everything, God is vindicated (12:1).

The very fact that Jeremiah dared to remonstrate with Yahweh

---

[97] Cf. H. Wildberger, *Jahwewort und prophetische Rede bei Jeremia* (Zürich: Zwingli, 1942); H. Reventlow, *Liturgie und prophetisches Ich bei Jeremia* (Gütersloh: Mohn, 1963).

[98] W. Baumgartner, *Die Klagegedichte Jeremias* (Giessen: Töpelmann, 1917); H. J. Stoebe, "Seelsorge und Mitleiden bei Jeremia," *Wort und Dienst,* 1955, pp. 116 ff.

shows that something new has appeared in the spiritual history of Israel. A period of questioning has begun; Jeremiah is unable simply to accept everything as it comes, he must understand, and events will not fit into the traditional schema.[99] As we have already mentioned, the writer of the Book of Job is soon to pose similar questions.

Occasionally, positive hopes are also expressed in the book of Jeremiah. The oracles against the foreign nations found in 25:15-38 and 46—49[100] may be assigned to this category, since they predict the destruction of Israel's enemies. The destruction is brought about through military catastrophes, but the agents are not so much enemy nations as Yahweh himself. It has been pointed out that this conception is strikingly reminiscent of the holy war; this would imply that Jeremiah is here speaking after the fashion of a cult prophet.[101] This raises the question whether Jeremiah's familiarity with these forms may not have been due to his position as priest or cult prophet.

It is impossible simply to include Jeremiah among the professional prophets. It was precisely these prophets of peace and prosperity whom he attacked most bitterly. During the reign of Zedekiah, when Jeremiah was expecting the victory of the Babylonians and urging the people to submit to them, he had to contend with a group of prophets proclaiming victory. With one of them, Hananiah, he came into violent conflict (Jer. 28). In this argument with Hananiah and in another passage (23:9 ff.) he outlines the criteria that distinguish a true prophet, i.e., one commissioned by Yahweh, from a false prophet. A prophet who promises that everything will go well is suspect, he says in another passage (23:16, 25 ff.); such prophecies do not come to pass (28:9). Obviously it was not easy to find a definite criterion.[102] But Jeremiah was convinced that he was proclaiming the living and mighty word of Yahweh (23:29).

Prophecies of salvation in the strict sense referring to Israel occur frequently in Jeremiah. Even the words about the potter in chapter 18 contain positive elements. The potter can indeed destroy the spoiled vessel, but he does so in order to make something new. So also Yahweh can destroy Israel, but in order to accomplish a definite purpose.[103] Jeremiah sent a letter to the Israelites carried away to Babylon in 597, exhorting them to labor peacefully in the new land, where they would have to remain for a long time. But this is not the final word. "For I know the plans I have for you, says Yahweh, plans for welfare and not

---

[99] Von Rad, *Theologie des Alten Testaments*, II, 216 f.

[100] Chapters 50 and 51 do not come from Jeremiah.

[101] Von Rad, *Theologie des Alten Testaments*, II, 211.

[102] Cf. G. Quell, *Wahre und falsche Propheten* (Gütersloh: Bertelsmann, 1952).

[103] H. H. Rowley, *The Biblical Doctrine of Election* (London: Lutterworth, 1950), pp. 40 f.

for evil, to give you a future and a hope" (29:11). And during the final siege of Jerusalem, Jeremiah buys a field and says, "Houses and fields and vineyards shall again be bought in this land" (32:15).

Much clearer and more important for our study is what Jeremiah says about the new covenant (31:31 ff.). We have here an expansion of an oracle that Jeremiah in his early period had directed to the Northern Kingdom (cf. 30:1-3), but toward the end of his life supplemented and revised:

> Behold, the days are coming, says Yahweh, when I will make a new covenant with the house of Israel [and the house of Judah],[104] not like the covenant which I made with their fathers when I took them by the hand to bring them out of the land of Egypt. . . . But this is the covenant which I will make with the house of Israel after those days, says Yahweh: I will put my law within them, and I will write it upon their hearts; and I will be their God, and they shall be my people. . . . For I will forgive their iniquity, and I will remember their sin no more.

Obviously Jeremiah is still thinking in the categories of the Sinai covenant. He makes use of the ancient covenant formula, "I their God, they my people"; he speaks of the law associated with the covenant. Israel's disobedience has broken the old covenant, but Yahweh will institute a new covenant. What is new is that obedience to the law will not, so to speak, be imposed from without, but will be effected by a new creation in the heart of men. This is the logical conclusion of the conviction frequently expressed by Jeremiah that man is incapable of ordering his life properly by himself (10:23; cf. 2:22; 13:23); a new act of creation by God is necessary (cf. also 32:37 ff.; 24:7).[105]

This prophecy was to have incalculable consequences. Reform movements in Judaism, e.g., the Qumran community, have looked upon themselves as its fulfillment. The same is true of Christianity, which even calls its sacred documents "the New Covenant" or "the New Testament."

In Jeremiah's view of the future the concept of the Sinai covenant plays the central role. But there are also references to the Davidic covenant, in other words, messianic prophecies. One passage, which probably contains an allusion to the name Zedekiah ("Yahweh my righteousness"), promises a new David, who shall reign with justice and righteousness and whose name will be "Yahweh is our righteousness" (23:5-6). The language used shows that Jeremiah is thinking in the categories of the royal ideology, and expecting an ideal king. In the Book of Comfort again we find the promise of a ruler who will live in intimate association with God: "I will make him draw

---

[104] Probably an addition.
[105] Von Rad, *Theologie des Alten Testaments,* II, 228 f.

near, and he shall approach me" (30:21). This hope was intimately connected with the idea of the new covenant, which is itself characterized by immediate communion with God.

According to the data contained in his book, which are probably reliable, Ezekiel exercised his ministry among the people deported to Babylon in 597.[106] There, in 593, he experienced his call to be a prophet. Like Isaiah, he beheld Yahweh upon a throne; but his description verges on the fantastic and, by piling up such expressions as "one like . . ." and "something that resembled . . .," suggests the indescribable nature of what he saw. The fact that mythological conceptions contributed to the shaping of the vision does not mean that the experience was not genuine. Ezekiel then received the commission to warn the rebellious children of Israel. Part of this commission involved a striking symbolic action: the prophet had to eat a scroll on which prophecies were written, and in his mouth it was "as sweet as honey" (3:3). This action clearly symbolizes the prophet's assimilation of God's message; but it is also reminiscent of taste sensations experienced by certain mystics.[107]

Even in his call we sense the peculiar psychical makeup of Ezekiel, which appears in various ways in the course of his subsequent ministry. He feels himself lifted by the Spirit and transported to distant places (8:3; 11:1, 24), he lies for a long time without moving (4:4 ff.), he becomes dumb (3:26), etc. The available data are insufficient for a precise psychological diagnosis; it is important to note, however, that these psychological phenomena constitute an integral part of Ezekiel's preaching, because he makes use of them as symbolic actions.

Ezekiel was a priest, and this fact leaves its particular stamp on his message. He is less concerned about social injustice than about cultic aberrations. "When Ezekiel speaks of sins, he means primarily offences against sacral ordinances."[108] Israel's sins and especially its idolatry have made it "unclean"—Ezekiel here uses a cultic expression, just as elsewhere, too, he is fond of judging according to such categories as "sacred" and "profane." Israel's sin consists in transgressions of

---

[106] A. Bertholet, *Hesekiel* (Tübingen: Mohr, 1936), pp. xiii ff., advocated the theory that the prophet's activity was partly in Jerusalem, partly in exile; there are grave objections to this view. For a bibliography on Ezekiel, see C. Kuhl, *ThR*, V (1933), 92 ff., XX (1952), 1 ff., XXIV (1956), 1 ff., XXVIII (1962), 261 ff.; H. H. Rowley, "Ezekiel in Modern Study," *BJRL*, XXXVI (1953), 146 ff., reprinted in *idem, Men of God*, pp. 169 ff. Cf. G. Fohrer, *Die Hauptprobleme des Buches Ezechiel* (Berlin: Töpelmann, 1952); H. Reventlow, *Wächter über Israel* (Berlin: Töpelmann, 1962). Good commentaries include those of G. Fohrer and K. Galling (in Eissfeldt's "Handbuch zum Alten Testament"), W. Zimmerli ("Biblischer Kommentar"), W. Eichrodt ("Das Alte Testament Deutsch"), and Cooke (International Critical Commentary).

[107] See above, p. 254.

[108] Von Rad, *Theologie des Alten Testaments*, II, 237.

Yahweh's "ordinances and statutes" (*ḥōq, mišpāṭ*)[109]—here again we have priestly terminology, this time alluding to the instruction given by the priests. The very language Ezekiel uses is influenced by priestly and sacral stylistic forms. The prophet's invective in 14:1-11 contains phrases from the language of sacral law (e.g., vs. 4: "Any man from the house of Israel who takes his idols into his heart . . . "; vs. 7: "Any one of the house of Israel, or of the strangers, . . . who separates himself from me . . . ").[110] The theological treatise on individual responsibility, contained in chapter 18, is in theoretical and didactic style, full of such declaratory priestly formulas as "he is righteous," "he shall live," or "he shall die."[111]

During the first period of his prophetic activity, Ezekiel concerns himself to an astonishing degree with the situation in Jerusalem. This fact has led some scholars to conclude that Ezekiel was active in Judah for a period. But the exiles clearly kept in such close touch with those who remained in Jerusalem that Ezekiel's concern for affairs there is quite understandable.

Ezekiel predicts the imminent end of Jerusalem. In a series of symbolic actions, he represents the siege of the city (chap. 4), the slaughter of the inhabitants (chap. 6), and the coming exile (chap. 12). In a vision he sees terrible idolatry going on in the Jerusalem Temple: sun worship, Egyptian (?) idols, the Tammuz cult; he proclaims Yahweh's fury at these practices (chap. 8). He also attacks the idolatry practiced upon "the mountains of Israel" (chap. 6)— apparently a reference to the Canaanite high places.

In two allegorical sermons, Ezekiel outlines all of Israel's history as he sees it. In the first, he is clearly taking an old story of a foundling as his point of departure. Israel is the child, found by Yahweh, brought up by him, and taken to wife. But Israel has been unfaithful from the very beginning (chap. 16). Here, as in the parable of the wood of the vine (chap. 15), Ezekiel expresses the idea that Israel was not chosen because of its worth or merit, but through a free act of Yahweh's grace. The other allegorical sermon (chap. 23) depicts Israel and Judah as two lascivious sisters. Ezekiel's theology is typified by the view that Israel has been unfaithful to Yahweh from the very beginning, but that he has nevertheless poured out his grace upon her for his name's sake, i.e., for his own honor (see especially chap. 20). His interpretation of the catastrophe that befell Jerusalem, contained in 11:22-25, is also characteristic: the glory (*kābôd*) of Yahweh, the sign of his constant presence in the Temple, departs from Jeru-

---

[109] *Ibid.*, p. 230.

[110] W. Zimmerli, "Die Eigenart der prophetischen Rede des Ezechiel," *ZAW*, LXVI (1954), 1 ff., reprinted in *idem, Gottes Offenbarung* (Munich: Kaiser, 1963), pp. 148 ff.

[111] W. Zimmerli, "Leben und Tod im Buche des Propheten Ezechiel," *TZ*, XIII (1957), 494 ff., reprinted in *idem, Gottes Offenbarung*, pp. 178 ff.

salem and moves to the east. Here Ezekiel's priestly background
betrays itself once more.[112]

Ezekiel thinks of himeslf as a watchman (33:1-9; 3:16b-21). His
duty is to warn his countrymen, as a watchman warns the inhabitants
of a city that the enemy is approaching. Just as the watchman is
responsible for the life of those who dwell in the city, so the prophet,
too, bears a grave responsibility: he must proclaim the warning
message of Yahweh in full. Those who hear him are free to take heed
or not. This view in itself implies the possibility of repentance. The
precise conditions are laid out in a short theological treatise, chapter
18. It is not true, says Ezekiel, that the children must suffer for the
sins of their fathers; to each generation the possibility of repentance is
given. Every man is responsible only for himself; indeed, if he does
repent, even his earlier sins are blotted out. Jeremiah, also, expressed
similar ideas, although he connects this new principle with the time
of the new covenant (Jer. 31:29 f.). Clearly the age of Jeremiah and
Ezekiel looked upon the individual in a completely new light.

Ezekiel's unconditional oracles of salvation presumably come for
the most part from the later period of his activity, after the fall of
Jerusalem. It is significant that, for Ezekiel, the restoration of Israel
clearly belongs in the category of divine miracles. In the impressive
vision of the dead bones, the prophet sees how the divine spirit enters
the bones and, contrary to all expectations, restores them to life
(37:1-14). Similarly, Israel is dead for the present, but can be
restored through a divine miracle. (This pericope does not contain any
doctrine of the resurrection of the dead, however.)

In chapter 36, Ezekiel gives clear expression to his hope for the
future. The scattered children of Israel will return out of all lands, the
land will be inhabited once more, the cities will be fortified and the
fields cultivated, and Yahweh will bless the land with fertility. But,
what is even more important:

> I will sprinkle clean water upon you, and you shall be clean from
> all your uncleannesses, and from all your idols I will cleanse
> you. A new heart I will give you, and a new spirit I will put
> within you; and I will take out of your flesh the heart of stone
> and give you a heart of flesh . . . and cause you to walk in my
> statutes and be careful to observe my ordinances . . . and you
> shall be my people, and I will be your God. (36:25-28)

Here Ezekiel has many points in common with Jeremiah. A new
obedience will be brought about through a new creation. The presupposition is the forgiveness of sins (here conceived in typically
priestly fashion as a ritual purification), and the result is a renewal
of the covenant relationship, which, as in Jeremiah, is characterized

---

[112] Cf. above, pp. 90 f.

by the ancient covenant formula. The significant point in Ezekiel, however, is that Yahweh will do all this for the sake of his holy name:

> It is not for your sake, O house of Israel, that I am about to act, but for the sake of my holy name, which you have profaned among the nations to which you came. And I will vindicate the holiness of my great name, which has been profaned among the nations . . . and the nations shall know that I am Yahweh . . . when through you I vindicate my holiness before their eyes. (36:22 f.)

Because of the dispersion of Israel, Yahweh's honor has been injured and his name profaned. Yahweh must protect his honor; he will vindicate his holiness in the eyes of the nations by making them acknowledge that he is the mighty God.

As Israel's leader there appears a new David, who is to be prince and shepherd (34:23 f.; 37:25 ff.).

These oracles of salvation are followed by two sections that probably derive only in part from Ezekiel. These are the Gog oracle (chapters 38—39) and the so-called vision of the restored community (40—48). The former describes a final assault of foreign nations (Gog, from the land of Magog in the far north) upon Israel and the defeat of the enemy. Here elements of the old Zion tradition (the assault of the nations) are mingled with the concept, originally mythological, of the foe from the north, together making up prophecies that prepare the way for apocalyptic. In chapters 40—48, the author draws a picture of the restored Temple and the organization of the Temple worship in the new Israel. Especially notable are the return of the *kābôd* of Yahweh to the new Temple (43:1-5) and the life-giving water flowing from the Temple (47:1-12). In addition, the prince (the word "king" is avoided) is remarkably subordinate to the priests.

In conclusion, several oracles against foreign nations (especially Tyre and Egypt) should be mentioned; they illustrate both Ezekiel's interest in world politics and his fund of mythological knowledge. The oracle against Tyre in chapter 28 is especially significant, since it has preserved some elements of the ancient royal ideology and also a myth of the first king or first man upon the mountain of God, a variant of the Paradise idea.[113]

Deutero-Isaiah ("second Isaiah") is the designation commonly applied to chapters 40—55 of the book of Isaiah.[114] Their author is

---

[113] For a discussion of Ezek. 28, see above, p. 111.

[114] Studies of Deutero-Isaiah: L. Köhler, *Deuterojesaja, stilkritisch untersucht* (Giessen: Töpelmann, 1923); J. Begrich, *Studien zu Deuterojesaja* (Stuttgart: Kohlhammer, 1938); I. Engnell, "The Ebed Yahweh Songs and the Suffering Servant in Deutero-Isaiah," *BJRL*, XXXI (1948), 54 ff.; P. H. de Boer, "Second Isaiah's Message," *OTS*, XI (1956); G.

unknown; historical allusions, however, betray the fact that he lived and worked during the final years of the Babylonian exile. Sylistically, his "book" shows a striking similarity to the poetry of the cult, especially the so-called enthronement psalms; the typically prophetical *Gattungen* are but slightly represented.

A section in chapter 40 is often interpreted as the inaugural vision of the prophet:

> A voice says, "Cry!
>   And I said, "What shall I cry?
> All flesh is grass,
>   and all its beauty is like the flower of the field.
> The grass withers, the flower fades,
>   when the breath of Yahweh blows upon it."
>   "Surely the people is grass.
> The grass withers, the flower fades;
>   but the word of our God will stand for ever." (40:6-8)[115]

Even though it is very doubtful whether this section really does represent the call of the prophet, he definitely knows that the word of God has been entrusted to him and that this word has power. Toward the end of his "book," he returns to this theme:

> For as the rain and the snow come down from heaven,
>   and return not thither but water the earth,
> making it bring forth and sprout,
>   giving seed to the sower and bread to the eater,
> so shall my word be that goes forth from my mouth;
>   it shall not return to me empty,
> but it shall accomplish that which I purpose,
>   and prosper in the thing for which I sent it. (55:10 f.)

Not only, then, is the prophetic word true; it also brings about what it predicts, because ultimately it is God's word. There can be no doubt, therefore, that Deutero-Isaiah thought of himself as a prophet truly called by God.

The outward occasion for Deutero-Isaiah's appearance was clearly the victorious advance of Cyrus, the Persian king, who had just conquered Croesus of Lydia and overrun Asia Minor. The prophet looks upon him as the deliverer of Israel, who has been aroused by Yahweh to crush Babylon and liberate the captured Israelites (41:25 ff.; 44:24—45:7; 46:8-11). Here the ancient prophetical conception of Yahweh as lord of human history achieves its highest expression.

Rignell, *A Study of Isaiah Chapters 40—55* (Lund: Gleerup, 1956). An excellent commentary in English is that of J. Muilenburg in *The Interpreters' Bible.*

115 [The translation given is that of the RSV except for the placing of quotation marks, which follows the author's translation.—TRANS.]

Deutero-Isaiah's message is accordingly a message of comfort. His book begins:

> Comfort, comfort my people,
>> says your God.
> Speak tenderly to Jerusalem,
>> and cry to her
> that her time of service is ended,
>> that her iniquity is pardoned. (40:1 f.)

In other words, Israel has now suffered enough; now the hour of deliverance is near.

This message has to a large extent been clothed in the forms of the enthronement festival, which has been associated with the motifs of the exodus tradition. For example, Yahweh is about to appear in triumph, like a king:

> A voice cries:
> "In the wilderness prepare the way of Yahweh,
>> make straight in the desert a highway for our God.
> . . . .
> And the glory of Yahweh shall be revealed." (40:3, 5)

Messengers announce his coming:

> How beautiful upon the mountains
>> are the feet of him who brings good tidings,
> who publishes peace, who brings good tidings of good,
>> who publishes salvation,
>> who says to Zion, "Your God reigns." (52:7)

Here we find almost word for word the acclamation of the enthronement psalms: "Yahweh is king."[116] From the fact that Yahweh is the creator of the world—a motif that also plays an important role in the enthronement psalms—the prophet draws the conclusion that Yahweh is unique and incomparable, the lord of all the world and its history:

> It is he who sits above the circle of the earth,
>> and its inhabitants are like grasshoppers;
> who stretches out the heavens like a curtain,
>> and spreads them like a tent to dwell in;
> who brings princes to nought,
>> and makes the rulers of the earth as nothing.
> . . . .
> To whom then will you compare me,
>> that I should be like him?
>> says the Holy One. (40:22 ff.)

---

[116] A. Haldar, *Associations of Cult Prophets Among the Ancient Semites,* p. 129, also sees in the messengers a reflection of cultic ceremonies (cf. Mal. 3:1).

He created the countless stars, "he brings out their host by number, calling them all by name . . . and not one is missing" (40:26). The prophet sees in this a proof that Yahweh is also able to help his people:

> Why do you say, O Jacob,
>   and speak, O Israel,
> "My way is hid from Yahweh,
>   and my right is disregarded by my God?"
> Have you not known? Have you not heard?
> Yahweh is the everlasting God,
>   the creator of the ends of the earth.
> He does not faint or grow weary,
>   his understanding is unsearchable. (40:27 f.)

In order to understand this, the reader must remember how logical it appeared to the Israelites of that period to conclude from the course of history that Yahweh was impotent, because the gods of Babylon had triumphed over him. Deutero-Isaiah counters this idea with his conviction, rooted in the ancient cultic traditions of Israel, that Yahweh is the almighty creator and lord. Developing an idea already embryonically present, for example, in Psalm 96:5 ("all the gods of the peoples are idols"), Deutero-Isaiah pursues the theme that the idols of the pagans, fashioned by human hands,[117] are powerless (40:19 f.; 44:12-20; 46:5-7): they are not gods at all, only Yahweh is God (44:6; 45:18, 22; 46:9). Never before has monotheism been so clearly expressed in Israel.

To this God—as in the enthronement psalms—all the world must sing a new song (42:10; cf. Pss. 96:1; 98:1); this God—as in the enthronement psalms—is called upon to awake and triumph over his enemies.

> Awake, awake, put on strength,
>   O arm of Yahweh;
> awake, as in the days of old,
>   the generations of long ago.
> Was it not thou that didst cut Rahab in pieces,
>   and didst pierce the dragon?
> Was it not thou that didst dry up the sea,
>   the waters of the great deep;
> that didst make the depths of the sea a way
>   for the redeemed to pass over?
> And the ransomed of Yahweh shall return,
>   and come with singing to Zion. (51:9-11)

In these verses we have a summary of the entire message of Deutero-Isaiah. Creation, the exodus, and the liberation of the exiles are here

---

117 The description is reminiscent of the manufacture of idols at the Babylonian New Year's festival (cf. *ANET*, pp. 331 ff., ll. 193 ff.).

fused in unique fashion, becoming one great saving event. Just as
Yahweh long ago slew the chaos monster, just as he dried up the
Reed Sea, representing the powers of chaos, so now he will overcome
all the powers of the enemy and deliver his people from their captivity. This intimate association between creation and redemption
typifies Yahweh's eternal saving purpose in a manner characteristic
of Deutero-Isaiah.[118]

The liberation of the exiles is conceived as a new exodus. But this
time it is a triumphal procession through a desert, which is transformed into a fertile plain with abundant water. Forget the first
exodus, says the prophet, for now Yahweh is doing something new
(43:18 f.):

> I will make a way in the wilderness
> and rivers in the desert.
> The wild beasts will honor me,
> the jackals and the ostriches;
> for I give water in the wilderness,
> rivers in the desert,
> to give drink to my chosen people,
> the people whom I formed for myself
> that they might declare my praise. (43:19-21)

The new exodus is not, like the first, a hasty flight:

> For you shall not go out in haste,
> and you shall not go in flight,
> for Yahweh will go before you,
> and the God of Israel will be your rear guard. (52:12)

The covenant, too, is renewed. Just as Yahweh once promised to Noah
by means of a covenant that he would never again destroy the earth
with a deluge, so now he will swear never again to vent his wrath
against Israel (54:9).

> For the mountains may depart
> and the hills be removed,
> but my steadfast love shall not depart from you,
> and my covenant of peace shall not be removed,
> says Yahweh, who has compassion on you. (54:10)

Here we are not dealing with a new covenant, for, according to
Deutero-Isaiah, the old covenant has never been renounced by Yahweh.
Again he says that Yahweh has not given Israel a bill of divorce, that
the marriage is still in effect (50:1).

The Davidic covenant, too, is renewed: "I will make with you an

---

[118] Von Rad, *Theologie des Alten Testaments*, II, 254 f.; cf. R. Rendtorff, "Die theologische Stellung des Schöpfungsglaubens bei Deutero-
Jesaja," *ZThK*, LI (1954), 1 ff.

everlasting covenant, my steadfast, sure love for David" (55:3). Now a new feature appears: "Behold, I made him a witness to the peoples, a leader and commander for the peoples. Behold, you shall call nations that you know not, and nations that knew you not shall run to you (cf. the similar statement about David in Ps. 18:44 [Eng. 18:43]), because of Yahweh your God, and of the Holy One of Israel" (55:4 f.). Here the Davidic tradition is combined with a motif of the Zion tradition, namely, the pilgrimage of the nations: all nations assemble at Jerusalem to worship the true God (cf. also Isa. 45:14; 49:14-23). This has been described as universalism. It must be remembered, however, that there is an important restriction on this universalism: Israel is the dominant nation, and the Gentiles will serve Israel and its God.

Up to this point the message of Deutero-Isaiah is clear and unambiguous. There are four remaining passages, however, that are among the most difficult sections of the Old Testament, concerning which no consensus has yet been reached: the four servant songs, Isaiah 42:1-4 (or 42:1-9); 49:1-6 (or 49:1-9); 50:4-9 (or 50:4-11); and 52:13—53:12.[119] Ever since Duhm, Deutero-Isaiah's authorship of these songs has been disputed. It seems, however, that the reasons given for denying their genuineness are hardly sufficient; and in point of fact the view that the songs do come from Deutero-Isaiah is gaining ground.[120] In all probability, these songs deal with an individual, who is referred to as the servant of Yahweh (Ebed Yahweh). We learn that he was chosen by Yahweh (from the very womb of his mother; 49:1) and endowed with his spirit, in order to bring righteousness and truth upon earth; he will be "a light to the nations" (49:6). He labors without success, but Yahweh will help him (50:4 ff.). The fourth song describes his suffering and death, which he undergoes vicariously on behalf of "many." In the end, though, he will prosper and astonish the world.

Who is this servant? The New Testament saw in him the Messiah, and this remained the interpretation of the Christian church. Jewish exegesis has usually understood the servant to be a symbol for the people of Israel. Critical scholarship has cast doubt on these interpretations, but without being able to offer any solution as a satisfactory alternative. The usual suggestion has been the prophet himself or some historical figure (Moses, Jeremiah, Hezekiah). In recent years, royal

---

[119] For a bibliography on the Ebed Yahweh problem, see G. Fohrer, *ThR*, XIX (1951), 298 ff., XX (1952), 228 ff. See also H. H. Rowley, *The Servant of the Lord* (London: Lutterworth, 1952), pp. 1 ff.

[120] E.g., A. Bentzen, in his commentary on Isaiah; I. Engnell, "The Ebed Yahweh Songs," pp. 10 f.; D. N. Freedman, "The Slave of Yahwe," *Western Watch*, March, 1959, pp. 1 ff.; J. Lindblom, *The Servant Songs in Deutero-Isaiah* (Lund: Gleerup, 1951).

motifs have been pointed out in the songs, and attempts have been made to utilize these as a key to their interpretation.[121]

Any interpretation must first take into account the fact that the servant songs stand in the context of Deutero-Isaiah and in all probability are an integral part of this book; in addition, the historical background of the various motifs must be considered. The first point to note is that the task of the servant somehow combines royal and prophetic features. Von Rad thinks it is necessary to decide between the two choices, and decides in favor of the prophetic office.[122] Kaiser emphasizes the royal components, but finds it difficult to assign the third song to this category.[123] Engnell interprets all four songs on the basis of the royal ideology, and sees in the servant of Yahweh a messianic figure.[124]

That the servant is not a king or messiah in the usual sense is undeniable. But neither does the prophetic office really fit, at least if one is searching for a concrete individual. The suffering in particular raises difficulties, even if suffering and intercession must be admitted to form part of the prophetical ideal of the period (Isa. 53:12). Von Rad discovers precisely these two features in the idealized figure of Moses, and makes the servant the second Moses, the ideal prophet.[125]

The question remains, however, whether the royal interpretation, in a somewhat modified form, does not come closest to doing justice to the facts. We have seen that in one passage Deutero-Isaiah transferred the promises of the Davidic covenant to Israel (55:5). In addition, outside the actual servant songs, Israel is frequently called the servant of Yahweh. Finally, such an interpretation seems appropriate to the liturgical style of the whole.

If this interpretation is right, the servant would be Israel, the ideal Israel, described with the aid of royal categories.[126] The prophetical features might then easily be derived from the figure of Moses; for Moses was in fact a leader of the people, and is occasionally depicted by means of royal categories. But it must not be forgotten that, in the ancient Near East, the king himself was frequently thought as a revealer of the divine will.[127] The suffering of the king also has parallels in Babylonia: the Babylonian king suffers symbolically at the New

---

[121] Engnell, "The Ebed Yahweh Songs"; V. de Leeuw, *De Ebed Jahweh-profetieen* (Assen: Van Gorcum, 1956); O. Kaiser, *Der königliche Knecht* (Göttingen: Vandenhoeck & Ruprecht, 1959).

[122] Von Rad, *Theologie des Alten Testaments,* II, 271.

[123] Kaiser, *Der königliche Knecht,* pp. 66 ff.

[124] Engnell, "The Ebed Yahweh Songs," pp. 38 ff.

[125] Von Rad, *Theologie des Alten Testaments,* II, 271 ff.

[126] H. Ringgren, "König und Messias," p. 147; cf. C. Lindhagen, *op. cit.,* p. 215; Kaiser, *Der königliche Knecht,* p. 132.

[127] G. Widengren, *The Ascension of the Apostle and the Heavenly Book* (Uppsala: Lundeqvist, 1950), pp. 7 ff.; *idem, Sakrales Königtum,* pp. 30 f.

Year's festival for the sins of the people.[128] The details have not been explained completely. Perhaps it is in this context that we shall find the explanation for the similarities between the servant songs and the songs of the Tammuz cult, since in this cult the king acted as the representative of Tammuz.

The message of the servant songs would then be somewhat as follows: Israel is called to a position of leadership among the nations; this consists primarily in making known to the nations the will of Yahweh. The suffering of the people is not meaningless. Indeed, it has a profound significance, because it is vicarious and makes "many" to be accounted righteous. The objection that Israel did not suffer silently and without complaint may perhaps be met (following Kaiser[129]) by assuming that the prophet's intention is not to depict the patient acceptance of suffering, but to summon Israel to this ministry.

The figure of the servant shows both individual and collective features. This is the result of the metaphorical application of an individual motif to the people as a collective entity, and may be considered an impressive example of what Robinson calls "corporate personality."[130] In other words, an individual is looked upon not only as a leader, but as the personal embodiment of a group (just as the king, for example, embodied and united the people). This conception could also justify the Christian, messianic interpretation of the servant; but this would take us beyond the limits of the history of religion.

---

[128] A point particularly emphasized by Engnell, "The Ebed Yahweh Songs."

[129] *Der königliche Knecht,* p. 110.

[130] H. W. Robinson, *The Hebrew Conception of Corporate Personality* (Giessen: Töpelmann, 1936), pp. 49 ff.

III.

THE EXILE AND POSTEXILIC PERIOD (JUDAISM)

1.

HISTORICAL INTRODUCTION

The fall of Jerusalem in 587 was in many ways of decisive importance for the subsequent development of the Israelite religion. In the first place, the loss of the Temple compelled the Jews to seek the forms of worship. The downfall of the royal dynasty was a terrible blow to those who had based their hopes upon the Davidic dynasty. The destruction of Israel as a political entity must have been interpreted by many as the defeat of Israel's God. It forced others to re-think their theology. The political and religious leaders were deported: those who remained behind lacked religious leadership, while the bearers of the religious tradition were in Babylon. Thus the way the Israelite religion developed among the exiles gradually became determinative for all Judaism. The influence of the exile should therefore not be considered totally negative; quite the contrary: it determined the direction in which the Israelite religion was to develop in the future.

The mood of those who remained in Judah is expressed in the Book of Lamentations.[1] Here we find bitter lamentations over the fate that has befallen the land and the city, in particular the destruction of the Temple, the cessation of the cult, and the end of the kingship. Yahweh has become like an enemy, he has destroyed Israel (Lam. 2:5). This makes the situation even more unbearable. But Yahweh is still in the right: Israel rebelled against his word, and is now receiving the reward of her sins (1:18). The people try to appease Yahweh's wrath through confession and penance. One section (chap. 3) devotes some space to more optimistic thoughts: Yahweh has mercy on those who hope in him (3:21-26).

It is possible that these poems were recited during memorial observances or as communal laments. Jeremiah 41:5 also bears witness to mourning rites connected with pilgrimages to the site of the ruined

---

[1] See N. H. Gottwald, *Studies in the Book of Lamentations* (London: SCM, 1954); and the commentaries of H. J. Kraus ("Biblischer Kommentar," 1956) and A. Weiser ("Das Alte Testament Deutsch," 1958).

Temple, and Zechariah 7:3 mentions mourning and fasting in the month of Jerusalem's destruction. What other forms the religious and cultic life took we unfortunately do not know.[2] Probably the syncretistic cults, whose existence during Judah's last days is witnessed to by prophets like Ezekiel (chap. 8) and Jeremiah (e.g., chap. 44), continued to exist in the exilic period. In two sections of so-called Trito-Isaiah (Isa. 56—66), which date from the early postexilic period, reference is made to a whole series of syncretistic practices; it seems unlikely that these were introduced only after the return of the exiles. Here the prophet speaks of fertility rites "under every green tree" and upon the mountains, of child sacrifice and other pagan sacrifices (swine's flesh; Isa. 65:4), of astrology, etc. (Isa. 57:3-10; 65:3-7, 11). In addition, mention is made of Canaanite deities such as Melech (Molech; Isa. 57:9), Gad, and Meni (Isa. 65:11).[3] In the desperate situation after the fall of Jerusalem, the people obviously clung to all conceivable deities and cults, since Yahweh had shown himself to be impotent.

Among the Jews taken to Babylonia as captives, the situation was quite different. The most important concern of those former religious and secular leaders was to preserve the distinctiveness of the Israelite religion by concentrating on what was possible and also religiously essential without the existence of a Temple. Since sacrificial worship and the Temple feasts had to be discontinued, the major emphasis fell on those religious duties that could be fulfilled by the individual in the context of the family. In this situation, circumcision acquired special significance as the sign of membership in the people of Yahweh. In several exilic or early postexilic texts (Isa. 56:1-8; 58:13 f.; perhaps Jer. 17:19-27), the Sabbath also is singled out as a signal mark of obedience to the covenant. Ezekiel calls it a sign that Yahweh is the God of Israel (20:12). Probably the Sabbath was the occasion for religious assemblies, at which the priests provided instruction and prayers were recited. Questions of ritual purity seem to have had an important place in the instruction (Ezek. 4:12-15; 22:26; 44 ff.). In the midst of an unclean, pagan nation, it was especially important to preserve the purity and holiness of the people of God (Ezek. 4:13).

Although there is no direct evidence, we must assume that there was a revival of interest in the ancient religious and historical traditions of Israel. Large sections of the laws and of the historical books were probably collected and reduced to writing during the exile. That part of the Pentateuch which is called P in all probability was assembled during the Babylonian captivity.

[2] For a discussion of these questions, see E. Janssen, *Juda in der Exilszeit* (Göttingen: Vandenhoeck & Ruprecht, 1956).

[3] [These proper names are translated by the RSV as Fortune and Destiny.—TRANS.]

Throughout all this period the hope for restoration remained alive. The prayer of Lamentations, "Renew our days as of old!" (Lam. 5:21), was also the prayer of the exiles. There may also have been formal assemblies for prayer and lament.[4] Ezekiel frequently voices his hope for a restoration. This expectation was given new life by the victorious advance of Cyrus, which occasioned Deutero-Isaiah's oracles of salvation and comfort.

The overthrow of the Neo-Babylonian empire by Cyrus (539) made it possible for the Jews to return to their land. Although not all the exiles were immediately prepared to undertake this long journey, a considerable number of them seized this opportunity to return home to Jerusalem and Judah.

The first project undertaken by the returnees was the building of an altar where the Temple had stood and the celebration of the feast of booths (Ezra 3). The sacrificial cult was thereby set in motion once more, although the Temple had not yet been rebuilt. In point of fact, economic and political conditions were wretched, and work on the Temple ceased almost as soon as it had begun. Only in the year 520, under the influence of the encouraging message of the prophets Haggai and Zechariah, was work on the Temple begun once more; and in 515 the new Temple was dedicated.

Obviously conditions in Jerusalem were still somewhat precarious and confused. Following the dedication of the Temple, our historical sources fall silent for many decades; when they begin to speak once more, Nehemiah and Ezra are active as strong organizers of the Jewish community. The problems of chronology are very complicated at this point—it is not even certain which of the two made his appearance on the scene first; but these problems need not delay us.[5] Our sources do show unambiguously that Nehemiah was primarily concerned with the rebuilding of the city wall, and that Ezra was a religious leader. According to Ezra 8 f., the latter held an assembly at which the law he had brought from Babylon was publicly recited and the people engaged themselves to observe it. Both Ezra and Nehemiah are associated with the prohibition against marrying non-Israelite women.

Unfortunately, it is impossible to identify the law read by Ezra and

---

[4] This is the conclusion reached by H. E. von Waldow, *Anlass und Hintergrund der Verkündigung des Deuterojesaja,* Dissertation, Bonn, 1953; cf. G. von Rad, *Old Testament Theology,* trans. D. M. G. Stalker (Edinburgh & London: Oliver & Boyd), p. 84.

[5] See M. Noth, *The History of Israel* (2nd ed.; New York: Harper, 1960), pp. 318 ff.; J. Bright, *A History of Israel* (Philadelphia: Westminster, 1959), pp. 375 f.; H. H. Rowley, "The Chronological Order of Ezra and Nehemiah," *Goldziher Memorial Volume,* 1948, pp. 117 ff., reprinted in *idem, The Servant of the Lord* (London: Lutterworth, 1952), pp. 131 ff.; H. Cazelles, "La mission d'Esdras," *VT,* IV (1954), 113 ff.; V. Pavlovsky, "Die Chronologie der Tätigkeit Esdras," *Biblica,* XXXVIII (1957), 275 ff., 428 ff.

to say whether it was the Pentateuch or a portion thereof. This story definitely illustrates one basic fact, however: from this time on, the religion of Israel is a religion based on written authority. The obligation to keep the law is one of the two foundation stones upon which the newly constituted Jewish community rests. The other is membership in the Jewish people, whose purity the commandment against mixed marriages is intended to guarantee. This does not necessarily imply racial purity, however, but religious purity.

Ezra and Nehemiah are again followed by a period without historical documentation. This is the more tragic because a very important event must have taken place during this period. The Samaritan community, composed of the inhabitants of what had been the Northern Kingdom and the foreigners who had settled there, broke off all relations with the Jerusalem community.[6] Since the Samaritans look upon the Pentateuch as Holy Scripture, the separation must have taken place after its final redaction; but unfortunately we do not know the precise date of this latter event, either. A few allusions to this schism have been found in Haggai (2:10-14) and in the latter part of the Book of Zechariah (11:4 ff.),[7] but these do not permit us to arrive at any detailed conclusions about when and how the separation took place. It is known, however, that in the first half of the second century B.C. a Samaritan sanctuary had already been in existence for some time (II Macc. 6:2). Josephus may be right in dating the schism at the end of the fourth century B.C.

In the first half of the second century, some light is shed once more on the history of Israel's religion. Palestine now is part of the Seleucid empire, and is exposed to the policy of hellenization carried out by Antiochus IV Epiphanes. This emperor was apparently seeking an accommodation between the religions of Hellenism and Judaism. The introduction of the cult of the Greek Zeus at Jerusalem and upon Gerizim (in December, 167) should be considered one element in these efforts. The Jews who opposed this measure were persecuted, and the immediate result was open revolt against the emperor. This situation, described in the two books of the Maccabees, produced the Book of Daniel, which was designed to encourage the Jews to resolute resistance. The Jews finally achieved victory, and after three years could rededicate the desecrated Temple.

---

[6] H. H. Rowley, "Sanballat and the Samaritan Temple," *BJRL*, XXXVIII (1955), 166 ff.; *idem*, "The Samaritan Schism in Legend and History," *Israel's Prophetic Heritage*, ed. B. W. Anderson and W. Harrelson (New York: Harper, 1962), pp. 208 ff.; T. Gaster, *The Samaritans, their History, Doctrines and Literature* (London: Oxford University Press, 1925); J. MacDonald, *The Theology of the Samaritans* (London: SCM, 1964), which includes an exhaustive bibliography.

[7] K. Elliger, *Das Buch der zwölf kleinen Propheten* (Göttingen: Vandenhoeck & Ruprecht, 1949), II, 160 ff.

The following period, during which the Jews were at first independent, but later (67 B.C.) came under Roman rule, gave rise to the apocryphal and pseudepigraphical writings. These give us once more an opportunity to describe the Jewish religion in more detail. Unfortunately, these writings represent only one tendency within Judaism; those tendencies that were later to be considered orthodox are not heard from in any detail. The material relating to these latter tendencies was only collected in the Mishna and Talmud, and therefore belongs to a later phase in the development of the Jewish religion.

2.

GENERAL CHARACTERISTICS
OF LATER JUDAISM: THE LAW

The rebuilding of the Jewish community at Jerusalem was by no means a simple repristination of the pre-exilic cultic community. Although the Temple was restored, the pre-exilic cult of the covenant and the kingship were not revived. The leading men of this period were primarily concerned with preserving the religious uniqueness of the Jewish people against all foreign influences. They needed a unifying element taken from the ancient heritage of Israel around which the new community could unite in order to survive. This they found in the law, which thereby became the dominant element in the further development of Judaism.

Actually, this process had already started before the exile. Josiah's reformation was carried out on the basis of a book, and Deuteronomy lays special emphasis on the book of the law: the king is to study and obey it (Deut. 17:18 f.), the Levites are to preserve it and read it in public (Deut. 31:11, 26), the people are to obey all its commandments and ordinances (Deut. 30:10), nothing must be added to it or taken from it (Deut. 4:2; 12:32).

But in the pre-exilic period the Temple still existed, the old cult of the covenant was still observed, and the kingship was still functioning. The exile forced Israel to concentrate on that portion of the ancient heritage that could be saved after these things were lost; the law became, as it were, the sum total of these traditions. Attempts were made to restore the Davidic kingship under Zerubbabel, as we read particularly in Haggai 2:21-24 and Zechariah 4; 6:9-15 (in its original form). These attempts failed, however, and only the law was left. The new Temple could not compete with the law; it was the place where the sacrifices and ceremonies prescribed by the law were carried out.

Of course we do not know what kind of a law book Ezra read to the people, but very soon the law (*tôrâ*) and the Pentateuch became identical concepts. The origin of the Pentateuch remains unknown to us; but we may probably assume that the selection and redaction of the old traditions involved a mutual interaction between the ancient material and the needs of the present. On the one hand, an attempt was made to constitute the Jewish community in accordance with the old traditions; on the other, those particular traditions were utilized which could be made to apply to the community.

This esteem for the law had several interesting and important consequences for Judaism. First of all, the codification of the law gave rise to the idea of canonical Holy Scriptures. Soon more steps were taken in this direction. The so-called Deuteronomistic History ("the former prophets") and the writings of the prophets gained canonical status, a process which must have been essentially finished around 200 B.C. As far as the third portion of the canon, the so-called writings, is concerned, a long time was to elapse before consensus was reached concerning the books to be accepted. As late as the Synod of Jamnia, around A.D. 100, there were still differences of opinion concerning such books as Ecclesiastes, the Song of Solomon, and the book of Esther.

In the second place, it became an important task to apply the law to all the concrete details of daily life and to lay down precise rules for the Temple cult. The law was given by God to direct and guide men's lives; but in cases for which the existing law did not contain any concrete regulations, it now appeared imperative to supplement the law with concrete rules. In the pre-exilic period, the living tradition of the priests had regulated these matters; now all the individual regulations had to be derived from the fixed law code. Thus arose the profession of the scribe (*sōpēr*), whose task it was to study the Holy Scriptures and interpret them. Tradition considered Ezra the first scribe.

Ecclesiasticus contains an interesting passage depicting the ideal scribe:

> On the other hand he who devotes himself
>   to the study of the law of the Most High
> will seek out the wisdom of all the ancients,
>   and will be concerned with prophecies;
> he will preserve the discourse of notable men
>   and penetrate the subtleties of parables;
> he will seek out the hidden meanings of proverbs
>   and be at home with the obscurities of parables.
> He will serve among great men
>   and appear before rulers;
> . . . .
> He will direct his counsel and knowledge aright,
>   and meditate on his secrets.
> He will reveal instruction in his teaching,
>   and will glory in the law of the Lord's covenant.
> (Ecclus. 39:1-4a, 7-8)

This passage shows that the scribes studied not only the law, but all varieties of the religious tradition.

Naturally the scribal interpretation of the law depended for the most part on living tradition, especially that of the priestly circles, even though the demand was often made that the applications be derived from the words of scripture. Gradually, however, the theory of the oral Tora developed: God gave Moses not only the written law, but also additional instruction, and this latter has been transmitted orally ever since. This oral tradition was called the Mishna ("repetition"). Through this theory, the learned interpretation acquired almost the same authority as the Tora itself. This interpretation was long restricted solely to oral transmission; only in the second century C.E. was it reduced to writing.

In the third place, the triumph of the law can also be traced in the other literary *Gattungen*. The wisdom literature had previously developed an ideal of wisdom, which is identical with the fear of God and expresses itself in righteousness. As we have seen (p. 133), this wisdom consists in the submission to the order God has decreed for the world. Now in the book of Ecclesiasticus we find a completely new orientation.[1] Wisdom is now equated with the law (especially in chap. 24); in other words, the law is an expression of divine order, it instructs men in proper conduct. Wisdom and the law are both incarnations of God's revelation and therefore equal. Earlier, wisdom frequently appeared as the common possession of mankind; now, as law, it is God's gift to his chosen people Israel. The dynamism of the earlier wisdom has become static.

Fourthly: reflection on the law and its origin goes further. The law begins to be thought of as an absolute, eternal quantity. For Philo, it is a reflection of the eternal order of the cosmos.[2] In the *Pirqe Abot* (III, 14), we read that the law is the instrument by which the world was fashioned.

In practice, the law was the criterion of proper conduct, through which man could attain life. "Where there is much Tora, there is much life," says Hillel (*Pirqe Abot,* II, 7). But to obey the law presupposes thorough knowledge of the law; therefore study of the Tora becomes a sacred obligation. The first psalm in the psalter already bears witness to this attitude:

---

[1] O. Kaiser, "Die Begründung der Sittlichkeit im Buche Jesus Sirach," *ZThK,* XXXV (1958), 51 ff.; E. G. Bauckmann, "Die Proverbien und die Sprüche des Jesus Sirach," *ZAW,* LXXII (1960), 33 ff. See also J. L. Rylaarsdam, *Revelation in Jewish Wisdom Literature* (Chicago: University of Chicago Press, 1946), pp. 27 ff.

[2] Cf. below, p. 348; W. Bousset and H. Gressmann, *Die Religion des Judentums im späthellenistischen Zeitalter* (Tübingen: Mohr, 1926), p. 120.

Blessed is the man

. . . .

Whose delight is in the law of Yahweh,
and on his law he meditates day and night. (Ps. 1:2)

But this verse also demonstrates that study of the Tora was not felt to be onerous; on the contrary, we repeatedly find examples of great delight in the law. Even though individual commandments are sometimes not associated with any guiding principle, leading one to expect that they would be considered restrictive and a heavy burden for the individual, this turns out not to be true. The basic attitude toward the law is overwhelmingly positive.

The law is God's gift to Israel. It gives to Israel, as bearer of God's revelation, a special place among the nations. This creates a tension clearly visible in the life of postexilic Israel. On the one hand, Israel must keep itself distinct from the other nations in order to preserve the purity of the revelation. On the other hand, if it takes seriously the doctrine of the one God who is lord of all the world, it must hope for and promote recognition of Yahweh among the nations. The former tendency unquestionably dominates postexilic Judaism; for, after the return from Babylon, the most important task was to preserve what was specifically Israelite. The measures taken by Ezra and Nehemiah must be judged in this light. Other exponents of this point of view include the books of Esther and Judith and the Book of Jubilees.

Alongside this dominant tendency, nationalistic and particularistic, another tendency also appears, which is universalistic. In this regard the Book of Jonah[3] occupies a special position. We are dealing here with a legend that has no historical basis, which some scholars even interpret as an allegory.[4] It tells of a prophet Jonah whom Yahweh sent to Nineveh to announce its imminent punishment. The Ninevites are moved to do penance, and Yahweh withholds his punishment. Jonah, however, is furious, and thinks that Yahweh should not have spared the city. Through a sign, God makes clear to him that mercy is to be extended even to the non-Israelite nations. The point is obvious. Yahweh is the God of all nations, and is concerned for them all. God's revelation is valid for all nations, and the Jews must not evade the task of making it known to the others.

---

[3] H. Schmidt, *Jona, eine Untersuchung zur vergleichenden Religions-Geschichte* (Tübingen: Mohr, 1907); A. Feuillet, "Les sources du livre de Jona," *RB*, LIV (1947), 161 ff.; *idem*, "Le sens du livre de Jona," *ibid.*, pp. 340 ff.

[4] E.g., J. A. Smart, "Jonah," in *The Interpreter's Bible* (Nashville: Abingdon, 1956), VI, 871 ff.

The book of Ruth is commonly held to exhibit this same tendency,[5] since it tells of a Moabite woman who married an Israelite and thus became an ancestress of David. There are objections, however, to the postexilic dating of the book.[6] One would also expect that if such a tendency were really present, it would be more in evidence.

The postexilic prophets, however, do contain several passages that follow Deutero-Isaiah in expressing universalistic sentiments. Zechariah speaks of a time when the nations will come to Jerusalem to worship Yahweh (Zech. 8:20-22).[7] In the postexilic sections of the book of Isaiah ("Trito-Isaiah"), we find references to "foreigners who have joined themselves to Yahweh" (Isa. 56:3), that is, Gentile converts to the Jewish religion. These cases naturally presuppose that the Gentiles acknowledge Yahweh as the only God and Israel's special position. We do not have here an unconditional universalism. When Malachi says that the nations present pure offerings to Yahweh (Mal. 1:11), he probably does not mean that the Gentiles worshiped Yahweh; he is using here an exaggerated mode of expression to make his listeners ashamed: even the Gentiles worship God with purer worship than do the Israelites.

In postexilic Israel, then, there is no single or unambiguous answer to this question. On the whole, the nationalistic and particularistic tendency carried the day, although there were always proselytes, i.e., Gentiles who conformed to Judaism.[8]

---

[5] Cf. W. E. Staples, "The Book of Ruth," *AJSL*, LIII (1937), 145 f.; A. Jepsen, "Das Buch Ruth," *Theologische Studien und Kritiken*, CVIII (1937/38), 416 ff.

[6] Cf., for example, H. W. Hertzberg, *Die Bücher Josua, Richter, Ruth* (Göttingen: Vandenhoeck & Ruprecht, 1959), p. 259.

[7] This passage may be a later addition.

[8] Cf. Bousset and Gressmann, *op. cit.*, pp. 76 ff.; G. F. Moore, *Judaism in the First Centuries of the Christian Era* (Cambridge: Harvard, 1927), I, 323 ff.; W. G. Braude, *Jewish Proselyting* (Providence: Brown, 1940); P. Dalbert, *Die Theologie der jüdisch-hellenistischen Missionsliteratur* (Hamburg: Reich, 1954).

3.

GOD AND THE ANGELS

The God of postexilic Judaism is of course the same Yahweh worshiped by Israel since the time of Moses. In general, the postexilic concept of God is identical with that which preceded it. God continues to be holy, great, almighty, omniscient, wise, just, good, and merciful.[1] Nevertheless, a certain unmistakable shift does take place in the concept of God.

First, there are numerous passages emphasizing God's uniqueness. In the pre-exilic period, we found such passages only in the enthronement psalms. Deutero-Isaiah, using these passages as a basis, was the first to arrive at formulations that can definitely be termed monotheistic. Now such statements are quite common in the Apocrypha and pseudepigrapha. "He alone is God," we read in II Maccabees 7:37, nor "is there any other god" (Wisd. of Sol. 12:13). In contrast to the "dumb idols of the heathen, which can neither speak nor aid" (III Macc. 4:16), stands God the living Lord (II Macc. 7:33; 15:4), the true God (III Macc. 6:18), the king of the universe (II Macc. 7:9), the sovereign of all authority (II Macc. 3:24). We find such new epithets as "the everlasting God" (*theos aiōnios*; e.g., Eth. Enoch 75:3; Jub. 12:29; 13:8; Bar. 4:8, 10, 14; etc.); the Immortal One (in the Sybilline Oracles).[2] Of course Yahweh had always been "the living God," but Hellenistic influence is probably at work here, at least indirectly.

Second, special emphasis is placed on those epithets that stress God's exalted transcendence. Terms such as the Almighty (*pantokratōr*), the Exalted One, the Great Holy One, the Lord of Glory, the Lord or God of Heaven, the Lord of Lords, the King of Kings, and the God of

---

[1] Abundant citations can be found in L. Couard, *Die religiösen und sittlichen Anschauungen der alttestamentlichen Apokryphen und Pseudepigraphen* (Gütersloh: Bertelsmann, 1907), pp. 36 ff.; W. Bousset and H. Gressmann, *Die Religion des Judentums im späthellenistischen Zeitalter* (Tübingen: Mohr, 1926), p. 312, note. Cf. also H. J. Wicks, *The Doctrine of God in the Jewish Apocrypha and Apocalyptic Literature* (London: Hunter & Longhurst, 1915).

[2] Bousset and Gressmann, *op. cit.*, pp. 311 f.

Gods are typical. In this category we also find the translation of 'elyôn as the Most High (hupsistos).

Third, this tendency is associated with the avoidance of the divine name "Yahweh."[3] The Septuagint renders it as kurios, "Lord." According to the Mishna, the name "Yahweh" was pronounced only in the Temple cult; elsewhere it was replaced by ădōnāy, "Lord." It is impossible to determine precisely when this custom came into use. The documents from Qumran also tend to avoid the name of Yahweh;[4] they do not, however, use ădōnāy as a substitute.

A considerable number of such circumlocutions were used to avoid using the name of God directly. The book of Daniel speaks of the "ancient of days" (Dan. 7:9); in Ethiopic Enoch we read, "I saw therein a high throne . . . and on it sat the Great Glory [i.e., God]" (Eth. Enoch 14:18 f.; cf. also Ecclus. 17:13; Tob. 3:16). The writer often refers to "heaven" when he actually means God (Dan. 4:23; Eth. Enoch 22:5 f.; and especially the books of the Maccabees). (We also find this phenomenon in early Persian sources, particularly when they are speaking of God as Fate.[5]) In colloquial speech, haššēm, "the name," is used in place of "God."

God's presence is referred to by the word "Shekinah" (šekînâ, lit. "dwelling"). It originally referred to God's presence in the Temple; it therefore comes to be used when God enters into relationship with men.[6] The Targumim often avoid literal translation of such phrases as "God said," or "God spoke"; they choose instead to use periphrases involving such words as dibbûr, mēmrâ, "speaking," or "the word."[7] Thus the translation runs "Speaking said . . ." or "The word spoke . . . ." The word, as it were, becomes semi-autonomous, interposing between God and man, and serving as a channel used by God to communicate his will to man.[8] The Old Testament itself contains the roots of this idea; there the word (dābār) can occasionally appear as a semi-autonomous entity.[9] The Johannine concept of the Logos probably cannot be completely divorced from this complex of ideas, although Hellenistic concepts may also be involved here. The later Jewish conception of the bat qôl, the voice of God speaking from heaven,

---

[3] Ibid., pp. 307 ff.

[4] H. Ringgren, The Faith of Qumran: Theology of the Dead Sea Scrolls, trans. E. T. Sander (Philadelphia: Fortress, 1963), pp. 47-48.

[5] H. Ringgren, Fatalism in Persian Epics, 1952, pp. 49 ff.

[6] Bousset and Gressmann, op. cit., p. 315; M. Kadushin, The Rabbinic Mind (New York: Jewish Theological Seminary, 1952), pp. 222 ff.

[7] V. Hamp, Der Begriff "Wort" in den aramäischen Bibelübersetzungen, 1938.

[8] H. Ringgren, Word and Wisdom (Lund: Ohlsson, 1947), pp. 157 ff.

[9] L. Dürr, Die Wertung des göttlichen Wortes (Leipzig: Hinrichs, 1938), pp. 122 ff.

seems to represent a further development of the *dibbûr* and *mēmrâ* concept.[10]

Behind all of this there lies, of course, a dread of profaning what is holy, so to speak, by too great familiarity. This emphasis on God's transcendence by no means implies a lack of appreciation for God's work in the human world. These circumlocutions were in fact created in order to express God's close relationship to man while preserving his holiness and majesty.[11]

In many, perhaps most, cases, what we are dealing with here is merely a stylistic device, a substitute for the divine name and God's activity. Occasionally, however, the abstract concept becomes semi-autonomous, appearing as an almost independent entity, half personified. This process is called hypostatization.[12] Among the concepts discussed above, this tendency operates most noticeably on the word; but other concepts were personified to an even greater degree. This is especially true of the spirit and wisdom.

The spirit or the holy spirit[13] appears in the Book of Wisdom, for example, as a holy, ethical principle in the world, a divine force that permeates the world and holds it together (Wisd. of Sol. 1:7) and teaches men God's will (Wisd. of Sol. 9:17). In one passage (Mart. Isa. 5:14), the spirit is depicted as a personal being, with whom Isaiah speaks. In the same work, the spirit seems several times to be thought of as an angel (4:21; 9:39 f.; 10:4; 11:4). In Judith 16:14, the spirit of God appears as a creative principle: "For thou didst speak, and they [all creatures] were made. Thou didst send forth thy Spirit and it formed them." In the rabbinic writings, the holy spirit (or more literally, the spirit of holiness, *rûaḥ haqqōdeš*) appears primarily as the mediator of divine revelation in the Holy Scriptures. When quoting a passage from Scripture, a writer often uses the words, "The holy spirit says."

Wisdom (Heb. *ḥokmâ*, Gk. *sophia*) is already personified in the introductory chapters of the Book of Proverbs.[14] She was called into being before the beginning of the earth and assisted when God created the world (Prov. 8:22-31). She has built a house and invites men to her feast (Prov. 9:1-6; cf. also 1:20 f.). This figure thus represents

---

[10] Cf. S. Liebermann, *Hellenism in Jewish Palestine* (New York: Jewish Theological Seminary, 1950), pp. 194 ff.; Kadushin, *op. cit.*, pp. 261 ff.; K. Schubert, *Die Religion des nachbiblischen Judentums* (Freiburg: Herder, 1955), p. 6.

[11] This point is especially emphasized by J. Abelson, *The Immanence of God in Rabbinic Literature* (London: Macmillan, 1912).

[12] Cf. H. Ringgren, "Hypostasen," *RGG*, cols. 504 ff.

[13] P. Volz, *Der Geist Gottes und die verwandten Erscheinungen im Alten Testament und im anschliessenden Judentum* (Tübingen: Mohr, 1910); Ringgren, *Word and Wisdom*, pp. 165 ff.

[14] Ringgren, *Word and Wisdom*, pp. 95 ff.

both the divine wisdom that was revealed in creation and the divinely sanctioned instruction of the teachers of wisdom, the goal of which is to discover the order that upholds the world. In other words, wisdom is both a divine attribute, a universal principle, and also a guiding revelation; these two features are present when wisdom is hypostatized. In Ecclesiasticus, where wisdom is identified with the law, we find the same personification:[15] wisdom was created by God (Ecclus. 1:9); she dwells in heaven and permeates the universe, but seeks a place to lodge and finds it in Israel (Ecclus. 24:4-11). Here wisdom is conceived as a universal principle and divine revelation, which takes concrete form in the law. There are also several interesting passages, both in Proverbs and in Ecclesiasticus, that depict the relationship between wisdom and her disciples in terms of love or marriage:[16]

> Say to wisdom, "You are my sister,"
> and call insight your intimate friend. (Prov. 7:4)
> Do not forsake her, and she will keep you;
> love her, and she will guard you. (Prov. 4:6)
> Blessed is the man who meditates on wisdom,
> . . . .
> He who peers through her windows
> will also listen at her doors.
> . . . .
> She will come to meet him like a mother,
> and like the wife of his youth she will welcome him.
>   (Ecclus. 14:20, 23; 18:2)
>
> My desire yearned for her,
> and my face did not turn away from her.
> My hand opened her gates,
> and I circled her and gazed upon her. (Ecclus. 51:19)[17]

Probably wisdom is here introduced as the superior counterpart to a mother-goddess or goddess of love: the disciple of wisdom should forsake idolatry and devote himself to the study of wisdom. Thus the hypostatization may have taken place under the influence of other deities, gaining thereby a more concrete form.[18]

In the postexilic period, the ancient conception of Yahweh's heavenly court is transformed into a highly developed doctrine of angels.[19] The

---

15 *Ibid.,* pp. 106 ff.

16 *Ibid.,* pp. 106, 111 f.

17 [This final passage is the author's own translation, based upon the Hebrew text; the Greek is considerably different (cf. RSV).—TRANS.]

18 Ringgren, *Word and Wisdom,* pp. 133 f.; cf. G. von Rad, *Old Testament Theology,* trans. D. M. G. Stalker (Edinburgh & London: Oliver & Boyd, 1962), p. 444.

19 E. Langton, *The Ministries of the Angelic Powers,* 1937; G. W. Heidt, *Angelology of the Old Testament* (Washington: Catholic University of

angels are thought to wait upon God and to serve him. According to Jubilees 2:2, they were made on the first day of creation. They were holy, eternal, and immortal beings (Eth. Enoch 15:4, 6; Jub. 1:25; 15:31). In heaven they stand before God, praising and glorifying him (Ecclus. 42:17; Eth. Enoch 39:12); but their primary function, as God's servants, is to carry out his will (Tob. 12:18; Ecclus. 43:26). They are commissioned by God to protect mankind and intervene in perilous situations. They receive the prayers of men and bring them before God's throne (Tob. 12:15); they also act as intercessors (Eth. Enoch 9:4 ff.; 15:2; 39:5; Test. Levi 3:5). The nation of Israel as a whole has a guardian angel, whose name is Michael (Dan. 10:13, 21; 12:1). In addition, all the other nations have their own guardian angels (Ecclus. 17:17).[20] Other angels function as avenging angels, i.e., they carry out God's punishment against the wicked (Eth. Enoch 56:1 ff.; 62:11; 63:1; Test. Levi 5).

In contrast to the views of earlier periods, Judaism divides the angels into various ranks. The first rank comprises the angels of the presence (Heb. *mal'ak pānîm*)[21] or archangels (Gk. *archangelos*). Their number is not known; we usually hear of four or seven archangels. The names of the four are Gabriel, Michael, Raphael, and Uriel (Eth. Enoch 9:1. Cf. Tob. 3:16; 5:4; etc. where only the first three are mentioned. Eth. Enoch 20 names six: Uriel, Raphael, Raguel, Michael, Sariel, and Gabriel. IV Esdras 4:36 adds a seventh, Jeremiel). Various other classes of angels are also mentioned: powers, dominions, princes, throne angels, etc., as well as individual figures like the angel of peace ("mediator between God and man for the peace of Israel," Test. Dan 6). Ethiopic Enoch 61:10 speaks of "powers that are upon the land and over the water"; each of them rules over one element of nature (hence the name "elemental spirits"): we find, for example, the angel of fire, of wind, of darkness, of snow, of lightning, etc. (Jub. 2:2; Eth. Enoch 60:11-21; cf. also ${}_1$QH i.8-15). The Qumran documents mention a great number of angels or spirits,[22] and declare that thousands and tens of thousands of angels are present in the midst of the community (${}_1$QM xii.1-9).[23] The Mishna expressly forbids angel worship[24]—worship belongs to God alone; the angels are only his servants.

America, 1949); H. Bietenhard, *Die himmlische Welt im Urchristentum und Spätjudentum* (Tübingen: Mohr, 1951).

[20] A. V. Ström, *Vetekornet* (Stockholm: Svenska kyrkans bokförlag, 1944), pp. 143 ff.; cf. W. Lueken, *Michael* (Göttingen: Vandenhoeck & Ruprecht, 1898).

[21] Bousset and Gressmann, *op. cit.,* pp. 325 ff.

[22] J. Strugnell, "The Angelic Liturgy at Qumran," *SVT,* VII (1960), 330 ff.

[23] H. Ringgren, *The Faith of Qumran,* pp. 84 f.

[24] Lueken, *op. cit.,* pp. 6 f.

A further question deserves at least to be stated: did Judaism's angelology develop under foreign influence? With reference to the archangels, for example, scholars have pointed to the Persian Amesha Spentas or the astral deities of Babylonia.[25] But the very fact that there is no fixed number of archangels speaks against a direct borrowing. Furthermore, the functions of the Jewish archangels by no means correspond to those of the Amesha Spentas or the planet gods. It is possible, however, that the number of the archangels was fixed at six or seven because of Persian or Babylonian influence. The other aspects ancient concept of the heavenly court.[26] This explanation seems all of angelology, though, can probably be explained on the basis of the the more likely because the apocalyptic writings, with their mythological overtones, made the most extensive use of a highly developed angelology. The idea of elemental spirits may have some connection with Hellenistic concepts.

[25] Bousset and Gressmann, *op. cit.*, pp. 325 ff., 499 ff.
[26] K. Schubert, *TLZ*, LXXVIII (1953), col. 502.

4.

SATAN AND DEMONS

Pre-exilic Israel believed that everything, both good and evil, came from Yahweh. "He kills, and he brings to life."[1] Deutero-Isaiah still emphasizes that both light and darkness come from God (Isa. 45:7). In the postexilic period, this conception begins to change. The conclusion has been reached that Yahweh, the exalted and holy God, is exclusively good; the origin of evil must be sought elsewhere. Now the figure of Satan makes its appearance as God's antagonist.[2]

Satan appears only three times in the canonical books of the Old Testament. He appears in the prologue of the Book of Job, called "the adversary" (with the definite article, and therefore not a proper name); he seems to be a kind of prosecuting attorney in the heavenly council, bringing charges against Job (Job 1:6 ff.; 2:1 ff.). He performs a similar function in one of the night visions of Zechariah: there he accuses Joshua the high priest before God (Zech. 3:1 ff.). In these two cases, he stands in God's service and is not thought of as an evil being. The third passage is somewhat different. II Samuel 24:1 tells how Yahweh incited David to carry out his disastrous census. When the Chronicler came to describe the same event, the idea that Yahweh could be the author of anything evil offended his theological sensibilities, and he therefore changed the verse to read, "Satan [no article!] stood up against Israel, and incited David to number Israel" (I Chron. 21:1).[3]

In the pseudepigraphic literature—and therefore primarily in the realm of apocalyptic—the development continues.[4] As author and

---

[1] See above, pp. 72 f.

[2] H. Ringgren, *Word and Wisdom* (Lund: Ohlsson, 1947), pp. 169 f., with additional bibliography; B. Noack, *Satanas und Soteria*, 1948, pp. 13 f., 19 ff.

[3] In similar fashion, the Book of Jubilees reinterpreted the statement of Exod. 4:24 that Yahweh met Moses and tried to kill him, saying instead that Mastema attacked Moses (Jub. 48:2).

[4] W. Bousset and H. Gressmann, *Religion des Judentums im spät-*

313

representative of evil we find here a prince of the evil spirits, who
bears various names: Satan, Mastema (only in the Book of Jubilees),
Belial or Beliar (Heb. *beliya'al*, "worthlessness"; primarily in the
Testaments of the Twelve Patriarchs and the Qumran documents),
and, in Greek, *diabolos* ("slanderer"). He, together with his angels
and powers, constitutes the realm of evil, and seeks to lead men to
destruction and ruin. It was he who tempted the first human beings
to sin; it was he who aided the Egyptians before and during the exodus
of the Israelites; it is he who causes all evil and all sins. Through him
death entered the world (Wisd. of Sol. 2:24). He is the prince of
lawlessness, the ruler of this world (Mart. Isa. 2:4); he stands in complete antithesis to God. At the end of the world, he will be conquered,
bound, and destroyed by God.

There was naturally much speculation about the origin of Satan. It
is noteworthy that the conclusion was never drawn that Satan had
existed beside God from the beginning. Judaism has never taught a
thorough-going dualism. Attempts have instead been made somehow
to explain the appearance of evil as a fall within God's creation, because it is impossible that God, who is good, could have created evil
beings. Recourse has usually been had to the story of the fallen angels
in Genesis 6:1 ff. These angels (or "sons of God," as they are called)
were once created good by God; but they fell and were imprisoned.
Their descendants, the demons, inhabit the earth. We find this explanation primarily in Ethiopic Enoch (15:8—16:4; cf. also Jub. 4:22;
5:1 ff.).[5] A later work, the Life of Adam and Eve, informs us that
Satan was an angel who refused to worship Adam as the likeness of
God, exalted himself above the stars, and was therefore cast down
from heaven. There is probably some connection between this story
and the myth of the fallen Day Star (Isa. 14:12 f.). Since the Latin
term for the Day Star is Lucifer, "Lucifer" later became another term
for Satan. The Qumran documents present a third explanation: God
created both a good spirit and an evil spirit, and gave them authority
over mankind.[6] Nowhere, then, do we find two equivalent powers, i.e.,
a real dualism.

This observation is important when any attempt is made to determine the origin of the figure of Satan. An outspoken dualism in

hellenistischen Zeitalter (Tübingen: Mohr, 1926), pp. 332 ff. Satan appears
only once in the Apocrypha: Wisd. of Sol. 2:24 (*diabolos*), translated
"the devil" by the RSV.

5 B. Reicke, *The Disobedient Spirits* (Copenhagen: Munksgaard, 1946),
pp. 52 ff.

6 H. Ringgren, *The Faith of Qumran*, trans. E. T. Sander (Philadelphia:
Fortress, 1963), pp. 68 ff. "Spirit" may here be meant in a psychological
sense, equivalent to "disposition." In this case, there would be no mention
of two beings. Cf. P. Wernberg-Möller, "A Reconsideration of the Two
Spirits in the Rule of the Community," *RQ*, III (1961), 413 ff.; M.
Treves, "The Two Spirits in the Rule of the Community," *ibid.*, pp. 449 ff.

proximity to Judaism is to be found in the Persian religion, where
Ormazd and Ahriman appear as the good god and the evil god. It is
hardly conceivable that the limited dualism of Judaism came into being
without Persian influence. Any attempt to give more particulars about
the nature of this influence, however, runs into difficulties.[7] The closest
approach to the Persian view is found in the Qumran community, with
their doctrine of the two spirits created by God; this agrees precisely
with the conceptions of Zervanism.[8] With this exception, though, the
Jewish conceptions of Satan can hardly derive immediately from Persia.
Perhaps instead we should think in terms of a general tendency to seek
a solution to the problem of evil in a more or less thoroughly dualistic
frame of reference, a tendency intensified within Judaism by Iranian
influence.[9]

As is always true when ideas are borrowed, certain necessary conditions for these developments were already present, in this case even
before the exile.[10] The idea that everything, even evil, comes from
Yahweh sometimes assumed strange forms and was presented in very
concrete terms. When Yahweh's spirit departs from Saul, an evil spirit
from Yahweh comes upon him (I Sam. 16:14; 18:10; 19:9). In the
remarkable encounter between Micaiah and the false prophets, the
spirit of God becomes a lying spirit, which puts lies in the mouth of
the false prophets (I Kings 22:22). In other words, we find a tendency to give concrete expression to the power that goes forth from
God: sometimes it is a good spirit, sometimes an evil spirit. The
obvious next step is to concentrate the forces of evil in a personal
figure. This figure was associated with the conception of the accuser
in the heavenly council. Finally, with an admixture of Persian ideas,
the Jewish conception of Satan developed.

As far as the other evil spirits are concerned,[11] one fact deserves
special emphasis. In the apocalyptic writings, the primary function of
the evil spirits is to tempt men into sin. The criteria are therefore
ethical. In the Testaments of the Twelve Patriarchs, specific sins are
even personified as evil or lying spirits (Test. Reub. 2:1; 3:3 ff.). This
fact is clearly associated with the general tendency of the Testaments

[7] On the question of Persian influence in general, cf. J. Duchesne-
Guillemin, *Ohrmazd et Ahriman,* 1953, pp. 71 ff.; G. Widengren, "Stand
und Aufgaben der iranischen Religions-Geschichte," *Numen,* II (1955),
107 ff.

[8] K. G. Kuhn, "Die Sektenschrift und die iranische Religion," *ZThK,*
XLIX (1952), 296 ff.; H. Michaud, "Un mythe zervanite dans un des
manuscrits de Qumran," *VT,* V (1955), 137 ff.; J. Duchesne-Guillemin,
"Le Zervanisme et les manuscrits de la Mer Morte," *IIJ,* I (1957), 96 ff.

[9] Cf. G. Widengren, *op. cit.,* p. 108.

[10] See H. Ringgren, *Word and Wisdom,* pp. 168 f.

[11] E. Langton, *Essentials of Demonology* (London: Epworth, 1949);
B. Noack, *op. cit.*

to term psychological traits and attitudes "spirits." In other words, in accord with normal Hebrew usage, the approximate meaning of "spirit" here is "disposition"; the vivid language of the Testaments personifies this concept.[12] Only occasionally do we find in the pseudepigrapha instances of demons that bring misfortune or are associate with magic, etc. (Eth. Enoch 15:11; 69:12; CD 14:5).

In rabbinic literature, on the other hand, the demons' function is to cause injury to life and limb; they are bearers of disease, for example. Spirits as tempters are rarely mentioned. This rabbinic conception is closest to the ancient belief in demons, and is also found occasionally in the Apocrypha. Asmodeus, in the Book of Tobit (3:8, 17; 6:7, 14 ff.), is such a destructive demon. His name (probably derived from *aēšma daēva*), furthermore, may suggest a Persian origin.[13]

Occasionally the evil beings appear to fall into two distinct classes. In Tobit 6:7, we find a demon (*daimonion*) and an evil spirit (*pnuema ponēron*) presented side by side as alternatives. Ethiopic Enoch 19:1 says that the spirits of the fallen angels tempt men to offer sacrifice to the demons—here, then, the evil spirits are distinct from the demons, which apparently represent pagan gods. Evil spirits are commonly found in the apocalyptic writings and are ignored by the rabbinic writings; demons simply represent a continuation of ancient beliefs, surviving especially among the common people.

Thus arose the conception of a structured realm of evil hostile to God's sovereignty, in which all kinds of evil beings serve as Satan's ministers or angels. This view had important consequences for the history of religion, because it was the world view taken for granted by early Christianity.

---

[12] Cf. R. Eppel, *Le piétisme juif dans les Testaments des douze patriarches*, 1930, pp. 121 f.; B. Otzen, "Die neugefundenen hebräischen Sektenschriften und die Testamente der zwölf Patriarchen," *STh*, VII (1953), 125 ff., esp. 136 ff.

[13] Admittedly there is no instance in Persia of the combination *aēšma daēva*; rabbinic sources derive the name from the verb *šāmad*, "destroy." Cf. *RGG*, I, col. 649.

5.

GOD AND THE WORLD

There has never been any doubt that God is the unique creator of the heavens and the earth, along with the entire universe. In this regard the postexilic period has nothing new to offer. One fact only deserves mention in this connection. There are a few passages that give evidence of reflection on how creation took place and some new conclusions arrived at.

Wisdom of Solomon 11:17 says that God's all-powerful hand created the world out of formless matter (*ex amorphou hulēs*). This may show the influence of Hellenistic ideas, especially from Platonism;[1] but in the last analysis this passage does not go beyond the creation account of Genesis 1, which also says that the world was created out of chaos.

II Maccabees 7:28 presents a completely different conception. Here we read, "Recognize that God made them out of things that did not exist" (*ouk ex ontōn*), which probably should be understood as meaning creation *ex nihilo*. A few other passages refer to the creative word of God (Ecclus. 43:10; Wisd. of Sol. 9:1; Jth. 16:14; Pr. Man. 3) without saying anything on the problem of creation *ex nihilo*.

The conviction that God upholds the world and guides the course of history remains a basic tenet of the Jewish faith. But apocalyptic so heightens the conception that God guides history that we can speak of historical predestination in the strict sense. "He has weighed the age in the balance, and measured the times by measure, and numbered the times by number; and he will not move or arouse them until that measure is fulfilled" (II Esd. 4:36 f.). When the time determined by God comes, all things, which he alone created, will also find their end in him (II Esd. 6:61). In the Qumran documents, this idea appears in its most extreme form: "From the God of knowledge comes all that is and that is to be, and before they came into being he prepared all their thoughts. And when they came into being according to his predestination, according to his glorious plan, they fulfill their work; without anything being changed" (1QS iii.15 f.). ". . . according to God's will and predestination concerning that which will come to pass:

---

[1] But cf. J. Fichtner, *Weisheit Salomos* (Tübingen: Mohr, 1938), p. 45.

317

and it comes to pass, and it is not invalid, and without that nothing has come to pass, neither shall it come to pass, since the God of knowledge has prepared it, and there is none beside him" (1QH xii.9-11).[2] This strict doctrine of predestination was accepted only in certain circles, of course.

In his governance of the world, God is guided by his righteousness. When the wisdom literature can still state that good things and bad, life and death, poverty and wealth, come from the Lord (Ecclus. 11:14), it obviously implies that God apportions good and evil according to men's deeds. The religious man, who fulfills the law, receives good; the lot of the sinner is ruin. It should be noted that Ecclesiasticus substitutes the law for the divinely ordained order of earlier wisdom.

There is nevertheless no lack of evidence that men racked their brains over those cases for which the doctrine of reward and punishment does not hold true. The Book of Ecclesiastes ("The Preacher") speaks of the vanity of all human effort and the impossibility of understanding God's actions.[3] That there could be any relationship between man and the divinely ordained course of the world seems to him to be out of the question. Everything takes place in an eternal circle according to fixed laws; nothing can alter this. Fate treats the righteous and the sinner alike, all must die, and man's efforts are to no avail. All man can do is be on his guard and enjoy life as much as possible. This book is probably one Israelite's reaction to the dissolution of Israel's old homogeneous culture and the old concept of righteousness.[4]

The Wisdom of Solomon presents a completely different solution.[5] It speaks at length of the suffering of the righteous, but also supplies a positive answer: God created man, and the souls of the righteous are in his hand (Wisd. of Sol. 2:23; 3:1). Even when they seem to have died, their hope for immortality remains, and in the time of their visitation they will shine forth (Wisd. of Sol. 3:2, 4, 7). References to vindication after death can also be found elsewhere (e.g., II Macc. 7:9, 14, 36).[6]

---

[2] H. Ringgren, *The Faith of Qumran,* trans. E. T. Sander (Philadelphia: Fortress, 1963), pp. 53 f.

[3] K. Galling, "Stand und Aufgabe der Koheletforschung," *ThR,* VI (1934), 353 ff.; *idem, Die Krise der Aufklärung in Israel,* 1952; R. Gordis, *Koheleth, the Man and his World* (New York: Jewish Theological Seminary, 1955). W. Zimmerli's commentary in "Das Alte Testament Deutsch" contains further bibliographical material.

[4] J. Pedersen, "Scepticisme israélite," *RHPR,* X (1930), 317 ff.

[5] Commentaries: J. Fichtner, *op. cit.* (in Eissfeldt's "Handbuch zum Alten Testament"); J. Reider, *The Book of Wisdom* (New York: Harper, 1957). See also J. Fichtner, "Die Stellung der Sapientia Salomonis in der Literatur- und Geistesgeschichte ihrer Zeit," *ZNW,* XXXVI (1937), 113 ff.; G. Ziener, *Die theologische Begriffssprache im Buche der Weisheit* (Bonn: Hanstein, 1956).

[6] See also below, p. 322.

6.

MAN BEFORE GOD

A two-fold transformation can be observed in the anthropology of postexilic Judaism, especially toward the end of this period. In the first place, the distinction between spirit (*rûaḥ, pneuma*) and soul (*nepeš, psuchē*) becomes more and more vague; in many respects, the two are felt to be equivalent. In the second place, though, the old view of man as a unity is for the most part given up, so that body and soul now appear as essentially different components of man. This dichotomy is basically alien to the old Israelite conception; it doubtless arose under Greek (Hellenistic) influence.[1] The development outlined here only took place toward the end of the period we are considering. It is intimately associated with the idea of the immortality of the soul and the conception of individual retribution after death.

The idea of immortality is unknown to the earlier apocryphal books. Ecclesiasticus and I Maccabees are unacquainted with it. The Book of the Wisdom of Solomon, however, states clearly that man was created for incorruption (Wisd. of Sol. 2:23), and the righteous are promised immortality and eternal life (1:15; 4:1; 5:15 f.).[2] A clear contrast is made between the mortal body and the immortal soul (or spirit). In Ethiopic Enoch 103:5, for example, we read, "The spirits of you who die in righteousness shall live, rejoice, and be glad: their spirits shall not pass away." Jubilees 23:31 is probably making the same point: "Their bones shall rest in the earth, and their spirit shall have great joy." The so-called Fourth Book of Maccabees, which bears a markedly Hellenistic stamp, speaks quite unambiguously of the immortality of the soul (14:6; 18:23; *et al.*)[3]

---

[1] Cf. R. Meyer, *Hellenistisches in der rabbinischen Anthropologie*, 1957.
[2] H. Bückers, *Die Unsterblichkeitslehre des Weisheitsbuches* (Münster: Aschendorff, 1938); M. Delcor, "L'immortalité de l'âme dans le livre de la Sagesse et dans les documents de Qumran," *NRT*, LXXVII (1955), 614 ff.
[3] Cf. J. Frey, "La vie de l'au-delà dans les conceptions juives au temps de Jésus Christ," *Biblica*, XXXIII (1952), 129 ff.; J. van der Ploeg, "L'immortalité de l'homme d'après les textes de la Mer Morte," *VT*, II (1952), 171 ff.

Despite all this, the Hellenistic view that sees in the body something evil, a prison of the soul, and the origin of all sin never really took root in Judaism. The Book of the Wisdom of Solomon hints at it once in passing: "For a perishable body weighs down the soul, and this earthly tent burdens the thoughtful mind" (Wisd. of Sol. 9:15). On the other hand, the awareness persists that man is flesh, i.e., weak, imperfect, and mortal.[4]

No man is pure in the sight of God. This had already been stated by the Psalms (e.g., 130:3) and the Book of Job (e.g., 9:2 f.). The writings of later Judaism also express the idea frequently. In the Book of Jubilees (21:21; cf. also 23:17), we read, "All the works of the children of men are sin and wickedness, and all their works are impurity, condemnation, and defilement, and there is no righteousness in them." II Esdras puts it quite straightforwardly: "Who among the living is there that has not sinned?" (7:46) and "There is no one among those who have been born who has not acted wickedly" (8:35). The Thanksgiving Psalms from Qumran witness to a similar sense of sin: "God is righteous, but to the children of men belong the service of iniquity and works of deceit" (1QH i.27). Man is in a state of sin from his very birth, and guilty of faithlessness until his old age (1QH iv.29 f.). No man has righteousness; only the help of God makes his way blameless (*ibid.*, 30 f.), etc.[5]

Men now begin to meditate more on the origin and cause of sin; three major explanations are ventured in this realm. One we have already discussed, namely, the theory that Satan and his evil spirits bring sin into the world. There are occasional allusions to the consequences of the fall; one of the first is Ecclesiasticus 25:24: "From a woman sin had its beginning, and because of her we all die" (cf. also Wisd. of Sol. 2:24); later, II Esdras and the Syriac Book of Baruch frequently refer to this theory, e.g., "O Adam, what have you done? For though it was you who sinned, the fall was not yours alone, but ours also who are your descendants" (II Esd. 7:118).[6]

A third attempt at a solution is represented by the assumption of an evil inclination in man; this solution takes Genesis 6:5 and 8:21 as its point of departure. We find it already in Ecclesiasticus 15:14 f.: "It was he who created man in the beginning, and left him in the power of his own inclination. If you will, you can keep the commandments, and to act faithfully is a matter of your own choice."

---

[4] Cf. K. G. Kuhn, "Peirasmos—hamartia—sarx im NT," *ZThK*, XLIX (1952), 200 ff.; E. Schweizer, "Röm. 1,3 f. und der Gegensatz von Fleisch und Geist vor und bei Paulus," *ETh*, I (1955), 563 ff.; also E. Schweizer and R. Meyer, "Fleisch im Judentum," in *TWNT*, VII, 109 ff.

[5] H. Ringgren, *The Faith of Qumran*, trans. E. T. Sander (Philadelphia: Fortress, 1963), pp. 101 f.

[6] W. Bousset and H. Gressmann, *Die Religion des Judentums im späthellenistischen Zeitalter* (Tübingen: Mohr, 1926), pp. 407 f.

This passage clearly means that God created man good, but also delivered him over (after the fall?) to his own evil inclination; the law, however, shows men how to overcome this inclination (cf. later Qiddushim 30 b). This same view is represented by II Esdras, which speaks of the "evil heart" and the "evil root" which are the cause of sin (3:20 ff.; 7:48).

The rabbinic writings systematize this doctrine, speaking of a good inclination (*yēṣer tôb*) and an evil inclination (*yēṣer ra‘*).[7]

Whoever sins is punished.[8] Every misfortune that befalls an individual or a nation is seen as God's punishment for sins that have been committed. But whoever acknowledges his sins and does penance can hope for God's mercy.[9] The Lord grants forgiveness to the man who humbles himself before him and confesses his sins. Ecclesiasticus warns against being overconfident and adding sin to sin, trusting in God's forgiveness (Ecclus. 5:5 ff.). But the dominent tendency on the whole is to eliminate the tension between God's wrath and his mercy through precise regulation of penance. Judaism places its primary emphasis on the fact that man is free to obey the commandments and thereby achieve life.

---

[7] G. F. Moore, *Judaism* (Cambridge: Harvard, 1927-31), I, 489 ff.; S. Schechter, *Some Aspects of Rabbinic Theology* (London: Adam & Black, 1909), pp. 264 ff.

[8] Å. Sjöberg, *Gott und die Sünder im palästinischen Judentum* (Stuttgart: Kohlhammer, 1939), pp. 30 ff., 72 ff., 95 ff.

[9] *Ibid.*, pp. 42 ff., 86 ff., 109 ff.

7.

RESURRECTION

In postexilic Judaism, opinions are sharply divided on the doctrine of the afterlife. Ecclesiastes expresses the conviction that man is basically no different from the animals: they die, and that is that (Eccles. 3:19 f.). Even in Ecclesiasticus we still find the conception of a realm of the dead (Gk. *hadēs*, i.e., Sheol), in which the departed lead a shadowy existence, and where one cannot sing God's praises (Ecclus. 14:16; 17:27 f.). But besides such statements we find, even in the earlier period, isolated passages looking forward to a resurrection of the dead.[1]

The earliest of these is probably Isaiah 26:19:[2]

> Thy dead shall live, their bodies shall rise.
> O dwellers in the dust, awake and sing for joy!
> For thy dew is a dew of light,
> and on the land of the shades thou wilt let it fall.

This divine promise constitutes the reply to a communal lament over the hopeless condition of the land, especially the small size of the population. The oracle promises God's intervention: the population will be miraculously increased when the dead are brought back to life. A regular doctrine of resurrection is probably not to be found here. It is noteworthy that the dead are brought to life by the dew, a phenomenon reminiscent of ancient Canaanite conceptions.[3] It should also be noted that what is really promised is the return of the shades (*rᵉpā'îm*) dwelling in Sheol; for this means in any case that Yahweh's power extends over the realm of the dead and that he is mightier than death.

---

[1] G. F. Moore, *Judaism* (Cambridge: Harvard, 1927-31), II, 279 ff.; P. Volz, *Die Eschatologie der jüdischen Gemeinde* (2nd ed.; Tübingen: Mohr, 1934), pp. 229 ff.; A. Nikolainen, *Der Auferstehungsglaube in der Bibel und ihrer Umwelt* (Helsinki: Finnische Literaturgesellschaft, 1944), esp. pp. 148 ff.

[2] The so-called Isaiah Apocalypse; cf. below, p. 332.

[3] See above, p. 247.

On the other hand, Daniel 12:2 states its belief in a resurrection in no uncertain terms: "And many of those who sleep in the dust of the earth shall awake, some to everlasting life, and some to shame and everlasting contempt." Here, then, the author is anticipating the resurrection of the dead (either all of them or, if we take the passage literally, only "many"): the righteous to eternal life, the wicked to eternal shame.

Of the Apocrypha, only II Maccabees mentions the resurrection; it speaks of the righteous being raised up to an everlasting renewal of life (II Macc. 7:9, 14, 36; 12:43 ff.), while the fate of the unrighteous is described in general terms as punishment (II Macc. 7:14, 31, 36), without any mention of their resurrection. That only the righteous are raised is also stated by the Psalms of Solomon (3:10 ff.; 14:3, 6, 9; 15:10; 16:2), in Ethiopic Enoch (22:13; 91:10; 92:3), in the Testaments of the Patriarchs (Test. Sim. 6; Test. Judah 25; Test. Zeb. 10), and elsewhere; the wicked accordingly remain in a state of death eternally (Ps. Sol. 14:6) or are destroyed (Test. Zeb. 10). Other passages, however, presuppose the general resurrection of all the dead: earth, sea, the realm of the dead, and Hell will then give up what was entrusted to them (Eth. Enoch 51:1; 61:5; II Esd. 7:32). In other words, one generally held doctrine of the resurrection does not exist. In addition, both Josephus and the New Testament show that the Sadducees did not believe in the resurrection; and up to now no unequivocal statement of belief in the resurrection has been found in the Qumran documents.[4]

How did this new idea come into being in Judaism? Unfortunately, none of the passages in question furnishes enough details about the mechanism of the resurrection to make possible any conclusions about the origin of the idea. An answer can be given only within the total context of general eschatology and apocalyptic. In this realm one must reckon with a comparatively powerful influx of Persian ideas, which suggests that the doctrine of the resurrection also drew its inspiration from that quarter.[5] It must be remembered, however, that the earliest text shows definite features of the ancient Canaanite syncretism.[6] It is likely that we have here one of the pillars on which the doctrine of the resurrection was based. In any event, Persian influences cannot explain everything. The old conviction that Yahweh is more powerful than death and Sheol[7] must have made some contribution.

---

[4] H. Ringgren, *The Faith of Qumran,* trans. E. T. Sander (Philadelphia: Fortress, 1963), pp. 148 ff.

[5] W. Bousset and H. Gressmann, *Die Religion des Judentums im späthellenistischen Zeitalter* (Tübingen: Mohr, 1926), pp. 510 ff.

[6] H. Riesenfeld, *The Resurrection in Ezekiel XXXVII and in the Dura-Europos Paintings* (Uppsala: Lundeqvist, 1948), pp. 10 f.

[7] See above, pp. 246 f.

8.

THE CULT AND THE PRIESTS

In the realm of the cult, the exile meant a break in the tradition. The postexilic cult is in many respects radically different from the pre-exilic cult. Several elements of the pre-exilic Temple cult were dropped, and many innovations were introduced. In addition, the cult itself forfeited some of its intrinsic importance, becoming subordinate to the idea of obedience to the law.

The new Temple[1] was built upon the site of the earlier Temple, according to the same plan, though with less magnificence and opulence. Around 300 B.C., Hecateus of Abdera describes it as a large building standing beside a stone altar; within it are an altar and a golden lampstand whose light never goes out.[2] The enthusiastic description of the Letter of Aristeas, which speaks of the magnificent and sumptuous interior of the Temple,[3] must probably be read with a grain of salt. In 20/19 B.C., King Herod (37-34 B.C.) began to build a new and magnificent Temple; but it was not completed until A.D. 64.[4] The plan remained the same. The Temple building proper was surrounded by two courts—the outer court was called the Court of the Gentiles, and could be entered even by non-Jews; the inner court was divided into three areas, intended for men, women, and priests. Inscribed stones have been discovered warning Gentiles not to enter the inner courtyards.

In addition to the Temple, the postexilic period saw the appearance of synagogues (a Greek word meaning "assembly"; Heb. *bêt keneset*) as places of worship.[5] Unfortunately we have no information about

---

[1] R. de Vaux, *Ancient Israel*, trans. J. McHugh (New York: McGraw-Hill, 1961), pp. 322 ff.; E. L. Ehrlich, *Die Kultsymbolik im Alten Testament und im nachbiblischen Judentum* (Stuttgart: Hiersemann, 1959), pp. 27 f.

[2] Josephus, *Contra Apionem*, I.22 (198 f.).

[3] E.g., R. H. Charles (ed.), *Apocrypha and Pseudepigrapha of the Old Testament* (Oxford: Clarendon, 1913), pp. 103 ff.

[4] Ehrlich, *op cit.*, pp. 28 f.

[5] Cf. K. Galling, "Erwägungen zur antiken Synagoge," *ZDPV*, LXXII (1956), 163 ff.; *idem*, "Synagoge," *RGG*, VI, cols. 557 f.

when this innovation came into being. A priori, it seems probable that the exiles in Babylon came together for reading from the Scriptures and for prayer; we have no information about the details, however. It is also possible that the synagogues gradually developed after the return to Palestine. No relevant archaeological finds antedate the first century c.e.[6] Inscriptions and documents on papyrus testify to the existence of "houses of prayer" (*proseuchē*) in Egypt from the middle of the third century b.c.[7]

In the Temple cult, sacrificial worship apparently predominated. The cultic regulations of the Pentateuch, which attained their final form during this period, have almost nothing to say about other ceremonies in observance of the great festivals. Malachi censures negligence in connection with sacrifice (Mal. 1:6-14), but says nothing of other cultic ceremonies.[8] The Book of Daniel stresses two points in connection with the interference of Antiochus Epiphanes with the Temple cult: he set up an image of Zeus, and brought an end to the offerings and sacrifices (Dan. 9:27; cf. 11:31, which mentions the continual burnt offering).[9] In the Greek version of Daniel, Azariah depicts the miserable condition of his people in a prayer: "At this time there is no prince, or prophet, or leader, no burnt offering, or sacrifice, or oblation, or incense, no place to make an offering before thee or to find mercy." Once again the cessation of sacrifice is felt to be a terrible disaster.[10] The last sentence is typical: the purpose of sacrifice is to gain mercy from God, a conception also expressed in the special position accorded to sacrifices for atonement in the post-exilic period. When Ecclesiasticus sings the praises of Simon the high priest, he emphasizes his sacrificial office (Ecclus. 50:11 ff.).

Simultaneously, a tendency to spiritualize the sacrifices asserts itself. In the prayer of Azariah quoted above, we read, "Yet with a contrite heart and a humble spirit may we be accepted, as though it were with burnt offerings of rams and bulls, and with tens of thousands of fat lambs" (vs. 16). And Ecclesiasticus says:

> He who keeps the law makes many offerings;
> he who heeds the commandments sacrifices a peace offering.

---

[6] The Inscription of Theodotus; see K. Galling, *Textbuch zur Geschichte Israels* (Tübingen: Mohr, 1950), p. 81. The earliest buildings discovered date from the 3rd century c.e. [For an English translation of the Theodotus Inscription, see I. Sonne, "Synagogue," in *The Interpreter's Dictionary of the Bible* (Nashville: Abingdon, 1962), IV, 480.—Trans.]

[7] Inscriptions from Schedia, Magdola, and Alexandria; cf. Philo, *In Flaccum*, VI.7, 14; *Leg. ad. Caj.*, XX.23, 43; Ehrlich, *op. cit.*, p. 86.

[8] T. Chary, *Les prophètes et le culte à partir de l'exil* (Tournai: Desclee, 1955), pp. 171 ff.

[9] *Ibid.*, pp. 268 f.

[10] *Ibid.*, pp. 257 f.

> He who returns kindness offers fine flour,
>> and he who gives alms sacrifices a thank offering.
> To keep from wickedness is pleasing to the Lord,
>> and to forsake unrighteousness is atonement.
>
> (Ecclus. 35:1-3)

Here proper conduct takes the place of sacrifice. But the author continues in a characteristic vein:

> Do not appear before the Lord empty-handed,
>> for all these things are to be done because of the commandment.
> The offering of a righteous man anoints the altar,
>> and its pleasing odor rises before the Most High.
> The sacrifice of a righteous man is acceptable,
>> and the memory of it will not be forgotten.
>
> (Ecclus. 35:4-7)

He thus places special emphasis on having the proper attitude while offering sacrifice: God cannot be bribed (35:12); he is not pleased with the offerings of the ungodly, and he does not forgive sins on account of a multitude of sacrifices (34:19).

One should not jump to the conclusion, however, that the post-exilic cult consisted solely of sacrifices and offerings. The Chronicles show a striking interest in the Temple functionaries responsible for the singing and music. We hear frequently of solemn occasions at which music played an important role (I Chron. 15:16 ff.; 29:20; II Chron. 5:12 f.; 20:21, 26, 28; 23:13; 29:27). The books of the Maccabees also make occasional mention of hymns and songs of praise, both in the Temple and elsewhere (I Macc. 4:54; II Macc. 10:7; 3:30 f.; cf. also I Macc. 4:24; 13:47, 51). In the Temple, the hymns were chanted by choirs, while the people responded with "Amen" or "Hallelujah" (Neh. 8:6; Ezra 3:11; I Chron. 16:36).

The great festivals were surely observed with additional ceremonies, although for the period we are studying it is exceptional to find any information about these other ceremonies. II Maccabees tells of the rededication of the Temple:

> And they celebrated it for eight days with rejoicing, in the manner of the feast of booths, remembering how not long before, during the feast of booths, they had been wandering in the mountains and caves like wild animals. Therefore bearing ivy-wreathed wands and beautiful branches and also fronds of palm, they offered hymns of thanksgiving to him who had given success to the purifying of his own holy place. (II Macc. 10:6 f.)

The Mishna also speaks of palm and willow branches and a festal thyrsus as elements of the feast of booths.[11] It also mentions drawing

---

[11] See above, p. 190.

water from the Pool of Siloam, followed by a drink offering. We have at least indirect evidence for this latter ceremony from the time of Jesus, since, according to the Gospel of John, Jesus invites the people to drink of the living water on the last day of the feast of booths (John 7:37). The ceremonies mentioned in the Mishna obviously are much older and were customary throughout the entire postexilic period.

The postexilic feast of booths continues only a part of the pre-exilic autumn festival. The enthronement motif has been dropped; other aspects of the ancient festival have been separated and distributed over various feast days. New Year's Day (*rō's haššānâ*) and the Day of Atonement (*yôm hakkippûrîm*) are the products of this process.[12] On the first of these days, the trumpet (*šôpār*) is blown to announce the New Year. This ceremony is called the *terû'â*, a term used in pre-exilic Israel to refer, among other things, to the acclamation of Yahweh as king. We have already described the ancient rites of the day of atonement;[13] it probably continues rites of atonement and penance once performed by the king, but also expresses in characteristic fashion the longing of the postexilic community for atonement and purification.

Two new festivals arose in the postexilic period. The feast of Purim, whose legend is contained in the Book of Esther, is probably of Persian origin, as the locale of the legend of Esther suggests. According to tradition, the feast celebrates the deliverance of the Jews from an intended persecution in Susa; in reality, however, it contains many elements deriving from Persian New Year's ceremonies, and has been given an historical interpretation through the legend.[14] It is primarily a joyous festival with banquets, gifts, and all kinds of processions. Traditionally, the feast of the rededication of the Temple, or Hanukka, is celebrated in memory of the rededication of the Temple in 165 B.C. Among the ceremonies belonging to it, the waving of palm branches and the lighting of lamps are singled out for special mention (II Macc. 10:6-8; 1:8, 18 f.). It is not impossible that the outward features of this festival have been influenced by Hellenistic feasts connected with the winter solstice.[15] The details remain largely unexplained.

---

[12] Ehrlich, *op. cit.*, pp. 58 ff.

[13] See above, pp. 173 f.

[14] V. Christian, "Zur Herkunft des Purim-Festes," in H. Junker and J. Botterweck (ed.), *Alttestamentliche Studien, Fr. Nötscher zum 60. Geburtstag* (Bonn: Hanstein, 1950), pp. 33 ff.; H. Ringgren, "Esther and Purim," *SEÅ*, XX (1955), 5 ff.

[15] O. S. Rankin, *The Origin of the Festival of Hanukkah* (Edinburgh: Clark, 1930); *idem*, "The Festival of Hanukkah," in S. H. Hooke (ed.), *The Labyrinth* (New York: Macmillan, 1935), pp. 161 ff.; Ehrlich, *op. cit.*, pp. 73 f.

The synagogue worship on the morning of the Sabbath[16] consisted of Scripture readings and prayers; we cannot describe the precise order of worship, since contemporary sources are lacking. The Theodotus Inscription from Jerusalem, mentioned above (p. 325), which antedates 70 B.C., describes the activities carried on in the synagogue as "reading of the law and instruction in the commandments." The New Testament witnesses to readings from the prophets accompanied by interpretation (Luke 4:16-21). In addition, the confession of faith called the šᵉmaʿ ("Hear"), made up of three selections from the Pentateuch (Deut. 6:4-8; 11:13-21; Num. 15:37-41), as well as certain formulas of prayer, appear to be ancient. According to Galling, Nehemiah 8:1-12 shows that the basic features of synagogue worship had already taken shape before time when the Chronicler's history was finished.[17]

With reference to the priesthood, too, certain changes may be noted. Since the priests were among the leaders of the people, the majority of them had to go into exile. It is clear that Zadokite priests alone returned with the first group of returnees.[18] But Ezra brought back with him a few priests who looked upon Ithamar as their ancestor (Ezra 8:2), and would therefore be descendants of Abiathar (cf. I Chron. 24:3; I Sam. 22:20), i.e., they belonged to a rival group, at odds with the Zadokites. However, since they, too, traced their lineage back to Aaron, in the postexilic period all priests could be termed "sons of Aaron." The Zadokite priesthood, though, retained its position of leadership. Later, when the Maccabean princes assumed the office of high priest, Zadokite groups broke away from the community and formed the Qumran community.

A few Levites were among the first and the second group of returnees (Ezra 2:40; Neh. 7:43; Ezra 8:15 ff.). They constituted an inferior class of priests, and were divided into various guilds, such as singers, musicians, gatekeepers, etc.

Thus there arose a well-organized hierarchy with precisely worked out genealogies. At its head stood the high priest, who now, after the fall of the monarchy, was the supreme authority in religious matters. In many respects, he seems simply to have taken over the functions of the king.[19] Zechariah 3:1-9 depicts the investiture of Joshua, the first postexilic high priest; the ritual is obviously modeled after the ancient royal consecration.[20] After a symbolic purification, he is dressed in

---

[16] I. Elbogen, *Der jüdische Gottesdienst* (4th ed.; Hildesheim: Olms, 1962), pp. 14 ff., esp. pp. 107 ff.

[17] K. Galling, *Die Bücher der Chronik, Esra, Nehemia* (Göttingen: Vandenhoeck & Ruprecht, 1954), pp. 233 f.

[18] De Vaux, *op. cit.*, pp. 388 f., 394 f.

[19] G. Widengren, *Sakrales Königtum* (Stuttgart: Kohlhammer, 1955), pp. 17 ff.; De Vaux, *op. cit.*, pp. 400 f.

[20] Cf. K. Elliger, *Das Buch der zwölf kleinen Propheten* (Göttingen: Vandenhoeck & Ruprecht, 1949), II, 122.

rich apparel; a turban is placed on his head, and an inscribed stone is placed before him. The turban is obviously the royal headdress (cf. Isa. 62:3; Ezek. 21:31 [Eng. 21:26]); the stone is probably the plate fastened to the turban of the high priest (Exod. 28:36), which bore the inscription "Holy to Yahweh" (seven letters!).[21] In addition, the breastpiece of the high priest (Exod. 28:15 f.) corresponds to similar ornaments worn by the Egyptian and Syrian kings.[22] With respect to the vesture of the high priest, Wisdom of Solomon 18:24 drops a valuable hint; there we read, "For upon his [Aaron's] long robe the whole world was depicted,[23] and the glories of the fathers were engraved on the four rows of stones, and thy majesty on the diadem upon his head." Here parts of the high-priestly vesture are interpreted symbolically: the dark blue robe, the turban, and the precious stones of the breastpiece (Exod. 28:31 ff.; also Exod. 28:15 ff., 36). The cosmic symbolism of the outer robe undeniably best fits a royal garment. According to Exodus 29:7 and Leviticus 8:12, the high priest is also anointed, which once more suggests the borrowing of a royal ceremony.

The hymn in praise of the high priest Simon II (218-192), contained in Ecclesiasticus 50:1-21, has many interesting aspects. Since this poem gives us a good idea both of the appearance of the high priest and also of some of his functions, as well as the Temple cult in general, we shall quote several verses from it:

> How glorious he was when the people gathered round him
>> as he came out of the inner sanctuary!
> Like the morning star among the clouds,
>> like the moon when it is full;
> like the sun shining upon the temple of the Most High.
> . . . .
> When he put on his glorious robe
>> and clothed himself with superb perfection
> and want up to the holy altar,
>> he made the court of the sanctuary glorious.
> And when he received the portions from the hands of the priests,
>> as he stood by the hearth of the altar,
> . . . .
> they surrounded him like the trunks of palm trees,
>> all the sons of Aaron in their splendor
> with Yahweh's offering in their hands,
>> before the whole congregation of Israel.

---

[21] *Ibid.*, pp. 123 f.

[22] De Vaux, *op. cit.*, p. 400; A. de Buck, "La fleur au front du Grand Prêtre," *OTS*, IX (1951), 18 ff.

[23] The text lacks the word "depicted"; the translation follows the interpretation of the Jewish Midrash; cf. C. Siegfried, *Philo von Alexandrien als Ausleger des Alten Testaments*, 1875, pp. 188 f., 223, 227.

Finishing the service at the altars,
>and arranging the offering to the Most High, the Almighty,
he reached out his hand to the cup
>and poured a libation of the blood of the grape:
he poured it at the foot of the altar,
>a pleasing odor to the Most High, the King of all.
Then the sons of Aaron shouted,
>they sounded the trumpets of hammered work,
they made a great noise to be heard
>for remembrance before the Most High.
Then all the people together made haste
>and fell to the ground upon their faces
to worship their Lord,
>the Almighty, God Most High.
And the singers praised him with their voices
>in sweet and full-toned melody.
And the people besought the Lord Most High
>in prayer before him who is merciful,
till the order of worship of Yahweh was ended;
>so they completed his service.
Then Simon came down, and lifted up his hands
>over the whole congregation of the sons of Israel,
to pronounce the blessing of Yahweh with his lips,
>and to glory in his name,[24]
and they bowed down in worship a second time,
>to receive the blessing from the Most High.

---

[24] That is, he pronounces the high-priestly blessing and also the divine name.

9.

ESCHATOLOGY AND APOCALYPTIC

At first, postexilic prophecy appears as a direct continuation of pre-exilic prophecy, modified to suit the prevailing conditions. Haggai and Zechariah assail the lack of enthusiasm for building the Temple and urge the Israelites to set to work once more. Their primary interest is not the Temple and the cult, but man's attitude toward God: any man who stands aloof from the Temple and the cult manifests thereby a lack of sufficient reverence for God.

The last eleven chapters of the Book of Isaiah (so-called Trito-Isaiah),[1] which date from the early postexilic period, attack cultic and social abuses such as idolatry and oppression of the weak among the inhabitants of Judah, and promise a better and happier time as a result of God's intervention. The oracles of salvation are obviously conditioned by the contemporary milieu.

The situation is similar in the case of Malachi.[2] He, too, is primarily concerned with the conditions of his period (5th century B.C.), supports more frequent and purer sacrifices (1:6—2:9) and regular tithing (3:6-12), attacks mixed marriages (2:10-16; but this passage may refer metaphorically to idolatry), and proclaims Yahweh's intervention to save his people.

In all these books we can observe a gradual theological change. The attitude toward the cult, the interest in what is clean and what is unclean, the nationalistic focus—all these are typical of postexilic religion. But there are no basic differences between these prophets and pre-exilic prophecy. They still speak to the situation at hand in terms of events within history.

But other features also appear that prepare the way for something

---

[1] K. Elliger, "Der Prophet Trito-Jesaja," *ZAW*, XLIX (1931), 112 ff.; H. Odeberg, *Trito-Isaiah* (Uppsala: Lundeqvist, 1931); W. Kessler, "Studien zur religiösen Situation im ersten nachexilischen Jahrhundert und zur Auslegung von Jesaja 56—66," *WZUH*, VI (1956/57), 41 ff.

[2] C. Lattey, *The Book of Malachy* (London: Longmans, Green & Co., 1934); E. Pfeiffer, "Die Disputationsworte im Buche Maleachi," *ETh*, XIX (1959), 546 ff.

new. Zechariah[3] receives his revelations in night visions. The message is clothed in strange and fantastic images. He sees horsemen patrolling the earth, who report that all is still and ready for God's intervention (Zech. 1:8 ff.); he sees smiths, who are to break the horns of the nations (1:18 ff.); he sees a golden lampstand and two olive trees, symbolizing the presence of God and the two anointed leaders Zerubbabel and Joshua (chap. 4); etc.

The eschatological nature of the prophet's vision of the future is further accentuated by having the decision come more or less outside the realm of history. The later redaction of the Gog oracle in Ezekiel 38—39[4] has a terrible nation from the distant north assault Israel and perish upon the mountains of Palestine. Here we have an intensification of the ancient motif of the assault of the nations, which transposes the event not only into the realm of the fantastic, but into the supra-historical realm.

In the book of Joel[5]—which, despite many arguments to the contrary, is probably postexilic[6]—a plague of locusts comes to assume the dimensions of a cosmic catastrophe: the day of Yahweh draws near, the sun is transformed into darkness, the moon into blood, the nations assemble for judgment, and Yahweh comes to dwell in Zion forever. In the so-called Isaiah Apocalypse (Isa. 24—27)[7] the fall of a great city (perhaps Babylon, in 485 B.C.) becomes a sign that the end is about to come. In the later additions to the Book of Zechariah (chaps. 9—14), also, historical events are mingled with supra-historical, eschatological elements.

All this can be considered preliminary to Israelite apocalyptic in the strict sense.[8] In this literature, the general purpose is to reveal

---

[3] G. Rignell, *Die Nachtgesichte Sacharja* (Lund: Gleerup, 1950); K. Galling, "Die Exilswende in der Sicht des Propheten Sacharja," *VT*, II (1952), 18 ff.; *idem*, "Serubbabel und der Wiederaufbau des Tempels," in A. Kuschke (ed.), *Verbannung und Heimkehr* (Tübingen: Mohr, 1961), pp. 67 ff.

[4] K. von Rabenau, "Die Entstehung des Buches Ezechiel in formgeschichtlicher Sicht," *WZUH*, V (1955/56), 681 f.

[5] A. Kapelrud, *Joel Studies* (Uppsala: Lundeqvist, 1948); R. E. Lattimore, *The Date of the Book of Joel*, 1951; M. Treves, "The Date of Joel," *VT*, VII (1957), 159 ff.; M. Bic, *Das Buch Joel* (Berlin: Evangelische Verlagsanstalt, 1960).

[6] [For a convincing defense of the postexilic dating, see the detailed commentary by H. J. Kraus in the "Biblischer Kommentar."—TRANS.]

[7] J. Lindblom, *Die Jesajaapokalypse*, 1938; E. S. Mulder, *Die teologie van de Jesaja-Apokalipse* (Groningen: Wolters, 1954).

[8] P. Volz, *Die Eschatologie der jüdischen Gemeinde* (2nd ed.; Tübingen: Mohr, 1934); H. H. Rowley, *The Relevance of Apocalyptic*, 1944; B. B. Frost, *Old Testament Apocalyptic*, 1952; J. Bloch, *On the Apocalyptic in Judaism* (Philadelphia: Dropsie College, 1952); O. Plöger, *Theokratie und Eschatologie* (2nd ed.; Neukirchen: Erziehungsverein, (1962). [Now see also D. S. Russel, *The Method and Message of Jewish Apocalyptic* (Philadelphia: Westminster, 1964).—TRANS.]

eschatological secrets, to depict the end of history and a new world in which God alone is sovereign. It is impossible to make a sharp distinction between prophecy and apocalyptic. Apocalyptic must doubtless be considered a further development of prophecy, but the transition took place gradually and passed through several intermediate stages. The apocalyptic features just mentioned in the prophetical books are matched by corresponding employment of prophetic motifs in the apocalyptic literature.

The earliest of the apocalyptic writings is the Book of Daniel, written during the Maccabean revolt.[9] It contains two kinds of material: legends, which use stories about the fortitude of Daniel and his friends as prisoners in Babylon to show that God helps those who remain faithful to him; and apocalyptic material, in which obscure visions are used to suggest that the readers are now living in the final age of oppression and will soon see deliverance. In visions ascribed to Daniel, who lived during the exile, the author depicts the succession of world empires allegorically as a series of animals (Dan. 7), the last of which stands for the Seleucid empire and Antiochus Epiphanes. The motivating idea is that, if Daniel's vision of the series of empires is correct, then his prediction of a happy outcome must also be reliable. The final vision in the book (Dan. 10—12) makes this even clearer. Here the author recounts in veiled language the course of history from the fall of Babylon down to Antiochus Epiphanes; the closer he comes to the Maccabean period, the more precise his description becomes, while numerous discrepancies appear with regard to the earlier period, purportedly closer to the time the author lived. Here, too, the vision concludes with a final period of severe oppression, which is, however, fairly brief. Then the archangel Michael will appear and bring victory to Israel. What we are dealing with, then, are *vaticinia ex eventu*, which only in conclusion refer to the future, describing events the author hopes for at any moment.

In the following period other apocalyptic works were written, all permeated by more or less the same basic view of history. One of the earliest and also most interesting is the so-called First Book of Enoch or Ethiopic Enoch (2nd century B.C.),[10] a somewhat heterogeneous collection of astronomical and cosmological speculations, visions, and allegorical representations of history. It claims to derive from Enoch, the grandfather of Noah. The Testaments of the Twelve

[9] W. Baumgartner, "Ein Vierteljahrhundert Danielforschung," *ThR*, XI (1939), 59 ff., 125 ff., 201 ff.; C. Lattey, *The Book of Daniel* (London: Longmans, Green & Co., 1948). Commentaries: A. Bentzen, *Daniel* (2nd ed.; Tübingen: Mohr, 1952); N. Porteous, *Das Buch Daniel* (Göttingen: Vandenhoeck & Ruprecht, 1962). Recently discovered sources of Daniel: J. T. Milik, "Prière de Nabonide," *RB*, LXIII (1956), 407 ff.; D. N. Freedman, "The Prayer of Nabonidus," *BASOR*, CXLV (1957), 31 ff.; R. Meyer, *Das Gebet des Nabonid* (Berlin: Akademie, 1962).
[10] R. H. Charles, *The Book of Enoch* (Oxford: Clarendon, 1912).

Patriarchs (partially pre-Christian, partially revised by Christians)[11] refer to the twelve sons of Jacob. They contain ethical admonitions and warnings, which look forward to the Last Judgment. Especially interesting is the fact that a position of leadership is claimed for Levi, which suggests priestly or Levitical origin.

The Second Book of Esra[12] was written considerably later, after the fall of Jerusalem in A.D. 70. It is especially important as a document revealing the dominant mood after that catastrophe. It asks why Zion, which had been chosen, is now rejected, and replies by referring to the new age that is imminent.

The War Scroll from Qumran[13] should probably also be included among the apocalyptic works; it describes the final battle between good and evil.

Jewish apocalyptic seems to be a phenomenon rooted almost exclusively in Palestinian soil. We cannot say with assurance what circles it arose in. Rabbinic Judaism, in any case, rejected it. The Book of Daniel must be associated with the groups that were faithful to the law, the so-called Hasidim of the Maccabean period. The fact that fragments of I Enoch and the Testaments of the Twelve Patriarchs were found at Qumran, together with the apocalyptic nature of the War Scroll, might suggest a connection with the Essenes. The Zealots, too, may have taken an interest in apocalyptic.

All the apocalyptic writings share the claim that they are revealing a secret wisdom, whether about the structure and nature of the universe, the course of history, or the eschaton and coming of the new world. In order to lend great authority to these revelations, their authors ascribe them to a sage or prophet of the distant past; for this reason, these writings are often called pseudepigraphic ("falsely ascribed").

The most popular form for apocalyptic revelation is the vision, which is frequently interpreted by an angel (*angelus interpres*). It is difficult to determine to what extent real visionary experiences lie behind these works; in most cases, the accounts of the vision give an impression of artificiality, and would be better described as allegories. The images are often unusual and fantastic; in many cases, the motifs are drawn from mythology. Numerology, too, plays an important role: symbolic numbers such as 3½, 4, 7, 70, and 12 occur frequently.

Apocalyptic is based on the view that the entire history of the world takes place according to a plan previously determined by God. The

---

[11] M. de Jonge, *The Testaments of the Twelve Patriarchs* (Assen: Van Gorcum, 1953); M. Burrows, *More Light on the Dead Sea Scrolls* (New York: Viking, 1958), chap. xvi.

[12] B. Violet, *Die Ezra-Apocalypse* (Leipzig: Hinrichs, 1910); G. H. Box, *The Ezra-Apocalypse* (London: Pitman, 1912); L. Gry, *Les dires prophetiques d'Esdras*, 1958.

[13] See below, p. 345.

meaning and purpose of the revelation is to reveal this plan. Since the *vaticinia ex eventu* show that up to the present everything has followed the eternal plan, this will also be true in the future. This conception of history is therefore quite deterministic: the course of history has already been determined by God's decree and is hastening remorselessly toward its hidden goal; there is a particular time for everything; even the present distress forms part of this divine plan, and is a sign that the end is near.

One of the basic ideas of apocalyptic is that the present age is rapidly approaching its end, and that it will be followed by a new age.[14] Only in the later writings do we find the two terms *hā'ôlām hazzeh* (Gk. *aiōn houtos*), "this world" or "this eon," and its counterpart *hā'ôlām habbā'* (Gk. *aiōn mellōn*), "the world to come" or "the eon to come"; the conception itself, however, occurs earlier, in more or less fully developed form. This eon, the period of history, has a definite duration, usually thought to be 6000 or 7000 years. Thus if a man knows the point in history at which he stands, he can calculate precisely how much time remains before the end. In order to facilitate this operation, the course of history is further divided into individual epochs. Frequently four empires or periods are used; this is true, for example, in Nebuchadnezzar's vision (Dan. 2) of the statue made of gold, silver, bronze, and a combination of iron and clay (here we may also have an echo of the golden age, the silver age, etc.). The vision of the four animals in Daniel 7 and the vision of the animals in Ethiopic Enoch 85—90, which distinguishes four epochs within the period of the seventy shepherds, should also be mentioned here. But other subdivisions are found, also. The Book of Daniel counts seventy "weeks of years" in which a day corresponds to a year from the destruction of Jerusalem (586 B.C.) until the end of the world (Dan. 9:24-27), etc.

The present age is in the power of evil and sin; it culminates in a furious assault of the forces of evil. Towards the end, the sufferings of the righteous are intensified to the limit. They are often described as the "birth pangs" or the "messianic woes," since they precede the appearance of the Messiah.[15] Strange portents will be observed. The order of nature is disturbed, the heavenly bodies are thrown into disorder,[16] terror reigns upon earth, and family ties are broken, so that close relations become enemies.[17] The devil appears under various

---

[14] Volz, *op. cit.*, pp. 34 ff.

[15] Mk. 13:18; Mt. 24:8; for rabbinic material, see Volz, *op. cit.*, p. 147.

[16] W. Bousset and H. Gressmann, *Religion des Judentums im spät-hellenistischen Zeitalter* (Tübingen: Mohr, 1926), pp. 250 f.; Volz, *op. cit.*, pp. 147 ff.

[17] Mic. 7:6; Eth. Enoch 99:5; 100:1 f. Cf. the Babylonian text in H. Gressmann, *Altorientalische Texte zum Alten Testament* (Leipzig: Gruyter, 1926-27), pp. 230 f.

names (Satan, Belial, etc.) as the leader of the powers of evil; but a human ruler also appears occasionally as the representative of evil.

There follows at once the intervention of God, the day of the Lord, the Great Judgment. God conquers the enemy and judges the evil ones. The righteous are set free and enter the new world, the Kingdom of God. The new eon has come.

The new life is conceived partially in earthly and nationalistic terms as a continuation of earthly life and the triumph of the people of God, partially in universalistic terms as untroubled communion with God and the destruction of sin. A renewal of all creation is also awaited: a new heaven and a new earth, under the dominion of God and goodness.

As has already been suggested, apocalyptic can be understood as a further development of certain tendencies of prophecy. It is not purely Jewish, however. The dualistic conception of history, the doctrine of the various ages, and the eschatological speculations had long been central to the Persian religion. It is scarcely conceivable that the Jewish ideas arose and developed without being influenced by Persian apocalyptic.[18]

In one respect, however, apocalyptic quite clearly builds upon the hopes of the prophets, namely, in belief in a Messiah. Even the pre-exilic prophets had visions of an ideal Davidic king, whom they described in the categories of the royal ideology. Passages like Isaiah 9:1 ff. (Eng. 9:2 ff.); 11:1 ff.; and Micah 5:1 ff. (Eng. 5:2 ff.) provide good examples of this belief.[19]

After the destruction of the monarchy, renewal of the Davidic kingship became a natural element of Israel's future hope. Even the description of the new Israel in Ezekiel 40—48, where words like "king" and "Messiah" are not found, speaks of a "prince" (*nāśî'*) who will reign over the restored nation and be responsible both for the cult and for secular affairs.[20] The prophets Haggai and Zechariah looked upon Zerubbabel as the Messiah (Hag. 2:20 ff.; Zech. 4:6 ff., and also 6:9 ff., although this latter passage has been reworked). Zechariah 9:9 f. depicts the future king in terms that remain completely within the realm of the old royal ideology:

> Lo, your king comes to you;
>> triumphant and victorious is he,
> humble and riding on an ass,
>> on a colt the foal of an ass.

---

[18] Bousset and Gressmann, *op. cit.,* pp. 507 ff.; G. Widengren, "Stand und Aufgabe der iranischen Religions-Geschichte," *Numen,* I (1954), 39 ff., II (1955), 108 f.; *idem, Iranische Geisteswelt,* 1961, pp. 181 ff.

[19] See above, pp. 272, 276.

[20] Cf. O. Procksch, "Fürst und Prophet bei Hesekiel," *ZAW,* LVIII (1940-41), 99 ff.; E. Hammershaimb, "Ezekiel's View of the Monarchy," in *Studia orientalia J. Pedersen dicata* (Copenhagen: Munksgaard, 1953), pp. 130 ff.

> I will cut off the chariot from Ephraim
>> and the war horse from Jerusalem;
> and the battle bow shall be cut off,
>> and he shall command peace to the nations;
> his dominion shall be from sea to sea,
>> and from the River to the ends of the earth.

Righteousness, victory, dominion over the nations—these are all features familiar from our study of the sacral kingship.[21]

Only later, in the postbiblical period, does the word "Messiah" become a technical term.[22] In the apocalyptic writings, in the Targumim, and later in the rabbinic writings, "Messiah," the anointed one, or "the King Messiah" is an eschatological concept. In addition, titles such as "the Chosen One," the Servant of the Lord, the Son of David, etc., are found. But the Messiah is still pictured as a human figure belonging to this world. He possesses extraordinary attributes, the ultimate degree of righteousness, wisdom, and power; but he still remains the king of the people of God.[23]

A typical description of the messianic ideal is found in Psalms of Solomon 17, a prayer for the coming of the Messiah. The psalm dates from the first century B.C., after Pompey's conquest of Jerusalem in 63. Following a lament over the desecration of the Davidic throne, we read:

> Behold, O Lord, and raise up to them their King, the Son of David, according to the time which thou seest, O God: and let him reign over Israel thy servant, and strengthen him with power that He may humble the sinful rulers: and may purify Jerusalem from the Gentiles who trample her down to destruction, so as to destroy the wicked from thy inheritance: and to break their pride like the potter's vessel: to break with a rod of iron all their firmness: to destroy the sinful Gentiles with the word of His mouth. (Ps. Sol. 17:21-24)

The last phrases are clearly derived from Psalm 2 and Isaiah 11. The author continues:

> He will gather together a holy people who shall exult in righteousness: and may judge the tribes of the people whom the Lord His God sanctifies: and He shall not any more suffer sin to lodge among them . . . for he will judge the Gentiles and the peoples in the wisdom of his righteousness . . . He, the righteous king, taught of God, is over them, because they are all righteous and their King is the Lord Messiah. (Ps. Sol. 17:26 f., 29, 32)

---

[21] H. Ringgren, "König und Messias," *ZAW*, LXIV (1952), 138 f.
[22] S. Mowinckel, *He that Cometh*, trans. G. W. Anderson (Nashville: Abingdon, 1954), p. 3.
[23] *Ibid.*, pp. 280 f.

The image of the Messiah as a righteous and wise judge agrees completely with the ancient royal ideal of Israel. As in ancient Israel, the coming king also claims world dominion:

> And He shall possess a people from among the Gentiles: that it may serve him under his yoke: and may praise the Lord openly over all the earth . . . that the Gentiles may come from the ends of the earth to behold His glory. (Ps. Sol. 17:30 f.)

The Messiah can do all this because he is chosen by God and trusts in God alone:

> For He will not trust on horse nor on his rider; nor on the bow: nor shall He multiply to himself gold and silver for war . . . for the Lord is His King: His hope and His strength are in the hope of God. (Ps. Sol. 17:33 f.)

This is also the reason for his ethical and religious perfection. The hopes expressed here go a little beyond the normal human level:

> He is pure . . . the head of a great people . . . and He shall not be weakened in His days from His God: because God hath made Him powerful by His Holy Spirit and wise in the counsel of the prudent with strength and righteousness, and with the blessing of the Lord in Him, and He shall not be weak. (Ps. Sol. 17:36-38)[24]

The Messiah, then, is a human being; there is no evidence that he was called a "son of God."[25] Only in isolated instances do we find the idea that he will die (II Esd. 7:29 f.: "And after these years my servant[26] the Messiah shall die, and all who draw human breath . . . And after seven days the world, which is not yet awake, shall be roused"). The appearance of the Messiah here precedes the new eon, which only comes after his death.

A remarkable transformation of the messianic expectation is found in the Testaments of the Twelve Patriarchs, with their priestly background, and in the Qumran documents.[27] Here hope centers not on one anointed figure, but on two. The Qumran documents speak of "the anointed of Aaron and Israel" (1QS ix.10 f.; cf. CD xii.23; xx.1). The Testaments do not use the term Messiah, but it is evident that both a priest and a king are awaited, the former of whom will have the higher rank. In Testament of Simeon 7:1 f., we read: "Obey

---

24 [R. Harris & A. Mingana, *The Odes and Psalms of Solomon* (London: Longmans, Green & Co., 1920), II, 431 f.—TRANS.]

25 Mowinckel, *op. cit.*, pp. 293 f. II Esd. 7:29 is an apparent exception (see below).

26 RSV "my son," Latin *filius meus;* but this probably translates Gk. *pais* and Heb. *'abdî.*

27 H. Ringgren, *The Faith of Qumran,* trans. E. T. Sander (Philadelphia: Fortress, 1963), pp. 167 ff.

Levi . . . the Lord will arouse a high priest from Levi, and from Judah a king." Testament of Judah 21:1-3 says: "Love Levi . . . for to me the Lord gave the kingship and to him the priesthood, and he subordinated the kingship to the priesthood."

Testament of Levi 18 has this to say of the priestly Messiah:

> And at the time of his priesthood all sin shall pass away, and the godless will cease to do evil, and he himself will open the gates of Paradise, and he will remove the sword that threatens Adam, and will give food to the holy ones from the tree of life, and the spirit of holiness will be upon him, and Beliar will be bound by him.

Here the priestly Messiah is accorded a saving function that cannot be connected with the royal Messiah: he will open once more the gate of Paradise, i.e., remove the consequences of sin.[28]

In other writings, the earthly Messiah is replaced by another eschatological figure,[29] rarely called Messiah (Eth. Enoch 48:10; 52:4),[30] but usually known by the name "Son of Man."

"Son of Man," Hebrew *ben ādām*, Aramaic *bar ĕnāšâ*, is an idiom for "an individual member of the human race" and would therefore better be translated "man" or "human being."[31] But we are not dealing here with an ordinary human being. The earliest passage, Daniel 7:13, indicates this clearly. At the end of a vision culminating in a description of the blasphemous deeds of Antiochus Epiphanes, we read: "I saw in the night visions, and behold, with the clouds of heaven there came one like a son of man (i.e., a human being) . . . And to him was given dominion and glory and kingdom, that all peoples, nations, and languages should serve him; his dominion is an everlasting dominion, which shall not pass away." The following interpretation of the vision explains the Son of Man as "the people of the saints of the Most High" (Dan. 7:27); but it seems very likely that the author has here reinterpreted a motif that he found ready to hand,[32] in which the Son of Man would presumably be a coming ruler who inaugurates the eschatological era.

The so-called Similitudes of Enoch (Eth. Enoch 37—71) describe the Son of Man at some length.[33] Here we learn first of all that he

---

[28] Mowinckel, *op. cit.*, p. 382, connects this passage with the conception of the Son of Man.

[29] *Ibid.*, pp. 346 ff.

[30] Perhaps also II Esd. 13:11; Mowinckel, *op. cit.*, pp. 423 f.

[31] J. Wellhausen, *Skizzen und Vorarbeiten* (Berlin: Reimer, 1899), VI, 187 ff.; G. Dalman, *Die Worte Jesu* (2nd ed.; Leipzig: Hinrichs, 1930), pp. 191 ff.; cf. Å. Sjöberg, *Der Menschensohn im äthiopischen Henochbuch* (Lund: Gleerup, 1946), pp. 40 ff.

[32] See the commentaries, e.g., Bentzen, *op. cit.*, pp. 33 f.; J. A. Emerton, "The Origin of the Son of Man Ideology," *JTS*, NS IX (1958), 225 ff.

[33] See especially Å. Sjöberg, *op. cit.;* Mowinckel, *op. cit.*, pp. 353 ff.

is pre-existent: "Before the sun and the signs of heaven were created, and before the stars of the sky were made, his name was named before the Lord of the spirits" (Eth. Enoch 48:3). "He was chosen and hidden before God, before the world was created" (48:6), but at the end of the world he reveals himself in order to aid the righteous who are suffering. Then he will sit upon the throne of his glory, and all kings and mighty ones shall see him and acknowledge him (62:3). "Then pain will come upon them as upon a woman who is in travail . . . they shall be terror-stricken, they shall lower their eyes, and pain will take hold of them, when they see that Son of Man upon the throne of his glory" (62:4 f.). He "will put down kings from their thrones and drive them from their kingdoms, because they do not acknowledge him" (46:5). "The righteous and the elect, however, will be delivered on that day, . . . with the Son of Man they will eat, lie down, and rise up for all eternity" (62:13 f.). The Son of Man will "be the light of the nations and the hope of those whose heart is sad" (48:4). On that day, says God, "my Elect—for that is a title of the Son of Man—will sit upon the throne of glory; . . . he will dwell in the midst of the elect people, and I will transform the heavens, making them an eternal blessing and light; I will transform the earth and make it a blessing and cause my elect people to dwell upon it" (45:1-5).

In II Esdras we find the Son of Man, also. Here he rises from the sea and flies with the clouds of heaven (cf. Dan. 7:13); he is attacked by an innumerable multitude of men, but slays them with a stream of fire that issues from his mouth. Then he summons a peaceful multitude, i.e., the righteous (II Esd. 13:1 ff.).

We are obviously dealing here with a figure of a savior that transcends the nationalistic and historical messianic hope. The Son of Man is here a transcendent figure, almost divine. The concept of a Messiah can be derived almost *in toto* from the royal ideology; such a derivation of the concept of the Son of Man runs into considerable difficulty. Undeniably, other motifs come into the picture here, motifs that do not originate in the Israelite royal ideology.[34] "Son of man" may indeed have been a term for the king (Ps. 8:5 [Eng. 8:4]);[35] but this observation is not sufficient to explain such features as pre-existence and coming upon the clouds of heaven. Probably we must think here in terms of influences deriving from the Persian concept of the Primordial Man.[36] This is naturally not intended to deny that elements of the royal and messianic ideology are also present.

---

[34] *Pace* I. Engnell, *Biblia Orientalis,* VIII (1959), 187 ff. (a review of Sjöberg, *op. cit.*).

[35] See above, p. 231.

[36] Mowinckel, *op. cit.,* pp. 427 f.

It has been stated that Ethiopic Enoch also speaks of the suffering of the Son of Man,[37] so that Jesus, who made use of the conception of the Son of Man, could draw upon a Jewish idea at this point. Unfortunately, all the evidence bearing on this problem is either obscure or indirect.[38] It still seems most probable that the New Testament conception of the Messiah represents a combination of the motifs associated with the messianic king and with the Son of Man, and that the idea of the suffering Messiah derives from the old royal ideology only indirectly, via the Servant Songs.

---

[37] This point has been particularly stressed by J. Jeremias, "Erlöser und Erlösung im Spätjudentum und Urchristentum," *DT*, II (1929), 106 ff.; N. Johansson, *Parakletoi* (Lund: Gleerup, 1940), pp. 113 ff.

[38] Å. Sjöberg, *SEÅ*, V (1940), 163 ff.; VII (1942), 141 ff.; Mowinckel, *op. cit.*, pp. 410 ff.

10.

PARTIES AND MOVEMENTS

Both in *The Jewish War* (ii.8.2 ff.) and in the *Antiquities* (xviii.1.2 ff.), Josephus tells of three "philosophic movements" in Judaism: the Sadducees, the Pharisees, and the Essenes.[1] He is obviously trying to interpret the religious tendencies within Judaism to the minds of his readers, who have been educated to think in Greek terms. This purpose probably accounts for some of his explanations. Furthermore, his interest centers almost exclusively in the "philosophic" views of the parties; he gives no information about their origins and their history. Other sources are meager or disputed. The New Testament also mentions the first two parties, but almost exclusively in polemical contexts and from a negative point of view. The rabbinic writings also contain references to the Pharisees. For the Essenes, we also have the accounts of Philo and of Pliny the Younger. Not all scholars are yet agreed that the Qumran documents are Essene in nature.

The origin of these sects appears to be associated with the hellenization policies of the Seleucid emperors and the religious policies of the Hasmonean rulers. The Jews who opposed the process of hellenization banded together under the name Hasidim, "pious ones," to preserve the uniqueness of their religion. In the struggle with Antiochus, they stood on the side of the Maccabees. In the course of time, however, when the Maccabees began to seek purely political goals, the Hasidim severed their connection with them and devoted themselves exclusively to religious exercises, including the study of the law. The Pharisees probably came from these circles. The Essene sect (presumably identical with the Qumran community) probably developed out of the opposition of Zadokite priests to the appropriation of the high-priestly office by the Hasmoneans, who were not Zadokites.

---

[1] J. Wellhausen, *Die Pharisäer und Sadduzäer* (2nd ed.; Hannover: Lefaire, 1924); G. F. Moore, *Judaism* (Cambridge: Harvard, 1927-31), I, 55 ff.; M. Simon, *Les sectes juives au temps du Jésus* (Paris: Presses universitaires, 1960).

We know least about the Sadducees.[2] They are said to have been conservative in their teaching, refusing to approve anything for which there was no evidence in the Pentateuch (or, perhaps better, in Holy Scripture).[3] Politically, they were conciliatory and were glad to enter into alliances with pagan powers. Their opponents represent them as men of the world untrue to their Jewish faith, who have adapted to Roman-Hellenistic culture. The rabbinic writings look upon them as heretics. They seem to have belonged primarily to the upper classes of society.

The Sadducees rejected all innovations such as angelology and the doctrine of the resurrection. Neither would they accept the theory of the oral law. According to Josephus, they did not believe in fate (*heimarmenē*),[4] and taught that the individual alone bore full responsibility for his destiny.

The Pharisees (Heb. *p*^e*rûsîm*, Aram. *p*^e*rîšayyâ*, "the separate ones")[5] are first mentioned around 135 B.C., during the regime of Hyrcanus II, when they are said to dispute the Hasmonean claims. Later on, they were not active in politics, but worked as a popular group favoring strict fidelity to the law.

The Pharisees place major emphasis on the interpretation and careful observance of the law, and separation from "sinners" (i.e., Gentiles and those Jews that associate with them). Scrupulously exact obedience to the regulations of the law is the mark of Pharisaism. In order to determine proper conduct they made great use of oral tradition. The rabbinic writings (the Mishna and Talmud) are for the most part a continuation of the Pharisaic doctrinal tradition. The leading Pharisees were therefore scribes; a certain antipathy to the uneducated (*'am hā'āreṣ*, "the people of the land") is clearly perceptible (cf. John 7:49: "This crowd, who do not know the law, are accursed"). Pharisaism nevertheless bore the stamp of a popular movement, and the Pharisees were greatly admired by the masses.

In doctrinal questions, the Pharisees approved of many innovations. The resurrection of the dead and angelology are typical examples. Josephus tells us that the Pharisees believed in fate (i.e., providence or predestination), but allowed for man's ability to engage in proper conduct. More precise information about the idea of predestination

---

[2] R. Lescynsky, *Die Sadduzäer*, 1912; J. Z. Lauterbach, *Rabbinic Essays* (Cincinnati: Hebrew Union College, 1951), pp. 23 ff.; cf. E. Stauffer, "Probleme der Priestertradition," *TLZ*, LXXXI (1956), 135 ff.

[3] Cf. Simon, *op. cit.*, pp. 23 f.

[4] Since Judaism actually is unacquainted with any concept of fate, it would perhaps be better to translate "providence" or "predestination."

[5] R. T. Herford, *The Pharisees* (London: Allen & Unwin, 1924); J. Z. Lauterbach, "The Pharisees and the Teachings," *HUCA*, VI (1929), 69 ff.; L. Finkelstein, *The Pharisees* (3rd ed.; Philadelphia: Jewish Publication Society, 1962); C. Rabin, *Qumran Studies* (London: Oxford, 1957).

is lacking, but free will was a natural presupposition for the view that righteousness can be attained through precise obedience to the commandments. *Pirqe Abot* iii.15 probably sums up the attitude of the Pharisees in these matters: "Everything is foreseen [i.e., by God], but free will is given."

The messianic hope was also alive among the Pharisees. Characteristically, they consider that strict fulfillment of the law can bring about the coming of the Messiah and the Kingdom of God. Apocalyptic speculations, however, are rejected.

The Pharisees constituted a kind of order, organized in closed groups called in Hebrew *ḥăbûrâ*, "fellowship"; the members were called *ḥābēr*, "comrade." Membership in the order was preceded by a time of probation. There were various grades within the order.[6]

Jesus and in fact the entire New Testament criticize the Pharisees for their self-righteousness and hypocrisy. This criticism is probably somewhat exaggerated. Most of the Pharisees were religious men, who really took the demands made by God seriously. But they did not completely escape the dangers of casuistry. Even the rabbinic writings contain criticisms of the extremes of Pharisaic piety, the observance of the letter of the law that leads to a multiplication of duties and a neglect of simple love for one's neighbor.[7]

The Essenes have recently attracted considerable attention because of the discovery of a number of Hebrew and Aramaic manuscripts of religious nature in the caves near Qumran, on the Dead Sea. Not all scholars agree in identifying the community from which the Qumran documents come with the Essenes; but at least this much must be admitted: if the two communities are not identical, they at least are so closely related that purely practical considerations demand that they be discussed together.[8]

The major documents of the Qumran community that have been preserved are: the Manual of Discipline (1QS), which contains a doctrinal summary and a collection of regulations governing the com-

---

[6] Cf. especially Rabin, *op. cit.*, pp. 11 ff.

[7] E. Stauffer, *Jerusalem und Rom zur Zeit Jesu* (Bonn: Francke, 1957), pp. 65 f.

[8] For a general discussion of the entire problem, a few comprehensive studies may be cited: M. Burrows, *The Dead Sea Scrolls* (New York: Viking, 1955); *idem, New Light on the Dead Sea Scrolls* (New York: Viking, 1958); H. Ringgren, *The Faith of Qumran*, trans. E. T. Sander (Philadelphia: Fortress, 1963); F. M. Cross, Jr., *The Ancient Library of Qumran* (2nd ed.; Anchor Books, 1961); J. T. Milik, *Ten Years of Discovery in the Wilderness of Judaea*, trans. J. Strugnell (London: SCM, 1959); and R. de Vaux, *L'archéologie et les manuscrits de la Mer Morte* (London, 1961). Bibliographies: W. S. LaSor, *Bibliography of the Dead Sea Scrolls* (Pasadena: Fuller Theological Seminary, 1958); C. Burchard, *Bibliographie zu den Handschriften vom Toten Meer* (Berlin: Töpelmann, 1959). Current bibliography and special articles may be found in *Revue de Qumran*, 1958 ff.

munity; the Thanksgiving Psalms (1QH), a collection of hymns that provides important information about doctrine; the War Scroll (1QM), an apocalypse describing the final battle between the Sons of Light and the Sons of Darkness. There are also several commentaries on Old Testament writings, applying words of Scripture to the contemporary situation; the most important of these is the Commentary on Habakkuk (1QpHab). The so-called Damascus Document (CD) also belongs here; it was discovered in a synogogue in Cairo, but, as fragments from Qumran demonstrate, it derives from these same circles.

The most important characteristic of the Qumran community is a dualistic point of view: God has created a good spirit and an evil spirit, which struggle with each other and determine human conduct.[9] This dualism is also described as an opposition between light and darkness, or between truth and lies. The will of God has assigned every man to the realm of one of these two spirits. God has preordained the course of history in all its details, and will finally destroy evil in a furious battle.

Man is completely sinful, but can be saved through the grace of God and received into the fellowship of the saints. Adherence to the dogmas of the sect appears to have played a crucial role in this process. In daily life, it is important to observe the law precisely. Such observance is a way to salvation. God's ultimate victory was clearly expected in the immediate future; man could prepare for God's coming by obeying his law. Two anointed figures ("Messiahs"), a priest and a king, will appear at the end and bring about God's triumph.

The community was founded by a priest who bears the title "Teacher of Righteousness." He is considered an inspired interpreter of Holy Scripture. His name is unknown. All attempts to identify him with any known historical figure have failed.

Excavations in the vicinity of the caves have revealed a building in which the members of the community lived. They were organized as an order, consisting of full members and various grades of novices. Whoever wanted to become a member was tested with regard to his understanding and conduct; when admitted, he had to swear to obey the commandments, to love the members of the order, and to hate outsiders. The life of the community was precisely regulated; strict discipline prevailed.

The cult of the community consisted of ceremonial washings and purifications; common meals with bread and wine, which were sacral, but probably not sacramental, in nature; and an annual renewal of the covenant (the community considered itself the fulfillment of the

---

[9] See above, pp. 311 f.

prophecy of the new covenant in Jer. 31:31). Study of the law occupied an important place.

The religio-historical significance of the Essenes cannot yet be evaluated in detail. A certain connection with John the Baptist is undeniable. Many points of agreement with primitive Christianity suggest certain lines of communication. The Johannine corpus in the New Testament must somehow derive from the same intellectual milieu as the Qumran documents. Less sure is the suggestion that the Qumran community represents an early stage of Gnosticism. Striking similarities to Mandaism suggest that there may be a relationship here that has not yet been brought to light.[10]

Finally, a few words should be said here about the Diaspora ("Dispersion"). The beginnings of Diaspora Judaism are obscure. Israelite commercial colonies are mentioned as early as the reign of Ahab (I Kings 20:34). In the fifth century B.C., we find Jewish mercenaries at Elephantine, in Egypt. The Israelites who were deported when the Assyrians and Babylonians conquered the two Israelite kingdoms must also have contributed to the growth of Jewish settlements outside Palestine. According to Jeremiah 42, a short time after the fall of Jerusalem a number of Jews fled to Egypt, followed in the third and second centuries B.C. by other emigrants. The Jewish population of the Roman Empire has been estimated at four million, of whom one million were in Egypt, one and a quarter million in Syria.

For the period we are studying, we know very little about the religion of the Eastern Diaspora. The fact that the Babylonian Talmud came into being in this region several centuries later suggests that at least the leading class of the Babylonian Jews did not deviate to any great extent from orthodox Judaism.

The development in Egypt is much more interesting. The colony at Elephantine exhibits several peculiarities. Not only is it remarkable that this community, independent of Jerusalem, possessed its own temple and full sacrificial worship; in addition, besides Yahweh (who is occasionally called the God or Lord of Heaven and Yahweh Sabaoth[11]), other deities were worshiped, e.g., Haram-Bethel, Ashim-Bethel, and the goddess Anat-yahu.[12] Unfortunately, we learn nothing more about this syncretistic cult, which was clearly brought from Canaan. The Elephantine documents also witness to the institution of the Sabbath and the feast of unleavened bread.[13]

---

[10] See especially Ringgren, op. cit., pp. 252 f.

[11] A. Dupont-Sommer, Rivista di Studi orientali, XXXII (1957), 403 ff.

[12] A. Vincent, La religion des judéo-araméens a Éléphantine (Paris: Geuthner, 1937); W. F. Albright, Archaeology and the Religion of Israel (4th ed.; Baltimore: Johns Hopkins, 1956), pp. 168 ff.

[13] P. Grelot, "Études sur le 'papyrus pascal' d'Éléphantine," VT, IV (1954), 349 ff., V (1955), 250 ff.

Another Jewish temple in Egypt was founded by the high priest Onias IV, exiled from Jerusalem about 162 B.C.[14] It was built after the model of the Jerusalem Temple, and continued to stand until A.D. 73, although the sacrificial cult practiced there was never recognized by the authorities at Jerusalem.

The Jewish Diaspora in Egypt rapidly assimilated Hellenistic culture and the Greek language. Thus a translation of Holy Scripture into Greek became necessary. It was begun about the middle of the third century. Legend tells that it was made by 72 men in 72 weeks, and was therefore usually referred to as the Septuagint ("Seventy").

The Septuagint is an extremely interesting source for the history of religions, since "like any non-scholarly translation, it transplants the text into a different intellectual world."[15] In many instances, a certain accommodation and assimilation to Greek thought can be observed.[16] A separate "religion of the Septuagint" has even been spoken of.[17] One may note, for example, a tendency to moderate the anthropomorphisms and the irrational element in the Old Testament depiction of God. The name Yahweh is translated *kurios,* "the Lord," or, as in Exodus 3:14, "he who is"; the epithets Shaddai and Sabaoth are replaced by *pantokratōr,* "the Almighty." Human reactions such as wrath and remorse seem inappropriate to God. Thus the concept of God is made more reasonable, and the immutability and transcendence of God are emphasized. There is a marked tendency to describe sin as blasphemous pride or hybris. Small changes make the ethics of the Book of Proverbs more acceptable to the Greek intellectual milieu.[18] The doctrine of the resurrection is read into many passages. Many other examples of this tendency could be cited, but those described probably make the general outline of the adaptation clear enough. In matters of detail, much work remains to be done in this field.

Greek philosophy also influenced Egyptian Judaism. Philo of Alexandria (approximately 20 B.C. to A.D. 45) is an outstanding

---

[14] E. Ehrlich, *A Concise History of Israel,* trans. J. Barr (London: Darton, Longman & Todd, 1962), p. 103, with bibliographical citations.

[15] P. Katz, "Septuaginta," *RGG,* V, col. 1706.

[16] H. St. J. Thackeray, *The Septuagint and Jewish Worship* (2nd ed.; London: Milford, 1923); C. H. Dodd, *The Bible and the Greeks* (2nd ed.; London: Hodder & Stoughton, 1954); H. S. Gehman, "The Theological Approach of the Greek Translator of Job 1—15," *JBL,* LXVIII (1949), 231 ff.; *idem,* "Hagios in the Septuagint," *VT,* IV (1954), 337 ff.; G. Bertram, "Vom Wesen der Septuagintafrömmigkeit," *Welt des Orients,* II (1956-59), 274 ff., 502 ff.; J. W. Wevers, "The Septuagint Text of 1 Ki. ii, 12—xxi, 43," *OTS,* VIII (1950), 300 ff.; I. L. Seligmann, *The Septuagint Version of Isaiah,* 1948.

[17] G. Bertram, *RGG,* V, cols. 1707 ff.

[18] G. Gerleman, "The Septuagint Proverbs as a Hellenistic Document," *OTS,* VIII (1950), 15 ff.

representative of Jewish thought upon Egyptian soil.[19] In him, Greek thought, especially of the Stoic and Platonic schools, united with the faith of Judaism and formed a unity. The ideas of philosophy are read into the Pentateuch by means of allegorical exegesis.

Philo holds firmly to the idea that God is the creator of the world. But he links this thought with the Platonic theory of ideas and with the Stoic theory of the World Mind or Logos. On the first day of creation, God conceived in his thoughts or in his mind (*logos*) the world of ideas, i.e., the ideal world, the pattern of the world perceptible to the senses. Ultimately, however, the Logos is identical with wisdom and with the revealed law. God works in the world through powers (*dunameis*) that share in the Logos. Occasionally Philo equates these powers with the angels.

Man is the likeness of a heavenly man or the Logos. He possesses a mortal body and an immortal soul. Thus he occupies a middle position between the divine world and the human world. In the world, he lives in ignorance and disobedience; but through the mediation of the Logos he can come to participate in divinity. The biblical revelation, the law, which is basically identical with the order of the universe, guides man on the path to perfection. Through practice and knowledge, man can approach God; but he can attain real communion with God only through faith (*pistis*), i.e., through firm belief in God's existence and trust in God's providence.

Thus Philo represents a synthesis between revealed religion and philosophy, which, although Hellenistic in form, must basically be described as Jewish. In the long run, however, rabbinic theology, which developed out of the teachings of the Pharisees, proved to be more vital than the speculative system of Philo.

---

[19] E. R. Goodenough, *By light, Light. The Mystic Gospel of Hellenistic Judaism* (New Haven: Yale, 1935); H. A. Wolfson, *Philo* (Cambridge: Harvard, 1947-62); E. Brehier, *Les idées philosophiques et religieuses de Philon d'Alexandrie* (3rd ed.; Paris: Vrin, 1950); H. Jonas, *Gnosis und spätantiker Geist* (Göttingen: Vandenhoeck & Ruprecht, 1954), II, 70 ff.; J. Danielou, *Philon d'Alexandrie* (Paris: Fayard, 1958). Cf. also H. Thysen, "Die Probleme der neueren Philoforschung," *ThR*, XXIII (1955), 230 ff.

CHRONOLOGY

ca. 1250 B.C. (?)	The Period of Moses and the Exodus
1200–1020	Occupation of Canaan; Period of the Judges
1020–1000 (?)	Saul
1000–961	David
961–922	Solomon
922	The Divided Kingdom
869–850	Ahab and Elijah (Northern Kingdom)
786–746	Jeroboam II and Amos (Northern Kingdom)
783—742	Uzziah (Southern Kingdom); 742, Call of Isaiah
735–715	Ahaz (Southern Kingdom)
722	Fall of Samaria and the Northern Kingdom
715–687/6	Hezekiah
640–609	Josiah and Jeremiah's Call; 622, Josiah's Reformation
587	Fall of Jerusalem
587–538	The Exile
520	Haggai and Zechariah
515	Rededication of the Temple
445 ff.	Governorship of Nehemiah
428 (?) 398 (?)	Ezra
333–323	Palestine under Alexander the Great
323–198	Palestine under the Ptolemies
198–164	Palestine under the Seleucids (Desecration of the Temple, 167; Book of Daniel)
164–63	Maccabean or Hasmonean Period
63 ff.	Palestine under Roman Control
A.D. 70	Destruction of Jerusalem

INDEXES

INDEX OF AUTHORS

INDEX OF PASSAGES CITED

GENERAL INDEX

Threshing floor, 158
———— of Arauna, 60
Throne, 225, 230
———— name, 223
———— of Yahweh, 48, 94
"Thus says Yahweh", 214, 252
thusia, 177
Thut-mose III, 223
Thyrsus, 326
Tiamat, 107, 188
Tiglath-Pileser, 273
Tigris, 110
tnt, 90
ṭôb, 321
Tobit, 14
tôdâ, 169
tōhû wābōhû, 106
tôrâ, 4 f., 39 n. 39, 119, 131, 135, 138, 207, 275, 302
Transhumance, 187
Treaty, 160
———— Hittite, 30, 35, 118, 260
Tree
———— cultic, 196
———— green, 96
———— of knowledge, 110
———— of life, 110, 224
———— sacred, 25 f., 158 f.
Trito-Isaiah, 9, 69, 298, 306, 331
trp, 26
Trumpet, 193 f., 215, 327
Trust, 130 f.
Truth, 85 f., 133
ttrp, 26
tummîm, 206
Turban, 329
Tyre, 23, 114, 261, 287
———— god of, 98
———— king of, 129, 231 f.

Ugarit, 81, 203
ûlām, 159
Uncleanness, 75, 131, 141 f., 207, 239 f., 270, 284
Underworld, 161
unio mystica, 130
Universalism, 10, 265, 292, 305 f.
Unleavened bread, 186
———— Feast of, 185 f., 346
Uppsala school, 7
Ur, 112
Uriel, 311
ûrîm, 206
Urim and Thummim, 52, 205 ff., 218, 224
Urukagina, 118
uṣurāti, 199
'uṭfah, 40
Uzzah, 61
Uzziah, 234, 266 n. 60

vaticinium ex eventu, 257, 333, 335
Vestments, 206, 328 f.
Victory, 83
Vision, 216
———— apocalyptic, 334
———— prophetical, 213, 253 f., 288
Voltumna, 42

War Scroll, 334 f.
Watchman, 219, 286
Water, 110
———— cultic use, 327
flowing from Temple, 287
———— holy, 84, 161
———— in Sheol 243
———— of chaos, 162
———— symbol of distress, 181
———— used in ordeal, 210
Weeks, Feast of, 186, 188
Weeping, cultic, 197
Wen-amun, 213
'wl, 67
Whole burnt offering, 169
Wisdom, 12, 111, 140, 304, 309 f.
———— at creation, 106, 108
———— literature, 133, 198, 304
———— of king, 231
———— personified, 198
Word
———— creative, 106, 317
———— of God, 308 f.
———— of Yahweh, 213, 252
Worship
———— false, 263 f., 270
———— of angels, 311
———— of dead, 241
———— of sun, 97 f., 285
———— synagogue, 328
Wrath, 79
———— cup of, 78 f.
———— day of, 10
———— of God, 76
———— of Yahweh, 268
Writings, 10

Xerxes, see Ahasuerus

yāda', 130, 242
yah, 33
yāhû, 33
Yahweh
———— angel of, 49, 89, 100
———— appearance, 70
———— atmospheric god, 71
———— beauty of, 154 f.
———— bull, 70
———— countenance, 89 f.
———— creator, 104, 289
———— Day of, 78, 199, 259 f., 265, 271, 276

Type, 9 on 11 and 9 on 10 Times Roman
Display, Bulmer and Times Roman
Paper, Standard 'R' Antique